Assessment and Classification of Juvenile Offenders

Assessment and Classification of Juvenile Offenders

A TREATMENT MANUAL FOR CRIMINAL JUSTICE PRACTITIONERS

Abu Mboka

California State University – Stanislaus

cognella
SAN DIEGO

Bassim Hamadeh, CEO and Publisher
Mary Jane Peluso, Senior Specialist Acquisitions Editor
Amy Smith, Project Editor
Abbey Hastings, Associate Production Editor
Jess Estrella, Senior Graphic Designer
Sara Schennum, Licensing Associate
Natalie Piccotti, Director of Marketing
Kassie Graves, Vice President of Editorial
Jamie Giganti, Director of Academic Publishing

Printed in the United States of America.

cognella® | CUSTOM
3970 Sorrento Valley Blvd., Ste. 500, San Diego, CA 92121

Brief Contents

Contents

Introduction

Criminal justice practitioners make contact with a variety of at-risk children daily and make critical decisions that profoundly affect the lives of those children, their families, and their communities. It is therefore particularly imperative for people who work with or aspire to work with children in the criminal justice system to understand protective, risk, and needs factors as well as the distinctions between legal and clinical classification and evidence-based interventions that serve youth in various behavioral groups, including sex, violent, controlled substance, general, and mental health-related offenders.

This book is written for all levels of juvenile justice practitioners who may or may not have adequate knowledge about delinquent and criminal behaviors and how to assess, classify, and correct such behaviors using the medical model, which relies heavily on the results of scientific inquiry into human thoughts and behaviors.

The phrase *medical model* refers to the identification of symptoms, determination of causes, identification of medication or intervention, administration of interventions, and reassessment of the effects on symptoms of evidence-based intervention. Shader (2004) explains:

> To evaluate a patient's risk of suffering a heart attack, a doctor commonly asks for the patient's medical history, family history, diet, weight, and exercise level because each of these variables has an effect on the patient's cardiac health. After this risk assessment, the doctor may suggest ways for the patient to reduce his or her risk factors. Similarly, if a youth possesses certain risk factors, research indicates that these factors will increase his or her chance of becoming a delinquent. A risk assessment may aid in determining the type of intervention that will best suit the youth's needs and decrease his or her risk of offending.

Drawn from the medical model, the behavioral science model used by criminal justice practitioners argues that criminality, and indeed delinquency, are illnesses that can be assessed, diagnosed, treated, and reevaluated like physical diseases. As a result, delinquency is viewed as a symptom of a disease that signifies one or more underlying disorder within the child (MacNamara, 1977). That is, the juvenile offender is mentally and/or socially sick but can be helped by accurate diagnosis and prompt treatment using evidence-based therapeutic interventions capable of altering antisocial behaviors. The behavioral science approach also recognizes that unlike physical illness, the notion of delinquency or criminality is based on political, social, and moral definitions (Balch, 1975; Akers, Sellers, & Jennings, 2017; Williams and McShane 2018). Further, risk assessment and classification are based on factors empirically related to future criminal and delinquent behaviors (Vincent, Guy, & Grisso, 2012; Hempel, Buck, Cima, & van Marle, 2013, p. 210; Aven, 2016; Walters, 2018).

The risk and needs assessment and classification process also operates under the shared belief that (1) children are less cognitively developed than adults and thus should be treated differently, (2) categorization of offending behaviors is based on the types of behaviors and circumstances that inform such behavior, and (3) the success of detention, probation, and parole interventions depends on the strength of the risk and needs assessment and classification systems that inform decision-making and on the strength of the evidence-based programs utilized.

Degree programs in criminal justice, social work, sociology, and psychology all provide academic training for future careers in the criminal justice system. Students from these fields become judges, attorneys, counselors, correctional staff, social service providers, clinical staff, and police, probation, surveillance, and parole officers, all of whom may well make contact with some of the most troubled offenders and hence make critical decisions that profoundly affect the lives of those offenders, their families, and the communities in which they reside. It is therefore imperative for criminal justice practitioners to possess knowledge about protective, risk, and need factors; legal and clinical classifications; needs and risk assessments; and clinical interventions. These skills are important for the development of effective therapeutic programs and for effectively interacting with youth whose antisocial behaviors can be categorized as sex-, drug-, violence-, controlled substance-, general delinquent, incorrigibility and criminality-, and mental health-related behaviors.

Indeed, knowledge about how the juvenile justice system works and about the politics that operate in the juvenile justice system are important. However, these factors are not as useful as information about risk, protective and needs factors, risk and needs assessment and classification, or the identification and application of evidence-based interventions. This is particularly true for juvenile detention, surveillance, probation, and parole officers as well as clinical staff and anyone charged with caring for at-risk youth because knowledge about the system does not equal knowledge about offenders or offending behaviors. On this note, this book breaks away from focusing on issues such as substantive and procedural rights of juvenile offenders and the history of how the juvenile court came into existence because in reality, juvenile justice practitioners are best prepared to positively impact offenders and public safety if they command adequate knowledge about clinical functions and responsibilities of the juvenile justice system. Equally, knowledge about risk, protective and needs factors and how to clinically manipulate risk and protective factors is vital. Certainly, ignorance of factors that inform various types of behaviors and how to analyze, classify, monitor, and constantly evaluate behavioral change does not serve the best interests of at-risk youth nor does it further public safety.

Risk and needs assessment and classification are the processes by which juvenile justice practitioners assess and classify the risks and needs of at-risk youth. Assessment and classification are also the scales used to develop and apply evidence-based clinical interventions and to continuously evaluate clinical outcomes (Savignac, 2010; Vincent et al., 2012; Office of Juvenile Justice and Delinquency Prevention, 2015; Bartol & Bartol, 2017; Taxman, 2017; James, 2018; Walters, 2018). On these grounds, the primary goal of this book is to demonstrate that delinquent or criminal behaviors can be manipulated for better or worse through careful assessment and classification processes that measure risks and needs associated with each at-risk youth. Hence, this book focuses on issues relevant to the assessment, classification, and rehabilitation of at-risk youth, guided by the belief that each delinquent child is unique and therefore requires distinct expertise and resources.

This book is thematically organized to provide a well-rounded understanding of what takes place or should take place after an-risk youth makes contact with the criminal justice system. In this regard, this book contains current empirical coverage of the rates and types of delinquent and criminal behaviors, the likely causes of such behaviors, sociological and criminological theories relevant to juvenile delinquency and criminality, existing evidence-based interventions, ways to assess and classify individual offender behaviors, and information required to effectively treat juvenile behaviors.

The 19 chapters in this book broadly cover delinquent and criminal offenses generally committed by youth, why youth commit such offenses, and how to prevent or control their criminal and delinquent behaviors using evidence-based interventions. Chapters are also thematically organized to provide broader understanding of what takes place—or what ought to take place—in the post-adjudication and prosecution phases of youthful offenders. Hence, chapters (1) provide a step-by-step discussion of the roles played by risk and protective factors, (2) cite assessment and classification tools used to assess and classify sex offenders, substance abusers, violent offenders, mental-health related offenders, and general offenders, (3) differentiate between legal and criminal offenders, and 4) discuss the contribution of critical domains such as attitudes and beliefs, family history, history of abuse, victimization, level of social skills, academic achievement, employment preparedness, use of free time, and mental health status. The chapters also devote significant attention to all categories of criminal and delinquent behaviors for which offenders make contact with the criminal justice system, with a strong clinical and theoretical focus that substantively distinguishes this book from other texts.

This book is written for people wanting to enter the field of criminal justice or social work, and for parents, counselors, and people already in the criminal justice system with the recognition that risk and needs assessment and classification are now key elements of the supervision, management, and rehabilitation of juvenile offenders as well as the prevention of recidivism in general. Thus, this book should be highly useful for students pursuing degrees in criminal justice, criminology, social work, psychology, and sociology who may work with at-risk youth and indeed for anyone charged with caring for and supervising children, especially adolescents.

REFERENCES

Akers, R. L., Sellers, C. S., & Jennings, W. G. (2017). *Criminological theories: Introduction, evaluation, and application* (7th ed.). New York, NY: Oxford University Press.

Aven, T. (2016). Risk assessment and risk management: Review of recent advances on their foundation. *European Journal of Operational Research, 253*(1), 1–13.

Balch, R. W. (1975). The medical model of delinquency: Theoretical, practical, and ethical implications. *Crime and Delinquency, 21*(2), 116–130.

Bartol, C. R., & Bartol, A. M. (2017). *Criminal behavior: A psychological approach.* Boston, MA: Pearson.

Hempel, I., Buck, N., Cima, M., & van Marle, H. (2013). Review of risk assessment instruments for juvenile sex offenders: What is next? *International Journal of Offender Therapy and Comparative Criminology, 57*(2), 208–228.

James, N. (2018). *Risk and needs assessment in the federal prison system.* Retrieved from the Federation of American Scientists website: https://fas.org/sgp/crs/misc/R44087.pdf

MacNamara, D. E. J. (1977). The medical model in corrections requiescat in pace: Requiescat in pace. *Criminology, 14*(4), 439–448.

Office of Juvenile Justice and Delinquency Prevention. (2015). *Risk/needs assessments for youths.* Retrieved from https://www.ojjdp.gov/mpg/litreviews/RiskandNeeds.pdf

Savignac, J. (2010). *Tools to identify and assess the risk of offending among youth.* Retrieved from the Public Safety Canada website: https://www.publicsafety.gc.ca/cnt/rsrcs/pblctns/tls-dntf-rsk-rprt/tls-dntf-rsk-rprt-eng.pdf

Shader, M. (2004). *Risk factors for delinquency: An overview.* Retrieved from the National Criminal Justice Reference Service website: https://www.ncjrs.gov/pdffiles1/ojjdp/frd030127.pdf

Taxman, F. S. (Ed.). (2017). *Handbook on risk and need assessment: Theory and practice.* New York, NY: Taylor & Francis.

Vincent, G. M., Guy, L. S., & Grisso, T. (2012). *Risk assessment in juvenile justice: A guidebook for implementation.* Retrieved from the National Juvenile Justice Network website: http://njjn.org/uploads/digital-library/Risk_Assessment_in_Juvenile_Justice_A_Guidebook_for_Implementation.pdf

Walters, G. D. (2018). Risk, need, and responsivity in a criminal lifestyle. In F. S. Taxman (Ed.), *Handbook on risk and need assessment: Theory and practice.* New York, NY: Taylor & Francis.

Williams, F. P., & McShane, M. D. (2018). *Criminological theory* (7th ed.). New York, NY: Pearson.

SECTION I

Explaining Delinquency and Criminality

CHAPTER ONE

Contexts and Complexity of Criminal Laws, Delinquency, and Criminality

A SOLID CONSENSUS now exists in and outside the scientific community that children are physiologically, cognitively, and behaviorally different from adults. There is also agreement, particularly within academic communities, that children (1) learn both good and bad behavior through interaction with others, (2) are vulnerable to physical, emotional, and sexual abuse and exploitation, (3) are different from adults in their mental ability to self-manage their own behaviors, (4) are more susceptible to certain predictive factors such as negative social and peer pressure, and (5) in general are less capable of developing and using good judgment, including the decision to commit offenses and the ability to calculate future consequences of the behavioral choices they make. Understanding the roles these factors play and how to respond to juvenile delinquency, criminality, incorrigibility, and other forms of deviance is critically important for criminal justice practitioners and for any student taking a course in juvenile delinquency and criminality.

Undeniably, it is important to acquire reasonable knowledge about the constitutional rights of juvenile offenders, juvenile justice procedures and practices, and ways to effectively articulate levels of threats to public safety posed by juveniles' delinquent and criminal behaviors. However, a juvenile justice professional is best prepared to fruitfully impact offenders and public safety when he or she commands adequate knowledge about the inner workings of the juvenile justice system and, more importantly, knowledge about risk and needs factors, including offenders' risk and needs levels. Furthermore, knowledge about factors that inform various types of criminal and delinquent behavior can enhance the overall quality of the services offenders receive. It is also critically important to note that knowledge about how to analyze, classify, monitor, and constantly evaluate delinquent behaviors and tendencies serves the best interests of at-risk youth and the public in general.

The issue of juvenile delinquency and criminality has been dealt with by every criminal justice system in the history of modern criminal law. Even today, juvenile delinquency and criminality continue to be a crucial part of public and scientific concern in terms of public safety and the welfare of at-risk children. In this respect, this chapter talks about the different ways that members of the public, policymakers, and lawmakers in the United States have responded to juvenile delinquency and criminality since the 17th century. Specifically, this chapter provides brief discussions of the complexity and multiplicity of criminal laws, the attention paid to children's criminal intent, the reformatory movement as a response to delinquency and criminality, the creation and enforcement of procedural rights of juveniles, support for the retributive response to delinquency and criminality, and the current emphasis on risk and needs assessment as a tool for addressing juvenile delinquency and criminality.

JUVENILES AND DELINQUENCY AND CRIMINALITY

What to do about juvenile offending behaviors, what makes a juvenile offender, and what constitutes child-like behavior have occupied the minds of criminal justice practitioners at various stages of the American juvenile justice system. History shows that answers to these questions change from time to time without altering the fact that laws are not scientific and do not even have to be logical. Laws do not also equal fairness, justice, or right. Rather, most penal laws are created by politicians with their personal political interests in mind and with the support of many voters who may have very little or no knowledge about juvenile offenders or offending behaviors. Consequently, laws are just laws, and there are too many to obey.

Human societies have been in existence for over 100,000 years, but the criminal laws children must obey today are relatively new. Even the Magna Carta, which codified the first known limitation of government's power over individuals—in this case the power of the British monarchy—is relatively new. In fact, the Hammurabi code, one of the oldest non-Mosaic codes of law, is known to have been created in 1752 BC.

In defense of at-risk behaviors, there is also hardly anyone in the United States over the age of 18 who has not committed a punishable offense (Fields & Emshwiller, 2011a), partly because there are too many laws on the books, so many that it is almost impossible for a normal person to live a crime-free life. For children in particular there are too many laws to obey, almost to a point where it is reasonable to argue that every child engages in behavior that could land him or her in the criminal justice system during the course of navigating childhood. In fact, there are sanctionable, criminal, social, or penal laws regarding what children can eat and drink, how they dress, where they sleep, stand, and sit, and what they hear and look at. Just about every aspect of children's lives are regulated by some form of active law, rule, norm, or tradition.

An American Bar Association study concluded in 1998 found that at the time of the study the number of federal offenses on the books was higher than three thousand. Another study done in 2008 by a Louisiana State University law professor puts the number of federal offenses on the books at 4,500 (Fields & Emshwiller, 2011a, 2011b). Evidently, the combination of those federal laws with laws enacted at state, municipal, and county levels would bring the estimated number of criminal laws each person in the United States has to navigate on a daily basis to between 8,000 and 10,000. Without doubt, this implies that the number of criminal behaviors that must be obeyed by children is too high, especially given that many of the laws are too complex and too broad (Fields & Emshwiller, 2011a). The Drug Abuse Prevention and Control Act, for instance, primarily criminalizes the felonious act of trafficking or possessing controlled substances, but it goes far beyond those two acts. The Act itself, about 130 pages long, prohibits additional behaviors, including the fraudulent mislabeling of controlled substances, tampering with drug containers or labels, the use of communication tools such as the Internet and phone to facilitate the commission of a felonious act, and the advertisement of controlled substances.

The number of people who have raped or who will likely rape another person, or who will commit a home invasion or commit dangerous crimes such as armed robbery, premeditated murder, terrorism, or arson in their lives is extremely low. However, many good-standing citizens have engaged in or will engage in felonious acts such as possessing a controlled substance or drug, willfully lying on taxes, using the telephone or the Internet to further the commission of felony, making false statements to law enforcement agents, tampering with evidence, engaging in fraud, endangering a child, and or contributing to the delinquency of a minor. Similarly, a high number of people have committed or will in their lives commit the crime of underage drinking, driving without a license, simple assault, theft, trespassing, engaging in malicious mischief, aiding and abetting, reckless driving, and/or driving under the influence of alcohol or a controlled substance.

CHILDREN AND CRIMINAL INTENT

The concept of criminal liability and responsibility, which holds that individuals choose to willfully engage in criminal conduct, is central to the traditions of the Anglo-American criminal justice system. As a result, only a few mental health exceptions can absolve a person of criminal or delinquent responsibility; thus, arguments about the role childhood plays in criminality has a long history. In this vein, "children were legally as responsible and punishable as adults" in both the 18th and 19th centuries (Bortner, 1984, p. 3). In the mid-18th century, lawmakers deliberated about not only what to do with juvenile offending behaviors or offenders but also what constituted a child for the purpose of criminal liability and what penal sanctions, including the death penalty, should be given to juvenile offenders who violated penal laws. In other words, the debate was also about the age at which a child should be viewed as capable of forming the "evil intent" required for certain crimes—most criminal laws punish mens rea, or the "evil intention," that produces the prohibited acts. The origin of intent or this common law concept is traceable to the 12th century concept that holds that there "can be no crime large or small, without an evil mind"; therefore, the essence of an offense is the 'wrongful intent' without which there would be no criminal or wrongful act, except in crimes of negligence (Chesney, 1939, p. 627).

It is less likely, for instance, that the criminal justice system would punish a person for accidentally throwing a rock at someone, but it will certainly punish a person for throwing a rock at someone to settle a grievance. The difference is that in the former there is no intention to cause harm to any person, but in the latter example, there is a clear intention to inflict physical harm on someone. In the same vein, if a friend unintentionally leaves a gas cooker on and hours later sets his friend's home ablaze when attempting to light a candle, that friend may not likely get prosecuted. However, if evidence shows that the friend intentionally wanted to set his friend's home on fire, then he or she would likely be charged with arson. The question, however, for criminal justice scholars in the 18th century was how old a child had to be to possess the legal ability to settle conflict by throwing rocks at another person or by intentionally setting a house on fire with the sole intention of settling grievances.

The ability to distinguish between lawful, unlawful, or "moral" behaviors develops gradually as one slowly drifts toward adulthood. Where the divergences arise is around the issue of the age of cognitive competence. So, the obvious question is at what age could a child reasonably foresee that leaving the gas cooker on without a flame for a prolonged period of time and later scratching a match would set a home on fire. Certainly, the answer to this question hangs in part on the child's age. In this case, what if the child is a 10-year-old? What if the culprit is a 14-year-old? How about a 16-year-old? Is a youth who is 17 years, 11 months, and 28 days old more capable of forming the requisite evil intent than an offender who is 18 years and one day old? What difference would it make if the person happened to be a six-, nine-, twelve-, fourteen-, seventeen-, or eighteen-year-old? At what age does criminal culpability fully develop? Is it at age 5, age 7, age 9, or at age 15? What about at age 17 years, 11 months, and 27 days? Criminal justice practitioners, including William Blackstone, were concerned with these questions in the mid-18th century.

In the 1760s, a prominent English lawyer, William Blackstone, took on these sorts of questions about how to distinguish between "infants" and "adults" in terms of criminal culpability in his *Commentaries on the Laws of England*. Under the subheading "Of the Persons Capable of Committing Crimes," Blackstone argued that infants or children below the age of seven lack the necessary mental capacity to develop the evil intention for certain crimes. They are too young to understand the consequences of their actions, Blackstone contended, and he went on to argue that they should not be held criminally liable.

Blackstone also argued that those between 7 and 10½ years old should not be held criminally liable unless evidence showed that an offender in this age group had the necessary intention, and even then, offenders in this category must be initially presumed incapable of forming intent. If the court found that the child was capable of distinguishing between good and evil, then he or she must be punished (Blackstone, 1765–1769). The children who were 10½ to 14 years of age may be punished, he argued, of course with lenience, if they were found to be capable of mischief. According to Blackstone, children 14 and upward should be held criminally liable, capitally or otherwise, and should be punished accordingly (Blackstone, 1765–1769). These policies and laws echo the notion that all 7-, 10-, and 14-year-olds have identical cognitive ability to delineate between good and evil, negative and positive, and right and wrong. This is problematic.

To Blackstone, the decision to adjudicate or prosecute should depend on the child's age and conditions, such as whether the child knew his action to be evil. The problem, however, is that Blackstone's classification did not recognize the fact that children are not identical or do not grow up in uniform environments. His argument also ignores the fact that the relationship between cognitive development and age with regard to the ability to rationally delineate between prohibited and lawful acts and to comprehend the possible consequences associated with each criminal behavior can differ significantly among the same age group. Similarly, the changes people go through, especially children, both in psychic and somatic senses as they progress in age, and the ability of the mind to comprehend certain skills depends on many factors and not exclusively on age.

AGE MATTERS, A LOT!

In his 18th century *Commentary on the Laws of England*, Sir William Blackstone talks about children being able to differentiate between "good and evil." He further treats the act of hiding (covering one's tracks) as a manifested evidence of "consciousness of guilt" and accuses children of making mischievous choices.

Ultimately, he argues that "dangerous children" are capable of committing "atrocious crimes with impunity" and thus qualify for capital punishment.

> But by the law, as it now stands ... the capacity of doing ill, or contracting guilt, is not so much measured by years and days, as by the strength of the delinquent's understanding and judgment. For one lad of eleven years old may have as much cunning as another of fourteen; and in these cases our maxim is, that "malitia supplet aetatem" ["malice is equivalent to age"]. Under seven years of age indeed an infant cannot be guilty of felony; for then a felonious discretion is almost an impossibility in nature: but at eight years old he may be guilty of felony.
>
> Also, under fourteen ... if it appear to the court and jury, that he ... could discern between good and evil, he may be convicted and suffer death. Thus a girl of thirteen has been burnt for killing her mistress: and one boy of ten, and another of nine years old, who had killed their companions, have been sentenced to death, and he of ten years actually hanged; because it appeared upon their trials, that the one hid himself, and the other hid the body he had killed; which hiding manifested a consciousness of guilt, and a discretion to discern between good and evil. ... Thus also, in very modern times, a boy of ten years old was convicted on own confession of murdering his bedfellow; there appearing in his whole behaviour plain tokens of a mischievous discretion: and, as the sparing this boy merely on account of his tender years might be of dangerous consequence to the public, by propagating a notion that children might commit such atrocious crimes with impunity, it was unanimously agreed by all the judges that he was a proper subject of capital punishment.

Source:

Blackstone, W. (1765–1769). Of the persons capable of committing crimes. In W. Blackstone *Commentaries on the laws of England* (*Vol. 4*). Retrieved from http://www.lonang.com/exlibris/blackstone/bla-402.htm

Whether arguments about prosecuting children nine years old or younger were informed by any meaningful scientific process, the "age debate" contributed significantly to the development of a distinct criminal justice system. Current juvenile justice systems separately process juvenile offenders and use punishment to address juvenile offending behaviors by various age groups, consistent with some aspects of Blackstone's classification system. For example, in every state in the United States there is support for laws and policies that allow some forms of criminal justice processing of children as young as seven years old (Windell & Mboka, 2019). States allow for the statutory prosecution of children as adults for certain violent crimes, such as aggravated armed robbery and murder. States also allow prosecutors to automatically charge certain age groups and permit courts to practice the so-called preventive detention laws that allow courts to detain juvenile offenders in order to prevent them from engaging in further criminal or delinquent activities. Of course, these laws and practices conflict with the views of reformers who believe that the human brain is not fully developed during childhood and that there is no reasonable scientific justification for policies that legitimize statutory or discretionary prosecution of children as adults.

REFORMATORY RESPONSES

The definition of juveniles as malleable persons who are subject to change and of delinquency as a failure to perform a required task was institutionalized by the American criminal justice system through efforts by reformers in the late 19th century. In this era, a group of humanitarians along with criminal justice practitioners known as reformers showed interest in the protection and reformation of juvenile offenders whom they viewed as people in need of state protection (Fox, 1996). It is therefore the case that the juvenile justice system was created with the noble intention that juvenile courts would serve as the best parents of at-risk children. These courts were charged with the important legal and moral responsibility to protect all children under the jurisdiction of any branch of the U.S. criminal justice system guided by the concept of *parens patriae*, or the commitment to protect such children against physical and psychological harm and to help any and all those malleable children to do what was required of them to become productive members of society (Levesque, 2011). As a result of this movement, the first juvenile court was established in 1899 in Cook County, Illinois.

Core beliefs that informed the establishment of the juvenile justice system at the end of the 19th century were that criminals or delinquent behaviors were treatable and thus delinquency and criminality could be prevented when properly diagnosed and treated. Furthermore, it was believed that "children are not truly capable of criminal intent and the state, embodying the principle of *parens patriae,* is their benevolent protector" who will shield those children from the abuses and exploitations they suffer at the hands of adults (Bortner, 1984, p. 1). In theory, therefore, the juvenile courts or justice system was designed to be a therapeutic and nonpunitive institution, charged with the responsibility to protect and guide children based on individual children's needs and characteristics.

THE PROCEDURAL RIGHTS ERA

In response to the failures of the criminal justice system to provide juvenile offenders with appropriate constitutional protections, the U.S. Supreme Court made a series of rulings in the 1960s and the 1970s that offered juvenile offenders a wide range of procedural safeguards. Thus, today children who make contact with the juvenile justice system enjoy the majority of rights adult offenders enjoy, including protection against double jeopardy, self-incrimination, and deprivation of the right to life, liberty, and or property without due process of law. Children also have the right to notice of charges, the right to confront and cross-examine witnesses, and the right to protection against self-incrimination. Offenders enjoy unquestionable rights to speedy judicial processing, to receive the assistance of effective counsel, and to protection against unreasonable search and seizure and warrantless searches. It worth noting that most of the rights juveniles currently enjoy did not exist at the beginning of the 20th century; rather, these rights were created or enforced by series of Supreme Court decisions (Vito & Kunselman, 2011).

The earliest court ruling that specifically addressed the juvenile justice system and juvenile offenders was the case of the Duke of Beaufort versus Berty (*Beaufort v. Berty*, 1721). In this case, the court ruled that the criminal justice system should treat children differently from adults. Although this ruling did not produce an immediate result, it established the fact that there ought to be a separate criminal justice system to handle juvenile offenders.

About four decades later, the principle of a separate justice system for underage offenders was further established in *Rex v. Delaval* (1763). The concept of *parens patriae* was, however, not established until 1828 by *Ellesley v. Ellesley* . These cases laid the foundation upon which the cases of *Kent v. United States* (1966), *In re Gault* (1967), *In re Winship* (1970), and *McKeiver v. Pennsylvania* (1971) created or recognized the rights juvenile offenders enjoy today.

In *Kent v. United States*, the Supreme Court ruled that when a case involves the transfer of a juvenile offender to the adult criminal justice system, the juvenile court must conduct a hearing. At a minimum, at that hearing the juvenile offender must be represented by counsel, given access to court records, and be given a statement of the reasons supporting such a waiver order. More importantly, the court expressed concern that delinquent children were being denied basic due process rights, noting that there "is evidence, in fact, that there may be grounds for concern that the child receives the worst of both worlds: that he gets neither the protections accorded to adults nor the solicitous care and regenerative treatment postulated for children" (*Kent v. United States*, 1996).

The most impactful U.S. Supreme Court ruling with respect to the due process rights of juvenile offenders was in 1967 in the case *In re Gault*. Simply stated, the court ruled that juvenile offenders are entitled to basic due process rights, specifically the right to be informed of charges, right to counsel, right to confront and cross-examine witnesses, and the right to protection against self-incrimination. The Supreme Court further noted that it is the job of criminal justice practitioners to predict with a certain degree of certainty where "may lay the brightest hope for progress in dealing" with juvenile delinquency issues (*In re Gault*, 1967).

Three years later, the U.S. Supreme Court ruled that when a juvenile offender is before a court in relation to criminal charges, findings of delinquency or guilt must be based on reason(s) "beyond a reasonable doubt" and not the "preponderance of the evidence," which is the standard generally used in civil cases (*In re Winship*, 1970). The last of the most important cases in this era is the case of *McKeiver v. Pennsylvania*. In this case, the court ruled that juvenile offenders are not entitled to a jury trial, noting that although juveniles enjoy basic due process rights, juvenile adjudication is not a civil or criminal proceeding (*McKeiver v. Pennsylvania*, 1971).

In recent years, the Supreme Court ruled in *Roper v. Simmons* that it is unconstitutional to impose the death penalty on an offender if that offender was under the age of 18 at the time of the alleged capital offense (*Roper v. Simmons*, 2005). This opinion obviously revised the 1989 *Stanford v. Kentucky* ruling that made it constitutional to impose such sanctions if an offender was at least 16 years old at the time of an alleged offense. In 2010, the Supreme Court also ruled in the case of *Graham v. Florida* that it is unconstitutional to impose a life sentence without the possibility of parole on a juvenile for a nonhomicidal crime because such action would violate the Eighth Amendment to the U.S. Constitution (*Graham v. Florida*, 2010). In 2012, the court added that it is unconstitutional to sentence a juvenile offender who was under the age of 18 at the time of an alleged crime to a mandatory life sentence without the possibility of parole and without prior due consideration of such offender's age (*Miller v. Alabama*, 2012).

The development of the rights of juvenile offenders produced unintended consequences. For example, the existence of these rights blurs the fundamental distinction between youth and adult offenders in terms of criminal liability. As Justice Potter Stewart argued in *In re Gault* (1967), the decision to extend full due process rights to juvenile offenders indirectly transformed juvenile proceedings into criminal prosecutions. Justice Stewart argues thus:

> Juvenile proceedings are not criminal trials. They are not civil trials. They are simply not adversary proceedings. Whether treating with a delinquent child, a neglected child, a defective child, or a dependent child, a juvenile proceeding's whole purpose and mission is the very opposite of the mission and purpose of a prosecution in a criminal court. The object of the one is correction of a condition. The object of the other is conviction and punishment for a criminal act. ... And to impose the Court's long catalog of requirements upon juvenile proceedings in every area of the country is to invite a long step backwards into the nineteenth century. In that era, there were no juvenile proceedings, and a child was tried in a conventional criminal court with all the trappings of a conventional criminal trial. (*In re Gault*, 1967)

In other words, the extension of the right to council, the Miranda warning, the right to question witnesses, and other procedural rights can be seen by many as equating juvenile offenders to adults—hence the saying that "if you do the crime, you must do the time." Many people may also believe that the "juvenile justice system not only fails to guide and treat, but equally important, it violates the basic tenets of fairness and due process" (Bortner, 1984, p. 6). It is therefore not surprising that the juvenile justice system became one of the major staging grounds for the zero-tolerance project or just desert desire for increased detention, adjudication, and/or prosecution of juvenile offenders.

ERA OF RETRIBUTION

The classical assumption is that harsh responses, in the form of prompt sanctions, to delinquency and criminality would teach offenders specific lessons and deter offenders from further delinquent and criminal behaviors. This approach to juvenile delinquency and criminality became a more visible public policy in the 1980s, peaked in the 1990s, and in many ways remains one of the underpinning forces of contemporary juvenile justice systems (Redding, 2010). Classicalism assumes that criminal or delinquent youth rationally choose to engage in bad deeds because of the goodies and pleasures they associate with such unlawful behaviors. Therefore, the only way to deter criminal or delinquent youth from continuously choosing bad behaviors over good ones is to compensate bad choices with proportionate sanctions that teach potential juvenile offenders that the painful consequences of criminal behaviors outweigh the envisioned temporary excitement—that is, punishment will serve as deterrence for youth who may be contemplating delinquency by purportedly sending clear signals to aspiring wrongdoers that delinquent or criminal behaviors do not pay.

FARTING IS A CRIME FOR KIDS

Yes indeed. If you are a kid, farting is an offense in some jurisdictions. So is burping and otherwise acting like a kid. In New Mexico, a "13-year-old was handcuffed and hauled off to a juvenile detention" center, and in addition he was suspended for the rest of the school year for "burping in class." Initial risk assessment at the detention facility classified the youth as low, a 2 on a scale of 1 to 10, with 10 being extremely dangerous (Cbsnews.com, 2011). A seventh-grader in the state of Ohio was suspended for farting, or "intentionally breaking wind," on the school bus (Huffpost, 2011). In New York City, the NYPD handcuffed a 5-year-old for "misbehaving" in kindergarten. The child suffered from attention deficit disorder, but the reason for his arrest was that he threw a tantrum at school. Also, he "apparently knocked items off a desk" while in the principal's office (Melago, 2008). In 2010, Texas police gave close to 300,000 Class C misdemeanor tickets to children for offences that used to be handled by phone calls to parents. Offenders included children as young as five years old whose offenses included behaviors like "throwing paper planes" and "failing to pick up crumbs" (McGreal, 2012).

Sources:

Cbsnews.com. (2011, December 1). *Student arrested for burping, lawsuit claims*. Retrieved from http://www.cbsnews.com/news/student-arrested-for-burping-lawsuit-claims/

Huffpost. (2011, November 15). *Ohio boy suspended for farting on school bus*. Retrieved from https://www.huffingtonpost.com/2011/05/12/boy-suspended-for-farting_n_861014.html

McGreal, C. (2012, January 9). The U.S. schools with their own police. *The Guardian*. Retrieved from http://www.theguardian.com/world/2012/jan/09/texas-police-schools

Melago, C. (2008, January 25). 5-year-old boy handcuffed in school, taken to hospital for misbehaving. *New York Daily News*. Retrieved from http://www.nydailynews.com/news/5-year-old-boy-handcuffed-school-hospital-misbehaving-article-1.341677

The just desert approach to juvenile delinquency and criminality also shares the belief that those who are identified by the criminal justice system as "criminals" or "delinquent" pose a particular set of threats to public safety; therefore, the only way to mitigate such threats is to closely monitor and control offenders. Consequently, the just desert era emphasizes arrests, longer incarceration periods, and intensive probation or parole in response to juvenile offending behaviors. Furthermore, the just desert stance supports laws that exclude certain categories of juvenile offenders from the jurisdiction of juvenile courts under what is usually known as automatic transfer laws. Advocates for just desert also favor the lowering of the age of criminal culpability, the expansion of the list of offenses that qualify at-risk juveniles for legislative or automatic transfer, judicial-discretionary or judicial transfer, and the expansion of discretionary or prosecutorial direct filing or the transfer of certain underage youth from juvenile justice systems to adult criminal justice systems. At the same time, advocates of this approach push for the reduction of judicial discretion and advance retributive policies and laws, such as preventive detention policies and laws that allow for the detention of suspects or delinquent youth for as long as necessary if such youth are considered threats to society or are believed to have the potential to commit or engage in any act that threatens public safety (Redding, 2010).

RISK AND NEEDS ASSESSMENT PERIODS

The concept of risk assessment has been around for more than two and a half centuries, but the methods of using risk and needs assessment as a tool for predicting future acts of criminality or delinquency is about a half-century old (Aven, 2016). Furthermore, the current risk and needs assessment instruments and processes have gone through a series of generational changes driven mainly by the desire to develop reliable and accurate actuarial risk and needs assessment instruments and processes, although risk assessment methods were used by social service agencies in the United States as early as 1928. It also worth noting that the process of using risk and needs assessment in response to juvenile delinquency and criminality became a common practice within key branches of the criminal justice system in the 1970s (Baird et al., 2013; Kehl, Guo, & Kessler, 2017; Schwalbe, 2007).

In fact, it is only in recent decades that the role played by risk and needs assessment became a cornerstone of every stage of the criminal justice process. That is, the clinical movement has been in the making for long time, but the popularity of risk assessment became more pronounced in the last two decades and continues to gain ground in secured care facilities, probation and parole departments, and in juvenile courthouses (James, 2018). Central to the push for risk and needs assessment is the belief that delinquency is a disease and that therefore the best response is that which treats antisocial behaviors as symptoms of a behavioral and or mental abnormality. The clinical approach argues that the rehabilitation of juvenile offenders must be predicated on gathering data, assessing, classifying, rehabilitating and continuously evaluating offenders. This approach employs the methods used by medical professionals: identification of symptoms (behavior), assessment of symptoms (behaviors), evaluation of assessment results, diagnosis of behaviors, prescription of intervention or treatment (medication), and evaluation of treatment effectiveness. Consistent with medical practice, most criminal justice interventions or treatment programs target one or more factors: risk, criminogenic, protective, needs, and or responsivity (James, 2018).

Criminal justice professionals use risk assessment tools to identify and assess each offender's needs, risk, protective, responsivity, and needs factors that are most apt to predict a youth's likelihood of committing crimes or engaging in delinquent and criminal behaviors and/or benefiting from clinical interventions. Risks predict the likelihood of an offender participating in delinquent and criminal behaviors, and protective factors reduce the chances of criminal behaviors. Criminogenic factors refer to behaviors that specifically increase an offender's engagement in criminal activities. Needs refer to the resources and interventions that an offender needs in order to reduce the risk of criminal or delinquent behaviors as well as to increase the number or strength of protective factors. Responsivity factors measure offenders' readiness and ability to benefit from interventions that address risk, criminogenic, and needs factors.

Most risk and needs assessment processes look at the degree and number of risk, criminogenic, needs, and protective factors associated with offenders' (1) attitudes and behaviors, (2) education, (3) employment, (4) mental health, (5) history of being sexually victimized, (6) history of sexually victimizing others, (7) peer influence, (8) alcohol and drug abuse, use, or dependency, (9) use of free time, (10) violence, (11) distorted thinking, (12) amiability to treatment, (13) community ties, and (14) family dynamics. Criminal justice practitioners also use these factors to create an understanding of prior, current, and future behaviors and tendencies as well as to develop and carry out interventions designed to serve each offender's clinical needs.

The ways that risk scores are calculated and used is similar to how risk is calculated and used socially and by businesses and institutions. For example, those with college degrees are viewed by many employers slightly differently because they are presumed to be better disciplined and privileged in many ways than people with no bachelor's degree. Those with high school diplomas also are viewed more favorably in many instances than those without such qualifications. Similarly, those with high credit scores tend to enjoy the special benefits associated with such scores. The same form of classification system operates in the form of clinical classification with correctional and community correctional institutions. For instance, two speeding citations in a month's period may place an individual at a higher risk of engaging in an accident than someone with one speeding ticket within the same period. If a driver with multiple tickets is cited for the third time, he or she likely will not receive sympathy from a traffic court judge and thus may be disqualified from attending traffic school and may incur suspension of driving privileges. The person's vehicle insurance premium too may go up based on the assumption that the driver is at high risk of causing accidents or filing claims.

CONCLUSION

Of the five phases in the history of the juvenile justice system and in response to juvenile delinquency and criminality as discussed in this chapter, the current risk and needs assessment era is the only one that is well-grounded in science and thus is less reliant on criminality or legality of behaviors. Consequently, and as a response to delinquency and criminality, the current risk and needs assessment approach is highly attentive to causes of delinquent, criminal, and antisocial behaviors in general. This phase of the juvenile justice system also holds the broadest form of response that covers offenders' behaviors, risk, needs, and protective factors while at the same time holding offenders accountable for their bad behaviors. The clinical approach is also the only intervention that places importance on each offender's readiness for treatment and their ability to fully benefit from such interventions. Currently, risk and needs assessments are also increasingly being used by juvenile probation, parole, and correctional officers as well as by juvenile courts and social workers, including mental health practitioners.

CRITICAL QUESTIONS

1. There are more children within the American criminal justice systems than in other countries' criminal justice systems. Why do these differences exist?
2. Why did the reformatory era fail to sufficiently serve the needs of at-risk children despite the good intention that informed reformers' actions?
3. Of all the eras discussed in this chapter, the just desert attitude fails the most to improve the lives of at-risk youth. Why?
4. Why did it take so long for the criminal justice system in general to fully embrace risk assessment and classification as crucial and routine functions of criminal justice practitioners?
5. In terms of criminal culpability, how much importance should be placed on age differences, such as the difference between 15- and 16-year-old or a 17- and 18-year-old?

REFERENCES

Aven, T. (2016). Risk assessment and risk management: Review of recent advances on their foundation. *European Journal of Operational Research, 253*(1), 1–13. https://doi.org/10.1016/j.ejor.2015.12.023

Baird, C., Healy, T., Johnson, K., Bogie, A., Dankert, E. W., & Scharenbroch, C. (2013). *A comparison of risk assessment instruments in juvenile justice.* Retrieved from the National Council on Crime and Delinquency website: http://www.nccdglobal.org/sites/default/files/publication_pdf/nccd_fire_report.pdf

Beaufort v. Berty. (1721). England.

Blackstone, W. (1765–1769). Of the persons capable of committing crimes. In W. Blackstone *Commentaries on the laws of England* (Vol. 4). Retrieved from http://www.lonang.com/exlibris/blackstone/bla-402.htm

Bortner, M. A. (1984). *Inside a juvenile court: The tarnished ideal of individualized justice.* New York: New York University Press.

Chesney, E. J. (1939). The concept of mens rea in the criminal law. *Journal of Criminal Law and Criminology (1931–1951), 29*(5), 627–644. doi:10.2307/1136853

Fields, G., & Emshwiller, J. R. (2011a, July 24). As criminal laws proliferate, more are ensnared. *The Wall Street Journal.*

Fields, G., & Emshwiller, J. R. (2011b, July 23). Many failed efforts to count nation's federal criminal laws. *The Wall Street Journal.*

Fox, S. J. (1996). The early history of the court. *The Future of Children, 6*(3), 29–39.

Graham v. Florida, 560 U.S. 48 (2010).

In re Gault, 387 U.S. 1 (1967).

In re Winship, 397 U.S. 358 (1970).

James, N. (2018). *Risk and needs assessment in the federal prison system.* Retrieved from the Federation of American Scientists website: https://fas.org/sgp/crs/misc/R44087.pdf

Kehl, D., Guo, P., & Kessler, S. (2017). *Algorithms in the criminal justice system: Assessing the use of risk assessments in sentencing.* Retrieved from Harvard Law School, Responsive Communities Initiative, Berkman Klein Center for Internet & Society website: http://nrs.harvard.edu/urn-3:HUL.InstRepos:33746041

Kent v. United States, 383 U.S. 541 (1966).

Levesque, R. J. R. (2011). Parens Patriae. In R. J. R. Levesque (Ed.), *Encyclopedia of adolescence* (pp. 1962–1964). New York, NY: Springer.

McKeiver v. Pennsylvania, 403 U.S. 528 (1971).

Miller v. Alabama, 567 U.S. 460 (2012).

Redding, R. E. (2010a, June). *Juvenile transfer laws: An effective deterrent to delinquency?* Retrieved from the National Criminal Justice Reference Service website: https://www.ncjrs.gov/pdffiles1/ojjdp/220595.pdf

Rex v. Delaval (1763). England.

Roper v. Simmons, 543 U.S. 551 (2005).

Schwalbe, C. S. (2007). Risk assessment for juvenile justice: A meta-analysis. *Law and Human Behavior, 31*(5), 449–462. doi:10.1007/s10979-006-9071-7

Vito, G. F., & Kunselman, J. C. (2011). *Juvenile justice today.* Boston, MA: Pearson, Prentice Hall.

Windell, J., & Mboka, A. (2019). *Juvenile delinquency in American society: Race, class, and politics.* San Diego, CA: Cognella.

CHAPTER TWO

Theoretical Explanation of Crimes and Delinquency

THE BROAD RANGE of academic interest in criminological theories, as evidenced by the amount of attention many criminal justice-related textbooks devote to the understanding of human behavior, show that "crime is not a unitary phenomenon explicable in terms of a single cause" (Walsh & Stohr, 2010, p. 5). The multiplicities of factors that inform prosocial and antisocial behaviors and tendencies have produced many criminological theories that collectively try to explain criminal and delinquent behaviors and tendencies. These theories are constantly evolving and as a result are continuously being defined, redefined, and subjected to rigorous academic scrutiny. Understanding these theories is a critical step towards predicting and effectively responding to criminal and delinquent behaviors and tendencies.

In an effort to create frameworks for looking at many of the factors that inform and explain delinquent or criminal behaviors as well as prosocial behaviors and tendencies, this chapter discusses some of the key sociological and criminological theories most frequently cited by practitioners when talking about delinquent and criminal behaviors and when explaining the ways in which certain predictive factors impact prosocial and antisocial behaviors. This chapter focuses on social learning theory, differential association theory, social control theory, social bond theory, routine activities theory, rational choice theory, labelling theory, social organization theory, subcultural theory and strain theory. These theories have been frequently refined and emphasized by scholars and researchers, and collectively they provide the most eloquent and well-defined criminological and sociological framework for understanding the relationships between risk, criminogenic, needs, responsivity, and protective factors and prosocial and antisocial thinking and behavior (Wells & Rankin, 1998; Akers, Sellers, & Jennings, 2017; Williams & McShane, 2018).

DIFFERENTIAL ASSOCIATION THEORY

Criminal or deviant behaviors in most cases are not invented by offenders but are learned through social interactions. Therefore, differential association theory focuses on the level of sophistication a criminal or delinquent youth possesses as a result of his or her interactions with people primarily with whom the offender has close relationships. The act of learning delinquent and criminal behavior takes place through verbal and nonverbal communication with close members of an offender's social world. The learned behaviors can be expressed and relearned through repetitions or imitations of what an offender has seen, heard, smelt, touched, and felt. It is through such interactions that behaviors such as substance abuse and the use of violence to solve social problems are learned. The process of learning skills needed for criminal or delinquent behavior therefore incorporates knowledge about how to engage in prohibited acts learned through observation, actual experience, or participation in the prohibited act (Sutherland & Cressey 2011; Akers et al., 2017; Williams & McShane, 2018).

When the learned criminal or delinquent behavior enhances the techniques required for a criminal or delinquent act, an offender's risk level goes up. For example, offenders who master the art of picking locks, breaking into cars, grooming sexual victims, or justifying antisocial behavior in interactions with family members or friends have greater chance of continuing to pick locks, break into cars, groom potential sexual victims, and justify antisocial behaviors. Furthermore, specific techniques are learned from the people with whom a potential offender interacts, and the extent to which a potential offender acquires antisocial techniques and skills depends on many factors, such as the duration of exposure, the type and frequency of the exposure, and the overall impact of the exposure on a potential offender's behavior. More often, the longer and the more severe exposure to delinquent or criminal behavior, the stronger the resulting effect will be on the potential offender's behavior (Walsh & Stohr, 2010).

The rationalization of antisocial behaviors is also learned, at least in part, from close members within an offender's social world. Typically, rationalization involves an offender adopting certain antisocial definitions that are favorable to the commission of criminal or delinquent acts. For example, an offender who steals a puppy from a pet store can rationalize the behavior by arguing that he or she felt sorry for the puppy, and as a result, the puppy was only removed from the store to end its loneliness and to provide it with a warm and loving home. A person who sexually abuses children can be taught to rationalize sexual interactions as "making love" or as something that does not "hurt" as opposed to sexual molestation or sexual victimization that causes physical and psychological harm.

Delinquents' rationalizations can also be informed by attitudes or vis-à-vis. Attitudes in this case means the feeling before, during, and after a criminal or delinquent act. For instance, the extent to which an offender gets excited about the prospect of sexually molesting a child depends on whether that offender views the behavior as an act of "love making" or as the act of sexual molestation. Similarly, the interpretation of removing a puppy from a pet store with the sole purpose of permanently depriving its owner access, or in other words referring to the stealing of a puppy as "rescuing a puppy" can significantly impact the degree to which an offender feels happy or guilty about such behavior. Differential association theory argues that those who view such a behavior as "stealing a puppy" are least likely to feel happy about their actions and therefore least likely to repeat such behaviors. Those who view the same behavior as a good act of humanity aimed at "rescuing animals" are unlikely to repent and are most likely to continue to steal puppies.

Rationalization and antisocial attitudes can also be informed by motives and drives that push an offender to act. In this case, if an offender is motivated to molest children because such behavior is the only means through which "full sexual pleasure" can be achieved, he or she is most likely to devote more energy to formulating reasons to justify the act and is most likely to feel excited about the prospect of molesting children. Equally so, an offender who is really motivated and driven by the desire to save puppies from their bondage and loneliness in pet stores' cages will most likely develop a distorted rationale to validate the act of stealing the puppy, and such a rationale will certainly dictate the types of feelings such offenders will derive from "rescuing" puppies in such a way. Of course, in these examples an offender's risk of continuing to molest children or an offender's risk of continuing to steal puppies increases.

NOT IN ALL CASES: POSSESSION OF ALCOHOL ACCEPTABLE IN THE UNITED SATES BUT A SERIOUS CRIME IN OTHER PLACES

Note that in many cases the mere subscription to one set of cultural expectation places an actor in direct confrontation with other cultural expectations. Therefore, what might be culturally deviant or illegal in one society might be culturally normal or legal in other societies (Akers et al., 2017). In this vein, the presence of firearms in an offender's home in a country where citizens are prohibited from possessing firearms might qualify as a risk factor, but the same behavior might have no clinical value on individual criminality or delinquency in the United States, where citizens are expected to possess firearms. Similarly, while possession or consumption of a can of beer in Saudi Arabia may qualify as a risk factor, the same behavior has no clinical value in the United States.

Indeed, it is a crime to possess or consume alcohol in Saudi Arabia. A 74-year-old British citizen, Karl Andree, learned it the hard way after he was arrested for possession, "caught with homemade wine" by Saudi religious police and imprisoned for more than a year and barely spared 360 public lashes because of his age and ill health (Cacciottolo 2015).

Equally, street prostitution is a risk factor in every American city except at legal brothels in the state of Nevada. It therefore makes sense to attach clinical values only to behaviors that are universally accepted crimes or antisocial behaviors.

Sources:

Akers, R. L., Sellers, C. S., & Jennings, W. G. (2017). *Criminological theories: Introduction, evaluation, and application*. New York, NY: Oxford University Press.

Cacciottolo, M. (2015, October 13). Saudi Arabia drinking: The risks expats take for a tipple. *BBC News*. Retrieved from https://www.bbc.com/news/uk-34516143

The impact of a learned behavior can therefore be measured by looking at (1) the means through which an offender learns techniques needed for engaging in a particular antisocial or prosocial behavior, (2) the dominant motives that drive an offender's criminal and delinquent behavior, (3) an offender's attitudes about the behavior, especially before, during, and after particular prosocial and antisocial activities, and (4) the sophistication of the distorted rationalizations an offender advances to validate antisocial behaviors.

SOCIAL LEARNING THEORY

As an extension of the differential association theory, the central premise of social learning theory is that family members and friends provide venues for incubating delinquent and criminal behaviors, which are learned through social interactions. The actual process of learning takes place through physical experience, observation, and verbal and nonverbal interactions and communication (Akers et al., 2017; Williams & McShane, 2018). The logic is that children learn and imitate what they are taught or made to see, feel, hear, taste, and smell as they interact with friends, family members, and other important social institutions such as school and social organizations. The learned behaviors and beliefs inform antisocial thoughts and beliefs such as mistruth, belief in stereotypes, animosity, prejudice towards certain people and institutions, and ways to validate antisocial thoughts and behaviors.

Criminal and delinquent experiences formed through participation in or observation of delinquent and criminal activities in the company of friends and family are reinforced through verbal and nonverbal communication, rationalization of antisocial behavior, practical validation, imitation, role modeling, repetition, and rewards in the form of praise, respect, and concessions that ultimately form the basis of antisocial and prosocial behaviors. In this context, the probability of an offender engaging in antisocial activities depends largely on each offender's experiences and on whether the family members, friends, and social institutions with whom a potential offender associates promote law abiding behaviors.

The level of risk might depend primarily on the strength of attachment, relationship, and level of validation or distorted interpretation of antisocial behaviors. Validation occurs in many forms, but most commonly it involves blaming others for one's own actions, justifying or minimizing delinquent and criminal behaviors. Behaviors are minimized when an offender argues that the negative consequences of his or her behaviors are less severe than the actual consequences. Justification occurs when an offender tries to explain the "justness" of delinquent and criminal behaviors so as to avoid taking full responsibility for wrongdoing. Other forms of validation are achieved by simply downplaying the importance of delinquent or criminal behavior so as to make an antisocial behavior appears less significant than others see it.

In some cases, an offender may also validate behaviors by casting his or herself as victim of his or her own behaviors, or by blaming other people for his or her own delinquent or criminal acts. For example, a rapist might attempt to justify his behavior by arguing that his victim wore a provocative dress or that the victim did not physically resist and thus must have consented to the assault. A gang member may justify criminal gang membership by claiming to be protecting his neighbors. The same criminal gang membership can be validated or reinforced through social rewards in the form of respect and praise from friends and family members. In all of these cases, the logic at work is that offenders who master the act of justifying, minimizing, or blaming others for their own actions are more likely to engage in criminal or delinquent activities. Offenders with little or no history of justifying or minimizing behaviors or blaming other people are less likely to engage in delinquent or criminal activities.

SOCIAL CONTROL THEORY

Social control theory is one of the most frequently cited criminological theories by criminal justice scholars (Wells & Rankin, 1998; Akers et al., 2017). This theory focuses on how positive relationships between a potential offender and other protective or prosocial institutions such as family, schools, workplaces, and community can deter such an at-risk youth from going astray. As a result, social control theory assumes that individual criminal or delinquent thinking and behaviors is controlled by key social control tenets: fear of punishment, desire to retain favorable reputation, degree of attachment, and the extent to which an offender identifies with a family, a school, or institutions capable of influencing a potential offender's behaviors (Wells & Rankin, 1998; Walsh & Stohr, 2010).

Social control theory also recognizes that not all ties to social institutions such as prosocial families, schools, and workplaces serve as protective factors because in order for an institution to qualify as a prosocial institution and thus a protective factor, it has to have the capacity to positively reinforce positive behaviors and sustain strong relationships with potential offenders, and the means to reward prosocial thinking as well as to punish antisocial behaviors. The power of an institution to shape behaviors includes the capacity to inform an offender's decisions about engaging or not engaging in a particular delinquent or criminal act. For example, if the institution is a school, it must be one that produces positive factors such as quality education and a crime-free environment and one that asserts some form of control through swift assignment of consequences and rewards. Furthermore, when an individual is making a decision to engage or not to engage in delinquent or criminal acts, the institution must serve as a meaningful source of positive aspiration.

The power to directly or indirectly influence a particular offender's behavior depends largely on how effectively an institution can manifest its power or control through the deliverance of rewards for good behaviors and consequences for bad behaviors. Thus, four types of control have been identified: direct, indirect, internalized, and opportunity-motivated controls. According to Wells and Rankin (1998), direct control occurs when a physical form of consequence is present, such as getting a ticket for speeding, getting arrested for drinking and driving, or receiving a life sentence for premeditated murder. The pain associated with getting a traffic ticket, being arrested, and receiving a life sentence has the power to deter specific offenders as well as potential drunks, speeders, reckless drivers, and murderers. Social control is the direct control of factors, such as fear of pain and discomfort inflicted by the traffic tickets, arrests, and sentences, that ultimately control individual behavior. This fear of receiving negative outcomes can also be internally generated by an individual's desire to achieve a particular end result. For example, love for and attachment to parents may urge a youth to do things that will please his or her parents. The internal force can also compel a student's pursuit of high grades as a way to satisfy his or her parents.

Internalized control is more of an internal or mental control mechanism that is based on what a potential offender personally believes and what beliefs have become parts of a potential offender's reality. Internalized control also includes how such notions of reality influence law breaking or antisocial behaviors. A student who believes that any grade less than an A is a disappointing grade is likely to be motivated by internalized notions of what constitutes a good grade to work harder in order to avoid getting any grade short of an A. Equally, the purpose for which a student views an A grade as worth pursuing may be primarily informed by the establishment of a link between the grade and future jobs and school opportunities. In these cases, future opportunities act as a compelling force that drives an offender to act positively in anticipation of receiving a particular reward associated with a behavior. This is similar to forces that push certain employees to work harder in anticipation of the opportunity to receive an employee-of-the-year award, and the same force may push a child to work really hard in school in anticipation of using his or her high-performing grades to win over the happiness and attention of parents. It is also similar to the invisible power that pushes a student to work harder to maintain a high grade-point average in anticipation of remaining or getting on a dean's list (Wells & Rankin, 1998).

Since social control theory views the absence of positive relationships between a youth and family and school as an absence of positive control and thus a license for delinquent and criminal activities, crime and delinquent behaviors are seen as the results of weakened social ties between an offender and those institutions. However, having a relationship is one thing and being committed to or appreciative of a relationship is another matter altogether and perhaps the most crucial for determining the impact of a relationship on an offender's behavior. Crucial in this process is the recognition of the inevitably intricate relationships between individual wants and collective wants.

Indeed, in many cases social conformity to collective norms or cultures "occurs at the cost of the repression of natural urges" and individual "wants and needs," which also mean personal needs "are inextricably linked to the wants and need of others" (Walsh & Stohr, 2010, p. 23). Therefore, an at-risk offender who recognizes the need to care about satisfying collective wants as a means through which his or her personal wants and needs can be achieved is more likely to succeed in maintaining a prosocial life than the one who neglects such connections. The assumption is that those who recognize the relationship between compliance with public laws and expectations and the attainment of individual needs tend to engage in prosocial activities. Those who neglect the connections between public needs and individual needs can be easily persuaded to take part in antisocial activities.

SOCIAL BOND THEORY

Social bond theory, introduced in 1969 by Travis Hirschi, argues that a potential offender's delinquent or criminal behaviors can be shaped by that offender's attachment and commitment to, involvement with, and belief in vital social institutions that primarily include prosocial families, schools, employers, and other social institutions, such as churches, mosques, or synagogues (Hirschi 1969). Many empirical efforts informed by this theory have resulted in the conclusion that a potential offender's weak attachment and commitment to, involvement with, and belief in vital social institutions such as families and schools increase that potential offender's chances of engaging in criminal or delinquent activities. At the same time, strong attachment and commitment to, involvement with, and belief in the same critical social institutions decrease the possibility of criminal or delinquent behaviors (Hirschi, 2011; Akers et al., 2017; Williams & McShane, 2018).

Attachment "involves an emotional connection to another person" (Hirschi, 2011, p. 215). Attachment is therefore the establishment or the recognition of deeper relationships between a potential offender and critical social intuitions—family, friends, schools, religious institutions, and community—that involve the sharing of interests and the identification with such institutions. Attachment can be expressed in many ways, but the real effect of a connection depends largely on the extent to which a youth becomes involved with such critical social institutions. For instance, the level of involvement with social institutions such as families and schools can be measured by the quality of a potential offender's attachment to and participation in activities that further those social institutions' goals and by the degree to which the potential offender adheres to the values and principles that those institutions share and promote.

Commitment includes the act of pledging to translate one's mental attachment into action by devoting time and effort to the physical pursuit of shared institutional goals and by participating in activities that are consistent with the shared goals of one's social institutions. Commitment also means the expressed desire and willingness to maintain one's attachment to and involvement with vital social institutions as well as the exercise of respect for the social institutions' goals. For example, commitment to schools can be exhibited through participation in extracurricular activities, and commitment to family can be manifested through one's participation in family gatherings, functions, and events. The greater the commitment to school- and family-related activities, the higher the involvement will likely be and the better the possibility for a potential offender to be swayed away from antisocial behaviors.

In terms of shaping behaviors, commitment to social institutions is more effective when such commitment is coupled with involvement in the perpetuation of the values and principles one's social institutions represent. Involvement in this context also refers to the manifestation of attachment and commitment through participation in family, extracurricular, religious, and civic activities. This process can be more rewarding when backed by expressed beliefs in the values and principles that are advanced by the social institutions to which potential offenders subscribe. At a minimum, such beliefs generally include show of respect for honesty, fairness, public laws, education, gainful employment, and responsibilities.

Within the context of social bond theory, the assumptions are that people who are attached to social institutions and who are involved in the pursuit of the common goals of those social institutions, and those who are committed to principles and values that are shared within those institutions, are more likely to veer away from criminal or delinquent behaviors and are also more likely to exercise belief in the common values and principles that those institutions represent. The stronger the relationship to those critical social institutions, such as schools and families, the firmer are the beliefs in those institutions' values and belief systems.

According to Hirschi (2011), healthy relationships between a youth and vital social institutions also make it more likely for that youth to care about what other members of those social institutions might "think of them" if they were to engage in delinquent or criminal acts. This line of thought creates a fear of being viewed negatively and thus has the power to compel potential offenders to restrain from engaging in criminal or delinquent acts, even in situations where opportunities for crime and delinquency might present themselves (Hirschi, 2011, p. 215). Furthermore, the stronger the bond between a potential offender and vital social institutions, the more likely the fear of disrupting the relationship or disappointing members of the social institution will shape the thinking and behavior of a potential offender.

Indeed, studies have shown that those youths with strong social bonds, as evidenced by their commitment to the pursuit of education, compliance with public laws, involvement in schoolwork, and participation in extracurricular and family activities, are less likely to engage in criminal and delinquent activities. A strong bond between these categories of youth and critical social institutions such as schools and families can also significantly enhance potential offenders' prosocial thinking and behaviors, and the absence of such a bond can drastically increase the offender's chances of engaging in delinquent or criminal activities. In other words, belief in, involvement with, and attachment and commitment to prosocial institutions such as families, peers, and schools can positively impact a potential offender's prosocial thinking and behaviors.

RATIONAL CHOICE THEORY

The differential association, social learning, and social control theories advance the notion that certain criminal or delinquent behaviors are influenced by external factors, such as dysfunctional families, delinquent peers, exposure to delinquent activities, or lack of bond between an offender and prosocial institutions. The search for a cure for criminal or delinquent behaviors and tendencies must therefore focus on those external factors. This positivist views clearly conflicts with the basic premise of rational choice theory, which at its core makes the classical argument that humans are created equal and endowed with the capability and free will to choose comfort over pain and pursue that which benefits them most. At a broader level, rational choice theory assumes that individuals have a standing social contract with their governments that binds them to obey laws and obligates states to punish lawbreakers (Akers et al., 2017).

The basic foundation of rational choice theory is the issue of personal choice derived from the notion of rationality. Thus, rational choice theory holds that (1) human are rational beings, (2) human rationality is regulated by end results, (3) criminal or delinquent behaviors are products of free choice based on rational calculations of pleasure versus pain, (4) human choices are influenced by the desire to maximize personal pleasure, and (5) that swift, certain, and proportionate punishments can deter criminal or delinquent choices. In other words, humans are rational. Therefore, they freely choose crime or delinquency because crime brings them pleasure; hence, punishment is the only thing that can stop them from making bad choices (Williams & McShane, 2014).

Rationality is understood as a calculated process driven primarily by selfish needs for self-preservation. Rationality is also understood as an individual's ability to make sound judgments that produce a planned behavioral outcome or results that further individual self-preservation. The process of reasoning involves the recognition of problem, such as a hungry and penniless person wanting a loaf of bread. In this case since the hungry and penniless individual wants the bread, stealing it is more rational in terms of the time needed to end his or her hunger: after all, the bread is right there and all that it takes is reaching for it and walking away. Of course, the alternative would be to find a job and use earned pay to buy the bread. However, that would take a much longer time; besides, there is no guarantee that the individual would get a job, and even if a job were to be secured, working on an empty stomach would be a very painful undertaking. The logical assumption, therefore, is that stealing the loaf of bread is a quicker way to address the hunger.

The premise of rationality is that by virtue of human ability to distinguish between comfort and pain, criminals or delinquent offenders carefully weigh the benefits of their choices against the likelihood of getting caught. Thus, since crimes or delinquent behaviors are products of rational thinking that further the pursuit of personal gain, satisfaction, and comfort as well as the attainment of the quixotic goodies offenders associate with their behavior, the best way to prevent people from engaging in criminal or delinquent acts is to swiftly punish bad choices. That is, as a response to criminal or delinquent behaviors, the logical way to deter people from continuously choosing bad behaviors that bring them comfort over painful behaviors that bring them pleasure is to punish bad choices.

The primary purpose of punishment is to specifically deter the offender and to send a message of deterrence to all would-be offenders that they too will be punished accordingly. In order to achieve maximum deterrent effect, the punishment must be swift, certain, and proportionate. Certainty has the effect of assuring all potential offenders that they too will receive the same punishment if they were to engage in similar actions. Swiftness reinforces certainty and guarantees future punishment by minimizing the possibility of intervening circumstances that could potentially make irregularity more permissible. Proportionality presents punishment as a product of one's choice and reassures potential offenders that the degree to which the offender suffers is dictated by the level of criminal or delinquent choices.

"FREE WILL" IS ALWAYS DEBATABLE

It is logical to say that the opposite of classicalism, which is the basis of rational choice theory, is positivism. For example, positivism argues that the concept of "free will" is not always practical because rational choices are subjective, often depending on many competing variables. Factors such as mental health condition, socioeconomic status, and natural, physiological, and psychological conditioning as well as environmental, historical, and legal reasons or circumstances can significantly shape decisions that lead to the commission of crimes. In other words, criminal or delinquent behaviors are informed by many risk or protective factors, consistent with the view of many criminological theories including the differential association, social learning, social bond, and social control theories.

The mental proximity and certainty of punishment have the effect of stopping potential offenders from intentionally choosing crimes or delinquency over law abiding behaviors because punishment teaches potential offenders that the painful consequences of criminal or delinquent behaviors outweigh the temporary excitements that are usually associated with particularly crimes against persons. In this case. harsh treatment such as detention specifically deters offenders from victimizing other members of the public and also has a general deterrent effect because it assures would-be offenders that crimes or bad choices do not pay; rather, they produce pain and suffering (Cornish & Clarke, 2011; Cullen & Agnew, 2011). Of course, these conclusions are inconsistent with positivism.

STRAIN THEORY

One of the common suspects of delinquent and criminal behaviors is nonconformity to social norms. Strain theory generally looks at the avoidance of stressful life predicaments as another source of frustration and strain for juveniles. That is, failure to conform to what society usually expects of its members creates social difficulties or strains that make it even harder to compete with the rest of society for meagre public resources. The term *strain* refers to the difficulties or stressors associated with an individual's failure to lawfully achieve the social status needed to be viewed and treated as successful in society, in part because they lack adequate social resources (Akers et al., 2017; Williams & McShane, 2018). In terms of why this happens, Lilly, Cullen, and Ball (2011) explain:

> Social structure limits access to the goal of success through legitimate means (e.g., college education, corporate employment, family connections). Members of the lower class are particularly burdened because they start far behind in the race for success and must be exceptionally talented or fortunate to catch up.

Feeling unable to attain meaningful education, employment, and social status leaves some people with the false assumption that they have no alternative path than criminal and delinquent behavior. As a result of the strain or stressors, the offender develops negative emotions and becomes frustrated at their inability to achieve desired goals. Consequently, they may become angry and desire to seek revenge against the perceived source of the strain.

Strain theory therefore focuses on the things that society values and the means to achieve such goals. Thus, the theory maintains that when mainstream norms pressure people to produce socially acceptable results without first facilitating the means or access to resources, generally in the form of financial, material, and educational help required to achieve such goals, some people turn to criminal and delinquent activities to compensate for their failure to achieve conventional success. In this case, crime may be used to reduce the strain or avoid the stress and to take revenge on perceived sources of socioeconomic impotence characterized by the inability to achieve social success or the status of middle class.

ROUTINE ACTIVITY

The argument made by routine activity theory is very simple: For most criminal and delinquent behavior to take place, three factors must be present. First, there must be a motivated offender or person willing to commit the crime. Second, there must be a suitable target in the form of a person or interest that can be legally violated. Third, contact between the motivated offender and the suitable target must happen in the absence of a guardian or authority capable of preventing the victimization. That is, delinquency is likely to take place when the offender and a target are present in the same location and in the absence of an authority or suitable guardian. Delinquency is also less likely when the offender and an authority are present in the presence of a target (Cohen & Felson, 1979; Williams & McShane, 2014).

WHY A FIVE-YEAR-OLD MAY WAIT FOR MOM TO WALK AWAY BEFORE REACHING FOR CANDY

If you ever wonder why banks make sure to let you know that you are being videotaped or why security officers stand outside banks, routine activities theory has the answers. Banks are suitable targets for many motivated offenders (bank robbers). So, the physical presence of the security guard greeting people as they enter and leave and customers' knowledge of being videotaped are designed to remind motivated offenders that a suitable guardian (security officer or video camera) is present. Routine activity theory also explains why children wait for their parents (suitable guardians) to walk away before dipping their hands into the candy jar and why children refrain from mischief when parents (suitable guardians) are present. This theory also explains why police departments make their officers and vehicles visible in areas where criminal activities are common.

A capable guardian includes any person or object that has the capacity to at least deter a motivated offender from engaging in a particular delinquent or criminal act. Thus, suitable authorities include police officers, security guards, probation and parole officers, and prosocial friends and family. The presence of a working closed-circuit television (CCTV) that is visible to the offender can also serve as a capable guardian. It is therefore not surprising that supervision of offenders is stressed at every level of the criminal justice process, including probation, detention, and parole. This theory also explains the reasons behind policies such as supervised visitation and restriction of certain offenders from working with vulnerable populations, such as children, in certain areas and capacities. For instance, sex offenders are generally prohibited from working with children or participating in any unsupervised interaction with children. Abusive parents may also be asked to have supervised interaction with their children. In both instances, the presence of capable guardians prevents the offender from recidivating.

LABELLING THEORY

It is common to hear labels such as criminal, delinquent, addict, and repeat offender thrown around in the halls of juvenile probation, parole departments, and courts. Unfortunately, however, while such titles make it easier to identify and serve offenders, the habit of labelling individuals, especially children, can produce negative consequences (Williams & McShane, 2018; Akers et al., 2017). Labelling theory is therefore concerned with the effect of labels that designate children as criminals, deviants, delinquents, failures, dropouts, or dangerous persons both in terms of how others respond to the labels and how the acceptance of the label by offenders increases their risk of future delinquency and criminality.

The basic premise of labelling theory is that the social meaning ascribed to children as a result of certain acts can influence new behaviors because labels for such acts connote specific social expectations and moral evaluations of both the act and the individual to whom the label is applied (Albrecht & Albrecht, 1978). Assumptions are that labels dictate how offenders are viewed and treated by society, how offenders view and treat others in society, and how offenders view their behaviors in relation to others. The key premise is that people who are labeled as delinquents or criminals tend to be treated as delinquent or criminal by members of the public and by the very people within vital institutions, such as schools and the criminal justice systems, who assign them the labels. Consequently, labeled children accept that they are what their labels says, and as a result, they may act in accordance with their assigned labels. The treatment that labeled children receive from the public in turn reinforces public perceptions and the offenders' own views, and that the offender is what the label says.

Labelling theory also views deviance as a matter of social definition or social meaning given to behaviors by those who view such behaviors as constituting acts of deviance. The initial label is the consequence of the offender's being caught and officially labeled as deviant. The labels attracted by the primary act of deviance can, however, have serious, unintended negative consequences, including an increase in the labeled offender's risk of future delinquency or deviance because such a label limits the offender's access to prosocial institutions and to crucial opportunities and resources. The label reduces the child's chances of succeeding in school or participating in certain legitimate activities and makes them feel that they are expected to behave in accordance with the labels that they have been assigned. As the doors for prosocial activities are closed as a consequence of labelling, opportunities open up for criminal behaviors, such as gang membership, as the only outlet for achieving the status they feel unable to attain through prosocial endeavors. The second labels depicting criminal, deviant, or delinquent behaviors, such as *gangster*, come as a reaction to the secondary deviant act, which is informed partly by the initial labelling. Obviously, the effect of labels varies in terms of the social attributes and the social consequences that are attracted (Williams & McShane, 2018).

Labelling theory is useful in that it reminds criminal justice professionals, including correction, probation, parole, and court officers as well as public institutions, that the mere placement of youth in secured facilities and the labelling of children who end up in the criminal justice system can have serious negative consequences on their future behaviors. The theory is also helpful in shaping the way juvenile offenders are treated both within and outside the criminal justice system. Furthermore, this theory makes the case that the assignment of negative labels to children has no valid clinical function; instead, the practice undermines the minimization of delinquency and criminality because it influences negative reactions to the youth's post-labelled behaviors by themselves and the public.

SOCIAL ORGANIZATION THEORY

The general hypothesis advanced by social disorganization theory says that low economic status and environmental and family disruption lead to social disorganization of societies, which in turn increases the risk of crime and delinquency committed by children living in such environments (Sampson & Groves, 1989). As the community becomes disorganized, neighborhood cohesion, social institutions, and collective efficacy weaken, and the social capacity that would normally regulate crimes and delinquency becomes incapable of doing so (Markowitz, Bellair, Liska, & Liu, 2001). The theory specifically emphasizes that variations in social structure, culture, and the local ecology, along with a lack of resources, shape social order, levels of social control, and social integration in communities.

Social disorganization theory therefore provides probation or parole officers as well as court officials with useful knowledge for decisions regarding the placement of juvenile offenders in certain neighborhoods and homes as well as the removal of children from localities that are by definition socially disorganized. At a systemic level, this theory advances support for public and collective investments in neighborhood appearance as a vehicle for mitigating delinquency and crime rates. It also provides support for the building of socially organized communities to prevent such communities from becoming socioeconomically disorganized and to significantly diminish the criminogenic risk of potential offenders there.

SUBCULTURAL THEORY

Members of society, subcultural theory argues, share a common value system that emphasizes certain norms over others. For example, it is the case that most societies expect members of their communities to individually possess some degree of authority, respect, status, and decent means of living. When the opportunities to achieve these goals become attainable mainly by privileged members of society, the less-privileged class feels left out (Akers et al., 2017; Williams & McShane, 2018). Additional constraints on potential offenders are made possible by the fact that public institutions such as schools reflect middle-class values and goals. These institutions use core societal values that are often not fully representative of disadvantaged or at-risk youth to evaluate every person with whom they come into contact.

For example, tardiness is an important breach of school rule. However, the behavior can be informed by factors beyond the control of a child, and by conditions such as economic difficulties and belonging to either a family that does not care about this important school rule or a family that is unable to fully comply. Unfavorable economic conditions can also prevent certain children and people from completing high school or college. In all of these situations, the failure to satisfy these core societal values may push a youth out of the mainstream.

As the subcultural theory argues, membership in a criminal subcultural group drastically increases the risk of engaging in criminal and delinquent activities, especially if the subgroup rewards criminal behavior. Consequently, as certain people are squeezed out of the mainstream, they become frustrated with the pursuit of status and values through legitimate means. Instead, they look for rebellious ways to defy the very authority that allegedly squeezed them out of legitimate means of achieving status and respect. Potential offenders accomplish these goals by joining or creating a new subcultural system that may be sympathetic to their plight (Akers et al., 2017; Williams & McShane, 2018).

When the opportunity to participate in illegitimate adventures is made available by subcultural groups such as gangs, at-risk youth jump at it. This may explain why the majority of street gang members are African Americans and Hispanics, and only a fraction of street gang members are Whites (Howell, 1998). Indeed, despite the fact that the United States is a culturally diverse society, the dominant or mainstream culture and values favor White, Anglo-Saxon, and Protestant Americans, and thus Whites naturally have some competitive edge in most cases (Weaver, 1999). Subcultural theory also explains why in every major America major city there tend to be more cliques of street gangs than schools. Further, this theory explains why street gang members share a few things in common; notably, members come from and operate in socioeconomically distressed environments that are known for high poverty rates and broken and highly disorganized families.

BLACKS AND HISPANICS TAKE THE LEAD IN GANG MEMBERSHIP

According to the National Gang Center, African Americans (or Blacks) and Hispanics (or Latinos) are first and second, respectively, in being members of criminal street gangs. On average, between 1996 and 2011 more than 82% of youth criminal gang members in the United States were Blacks and Hispanics.

TABLE 2.1 *Race/Ethnicity of Gang Members, 1996–2011*

YEAR	HISPANIC	BLACK	WHITE	OTHER
1996	45.2	35.6	11.6	7.5
1998	46.5	33.6	11.8	8
1999	47.3	30.9	13.4	8.4
2001	49	33.7	10.3	7
2002	47	35.7	10.4	6.9
2004	48.7	37.8	7.9	5.7
2005	50.1	32.6	9.5	7.7
2006	49.5	35.2	8.5	6.8
2008	50.2	31.8	10.5	7.6
2011	46.2	35.3	11.5	7

In comparison to Black and Hispanic youth, the number of White youth who are members of one or more criminal gangs at the local level is much smaller. Specifically, the number of White youth who are members of one or more criminal gangs in larger cities is 9.7%; in smaller cities, that number is 14.6%; in suburban counties, it is 9.1%; and in rural counties, the figure stands at 14.9%. The numbers for Blacks and Hispanics were also higher than for Whites in smaller cities (Blacks 20.3% and Hispanics 53.8%), in rural counties (Blacks 56.8% and Hispanics 24.8%), in larger cities (Blacks 39% and Hispanics 45.5%), and in suburban counties (Blacks 32.7% and Hispanics 51%).

It is to be remembered that race or ethnicity does not predict gang membership. Other factors such as poor socioeconomic status and lack of ties to prosocial institutions do. For instance, although poverty is a reality for many children in the United States, there are more Hispanic and Black adolescents who grow up in poverty than White adolescents. Blacks and Hispanics are also less likely to graduate from high school compared to Whites. These factors are important because all are good predictors of youth becoming gang members.

Source:

National Gang Center. (2019). *National youth gang survey analysis*. Retrieved from https://www.nationalgangcenter.gov/survey-analysis/demographics

Social disorganization theory views behaviors such as gang crimes as the result of efforts by underprivileged members of society to attain goals and status they feel could not be achieved using mainstream means, a framework for addressing crime and delinquent problems such as gang behavior. Indeed, gang membership can be seen as a symptom of youth who feel unprotected; come from disorganized and broken families and homes; are unable to achieve academic success; lack involvement in, or attachment or commitment to school; live in neighborhoods with active gangs; and believe that gang membership is a means for overcoming barriers that prevent them from achieving mainstream dreams. Thus, gang membership can shape criminal justice practitioners' supervisory and treatment responses to many criminal and delinquent activities.

CONCLUSION

Theories discussed in this chapter can be grouped under two distinct categories: institutional response theories and behavioral assessment and classification theories. The latter talk about what public policies should be implemented to mitigate the risk of delinquent and criminal behavior. The former talk about what the offender has done or should do to minimize the risk of criminal and delinquent behavior. For example, routine activity theory, labelling theory, social organization theory, and subculture theory shape the decisions made by criminal justice practitioners, especially probation, parole, court, and detention authorities, in relation to the treatment and supervision of offenders. They direct attention to offenders' environments and other conditions that influence delinquency and criminality.

Similarly, social learning theory, differential association theory, and social bond and social control theories point to offenders' manifested behavior as sources of vital factors that can be used to calculate the risk and needs levels of offenders. Differences between these behavioral assessment and classification theories and the institutional response theories also include the fact that theories such as social learning theory, differential association theory, social bond and social control theories focus on offender-acquired prosocial and antisocial behaviors—in other words, what the offender has done. On the contrary, institutional response theories focus on why children under certain conditions develop an interest in learning and engaging in delinquent and criminal behaviors. For example, social bond theory posits that children who are attached and committed to and involved with their schools have a high chance of generating prosocial results. The theory, however, does not explain why certain children fail to attach to, commit to, or be involved with their schools. For an answer to that question, one would have to turn to institutional response theories such as labelling, social organization, or subcultural theory.

DISCUSSION QUESTIONS

1. Name and discuss criminal justice policies currently in use by probation, parole, court, or detention authorities that are informed by these theories: routine activity, labelling, social organization, and subcultural.
2. What are some of the most impactful risk and protective factors advanced by each of the theories discussed in this chapter?
3. If you had to pick two theories that every probation or parole officer must read and use in formulating strategies for preventing offenders' future criminal or delinquent behaviors, which would those be and why?
4. If you had to pick two theories that every elected public officeholder charged with responding to juvenile delinquency and criminality must read and use in formulating strategies for preventing offenders' future criminal or delinquent behaviors, which would those be and why?
5. Which theoretical framework best explains racial differences in certain crime statistics?

REFERENCES

Akers, R. L., Sellers, C. S., & Jennings, W. G. (2017). *Criminological theories: Introduction, evaluation, and application*. New York, NY: Oxford University Press.

Albrecht, G. L., & Albrecht, M. H. (1978). A critical assessment of labeling in the juvenile justice system. *Justice System Journal*, *4*(1), 114–128.

Cacciottolo, M. (2015, October 13). Saudi Arabia drinking: The risks expats take for a tipple. *BBC News*. Retrieved from https://www.bbc.com/news/uk-34516143

Cohen, L. E., & Felson, M. (1979). Social change and crime rate trends: A routine activity approach. *American Sociological Review*, *44*(4), 588–608.

Cornish, D. B., & Clarke, R. V. (2011). Crime as a rational choice. In F. T. Cullen & R. Agnew (Eds.), *Criminological theory: Past to present* (4th ed.). New York, NY: Oxford University Press.

Cullen, F. T., & Agnew, R. (2011). Reviving classical theory: Deterrence and rational choice theories. In F. T. Cullen & R. Agnew (Eds.), *Criminological theory: Past to present* (4th ed.). New York, NY: Oxford University Press.

Hirschi, T. (1969). *Causes of delinquency*. Berkeley: University of California Press.

Hirschi, T. (2011). Social bond theory. In F. T. Cullen & R. Agnew (Eds.), *Criminological theory: Past to present* (4th ed.). New York, NY: Oxford University Press.

Howell, J. C. (1998). *Youth gangs: An overview*. Retrieved from the Office of Juvenile Justice and Deliquency Prevention website: https://www.ojjdp.gov/jjbulletin/9808/contents.html

Lilly, J. R., Cullen, F. T., & Ball, R. A. (2011). *Criminological theory: Context and consequences*. Los Angeles, CA: Sage.

Markowitz, F. E., Bellair, P. E., Liska, A. E., & Liu, J. (2001). Extending social disorganization theory: Modeling the relationships between cohesion, disorder, and fear. *Criminology, 39*(2), 293–319.

Sampson, R. J., & Groves, W. B. (1989). Community structure and crime: Testing social-disorganization theory. *American Journal of Sociology, 94*(4), 774–802.

Sutherland, E. H., Cressey, D. R. (2011). A theory of differential association. In F. T. Cullen & R. Agnew (Eds.), *Criminological theory: Past to present* (4th ed.). New York, NY: Oxford University Press.

Walsh, A., & Stohr, M. K. (2010). *Correctional assessment, casework, and counseling*. Alexandria, VA: American Correctional Association.

Weaver, G. R. (1999). *American cultural values*. Kokusai Bunka Kenshu (Intercultural Training). Retreived from https://www.airuniversity.af.edu/Portals/10/AFNC/documents/Negotiationsectionstef/American%20Cultural%20Values.pdf

Wells, L. E., & Rankin, J. H. (1998). Social control theories of delinquency: Direct parental controls. In S. Henry & W. Einstadter (Eds.), *The criminology theory reader*. New York: New York University Press.

Williams, F. P., & McShane, M. D. (2018). *Criminological theory* (7th ed.). New York, NY: Pearson.

CHAPTER THREE

Juvenile Justice Classification Labels

THOSE WHO WORK with juveniles at any level of the juvenile justice process use labels that are designed to distinguish one group of juveniles from another. In particular, the courts, correctional facilities, and departments of probation and parole each use unique classification systems that convey offenders' needs, risk, and responsivity as well as dictate how each group of juvenile offenders should be treated in comparison to other youth in the system. Labels communicate how juvenile offenders should be treated by every criminal justice practitioner with whom they interact. That is, in theory labels are designed to help criminal justice practitioners make informed decisions about each youth's likelihood of reoffending, placement options, supervision levels and strategies, and interventions that can effectively reduce the likelihood of recidivism (Vincent, Guy, & Grisso, 2012). Each designated label therefore comes with certain rights, privileges, consequences, and benefits that dictate how an offender is to be treated in terms of access to services and the degree of freedom that should be accorded them while under juvenile justice supervision.

This chapter provides an overview of labels used by legislators, juvenile courts, clinical staff, and juvenile corrections, probation, and parole officers regarding offenders who come under their control or care. It is important to note that each jurisdiction uses a unique system to clinically or legally distinguish one group of offenders from another in terms of needs, risk, responsivity, and behavior. Hence, this chapter covers what the labels *emancipated child, status offender, dependent child, incorrigible child, delinquent child, criminal offender, probationer,* and *parolee* mean when used by juvenile justice practitioners.

JUDICIAL AND STATUTORY CLASSIFICATION LABELS

One factor that distinguishes the adult criminal justice system from the juvenile justice system is that the latter uses unique labels when talking about offenders under its control. Also, the way offenders are processed generally differs from the way the former processes adult offenders. For example, unlike the adult system, where offenders are brought in by police officers and classified strictly on the offenders' escape or flight risk and danger to others or self within a secured facility, juveniles who come under the juvenile justice system's control or care make their contact through various means. Consequently, individuals charged with the initial assessment of juvenile offenders play important roles in determining the fate of each offender who enters the custody of the juvenile justice system, specifically in terms of assigning appropriate labels that describe offenders both in terms of behaviors and how they should be treated, cared for, and protected while in the custody of the juvenile justice system.

IDEAL REPONSES TO LEGAL LABELS

It would be perfectly acceptable if a juvenile court judge communicated the following labels in Table 3.1 toward youth who qualify for the label of emancipated or dependent and also offenders justly labelled incorrigible, delinquent, criminal, or status offenders.

TABLE 3.1 *Authority Responses to Labels*

LABELS	POSSIBLE RESPONSE
Emancipated Youth	Good luck, and remember that you are still a kid.
Dependent Youth	Are you okay? What can I do for you to ensure that you are safe?
Incorrigible Offender	Go home and obey your parents. Do what they tell you to do.
Status Offender	You need to stay out of trouble by obeying rules and being responsible.
Delinquent Offender	You are not going home today because you and I have to talk about serious stuff: your bad behaviors.
Criminal Offender	You are not going home. I am detaining you until your behaviors are addressed.

A well-informed probation or intake officer would also take similar approaches based on the criminal justice response each label legally or clinically demands. An emancipated or dependent youth generally needs help from the courts because the contact they make with the criminal justice system is entirely warranted by the need for protection. The incorrigible youth and the status offender may require a stricter warning because both cases involve the exhibition of antisocial behaviors. Incorrigible behaviors mostly take place at home and involve parents or legal guardians, where status offender's behaviors occur in the public arena. Also, emancipated youth do not qualify for probation, parole or detention because the label calls for protection and sanction. Under current federal law, status and incorrigible offenders do not qualify for parole. Delinquent and criminal youth represent more serious behaviors.

Juvenile court intake officers—or in some jurisdictions, probation officers—conduct initial assessments of juveniles who are brought under the control of the juvenile justice system for allegedly committing delinquent, criminal, status, or incorrigible offenses. The intake officer also processes youth who enter the system for dependence or emancipation-related cases. The person conducting the assessment is also generally charged with determining whether a youth is dependent, incorrigible, delinquent, or criminal. The intake officer's interaction with youth seeking emancipation orders may, however, be limited because that group of youth are not offenders; rather, they are children seeking court protection.

Emancipated Child

Juvenile courts deal with some youth whose only reason for contacting the juvenile justice system is to seek a declaration of emancipation from parental control. A petition for emancipation is an appeal to a juvenile court to terminate parental rights to exercise control over a youth. Hence, an emancipated child is a youth who legally becomes "adult" before his or her 18th birthday as a result of a judge declaring such a youth independent from his or her parents. The emancipated status frees the child from parental control and gives the child the right to live how and where he or she chooses.

Generally, the court approves an emancipation request when records show that such an order will be in the best interest of the minor. The court may also deny application for emancipation if records show that granting the order will not serve the best interest of the child. However, once attained, an emancipation order is generally permanent, although a court can revise its order if post-emancipation evidence shows that the child lied to the court or if the child becomes unable to take care of himself or herself.

According to the Legal Information Institute, all states in the United States have specific laws or legal processes regarding the right of children under certain circumstances to emancipate themselves from direct parental control. The states of Alabama, California, Colorado, Florida, Massachusetts, North Carolina, and Wyoming are examples of states that have specific laws devoted to emancipation proceeding (Centers for Disease Control and Prevention, 2018). In California, for example, the California Emancipation of Minors Law gives youth who are at least 14 years old the right to petition the court for emancipation from parental control if the child is legally married or enlisted in the United States Armed Forces. In the absence of these conditions, a child may still petition the court and get a declaration of emancipation order.

To acquire an emancipation order under California law, the child must file the appropriate documentation with the court and pay any relevant fees. A child's application for emancipation must also show that in addition to the child's express desire not to live under parental control, the parents must have no objection to the child becoming emancipated. This requirement explains why an application for emancipation must be signed by parents; their permission indicates approval of the applicant's desire to emancipate himself or herself from parental control. Additionally, the child must show the court that he or she can satisfactorily manage finances and show that they have ways to legally earn money. The applicant must also convince the court that an emancipation order would serve the applicant's best interest.

EMANCIPATION IS A MIXED BAG: A LITTLE FREEDOM AND A LOT OF RESPONSIBILITY

Emancipation is a great tool, especially for children at risk of suffering serious harm by being in their parents' custody. There is, however, the chance that some youth may mistakenly assume that this useful legal remedy for things such as sexual or physical abuse is a free ride or shortcut to adulthood. Indeed as shown in Table 3.2 in reality emancipation is a mixed bag of limitations and responsibilities, and the freedoms are costly and come with responsibility (Superior Court of Orange County, 2019).

TABLE 3.2 *Responsibilities and Rights*

NEW RESPONSIBILITIES	RIGHTS TO ENJOY
Support self financially	Live at any place of choice
Procure medical insurance	Legally enter into binding contracts—buy own car, boat, and home
Maintain legal and financial responsibilities	Take legal action against other people or companies
	Keep own earnings
	Work without parental consent
	Enroll at any school or college
	Make decisions regarding medical, dental, and psychiatric care
	Stay out as late as any adult—no more curfew
Not So Fast—Only Actual Grown Ups Can Do These	
Refuse to go to school, at least not until age eighteen or graduation from high school	
The number of paid work hours is limited—school still counts	
Parental consent is still required for marriage	
No sexual activity with older person(s)—statutory rape stays on the books	
No alcohol or illicit drug use that is legal for people twenty-one or older	
Voting is still not allowed, no matter how much the president, government, or mayor is hated	

Source:

Superior Court of Orange County. (2019). Minor emancipation. Retrieved from https://www.occourts.org/directory/probate/probate-case-types/minor-emancipation.html

When granted, the emancipation status comes with certain restrictions that do not apply to people aged 18 years or older. For instance, an emancipated child can apply for job, register at a school or college, or live where he or she likes like without parental approval. However, unlike 18-year-old adults, an emancipated child must attend school and must obtain parental permission if they want to marry before reaching the age of 18. The emancipated child must also remain under juvenile justice jurisdiction. If the emancipated child commits an offense, he or she will appear before a juvenile court judge and, if necessary, will be held at a juvenile detention center or correction institution. Where warranted, the emancipated child will come under the supervision of a juvenile correction probation or parole officer (Taylor, 2016).

Dependent Child

Courts can declare a child dependent and order the removal of that child from the custody of the child's parents when the court is convinced that the parents or legal guardians have failed to fulfill their parental roles. The evidence required for reaching this conclusion include parental abuse, neglect, or inability to supervise, protect and care for the child. A dependence status permits the court to order the parents and the child into counselling or to remove the child from the control or care of the parents.

Dependence cases are typically brought to the attention of the court by state or county social welfare employees. Of course, different states have different requirements for how dependence cases are processed. In the state of California, for instance, the Welfare and Institutions Code permits juvenile courts to classify as dependents certain children who make contact with the juvenile court if the child meets the following statutory conditions:

> The child has suffered, or there is a substantial risk that the child will suffer, serious physical harm or illness, as a result of the failure or inability of his or her parent or guardian to adequately supervise or protect the child, or the willful or negligent failure of the child's parent or guardian to adequately supervise or protect the child from the conduct of the custodian with whom the child has been left, or by the willful or negligent failure of the parent or guardian to provide the child with adequate food, clothing, shelter, or medical treatment, or by the inability of the parent or guardian to provide regular care for the child due to the parent's or guardian's mental illness, developmental disability, or substance abuse. (California Legislative Information, 2019)

For a youth to qualify as a dependent in California, the juvenile court must find that (1) the youth lacks parental care or protection, (2) the youth's parents are unable to provide for the child in terms of basic needs such as shelter, food, and safety, or (3) the youth is a victim of physical, psychological, or sexual abuse. In such cases, the court can remove the youth from the care of his or her parents to serve the best interest of the child. In this case, the judge relies on the preponderance of evidence.

Incorrigible Offenders

British House of Commons' Speaker John Bercow once rebuked a parliamentarian, shouting "You are an incorrigible delinquent at times. Behave yourself, man." By that, the Speaker meant that the parliamentarian refused to obey Bercow's lawful command as speaker, designed to maintain order during a Prime Minister's Questions session (Morris, 2014). Evidently, similar to the parliamentarian's action, in order to qualify for the "incorrigible" label in the juvenile justice system, a child must repeatedly engage in actions that are disruptive, dangerous, and/or disobedient, or refuse to obey lawful parental commands in ways that threaten the welfare and or safety of those with whom the youth interacts. Obviously, acts such as being disruptive, engaging in gang activity, or being involved with controlled substance use-related behaviors on school grounds would meet these requirements.

Incorrigibility is a more serious form of disobedience, worse than a simple or occasional defiance of authority. In fact, most acts of incorrigibility are status offenses that fall under the general definition of delinquency. Thus, the incorrigible status is seldom assigned to youth because in most cases incorrigibility is adjudicated as delinquent and because incorrigibility is also a precursor or symptom of delinquency, criminality, or status offenses. Of course, there are many cases where a child gets out of control in ways that make it almost impossible for the parent to exert full control over their behaviors. In such cases, a juvenile court can declare a child incorrigible and order the child removed from the care of his or her parents into the custody of the state. In 2017, the California State Supreme Court, for instance, ruled that state social workers can take custody of an out-of-control or incorrigible child from a blameless parent when such "child's behavior places her at substantial risk of serious physical harm, and a parent is unable to protect or supervise that child" (In re R.T., 2017).

case The offender in the California case was a minor who at the age of 14 started running away from home for days at a time. During her absences from home, she would refuse to attend school. At age 15 she gave birth to a child who become dependent on the juvenile court. A few year later, she gave birth to another child. During these periods, the offender's mother unsuccessfully tried to supervise and protect her daughter. Consistent with such endeavors, the offender's mother even sought help from the Los Angeles County Department of Children and Family Services as well as law enforcement agencies. At the same time, the offender falsely alleged that her mother was abusing her. Further, she reportedly challenged her mother's authority. The mother, who grew unable to control the child, even gave the grandparents oversight of the child hoping they could control her behavior. The mother's effort to control the minor, however, failed.

In 2014, when the child was 17, the state filed a petition with the court to classify the youth "a dependent of the juvenile court" on the grounds that the offender was facing substantial risk of serious physical harm or illness due to the failure or the inability of the mother to adequately supervise or protect the 17-year-old. Consequently, the court ordered that the child be placed elsewhere while reunification services were being provided with the ultimate goal of placing the youth back with her grandparents. The youth's mother appealed the decision, but the Court of Appeals agreed with the order of the juvenile court. Upon appeal, the Supreme Court of California ruled that a child could be declared incorrigible under section 300(b)(1) when that "child's behavior places her at substantial risk of serious physical harm, and a parent is unable to protect or supervise that child." The juvenile court was therefore authorized under section 300(b)(1) to classify the youth as dependent on the basis of incorrigibility (In re R.T., 2017).

In other states, including California, a child can be found incorrigible if evidence shows that the child leaves home without permission, violates curfew, threatens to or causes deliberate physical harm to family members, uses foul or abusive language toward family members, allows people into the parent's home in violation of parental directives, destroys property that belongs to other family members, steals money or property from family members, associates with undesirable people, uses alcohol or illicit drugs, refuses to follow reasonable directives, fails to attend school on a regular basis, or is disruptive in school environments. The more the offender's behavior fits this profile, the more he or she is qualified for the incorrigible designation.

Status Offenders

The category of status offender is a statutory designation for offenders who make contact with the criminal justice system for engaging in behaviors that are nondelinquent and noncriminal but that are prohibited when the offender is a person under the age of 18. Examples of status behaviors include curfew violations or behaviors that are prohibited for persons under the age of 18, while the same behavior is actually lawful when performed by adults. Status offenses also include behaviors that suggest ungovernability or that demonstrate that a child's parent, guardian, or custodian has failed to successfully control his or her behavior. Also qualifying as status offenders are children who run away from home or leave their parents', guardians', or custodians' home without permission and who fail to return home within a reasonable period. Of course, truancy or failure to attend school and the possession, use, or consumption of alcohol by persons under the age of 18 are also status offenses (Office of Juvenile Justice and Delinquency Prevention, 2015, 2018).

STATUS OFFENSES ARE FOR KIDS

The five most common status offenses are these: running away, truancy, curfew violations, incorrigibility, and underage possession or consumption of alcohol. The latest National Estimates of Petitioned Status Offense Cases disposed in 2016 showed that juvenile courts in the United States handled an estimated 94,700 status offense cases (Hockenberry & Puzzanchera, 2018a). Of that number, 8% of the offenders were runaways, 57% were truant, 6% violated curfew, 9% were incorrigible, 12% violated liquor laws, and 8% violated tobacco laws or committed other status offenses.

Source:

Hockenberry, S., & Puzzanchera, C. (2018a). *Juvenile court statistics 2016*. Retrieved from https://www.ojjdp.gov/ojstatbb/njcda/pdf/jcs2016.pd

In the 1970s, the status offender label gained more recognition as a result of the federal government's efforts to deinstitutionalize status offenders who make contact with the criminal justice system for minor behaviors. That effort resulted in the enactment of the 1974 Federal Juvenile Delinquency Act. The act demands "that youths charged with status offenses, and/or abused and neglected youths, shall not be placed in secure detention"; instead, the act encourages states "to divert status-offending youths away from the juvenile justice system and place them in less restrictive, service-intensive, community-based programs" (Office of Juvenile Justice and Delinquency Prevention, 2015). As a result, the federal government rewards states for keeping youth out of the correctional system and punishes those states that institutionalize status offenders. This policy applies to all states in the union because the Federal Juvenile Delinquency Act binds all states that receive federal funding from the Office of Juvenile Justice and Delinquency Prevention.

Delinquent Child

The label that most commonly comes up in conversations about the juvenile justice system is the delinquent child status. The Office of Juvenile Justice and Delinquency Prevention (OJJDP) defines delinquency as "an act committed by a juvenile for which an adult could be prosecuted in a criminal court, but when committed by a juvenile is within the jurisdiction of the juvenile court" (Office of Juvenile Justice and Delinquency Prevention, 2018). According to OJJDP, delinquent behaviors typically include crimes against persons, crimes against property, drug offenses, and crimes against public order. Hence, a delinquent youth is a minor who has been adjudicated for one or more penal offenses that range from misdemeanor-type behaviors, such as simple theft, to more serious felonies, such as aggravated assault, burglary, and trafficking in controlled substances.

Criminal Offenders

Certain criminal behaviors qualify youth for the most serious statutory or judicial classification, the criminal offender designation. This category is sometimes referred to as automatic transfer, statuary exclusion, or waiver of jurisdiction. Each of these labels refers to the authority to treat a juvenile offender as a criminal in adult criminal court because in the view of legislators, public prosecutors, or juvenile court judges, the offender's behavior warrants a harsh criminal justice response that is only available in the adult criminal justice system. Hence, an automatic transfer, statutory transfer, prosecutorial transfer, or juvenile court waiver means a youth's behavior has been classified by legislators, public prosecutors, or juvenile court judges as severe enough to warrant the treatment of that juvenile as an adult in the adult criminal justice system.

ADJUDICATED OFFENDERS

A judicial adjudication is the process of determining whether the offender before the juvenile court is responsible for the delinquent or status behaviors alleged in a petition. Allegations of a juvenile's delinquent or incorrigible behavior can be brought to the attention of the juvenile justice system by any law enforcement or social service agency, school, parent, or victim, or by any concerned citizen. Youth who are deemed appropriate for juvenile court processing can be committed to correctional institutions or placed in group homes or other residential facilities such as foster homes (Hockenberry & Puzzanchera, 2018a, 2018b). The most common labels used to discuss offenders during any of these processes are juvenile *detainees*, *probationers*, and *parolees*. In this regard, juvenile offenders who are waived over to the adult criminal justice system can be referred to as detainees or prisoners unless the petition is dismissed. Juvenile offenders who go through the normal juvenile justice process are called adjudicated offenders or adjudicated youth.

Indeed, the majority of youth who enter the juvenile justice system as a result of delinquent or criminal behavior are released into the community, and only a small number of such youth remain in secured facilities until their 18th birthdays. That is, the vast majority of juvenile offenders in secured facilities are released into the community as probationers or parolees. Some probationers and parolees with risk and needs levels that are too low to warrant continuous detention in secured facilities but are too high to warrant home placement may be placed in out-of-home facilities in the community, such as group homes, while others are returned directly to their original residences (Ryan, Marshall, Herz, & Hernandez, 2008; Rauktis, 2016).

A group home is a treatment center located in the community that offers short- and long-term services to juvenile offenders who are awaiting placement in a family or foster home or who are transitioning into independent living arrangements. Group homes are, however, more regulated and restricted compared to family homes; they are "considered less restrictive than juvenile detention centers but more restrictive than family foster care placements" (Office of Juvenile Justice and Delinquency Prevention, 2008). Group homes also differ from secured facilities in the sense that they allow youth to remain in the community and to live normal lives with opportunities to participate in normal activities such as attending school and securing employment. In other words, group homes try to make life as normal for youth as it can be outside secured facilities and group homes (Rabley, Preyde, & Gharabaghi, 2014).

GROUP HOMES ARE AN ANNUAL $8 BILLION BUSINESS

Studies show that children "nearly always fare best with their parents" compared to growing up in group homes, detention facilities, or in other institutionalized environments. Consistent with this view, the Family First Prevention Services Act, signed into law in 2018, prioritizes keeping families together, putting more money toward at-home parenting training, prevention of delinquency and criminality, mental health counseling, and substance abuse treatment. In the same respect, the Act puts limits on placing children in institutional settings such as group homes. Under the new law, the federal government will not fund group home placement for a child longer than two weeks except when the youth is pregnant or parenting a child (Wiltz, 2018).

Source:

Wiltz, T. (2018, May). *This new federal law will change foster care as we know it.* Retrieved from the Pew Charitable Trusts website: https://www.pewtrusts.org/en/research-and-analysis/blogs/stateline/2018/05/02/this-new-federal-law-will-change-foster-care-as-we-know-it

Juvenile Detainees

Detention of a juvenile offender takes place at different stages of juvenile justice processing (Hockenberry & Puzzanchera, 2018a). At each stage, an offender in a juvenile or adult correctional facility is considered a detainee. The label applies to all youth held in secured facilities, irrespective of whether the offender is detained while awaiting an adjudication hearing, disposition, placement in a group home or similar, transfer to adult criminal court, or a hearing in adult criminal court. Juvenile detainees enjoy all the rights constitutionally available to adults in addition to rights exclusively reserved for underage offenders, such as the right to therapeutic programming, to education, and to confinement separate from adult detainees.

Diverted Youth

Juvenile offenders brought into the criminal justice system for behaviors that are in the view of the initial assessment officer not significant enough to warrant detention or formal criminal justice processing usually benefit from the policy of diverting youth to mostly non-criminal justice institutions intended to hold youth accountable for their actions but at the same time designed to prevent the juvenile from being formally processed by the juvenile justice system as delinquent, incorrigible, or dependent. Diverted youth are therefore juvenile offenders who are sent to other agencies that are known for addressing the needs of offenders who have not been formally adjudicated in juvenile court.

Juvenile Probationers or Wards

What makes juvenile probation the core workhorse of the juvenile justice system is that the majority of youth who enter the juvenile justice system are released back into the community as probationers shortly after they are processed or adjudicated (Torbet, 1996). The juvenile justice system uses probation as a mechanism for sanctioning offenders and also as a way for diverting status offenders and offenders with low risk and needs levels from normal juvenile court processing (Hockenberry & Puzzanchera, 2018b).

The label *probationer* refers to an offender who is spared commitment to a secured facility and instead is placed in the community, generally in lieu of post adjudication detention. Probationers are therefore supervised by juvenile court judges or juvenile probation officers; hence, probationers are subject to a variety of supervision statuses depending on whether they are on intensive or standard probation. Probationers on standard probation typically require minimal supervision because their likelihood of engaging in criminal or delinquent behaviors is less compared to an intensive probationer. Offenders who are labelled as intensive probationers generally have high risk and needs levels compared to those on standard probation.

Juvenile Parolees

The overwhelming number of juvenile offenders committed to secured facilities are released into the community on parole prior to coming of age or prior to gaining absolute discharge from juvenile justice system jurisdiction. In theory and indeed in practice, juvenile probationers are not treated differently than juvenile parolees. However, the number of juvenile offenders committed to correctional facilities as a response to delinquent behavior is very small. Therefore, the number of juvenile offenders who are released from post adjudication detention facilities into the community is rather small.

Juvenile parolees too can be grouped under two sets of supervisory labels: *intensive* and *standard parolees*. The former implies that the offender is less likely to engage in delinquent or criminal behavior and thus needs minimal supervision. The latter implies that offenders with high risk and needs levels are more likely to engage in post-release delinquent or criminal activity than those with low risk and needs levels. Consequently, intensive parolees are subjected to more intensive supervision, such as having to report to their parole officers more frequently than those on standard parole. Intensive parolees are monitored more closely by parole officers to ensure compliance with conditions of their parole because their chances of violating conditions of their parole are greater than those on standard parole.

CONCLUSION

In general labels are useful, at least in terms of making it easier to distinguish between juvenile offenders without having to read through their entire field files. For instance, the labels *incorrigible, delinquent, transferred, probationer, parole,* and *detainee* communicate specific information about the types of offenses committed by an offender and the offender's likely risk and needs level. These labels also dictate how each offender should be treated by criminal justice practitioners and indeed by members of the public.

On the negative side, however, any criminal justice label can invoke stereotypical and prejudicial reactions and thus create opportunity for ill treatment of the offender. In fact, the practice of assigning labels to juvenile offenders is viewed as a risk factor. Indeed studies show that delinquent and indeed criminal behaviors can be influenced by some of the labels criminal justice professional use to describe or classify juvenile offenders who make contact with the juvenile justice system (Akers, Sellers, & Jennings, 2017; Williams & McShane, 2018). For instance, studies show that labels have the potential to increase the chances of antisocial behavior because negative labels such as *delinquent youth* or *incorrigible youth* easily catch the attention of the ordinary citizens and provide reasons, however groundless, for people to more closely watch the labeled offender, thereby making it easier to find reasons to reinforce the label. Furthermore, labels have the potential to be internalized by the labeled person.

CRITICAL QUESTIONS

1. There is an argument that labelling offenders increases the chances of future antisocial behaviors. Which of the labels described in this chapter may have the least influence on future antisocial thoughts and behaviors?
2. Is it possible to more effectively work with juvenile offenders without the use of labels, and if so, how would we therapeutically distinguish between juvenile offenders with certain/different needs and risks at different stages of the juvenile justice process?
3. In an attempt to avoid the negative consequences of being labelled by the criminal justice system, should cases involving emancipation orders and dependency be handled by noncriminal justice practitioners, such as social welfare officials? What would be the disadvantages and advantages of such policies?
4. The criminal justice system recognizes the importance and effect of labelling. As a result, the juvenile justice system uses different labels (*delinquent, minor,* and *school* instead of *criminal, prisoner,* and *prison*) when talking about juvenile offenders. Are there specific examples of how these terms reduce the stigma associated with particularly negative labels that are used to describe adults in the criminal justice system?
5. In terms of prevention of crime and delinquency, is it helpful to introduce children to the criminal justice system for status offenses?

REFERENCES

Akers, R. L., Sellers, C. S., & Jennings, W. G. (2017). *Criminological theories: Introduction, evaluation, and application* (7th ed.). New York, NY: Oxford University Press.

California Legislative Information. (2019). Welfare and Institutions Code Sec. 300(b)(1). Retrieved from http://leginfo.legislature.ca.gov/faces/codes_displaySection.xhtml?lawCode=WIC&sectionNum=300

Centers for Disease Control and Prevention. (2018). *Youth violence: Definitions.* Retrieved from https://www.cdc.gov/violenceprevention/youthviolence/definitions.html

Hockenberry, S., & Puzzanchera, C. (2018a). *Juvenile court statistics 2016.* Retrieved from the Office of Juvenile Justice and Deliquency Prevention website: https://www.ojjdp.gov/ojstatbb/njcda/pdf/jcs2016.pdf

Hockenberry, S., & Puzzanchera, C. (2018b). *Juvenile court statistics 2015.* Retrieved from the Office of Juvenile Justice and Deliquency Prevention website: https://www.ojjdp.gov/ojstatbb/njcda/pdf/jcs2015.pdf

In re R.T. 3 Cal.5th 622 (2017). Retrieved from Stanford University, Supreme Court of California Resources web site: https://scocal.stanford.edu/opinion/re-rt-34532

Morris, N. (2014, February 18). Ed Miliband and Nick Clegg back John Bercow's plans to reform PMQs—but Conservative backbenchers resist. *The Independent.* Retreived from https://www.independent.co.uk/

Office of Juvenile Justice and Delinquency Prevention. (2008). *Group homes.* Retreived from https://www.ojjdp.gov/mpg/litreviews/Group_Homes.pdf

Office of Juvenile Justice and Delinquency Prevention. (2015, September). *Status offenders.* Retrieved from https://www.ojjdp.gov/mpg/litreviews/Status_Offenders.pdf

Office of Juvenile Justice and Delinquency Prevention. (2018). *Statistical breifing book: Glossary.* Retrieved from https://www.ojjdp.gov/ojstatbb/glossary.html; See also *Performance measures: Glossary.* Retrieved from https://www.ojjdp.gov/grantees/pm/glossary.html

Rabley, S., Preyde, M., & Gharabaghi, K. (2014). A survey of adolescents' perceptions of their relationships with nonparental caregivers in group home settings: An attachment perspective. *Children and Youth Services Review, 40*, 61–70.

Rauktis, M. E. (2016). "When you first get there, you wear red": Youth perceptions of point and level systems in group home care. *Child and Adolescent Social Work Journal, 33*(1), 91–102.

Ryan, J. P., Marshall, J. M., Herz, D., & Hernandez, P. (2008). Juvenile delinquency in child welfare: Investigating group home effects. *Children and Youth Services Review, 30*(9), 1088–1099.

Superior Court of Orange County. (2019). *Minor emancipation.* Retrieved from https://www.occourts.org/directory/probate/probate-case-types/minor-emancipation.html

Taylor, J. (2016). *Kids and the law: An A-Z guide for parents.* Retrieved from the State Bar of California's Office of Media and Information Services website: https://www.advancingjustice-alc.org/wp-content/uploads/2012/11/Kids_2011_English.pdf

Torbet, P. M. (1996, March). *Juvenile probation: The workhorse of the juvenile justice system.* Retrieved from the National Criminal Justic Reference Service website: https://www.ncjrs.gov/pdffiles/workhors.pdf

Vincent, G. M., Guy, L. S., & Grisso, T. (2012). *Risk assessment in juvenile justice: A guidebook for implementation.* Retrieved from the National Juvenile Justice Network website: http://njjn.org/

Williams, F. P., & McShane, M. D. (2018). *Criminological theory* (7th ed.). New York, NY: Pearson.

Wiltz, T. (2018, May 2). *This new federal law will change foster care as we know it.* Retrieved from the Pew Charitable Trusts website: https://www.pewtrusts.org/

CHAPTER FOUR

Institutional Responses to Delinquent and Criminal Behaviors

MANY RENOWNED SCHOLARS have attempted to provide a universal explanation of justice as a clinical tool for correcting inequality and controlling crimes and delinquency. John Rawls, for instance, talks about justice from a distributive perspective among "proper ordering between equality and liberty with a particular concern for the needs of the least advantaged in **society.**" In contrast, Nozick, emphasizing individual liberty and private property rights, takes a retributive and procedural justice approach and thus defends a particular notion of "entitlement" with strong emphasis on a just world in which everyone gets exactly "what he or she is entitled to, without reference to equality or inequality" (Solomon & Murphy, 2000, p. 5; Rawls, 2001). However, the act of determining the therapeutic outcome of a criminal justice approach to delinquent and criminal behaviors is not always straightforward. At least, one has to first of all answer some fundamental questions.

Let's take sex offenders, for instance. Does sex offender registration provide deterrence or rehabilitative results, considering that the majority of sex offenders never get arrested or are never reported to police because most sex offenders are in fact family members, close relatives, friends, or acquaintances of their victims? Is sex offender registration more or less therapeutic if a sex offender has a history of being sexually molested or abused as a child? Is it therapeutic to respond to an offending behavior with the procedural mindset that ignorance of the law is not an excuse? The answer to each of these questions can be informed by at least one of four principles of justice: procedural, retributive, distributive, and restorative notions of why people offend and how to prevent or contain offending behaviors.

BEHAVIORAL DECEPTION: SEX OFFENDERS, GENERAL OFFENDERS, AND SUBSTANCE ABUSERS

Criminal justice practitioners are charged with correcting youth's behaviors. However, correctional staff always want to know the typology of each offender they serve, and sometimes the process of identification is not always straightforward. Terry's case is a good example. Terry was arrested for breaking into a motor vehicle and for illegally possessing a firearm. So, the obvious question is why he illegally carries a weapon and breaks into vehicles. The answer to these questions will depend on what a practitioner thinks will be the most effective way to correct Terry's antisocial thoughts and behaviors. A restorative justice practitioner will argue that Terry should take responsibility for his action and apologize to the owner of the vehicle as well as to the police for possessing a gun. A restorative justice practitioner believes that such a step will prevent Terry from possessing unlawful guns or committing break ins in the future. A retributive justice practitioner will argue that the state is not doing enough to enforce the laws on the books and so should aggressively pursue offenders like Terry and punish them for their antisocial behaviors because punishment specifically and generally deters future offending behaviors.

A distributive practitioner would argue that the lack of public resources to guide Terry is to be blamed for the break in and for Terry's firearm possession. That is, distributive justice practitioners believe that crime can be avoided if all offenders receive "fair shares" of public resources. Procedural justice practitioners believe in the principle of fairness and equality at all levels of the criminal justice process using established procedures. The shared assumption is that procedural fairness, irrespective of the offenses and the persons involved, significantly increases public faith in public laws and the ways such laws are enforced. Therefore, all that is needed is for Terry to have his days in court (Heery & Noon, 2017).

Source:

Heery, E., & Noon, M. (2017). *A dictionary of human resource management* (3rd ed.). London, England: Oxford University Press.

The history of crime and punishment shows that societies in different parts of the world and at different stages in human history have always struggled with how to deal with people who are convicted or adjudicated for penal violations both in terms of punishment and rehabilitation. Even today, the ways that institutions respond to violations of public laws are sharply different and informed by conflicting perceptions of what pushes offenders to break laws in the first place. Consequently, the answer to questions about the best therapeutic response to a particular delinquent or criminal act that will deter offenders and would-be offenders from engaging in prohibited acts is guided by a variety of interpretations that are mainly causational explanations of ways to prevent and contain criminal and delinquent behaviors.

Those who believe in procedural and retributive justice tend to advance classical responses to crime, and those who appeal to ideas of distributive and restorative justice generally respond to criminal behaviors from a positivist standpoint. Also, neoclassicism draws from both classicism and positivism. It is therefore important for criminal justice professionals to develop the capacity needed to identify different theoretical frameworks that inform institutional approaches and how best those methods serve the treatment needs of offenders and minimize offenders' risk of causing harm to themselves or society.

This chapter builds on criminological theories that explain why people commit criminal and delinquent acts to discuss theories that explain the different responses and reactions of states and local criminal justice institutions to certain delinquent and criminal behaviors. In doing so, this chapter discusses the concept of procedural, retributive, distributive, and restorative justice as well as how these theoretical frameworks inform criminal justice institutions' classical and positivist approaches to criminal behaviors as therapeutic frameworks for the prevention and containment of such behaviors.

THEORIES OF JUSTICE

Indeed, knowledge of dominant theoretical explanations of why people engage in criminal and delinquent behaviors for which they are convicted or adjudicated makes it easier to understand why institutions choose particular responses to criminal and delinquent behaviors. Such knowledge also makes a big difference because whether an institution is likely to take a classical approach or use a positivist method in response to criminal or delinquent behaviors depends largely on whether the same institutions' responses to crimes are informed by procedural and retributive justice or distributive and restorative justice. Of course, there is no universal answer to what constitutes a "right intervention" because what makes a therapeutic intervention right is often determined by different socioeconomic, cultural, political, legal, and other extralegal factors within the context in which the issue of rehabilitation arises. The important task, however, for criminal justice students and professionals is to develop the ability to articulate what is likely to work in a given situation.

Procedural Justice

A procedural approach to crime emphasizes due process, procedural fairness, and transparency of the process in general by which criminal justice decisions are made. Of paramount importance to those who look to this doctrine for just and therapeutic outcomes is the assumptions that without reference to social status or physiological or biological characteristics, a fair application of criminal law gives every citizen a just outcome and at the same time provides reasons for citizens to trust the criminal justice system. To accomplish these goals, those who ascribe to the procedural justice principle look to the fairness and transparency of the criminal justice process and the strict application of law and policies for clinical outcome. The claim is that offenders are more likely to exercise respect for public law and policies when they are subjected to a fair, transparent, and consistent public policies and laws. This categorization is, however, a key source of criticism.

Legal formalism—simple compliance with the "law"—does not produce equality or just outcomes and does not produce any effective clinical response to criminal and delinquent behavior (Savelsberg, 1992). For instance, one of those criticisms against procedural justice is that as a crime fighting tool, procedural justice fails to take into account that access to justice depends on many factors, such as the equitable distribution of public resources and the means to finance a private criminal defense as well as one's social background; therefore, it is impossible to assume that in all instances the fair application of law is possible and clinically useful (Rhode, 2004).

O. J. SIMPSON DID NOT MURDER NICOLE AND RON

In 1994, Orenthal James (O. J.) Simpson was tried on two counts of murder for the June 12, 1994, deaths of his ex-wife Nicole Brown Simpson, and her friend Ron Goldman. A procedural criminal justice practitioner who believes in the criminal justice system would argue that O. J. and the government had their days in court, and the jury found him not guilty. So legally, he did not murder Nicole and Ron. A retributive practitioner would, however, express disappointment because such a person would think that O. J. should have been punished. A distributive practitioner will, however, be more concerned with how this tragedy could have been prevented. A restorative justice practitioner would want O. J. Simpson to speak the truth and, if necessary, take responsibility for his actions, ask for forgiveness, and make peace with his victims' families and the rest of the American public.

Secondly, procedural justice is primarily concerned with whether the entity administering the justice acted fairly within the scope of the law, policies, and procedures and not simply in pursuit of a particular outcome of a criminal justice process, ignoring the fact that fair application of the law and compliance with due process may still convict or find an innocent child delinquent. Lastly, what is fair does not always equal lawful, and what is lawful in some cases may be unjust. There is, however, a clear distinction between procedural justice and retributive justice in that the former is concerned with the due process associated with adjudication or prosecution, and the latter deals exclusively with postconviction or adjudication sanctions.

Retributive Justice

Similar to procedural justice, retributive justice emphasizes objectivity without regard to individual psychological, biological, and physiological differences and limitations. The notion that offenders should suffer fair and determinate punishment in the form of incarceration, public denunciation, condemnation, shame, financial consequences, and sometimes death proportionate to the seriousness of each offense defines retributive justice. This principle of justice argues that if an offender is capable of committing a crime, he or she must also be capable of suffering the consequences. Punishment is believed to have both specific and general deterrent effects because it teaches the offenders a painful lesson and discourages others from engaging in criminal activities.

Retributive justice is also based on the belief that individuals have free will and hence are responsible for their decisions. Therefore, after having their days in court, offenders must suffer the consequences of their actions because they rationally chose to engage in bad acts in pursuit of the pleasure they derived from such acts. That is, the shared beliefs among retributive jurists is that society can achieve specific and general deterrence of crime and delinquency through the act of punishing criminal or delinquent acts—general deterrence occurs when those who witness the application of punishment refrain from engaging in similar unacceptable behaviors for fear of suffering similar consequences. For instance, if an offender is jailed for possessing marijuana, and the act of possessing marijuana is rewarded with jail time, the assumption is that the person jailed will avoid possessing marijuana in the future for fear of going to jail. At the same time, those with potential for possessing marijuana will refrain from doing so in fear of going to jail.

Retributive justice is a zero-tolerance approach to crimes and antisocial behaviors. It is based on the premise that criminals or delinquent offenders rationally choose to engage in prohibited acts because of the pleasure they derive from such acts; therefore, punishing wrongful acts will deter future criminals. The assumption is that by rewarding bad actions with punishment, fear of the pain punishment delivers compels those who are prone to engaging in the prohibited acts to avoid the acts altogether. This argument has, however, been widely refuted in many studies that focus on criminal and delinquent behaviors.

PUNISHMENT IS ONLY FOR THOSE WHO GET CAUGHT

The argument made by rational choice theory is simple: If Susan drives above the posted speed limit, she should receive a speeding ticket as punishment for choosing to speed. The ticket teaches a driver that speeding equals the cost of the ticket and the additional premiums charged by insurance companies. The next time Susan is tempted to speed, the cost of her previous speeding ticket and the fear of going through the same motions with the police, court, and insurance company will compel her to avoid speeding. This is called specific deterrence—the possibility of another ticket will specifically stop Susan from speeding in the future.

Most likely, Susan told her friends and family about her speeding ticket and the related headaches that came with her ordeal. Consequently, at least the people at the insurance company who raised her premium, the people at the court who processed her ticket, those who drove by during the traffic stop, and her personal associates who learned about the ticket will all be deterred from speeding in the future by their knowledge of Susan's pain and suffering Susan. This is called general deterrence because Susan's suffering is now deterring various members of the public.

Note, however, that criminal laws, and indeed traffic laws, punish only those who are caught and convicted. Hence, most offenders, including traffic offenders, come up with new ways to avoid getting caught for their behaviors—that is, a speeder may not stop speeding because of a ticket; instead, a speeder may learn how to avoid getting caught and also how to avoid statutory consequences when and if caught. These arguments are true in relation to juvenile offending behaviors and retributive responses to those behaviors.

The major criticism that is commonly levied against the retributive justice model is that retribution is difficult to achieve in the strict sense of "an eye for an eye" due to the practical difficulty of replicating past events. Study after study have also shown that punishment does not deter crime. This finding is not surprising because at the critical point of decision-making about whether to engage in a particular prohibited act, people convince themselves first and foremost that they will not get caught, and even if they do get caught, somehow they will not be held accountable to the fullest or may get away with the behaviors without any harsh repercussion.

Restorative Justice

The least popular and at the same time most helpful method of response to criminal and delinquent conviction or adjudication is restorative justice. This doctrine focuses on the restoration of socioeconomic, political, and moral equilibrium in which the humanity and in some cases the sanity of both the victim and the offender are respected and preserved. For this reason, restorative justice views crimes as harmful and hurtful acts against other individuals rather than the state. Thus, it mends fences and calls for the reparation of relationships between a victim and his or her offender and the community at large because the unification of offenders with victims creates special opportunities for both parties to repair damages in a way that reduces the risk of the offender engaging in future victimization and also provides emotional relief for the victim and at the same time advances community safety. In order to achieve this goal, restorative justice encourages face-to-face meetings between offenders and victims and active participation of victims in offenders' postconviction treatment. This approach holds offenders accountable for their actions but discourages the social humiliation and stigmatization of offenders with the sole goal of minimizing the possibility of the offender's reoffending.

SEX OFFENDER TREATMENT PROGRAMS AND RESTORATIVE JUSTICE

Restorative justice is commonly used by criminal justice practitioners who work with children who sexually molest their siblings or with family members who sexually abuse children in their families (Gilligan & Bumby, 2008). This process has been most commonly referred to as family reintegration, family reunification, or family preservation and reunification. Typically, the process involves the offender and victim working with separate clinical staff or therapists. The treatment focuses on the offender taking responsibility for the wrong behaviors and on learning about the full impact of the behavior on the victim. The treatment for the victim focuses on helping him or her deal with the impact of the victimization and on learning that victims are not responsible for their victimization. In the end, the two therapists bring the victim and the offender together during a supervised session. During the initial reunification session, the offender starts by taking responsibility for the wrong behavior. The offender apologizes for the pain and suffering the behavior caused the victim. In return, the victim expresses his or her feelings and experience and accepts the apology if so desired. In short, the critical stages of any reunification process start with the treatment of everyone (victim, offender, and family) and the assessment of each party's readiness for family unification session. The process ends with the reconnection or reunification of all parties. Studies find that family reunification reduces offenders' chances of reoffending, increases the chances of preserving family cohesion, and helps victims cope with the effects of their victimization.

Source:

Gilligan, L., & Bumby, K. (2008). Key considerations for reunifying adult sex offenders and their families. In J. V. Fenner (Ed.), *Sex offenders: Management, treatment and bibliography* (pp. 1–21). Hauppauge, NY: Nova Science.

Some of the major criticisms drawn by restorative justice are that it does not deliver a specific and general deterrence message; therefore, it fails to control crime and delinquency. Furthermore, the theory may not be suitable in certain cases, such as in domestic violence situations, because it requires the victim to make peace with the offender instead of empowering the victim to remove himself or herself from the offender. This process of removal might also be very helpful in situations where the distress experienced by the victim is excessive or overwhelmingly traumatic, such as in cases involving victims of rape and torture. Restorative justice theory also assumes that every society has social mechanisms in place to facilitate the restoration of relationships between offenders, victims, and society. It is difficult also to get a true and genuine apology for most victims because to escape the negative consequences of their actions, offenders naturally will do and say anything, including saying "I am sorry" without the requisite sincere intention (Daly, 2007).

Distributive Justice

The basic premise of distributive theory is that the inequality found in history, public policies, and the distribution of public wealth explain the rate and types of crimes a society experiences. In theory, those who argue for their "fair share of public resources" and who blame crime and delinquent behaviors on the absence of socioeconomic and political resources also argue that helping offenders meet their basic needs can prevent them from committing future crimes because the inequitable distribution of public goods, wealth, and access to public resources found in history and public policies define the scope, rates, and types of crimes people commit (Rawls, 2001). Hence the "fair share of public resources" can prevent or minimize many of the risk factors associated with high-risk behaviors.

Distributive jurists blame socioeconomic and political inequality and the unfair distribution of public resources for crimes, especially crimes committed by the least privileged members of society. The central argument is that inequitable distribution of public goods and wealth blocks the least-privileged citizens' access to critical resources, including access to the criminal justice system, which as a result pushes those least-privileged members further toward criminal and delinquent behaviors. A distributive response is a preventive measure that can minimize many of the risk factors associated with high-risk behaviors and tendencies when the distribution of public goods, wealth, and resources in society are equitably distributed. For example, fairly distributed public resources permit governments' involvement in the proper upbringing of children and facilitate rewards for good behaviors and choices.

Of course, the principle of distributive justice is accused of rewarding bad behavior with public resources by subsidizing social programs. That is, the provision of social programs to less-privileged citizens with the goal to veer them from engaging in antisocial behaviors amounts to a bribing scheme for criminals and delinquent youth who deserve nothing but exclusion from society. Furthermore, distributive justice theory is faulted for its view that resource rights come into existence simply by virtue of being a member of society. The theory also fails to account for how resources once possessed by another person suddenly become another person's entitlement and how one might correct the apparent injustice that emerges out of the distribution of public goods (Solomon & Murphy, 2000).

CLASSICAL AND POSITIVIST APPROACHES TO CRIMES AND DELINQUENCY

Right or wrong, proponents of restorative, distributive, procedural, and retributive justice advance their respective arguments in the name of the greater good or the public good or the common good—that is, the moral worth of an action should be dictated by the degree of the positive impact that action is likely to have on the greatest number of people. In another words, the extent to which an intervention qualifies as just and clinically productive is dictated by how many members of that society are likely to benefit from such an act. For example, proponents of the restorative doctrine argue that the mending of fences between a victim and an offender benefits society as a whole because the process minimizes the likelihood that other members of society will suffer from the same harm at the hands of the offender. Similarly, supporters of distributive justice believe that society as a whole benefits most when people are aided with public resources in pursuit of their individual goals.

Supporters of procedural justice steadfastly subscribe to the notion that equal treatment as a consequence of wrongful acts guarantees fair treatment of all people and lends credibility to the criminal justice system. Credibility, they argue, brings about greater public appreciation of the meaningful roles criminal justice systems play. Those who see events through the lenses of retributive justice unwaveringly argue that punishment deters crimes and that a society without crime is possible and highly desired by every citizen. Yet it is also clear that procedural and retributive justice share certain characteristics in common. Also, distributive and restorative justice have certain common features with regard to dealing with offenders as well as people at risk of participating in prohibited acts. As a result of these similarities, procedural and retributive jurists find comfort in classicism when responding to prohibited behaviors. Similarly, positivism shares many characteristics in common with restorative and distributive theories of how to respond to crimes and delinquency. Neoclassicism draws on retributive and restorative approaches to crimes and delinquency.

Classicism

The premise of classicism is that all persons are created equal and endowed with free will and physical and cognitive abilities to choose between right and wrong behaviors; therefore, people engage in prohibited acts after carefully considering the benefits and consequences of their behaviors, and it is only after the conscious decision to pursue the pleasures they associate with unlawful behaviors that they end up engaging in such behaviors. Classicism is therefore an extension of rational choice theory, because its approach to criminal behaviors holds the view that all humans are rational beings whose actions are dictated by the need to readily gravitate toward hedonism—the seeking of pleasure and avoidance of pain and suffering.

ALL MEN AND WOMEN ARE NOT CREATED EQUAL

Below is an excerpt from Deborah L. Rhode's book *Access to Justice*. As you read, note that while all men and women have equal human and constitutional rights on paper and by nature have the same aspiration for life, liberty, and the pursuit of happiness, in practice some men and women are more equal than others. Note also that fair procedural justice is an expensive commodity in the United States, and only those who are financially or politically well-placed can afford justice.

> "Equal justice under law" is one of America's most firmly embedded and widely violated legal principles. It embellishes courthouse entries, ceremonial occasions, and occasionally even constitutional decisions. But it comes nowhere close to describing the justice system in practice. Millions of Americans lack any access to the system, let alone equal access. An estimated four-fifths of the civil legal needs of the poor, and the needs of an estimated two- to three-fifths of middle-income individuals, remain unmet. Governmental legal services and indigent criminal defense budgets are capped at ludicrous levels, which make effective assistance of counsel for most low-income litigants a statistical impossibility. We tolerate a system in which money often matters more than merits and equal protection principles are routinely subverted in practice. (Rhode, 2001; Rhode, 2004)

Sources:

Rhode, D. L. (2001). Access to Justice. *Fordham Law Review*, *69*(5), 1785–1819.
Rhode, D. L. (2004). *Access to Justice*. New York, NY: Oxford University Press.

Classicism demands that responses to criminal behaviors must be laced with retributive responses that are designed to punish wrongdoers with the goal of compelling them to think of their behavior in terms of pain and suffering and not in terms of pleasure. The purpose of the sanctions is to specifically deter current offenders and at the same time deliver universal warnings to would-be offenders that they too will suffer similar consequences if they choose to participate in similar behaviors. That is, harsh treatments such as detention specifically deter offenders from victimizing other members of the public because it assures would-be offenders that crimes or bad choices do not pay; rather, such choices of behaviors produce pain and suffering in the form of sanctions (Cornish & Clarke, 2011; Cullen & Agnew, 2011).

In order to achieve retributive goals, sanctions must be prompt, certain, and identical for the same offense. The principle of proportionality demands that offenses must be rewarded with sanctions that are reasonably necessary and related to the achievement of specific and general deterrence of future delinquency or criminality. In other words, "sanctions should be scaled in proportion to each offender's blameworthiness, and equally culpable offenders should receive equally severe sanctions" (Frase, 2005). When sanctions are proportionate, they tend to deter crimes and delinquent behaviors by teaching offenders that the criminal justice system is fair in dishing out just deserts, what an offender deserves. In this case, offenders learn that government has a compelling interest in stopping criminal and delinquent behaviors and no interest in merely punishing its citizens. Proportionality also presents punishment as a product of the offenders' choices while at the same time reassuring potential offenders that the degree to which offenders suffer is dictated by the level of criminal or delinquent choices they make—the more serious the crime, the lengthier and more painful the sanction is expected to feel.

The presumed outcome of proportionality is further strengthened by the swiftness and certainty of sanctions, because certainty leaves no doubt in the minds of potential offenders that the choice to engage in criminal or delinquent acts is indeed a choice to suffer predetermined sanctions. Certainty, therefore, gives offenders and would-be offenders a mental proximity of the relationship between bad behaviors and punishment and also allows offenders to weigh the consequential and painful results of their criminal or delinquent behaviors against the temporary excitements that are usually associated with crimes and delinquent acts (Frase, 2005). Swiftness in this process reinforces the certainty of future sanctions by minimizing the possibility of intervening circumstances that could otherwise obscure the proper and timely delivery of retribution.

Classicism, however, ignores the actual effect of risk and protective factors on criminal and delinquent behaviors and consequently diverts attention and vital resources from the causes of crimes and delinquency to the incapacitation of the offender to temporarily stop the continuation of offending behavior and the so-called specific and general deterrent. Furthermore, studies show that classicism is least effective at deterring future crime, and in many ways its full implementation is practically impossible. For example, it is difficult to achieve complete proportionality in terms of matching sanctions with behaviors, and even if it were possible to proportionately sanction each crime or delinquent act, the possibility of unjust treatment or excessive retribution would exist because each crime is unique—some people, for instance, speed to avoid being late for important prosocial activities but others speed for the sake of pleasure. The concept of swiftness is also not easy to achieve because an increase in the severity of retribution generally has a positive correlation with an increase in procedural safeguards. For example, in most jurisdictions, capital punishment takes well over 10 years to carry out.

Neoclassicism

In essence, neoclassicism is a frame of reference that draws more on classicism and very little on positivism. Thus, neoclassicism emphasizes logic and symmetry in an effort to create an understanding of how age, mental health, and past criminal history should inform states' responses to delinquent and criminal behaviors (Abadinsky, 2015). At its core is the classical notion that individuals are rational beings whose behaviors are always motivated by the urge to satisfy both needs and wants. At the same time, while recognizing the important mitigating roles of mental health disorders and the ages of offenders, neoclassicists see past criminal histories as a legitimate aggravating factor for retributive policies (Savelsberg, 1992). Neoclassicists take those factors into account when considering post adjudication and conviction responses.

Neoclassicism has a positivist drive in that it recognizes the importance of classification, although in a limited way, based on age, psychological defect, and criminal history. The belief is that mental disorders, in their various forms and stages, do explain certain criminal behaviors. Therefore, clinical interventions ought to take note of such contributions. Neoclassicism also recognizes that age is a good predictor of cognitive ability and psychological development, especially in terms of the ability to fully understand the consequences of one's behaviors and how to proactively act in ways that would generate more protective factors (Abadinsky, 2015). However, the limitation on predictive factors—mental health, age, and criminal history—violates one of the core principles of positivism, which generally rejects much of the deterrent capability classicists and neoclassicists attribute to retributive and procedural justice.

Positivism

The central theoretical difference between classicism and positivism is that the latter rejects the classical concept of "free will" and the notion that the pursuit of hedonism explains some criminal and delinquent behaviors (Groves, 1985). Positivist criminologists therefore draw on contemporary deterministic and criminological theories such as strain, social control, and differential association theories to argue that human behaviors are instead informed by many different factors. That is, criminal and delinquent behaviors are products of many competing variables, such as family situation, educational achievement, mental health status, risk and needs levels of close friends and family members, history of abuse, level of social skills, employment preparedness, and relationships with controlled substance and illicit drugs. For these reasons, positivists believe in environmental and physiological determinism—the notion that behaviors are products of the environment in which the offender resides and of the offender's mental and biological makeup.

Positivist criminologists can deduce the degree and types of risk factors present in a society from information about the rate of crime in that society. Conversely, positivists can also predict the rates of crime and delinquency in a given society using only information about the type and degree of risk and protective factors present in that society (Young, 1988). For instance, information about elevated rates of child molestation in a society may suggests a high number of people who were molested as children in the same society. Similarly, an increase in gang presence in a community means an increase in street crime rates. Low school graduation rates can be used to predict high teen pregnancy as well as increased antisocial thoughts and beliefs. Increases in physical and sexual abuse mean increases in the number of future sex offenders, certain mental disorders, and substance abuse. In each of these cases, the behaviors of the offender are determined by events that happened around them or to them in the past. For instance, there is a strong relationship between sexual victimization and substance abuse behaviors and mental health disorders, and there are links between gang affiliation and participation in antisocial behaviors and high school dropout rates.

It is also true that people drink water to quench the pain of thirst, people sleep because of exhaustion, eat because of hunger, and attend college because of the need for education or employment. These needs lead positivist criminologists to reject the classical notion that behaviors are products of free will. It is for the same reasons that positivists emphasize clinically informed assessment and classification systems that are backed by empirical evidence that inform the assessment, classification, and calculation of risks and needs as well as the formulation of clinical responses to crimes and delinquency.

CONCLUSION

The explanations and approaches procedural, restorative, retributive, distributive, and indeed classicism and positivism advance in response to criminal behaviors collectively support the notion that for every criminal behavior there is an explanation that points to a particular risk or protective factor. The risk highlighted by the schools of thought discussed in this chapter include harsh socioeconomic conditions, mental defects, procedural fairness, and lack of healthy connections between offenders, victims, and their communities. Thus, although many agencies may emphasize one particular approach and ignore others, probation and parole officers and indeed criminal justice practitioners in general have the authority and ability to utilize approaches that have the most potential to prevent and minimize recidivism.

Unfortunately, however, the core principles that inform many criminal justice policies in the United States are based on the idea that certainty, severity, and celerity of punishment lead to specific and general deterrence; thus, the most effective way to ensure public safety is to utilize measures that emphasize harsh treatment of offenders. That is, punishment deters because any criminal behavior is a product of "choice and free will" and symbolizes a natural consequence of unrestrained human tendencies to always seek pleasure over pain (Gottfredson & Hirschi, 1990; Akers, Sellers, & Jennings, 2016). So far, in comparison to other developed countries, this traditional American retributive approach to crime and delinquency has failed to reduce the rate of substance abuse, sexual offending behaviors, violent crimes, and general offending behaviors. Sadly, these results are not very surprising. Certainly, while punishment may deter some people, punishments are, logically speaking, reserved for those who are caught, and most offenders commit crimes and delinquent acts with the strong conviction that they will not be caught.

DISCUSSION QUESTIONS

1. What are some of the key weaknesses of classicism with regard to the rehabilitation of offenders?
2. Which of the four principles of justice discussed in this chapter provides the most effective ways to reduce recidivism?
3. Should probation or parole officers totally ignore classicism in their approach to offender rehabilitation, and whether yes or no, why?

4. With regard to the prevention of recidivism and reduction of crime rates in general, what are the key strengths of positivism?
5. Why does classicism remain the core means of response to crimes and delinquency by the American criminal justice system?

REFERENCES

Abadinsky, H. (2015). *Probation and parole: Theory and practice*. New York, NY: Pearson.

Akers, R. L., Sellers, C. S., & Jennings, W. G. (2016). *Criminological theories: Introduction, evaluation, and application* (7th ed.). New York, NY: Oxford University Press.

Cornish, D. B., & Clarke, R. V. (2011). Crime as a rational choice. In F. T. Cullen & R. Agnew (Eds.), *Criminological theory: Past to present* (4th ed.). New York, NY: Oxford University Press.

Cullen, F. T., & Agnew, R. (2011). Reviving classical theory: Deterrence and rational choice theories. In F. T. Cullen & R. Agnew (Eds.), *Criminological theory: Past to present* (4th ed.). New York, NY: Oxford University Press.

Daly, K. (2007). The limits of restorative justice. In D. Sullivan & L. Tifft (Eds.), *Handbook of restorative justice: A global perspective*. New York, NY: Routledge.

Frase, R. S. (2005). Punishment purposes. *Stanford Law Review*, *58*(1), 67–83.

Gilligan, L., & Bumby, K. (2008). Key considerations for reunifying adult sex offenders and their families. In J. V. Fenner (Ed.), *Sex offenders: Management, treatment and bibliography* (pp. 1–21). Hauppauge, NY: Nova Science.

Gottfredson, M. R., & Hirschi, T. (1990). *A general theory of crime*. Stanford, CA: Stanford University Press.

Groves, W. B. (1985). Socialism, Capitalism, and the Reproduction of Crime. Crime and Social Justice, 23, 129–150

Heery, E., & Noon, M. (2017). *A dictionary of human resource management* (3rd ed.). London, England: Oxford University Press.

Rawls, J. (2001). *Justice as fairness: A restatement*. Cambridge, MA: Harvard University Press.

Rhode, D. L. (2001). Access to Justice. *Fordham Law Review*, *69*(5), 1785–1819.

Rhode, D. L. (2004). *Access to Justice*. New York, NY: Oxford University Press.

Savelsberg, J. J. (1992). Law that does not fit society: Sentencing guidelines as a neoclassical reaction to the dilemmas of substantivized law. *American Journal of Sociology*, *97*(5), 1346–1381.

Solomon, R. C., & Murphy, M. C. (Eds.). (2000). *What is justice? Classic and contemporary readings*. New York, NY: Oxford University Press.

Young, J. (1988). Radical criminology in Britain: The emergence of a competing paradigm. *British Journal of Criminology*, *28*(2), 159–183.

CHAPTER FIVE

The Juvenile Offenders

ANTISOCIAL, CRIMINAL, AND delinquent behaviors generally fall under one of five behavioral domains: sexual, violent, substance abuse, general, and mental health-related behaviors. To date, however, there are no empirically sound biological or physiological markers for who is likely to become or continue to be a violent, sex, substance abuse, general, or mental health-related offender, and there is no known way, at the present moment, to use psychological or physiological markers to separate would-be offenders from youth who are less likely to reoffend (Boyd, Hagan, & Cho, 2000, p. 1; Anthony & Stohr, 2010). A lot is, however, known about social and behavioral factors and markers that increase the chances of an offender being labelled as a violent, sexual, substance use, general, and or mental health-related offender.

This chapter talks about sexual, violent, general, substance abuse, and mental health-related offenders and the factors that increase their chances of recidivating and inform their behavioral patterns. In other words, this chapter provides broad working definitions and explanations of sex offenders, substance abuse offenders, violent offenders, general offenders, and mental health-related offenders. Each of these labels is used by correctional institutions, probation and parole officers, and the courts. Also, when used, each label commands specific criminal justice responses. In terms of risk and needs assessment and classification as well as the management and supervision of offenders, each of these labels suggests a unique social and psychological history and thus commands a specific criminal justice response.

CONTROLLED SUBSTANCE USE OFFENDERS

Substance use-related assessments measure relationships between substance use and offending behaviors such as committing crimes in order to fund controlled substance use habits, engaging in antisocial behaviors while under the influence of controlled substances, consuming increased quantities of a substance, using two or more types of controlled substances, and increasing the frequency of controlled substance use. Classification in this area also looks at whether an offender's use of a controlled substance has reached a life-threatening stage, whether the use of a controlled substance increases or exacerbates offenders' existing mental health-related problems or behaviors, and whether offenders feel physically and psychologically compelled to use certain controlled substances.

Controlled substance use refers to any illegal use of a substance that is intended to intoxicate or make the user feel high, or that alters the senses of the users and weakens the ability to function in a normal way. Controlled substances can include alcohol, marijuana, prescription drugs, opioids, and other substances such as glue, paint, and mushrooms. The use of prescription drugs for any reasons other than their medically prescribed purpose also constitutes substance abuse or dependence behavior, of course depending on the degree and frequency of the controlled substance use. Similarly, occasional excessive or daily heavy use of alcohol would qualify an offender as a substance abuser. The phrase "substance-related offender" is therefore meant to capture both controlled substance abusers and controlled substance dependents. Indeed, the labels "controlled substance abuser" and "controlled substance dependent" are often used interchangeably when talking about alcohol or drug use in general. However, there are specific differences between the two behaviors.

Substance abuse offenders are generally people who use one or more controlled or prohibited drugs that cause drowsiness and produce intense feelings of elation, sedation, stimulation, or hallucination. The substance abuser uses controlled substances in ways that result in failure to fulfill major work or school requirements or to successfully carryout other social commitments. Substance abusers also use controlled substances in manners that increase their chances of engaging in hazardous such as driving while intoxicated, engaging in behaviors that often lead to legal problems, or continuously using a controlled substance even when it is clear that the substance is making it difficult for them to meet basic social responsibilities and to satisfy interpersonal commitments (Bronson, Stroop, Zimmer, & Berzofsky, 2017a; Rehabs.com, 2018).

Controlled substance-dependent offenders are what one may refer to as advanced substance abusers. This group of offenders is different from substance abusers because unlike substance abusers, substance-dependent offenders tend to have high tolerance levels for controlled substances, and as a result, they consume increased amounts to achieve the euphoric effects of the substance. Controlled substance-dependent offenders also tend to suffer from severe withdrawal symptoms that are characterized by psychological and physical signs of abnormality when the use of the controlled substance ceases. This group feels unable to stop the use of controlled substances to a point where the offenders remain continuously dependent on controlled substances even while dealing with controlled substance use-related problems. Other physical symptoms may include nausea, vomiting, sweating, visible irritability, depression, anxiety, or fuzziness as well as failure to fully recognize the dangerousness of the controlled substance (Morrison, 2001; Anthony & Stohr, 2010; ALLPSYCH, 2018; Rehabs.com 2018).

CONTROLLED SUBSTANCE AND ALCOHOL ABUSE/DEPENDENCE ARE SERIOUS DISEASES

According to the U.S. Department of Justice, correctional facilities house and supervise many offenders who use, abuse, or are dependent on controlled substances. Specifically, the study shows that about 58% of offenders in state correctional facilities and 63% in county jails meet the *Diagnostic and Statistical Manual of*

Mental Disorders' criteria for controlled substance dependence or abuse. Similarly, 56% of adolescent boys and 40% of adolescent girls under criminal justice jurisdiction for various offenses also qualify as controlled substance abusers or dependents (Chassin 2008; Bronson et al., 2017).

Sources:

Bronson, J., Stroop, J., Zimmer, S., & Berzofsky, M. (2017). *Drug use, dependence, and abuse among state prisoners and jail inmates, 2007–2009*. Retrieved from https://www.bjs.gov/content/pub/pdf/dudaspji0709.pdf

Chassin, L. (2008). Juvenile justice and substance use. *The Future of Children, 18*(2), 165–183.

It is, however, important to note that despite what is known about substance use offenders, there is no specific marker for who is or is not a substance abuser or dependent or who is likely to be one. That said, comparatively, controlled substance abusers are at lower risk of future use of drugs than those who are dependent on a controlled substance. Conversely, however, every controlled substance user is at risk of becoming an abuser, and every substance abuser is at even greater risk of becoming dependent. Thus, in reality the dangerous journey to controlled substance dependency starts with the first use of a controlled substance. Similarly, the road to being controlled substance free begins each time an offender rejects an opportunity to use a controlled substance.

SEX OFFENDERS

In general, sex offenders are not heterogeneous; they come from every background and commit a wide range of offenses (Terry, 2006). Indeed, the stereotypical image of a sex offender as "a brutally depraved and oversexed monster who spends his time hunting" victims is not an accurate representation of sex offenders (Anthony & Stohr, 2010, p. 388). Adult sex offenders can consist of businessmen, priests, politicians, presidents, congressmen and congresswomen, physicians, teachers, attorneys, police officers, and persons from all walks of life. In the same vein, there is no formula for distinguishing a juvenile sex offender from a non-sex offender, although there are reliable formulas (risk assessment tools) that use behavioral, psychological, and social factors to distinguish those who are likely to commit sex offenses from those who are less likely to commit such offenses.

Juvenile sex offenders too come from a variety of backgrounds. Some offenders are high-performing pupils and others are low or average performing. Some have no history of behavioral problems, and others have moderate or serious histories of behavioral problems. Some juvenile sex offenders come from well-educated family backgrounds, and others come from somewhat educated family backgrounds while others come from families that do not have an established educational background. Certain juvenile offenders come from the middle class and upper class, and others from not so well-off families. In short, evidence shows that juvenile sex offenders come from just about every religious, cultural, national, socioeconomic, and political background. Of course, these diverse characteristics of juvenile sex offenders make it even harder to distinguish between those who are likely to sexually offend and those who are less likely to engage in deviant sexual acts.

NOT CANDIDATES FOR SEX OFFENDER REGISTRATION

In some cases, the identification of a juvenile sex offender is not an easy task. Hannah is a 13-year-old girl and Joseph a 15½-year-old boy who attend the same school. During one of their morning bus rides, they made out on board the school bus. Right when Hannah was pushing Joseph away, the bus driver looked into her rearview mirror and saw Hannah resisting. When the bus driver inquired, the girl acted as if she had not consented to the boy's advances. The bus driver reported the incident to school authorities, who informed the parents, consistent with local law. When Hannah's father arrived at the school, the girl denied that she had consented. The father contacted the police, and the boy was adjudicated for sex offenses. In this case, Joseph is legally a sex offender because of Hannah's age and the allegation that he attempted to sexually assault her. Clinically, however, Joseph is not a sex offender because although it is legally wrong to make out with a 13-year-old, the behavior was consensual. Furthermore, the circumstances surrounding the behavior and the age difference do not suggest that Joseph specifically pursued a child for sexual purposes.

Sex-offending behavior is also a unique category of delinquent and criminal behavior both in terms of government responses and public perception outside and inside the walls of correctional institutions. For instance, both in and outside correctional facilities, sex offenders are the most hated group compared to substance abuse, general, mental health-related, and even violent offenders. Sex offenders are also a group of offenders who can be civilly detained for indefinite periods of time. In addition, sex offenders are the only group who are required to register with local law enforcement agencies and whose criminal histories get published on the Internet by government agencies and disclosed to residents in the areas in which they physically reside (Anthony & Stohr, 2010).

Sex offenders are also the only category of offenders that are predominantly male, as only a fraction of sex offenses are committed by female juveniles (Keelan & Fremouw, 2013). A review of research on adolescent sex offenders also found that while the overwhelming majority of juvenile sex offenders are males, about three-quarters of their victims are females (Boyd et al., 2000).

Most juvenile sex offenders come from unhealthy family backgrounds. Some juvenile sex offenders have a history of sexual, physical, and or psychological violence during their childhood. For example, about 79% of adolescent sexual offenders under state supervision have reportedly witnessed intrafamily violence compared to only 20% of nonsexual offenders. Families of adolescent sex offenders also tend to have "very dysfunctional and severely disturbed" histories (Boyd et al., 2000, p. 138).

A history of sexual or physical abuse is one of the core predictors of future sex offending behavior among juvenile sex offenders. Such a history can, at a minimum, significantly affect an individual offender's "appraisal of subsequent potentially conflictive situations in such a way that" the overall chances of future acts of violence and the risk of engaging in sexual offending behaviors compared to those without such history increases (Averdijk, Van Gelder, Eisner, & Ribeaud, 2016, p. 282). The impact of such histories is even greater if the abuse occurs at an earlier stage in the offender's development because the younger an offender is at their first experience of sexual victimization, the higher the likelihood that they will mentally normalize their victimization and the higher the chances of exhibiting early behavioral problems that generally include abuse of controlled substance and aggressive or violent behaviors such as cruelty to animals or setting property on fire (Boyd et al. 2000).

Fire Setting and Animal Abuse

It might seem difficult to fully comprehend the connections between fire setting and animal cruelty or abuse and violent or sexual offending behaviors. However, understanding why offenders delinquently and criminally set fires and why people subject animals to torturous violence can be helpful, especially given that it is very common to come across juvenile sex or violent offenders who have a history of setting fires and or sexually or physically abusing animals. Obviously, both behaviors are violent in nature and in some cases also sexual. Also, the relationship between the two forms of behaviors and future acts of sex or violent offending behaviors is strong and understandable.

Logically, both fire setting and animal cruelty constitute deliberate attempts to cause harm to living creatures or to destroy property. Fire-setting behaviors are more common among juvenile offenders with low intelligence levels, histories of sexual trauma, cruelty to animals, and sexual deviancy than among those who do not have such histories. Such behaviors also predict other acts of delinquency and criminality. For instance, an examination of 182 fire-setting children and adolescents in a New Zealand Fire Awareness and Intervention Program over a period of 10 years shows that although arson recidivism rate among the group was only 2%, about 59% of the sample engaged in one or more delinquent and criminal acts during the follow-up period. The same study found that 15% of the sample were classified as serious offenders, 40% as medium-risk-level offenders, and 4% as minimum-risk-level offenders, and about 12.6% of the participants either served or were serving prison terms during the follow-up period (Lambie, Ioane, Randell, & Seymour, 2013).

Animal cruelty is a form of interpersonal violence, and a strong relationship exists between physical and sexual abuse of animals and future acts of violence and sexual offending behaviors. These abuses typically include shooting, kicking, hitting, choking, drowning, burning, sexually abusing, or torturing domesticated animals (Hensley & Tallichet, 2009; Levitt, Hoffer, & Loper, 2016). Studies have also found statistically significant relationships between childhood cruelty to animals and future acts of violence against humans, and thus violent offenders are "significantly more likely than nonviolent offenders to have committed acts of cruelty toward pet animals" (Merz-Perez, Heide, & Silverman, 2001, p. 556). Again, this is understandable because animal abuse is characteristic of someone wanting to unnecessarily harm living creatures that have the clear capacity to feel pain and distress just like humans. It is therefore not surprising that cruelty to animals, or animal abuse, is empirically linked to "serious violent behavior, especially among youthful offenders"—for example, one study found that 45% of school shooting perpetrators in the United States had a history of animal abuse (Ascione, 2001).

Offenders abuse animals and set fires for different reasons. Some abuse animals because they derive personal pleasure from watching animals suffer. Some subject animals to violence in order to hurt the feelings of a particular pet owner or to settle a grievance. Others hurt animals in order to shock the conscience of the public or to satisfy personal curiosity as to how a particular animal experiences pain. Some offenders do so to learn how a particular animal responds to certain kinds and levels of pain and suffering. Other offenders abuse animals in order to derive sexual pleasure or to imitate the abuse they suffered in the hands of one or more family members, relatives, or persons with whom they have had personal relationships (Ascione, 2001). Similarly, some offenders set fires because they derive sexual pleasure from watching flames they initiated themselves. Some engage in fire-setting behaviors because they enjoy public reactions to fire or want to know how much damage the fire can cause.

ARSON FLAMES ARE BEAUTIFUL AND SEXUALLY AROUSING

There no evidence that the offender in this case started setting fires during his childhood. However, his adult behaviors are good examples:

John Orr was a well-respected fire captain and arson investigator for the Glendale Fire Department in California. His coworkers admired him for his dedication and ability to quickly arrive on the scene of fire and to identify the nearest hydrants. He was also known for having the ability to come up with the best strategy for putting out fires as well as investigating the cause of each fire. What his coworkers didn't know, however, was that John was the arsonist behind many of the fires they were fighting. He would tie a burning cigarette to a book of matches with a rubber band, and once the cigarette burned, the matches would ignite, causing flame. In one instance, a fire at a local hardware store killed four people, including a two-year-old child. John was caught because he apparently left his fingerprint at one of the several fires he secretly initiated while he was attending an arson investigators' conference in Bakersfield, California, in 1987. He was arrested in late November 1991 after his 1987 fingerprint was matched to another found by fingerprint investigators at a suspicious fire in Los Angeles. During the investigation, police also found a manuscript in his possession. An excerpt from that transcript eerily reads: "To Aaron, the smoke was beautiful, causing his heart rate to quicken and his breathing to come in shallow gasps. He was trying to control his outward appearance and look normal to anyone around him. He looked around and saw nothing; the lot was empty. He relaxed and partially stroked his erection, watching the fire." Former LAPD detective and crime novelist Joseph Wambaugh told *Newsweek* that "if you read it [the manuscript], you'll encounter more erections than at the Playboy Mansion" (Blankstein, 1998; Thomas, 2007).

Sources:

Blankstein, A. (1998, May 7). Trial starts for former firefighter accused in blaze that left 4 dead. *Los Angeles Times.*

Thomas, E. (2007, October 27) Arson: The scorched-earth obsession. *Newsweek.*

In the end, evidence suggests that most juvenile sex offenders are older than their victims. Also, although many child sex offenders grow up to live normal lives without any sex offending behaviors, most adult sex offenders begin their acts of victimization at a very young age or prior to their 18th birthdays (Gibson & Vandiver, 2008). It is also common to find juvenile sex offenders with noticeable histories of being physically and or sexually abused—note that the number of offenders who have some history of being physically abused is generally higher than those who were sexually abused (Terry, 2006). Studies have also reported that high-risk juvenile sex offenders tend to have histories of prior sexual-offending behaviors and social isolation and tend to hold distorted thinking or believe that their victims enjoy being victimized. Of course, distorted thinking in general and specifically thinking errors such as minimization of antisocial behaviors, blaming victims, and denying responsibility for offending behaviors significantly reinforce sexual offending behaviors.

VIOLENT OFFENDERS

The Centers for Disease Control and Prevention (CDC) report that "youth violence negatively impacts youth" in all urban, suburban, and rural communities and affects thousands of people but that the "magnitude and types of youth violence vary across communities and demographic groups" (Centers for Disease Control and Prevention, 2018). Violent behaviors evoke several meanings in different jurisdictions as well as cultural and geographical settings. For example, the CDC defines violent offenders as offenders who intentionally use physical force toward a person or property with the sole purpose of causing one or more persons pain and suffering or damaging or destroying an object. Violent juvenile offenders fight, bully, threaten others with weapons or harm, and even murder or cause serious bodily harm to people.

Legally speaking, a violent offender is an offender who has been adjudicated delinquent for one or more violent behaviors designated as violent acts. Examples of criminal violent behaviors include the commission of acts such as armed robbery, rape, assaults of various degrees, homicide, setting occupied structures on fire, sexual assault, carjacking, criminal damage, animal cruelty, domestic violence, kidnapping, and similar acts of physical violence. Clinically, a violent juvenile offender can be described as someone who engages in uninvited or unwanted use of physical force against another person or property with the intention to cause psychological or physical harm or to physically damage or destroy property. Violent offenders are different from people who easily get angry or who are aggressive.

Although anger is an emotional response to an unpleasant event, it can lead to behaviors that are aggressive or nonaggressive or are violent or nonviolent. Hence, anger can be a protective or a risk factor depending on the behavior that follows the anger. For example, many children get angry, but instead of lashing out, they simply complain or verbally express themselves or cope with the sources of their displeasure or anger. Other youth, however, look for opportunities to aggressively or violently lash out at other persons, animals, or property.

Aggression refers more appropriately to assertive behaviors that are characterized by the overt use of verbal or nonverbal force. Aggression therefore includes verbal hostility such as sending threatening emails or phone calls or making threats, shouting, or swearing at persons when angry. That is, slamming a door when exiting a premise as a result of anger is often an aggressive act, but banging on or kicking a door as a result of anger is certainly an act of violence. In this regard, it is therefore worth noting that aggressive behaviors are not violent behaviors and violent acts do not always equal aggressive acts, and not all manifestations of force amount to violence. Yet, aggression is a basic ingredient of violent behaviors (Bartol & Bartol, 2017).

Common risk factors associated with violent offenders include "impulsive behavior, poor emotional control, and lack of social and problem-solving skills" as well as a history of having experienced past sex, violent and/or psychological victimization as a child (Centers for Disease Control and Prevention, 2018). Characteristically also, offenders with prosocial views of victims are less likely to engage in violent behaviors, but those who believe that the use of violence is an appropriate way to respond to life's problems are at greater risk of committing future violent offenses (Bowes & McMurran, 2013). Furthermore, as with other categories of offenders, violent offenders too come from wide ranges of backgrounds. Some violent offenders are predatory violent offenders who groom, set up, and pursue victims for the sole purpose of violent victimization, while others are nonpredatory violent offenders who engage in violent acts without premeditation or any serious thought. Most violent juvenile offenders commit their offenses against friends, relatives, acquaintances, or people with whom they have domestic relationships (Khoshnood & Väfors Fritz, 2017).

GENERAL OFFENDERS

Some studies have found that the effect of prior general delinquent behaviors on particularly future violent behavior is only moderate; thus, general offending behaviors are not a good predictor of future acts of particularly violent behaviors (Boyd et al., p. 139). General offending behaviors as a category of criminal and delinquent offending behaviors, however, cover a large segment of juvenile offenders. In fact, the majority of juvenile offenders are in some ways general offenders. Also, youth who qualify as sex, violent, substance abuse, or mental health-related offenders do commit or are at risk of committing a variety of general offenses as children and as adults.

The list of general offending behaviors is very long, and such a list would generally include behaviors such as theft, possession of stolen property, reckless driving, trespassing, public nuisance, and driving without a license. General offenses also include computer-related offenses, status offenses, and many types of acquisitive offenses that are not violent, sexual, substance abuse, or mental health-related. In fact, a 2016 report shows that general offenses such as burglary, motor vehicle theft, larceny-theft, obstruction of justice, and disorderly conduct accounted for the overwhelming majority of adjudicated youth crimes. In addition, the report also shows that a large number of youth who made contact with the criminal justice system did so for status offenses such as running away, truancy, curfew violation, governability, and other miscellaneous status offenses (Hockenberry & Puzzanchera, 2018).

MENTAL HEALTH-RELATED OFFENDERS

The most recent U.S. Department of Justice Indicators of Mental Health Problems among prisoners and jail inmates shows that 37% of prison inmates and 44% of jail inmates have been diagnosed by at least one qualified mental health practitioner as having one or more mental disorders that affect behavioral choices (Bronson et al., 2017a). Also, a review of studies looking at incarcerated youth and mental health shows that 92% of the 86 studies analyzed found that as the severity and number of mental health conditions go up, so does the likelihood of criminal behaviors (Bronson et al., 2017b).

Mental health-related behaviors encompass schizophrenia-related behaviors, self-abusive behaviors such as attempted suicide and self-cutting, and broadly speaking, any behavior that is a direct product of a known mental health condition. Obviously, mental illnesses affect the ways an individual receives, processes, and digests information as well as how an offender behaves under certain conditions. In certain cases, offenders may manifest symptoms that are associated with certain mental disorders such as mental retardation and development disabilities that may interfere with their behaviors. Evidence also shows that offenders who are suffering from certain mental illnesses such as schizophrenia or who hallucinate usually show fragmented thought processes and appear delusional. Furthermore, although not very commonly, some mental health offenders claim to have physical contact with entities such as "alien[s] from another universe" and may claim to listen in on such beings' conversations or to have the power to allegedly sense and hear things that are not there or are invisible to other people. Some mental health offenders engage in delinquent or criminal behaviors, claiming that they did so because of voices commanding them to commit certain offenses (Prins, 2016; Bartol & Bartol, 2017).

Mental health-related offenders also tend to manifest psychosis or current substance abuse or dependence problems, and to have some history of violence. Some studies have also found that youth with conduct disorder diagnoses, a history of prior suicide attempts, and multiple prior adjudications for offenses are at higher risk of reoffending (Mallett, Fukushima, Stoddard-Dare, & Quinn, 2013). Additionally, studies found that having a mental health condition increases the chances of antisocial behavior. In this regard, offenders with a history of psychosis or delusions and hallucination are four times more likely to engage in delinquent or criminal types of antisocial behavior than those without such backgrounds (Bronson et al., 2017a).

Most juvenile offenders can be labelled as mental health-related offenders, but having a mere label does not explain the extent to which mental health conditions are directly related to an offender's behavior; at least, the connection would not be as clear as is the relationship between mental health conditions and behaviors such as suicidal ideation and attempts, self-abusive behaviors, and claims of acting under direct verbal command of a god, devil, or other supernatural power. It should also be noted that while not everyone with a known mental health condition is a potential mental health-related offender, mental health-related offenders too are diverse in terms of how individual offenders mentally process, acquire, retain, and retrieve key pieces of information, and most importantly how those processes influence antisocial and prosocial thinking and behavior.

CONCLUSION

Knowledge of each of the domains or behavioral labels discussed in this chapter is "critical for designing effective intervention strategies" (Ascione 2001, p. 6). At a minimum, such knowledge is helpful in understanding some of the psychological, social, and behavioral factors that inform offending behaviors in each of the behavioral domains discussed in this chapter. However, there is no empirically backed anatomical, physiological, or genetic abnormality that can be relied upon as a factor that distinguishes between law breakers and non-law breakers or that distinguishes a sex offender, violent offender, substance abuser, or general offender from nonoffenders. Furthermore, none of the factors discussed in this chapter is a definitive predictor with regard to who is likely or not likely to engage in violent, sex, general, substance abuse, or mental health-related behaviors.

Additionally, legal and clinical descriptions such as sex, violent, substance abuse, general, and mental health-related behaviors do not explain many of the underlying factors that inform sexual, general, violent, substance abuse, or mental health-related behaviors, and thus these labels do not predict the likelihood of an offender behaving in a particular way. However, while there is no single path to delinquency, the "presence of several risk factors often increases a youth's chance of offending" in each behavioral domain (Shader, 2008, p. 1). That is, accumulation of factors can produce a cumulative effect. For example, having certain risk factors such as a history of physical, sexual, or emotional abuse can significantly increase an offender's chances of future criminality and delinquency in terms of sexual, violent, substance abuse, and mental health-related behaviors.

CRITICAL QUESTIONS

1. How effective is the policy of requiring certain sex offenders to register with local sheriffs' offices and online in an effort to prevent future sex crimes?
2. What are the stereotypical characteristics of a juvenile sex offender; substance abuser; violent, general delinquent, or criminal offender; and mental health-related offender not discussed in this chapter that conflict with what research has so far documented?
3. Identify factors not discussed in this chapter that may increase the chances of recidivism for a sex, violent, general, substance abuse, and mental health-related offender.
4. To what extent does the choice to engage in antisocial behaviors with or without full understanding of the consequences of such behaviors qualify an offender as a mental health-related offender?
5. How much effort should be directed at distinguishing between sexual experimentation and sexual offending behaviors?

REFERENCES

ALLPSYCH. (2018). *Diagnostic and Statistical Manual of Mental Disorders, 4th ed. (DSM-IV)*. Retrieved from https://allpsych.com/disorders/dsm/

Anthony, W., & Stohr, M. (2010). *Correctional assessment, casework and counseling*. Alexandria, VA: American Correctional Association.

Ascione, F. R. (2001). *Animal abuse and youth violence*. Retrieved from the National Criminal Justice Reference Service website: https://www.ncjrs.gov/pdffiles1/ojjdp/188677.pdf

Averdijk, M., Van Gelder, J.-L., Eisner, M, & Ribeaud, D. (2016). Violence begets violence ... but how? A decision-making perspective on the victim–offender overlap. *Criminology, 54*(2), 282–306.

Bartol, C. R., & Bartol, A. M. (2017). *Criminal behavior: A psychological approach*. Boston, MA: Pearson.

Blankstein, A. (1998, May 7). Trial starts for former firefighter accused in blaze that left 4 dead. *Los Angeles Times*. Retrieved from https://www.latimes.com

Bowes, N., & McMurran, M. (2013). Cognitions supportive of violence and violent behavior. *Aggression and Violent Behavior, 18*(6), 660–665.

Boyd, N. J., Hagan, M., & Cho, M. E. (2000). Characteristics of adolescent sex offenders: A review of the research. *Aggression and Violent Behavior, 5*(2), 137–146.

Bronson, J., Stroop, J., Zimmer, S., & Berzofsky, M. (2017a). *Indicators of mental health problems reported by prisoners and jail inmates, 2011–2012*. Retrieved from the Bureau of Justice Statistics website: https://www.bjs.gov/content/pub/pdf/imhprpji1112.pdf

Bronson, J., Stroop, J., Zimmer, S., & Berzofsky, M. (2017b). *Drug use, dependence, and abuse among state prisoners and jail inmates, 2007–2009*. Retrieved from the Bureau of Justice Statistics website https://www.bjs.gov/content/pub/pdf/dudaspji0709.pdf

Centers for Disease Control and Prevention. (2018, September 29). *Preventing youth violence*. Retrieved from https://www.cdc.gov/violenceprevention/pdf/yv-factsheet.pdf

Chassin, L. (2008). Juvenile justice and substance use. *The Future of Children, 18*(2), 165–183.

Gibson, C., & Vandiver, D. M. (2008). *Juvenile sex offenders: What the public needs to know*. Westport, CT: Praeger.

Hensley, C., & Tallichet, S. E. (2009). Childhood and adolescent animal cruelty methods and their possible link to adult violent crimes. *Journal of Interpersonal Violence, 24*(1), 147–158.

Hockenberry, S., & Puzzanchera, C. (2018). *Juvenile court statistics 2016*. Retrieved from the Office of Juvenile Justice and Delinquency Prevention website: https://www.ojjdp.gov/

Keelan, C. M., & Fremouw, W. J. (2013). Child versus peer/adult offenders: A critical review of the juvenile sex offender literature. *Aggression and Violent Behavior, 18*(6), 732–744.

Khoshnood, A., & Väfors Fritz, M. (2017). Offender characteristics: A study of 23 violent offenders in Sweden. *Deviant Behavior, 38*(2), 141–153.

Lambie, I., Ioane, J., Randell, I., & Seymour, F. (2013). Offending behaviours of child and adolescent firesetters over a 10-year follow-up. *Journal of Child Psychology and Psychiatry, 54*(12), 1295–1307.

Levitt, L., Hoffer, T. A., & Loper, A. B. (2016). Criminal histories of a subsample of animal cruelty offenders. *Aggression and Violent Behavior, 30*, 48–58.

Mallett, C. A., Fukushima, M., Stoddard-Dare, P., & Quinn, L. (2013). Factors related to recidivism for youthful offenders. *Criminal Justice Studies, 26*(1), 84–98.

Merz-Perez, L., Heide, K. M., & Silverman, I. J. (2001). Childhood cruelty to animals and subsequent violence against humans. *International Journal of Offender Therapy and Comparative Criminology, 45*(5), 556–573.

Morrison, J. (2001). *DSM-IV made easy: The clinician's guide to diagnosis.* New York, NY: Guilford Press.

Prins, H. A. (2016). *Offenders, deviants or patients? An introduction to clinical criminology.* New York, NY : Routledge.

Rehabs.com (2018). *Differences in treatment of abuse and dependence.* Retrieved from https://luxury.rehabs.com/drug-abuse/abuse-vs-dependence/

Shader, M. (2008). *Risk factors for delinquency: An overview.* Retrieved from the National Criminal Justice Reference Service website: https://www.ncjrs.gov/pdffiles1/ojjdp/frd030127.pdf

Terry, K. J. (2006). *Sexual offenses and offenders: Theory, practice, and policy.* Belmont, CA: Wadsworth.

Thomas, E. (2007, October 27) Arson: The scorched-earth obsession. *Newsweek.* Retrieved from https://www.newsweek.com

SECTION II

Delinquent and Criminal Behaviors

CHAPTER SIX

Violent Offending Behaviors

MANY CHILDREN HAVE never abused substances or committed any substance-related offenses or engaged in sexual offending behaviors; however, such a claim cannot be made about violent behaviors. That is, violence is a natural part of the life cycle of every child. Indeed, every child participates in violence, although some children engage in more violent acts than others. After all, most humans are born with some capacity and appetite to hit, scream at or fight with other people, and to destroy or break things. It is therefore important not only to keep abreast of the latest information on the proportion, characteristics, and trends of violent offenses but also to gather information about behaviors for risk assessment and classification. Such knowledge is particularly useful when working with juvenile offenders, who at their tender ages experiment with and/or are readily thrilled by acts of violence.

VIOLENT VICTIMIZATION ON THE INCREASE

Compared to the previous decades or years, violent victimization is on the increase. The 2017 criminal victimization report by the U.S. Department of Justice indicates that the rate of violent victimization is on the increase (Morgan & Truman, 2018). Specifically, the number of persons age 12 or older who were victims of violent crimes increased from 2.7 million in 2015 to 2.9 million in 2016, and in 2017 the figure rose to around 3.1 million. That is, the 2017 victimization rate is 17% higher than the rate for 2015. In terms of specific criminal or delinquent behaviors, the rate of robbery victimization increased from 1.7 per 1,000 persons in 2016 to 2.3 per 1,000 persons in 2017. The percentage of rapes or sexual assaults that were reported to police also increased from 23% in 2016 to 40% in 2017. The number of people age 12 or older who were victims of assault in 2017 rose by 420,300, and the number of people who were victims of simple assault also rose by 334,700 in 2017. These figures are obviously disturbing because only about 45% of violent victimization acts were reported to police in 2017.

Source:

Morgan, R. E., & Truman, J. L. (2018). *Criminal victimization, 2017*. Retrieved from https://www.bjs.gov/content/pub/pdf/cv17.pdf

The ability to categorize deviant, criminal, and delinquent behaviors is also vital in determining the type and level of scrutiny or supervision each offender deserves to fully benefit from services available. This chapter is therefore concerned with those violent behaviors that rise to the level of crime and delinquency and those that qualify as deviant. The list of such violent criminal, delinquent, and deviant behaviors covers arson (involving occupied structures or disregard for human lives), aggravated assault, simple assault, intimidation, vandalism, destruction of property, kidnapping, robbery, and certain instances of disorderly conduct. In the case of children, these and other acts of violence can be grouped under violence associated with hate, domestic interactions, school, gangs, Internet or cellphone technologies, and other general violence. At a minimum, an effective violent risk assessment must be informed by up-to-date knowledge of the current trends of these behaviors among children.

CATEGORIES OF VIOLENCE

Juvenile offenders actively participate in some of the most troubling violent behaviors, such as murder, forcible rape, robbery, aggravated assault, arson, and cruelty to animals. As reflected in Table 6.1, each year between 2004 and 2015, an estimated 77,891 juveniles were arrested for various forms of violent behavior. On average, authorities arrested 1,025 juveniles for murder and nonnegligent manslaughter, 3,000 for acts of forcible rape, 26,675 for robbery, 46,383 for aggravated assault, and 5,525 for arson (Office of Juvenile Justice and Delinquency Prevention, 2017). These figures represent a small fraction of the violent behaviors that occur but do not come to the attention of law enforcement authorities.

TABLE 6.1 *Estimated Number of Juveniles Arrests, 2004 to 2015*

YEAR	TOTAL ARRESTS	TOTAL VIOLENT CRIMES	MURDER	RAPE	ROBBERY	AGGRAVATED ASSAULT	ARSON
2004	2,064,200	90,800	1,100	4,200	25,300	60,200	7,700
2005	2,039,400	95,600	1,300	4,000	29,000	61,300	8,000
2006	2,098,900	100,200	1,300	3,600	34,800	60,500	8,100
2007	2,061,900	96,500	1,300	3,600	34,400	57,200	7,200
2008	1,991,600	95,700	1,300	3,300	35,200	55,900	6,500
2009	1,812,900	85,900	1,200	3,100	31,700	49,900	5,300
2010	1,642,500	75,900	1,000	2,900	27,200	44,800	4,600
2011	1,47,0000	68,100	800	2,800	23,800	40,700	4,900
2012	1,319,700	61,100	700	2,500	21,500	36,300	4,400
2013	1,081,400	56,500*	700	2,000*	19,200	30,900	3,700
2014	1,023,800	55,800*	800	2,000*	19,500	30,300	3,200
2015	921,600	52,600*	800	2,000*	18,500	28,600	2,700

Source: Office of Juvenile Justice and Delinquency Prevention. (2017). *OJJDP statistical briefing book: Estimated number of juvenile arrests, 2015*. Retrieved from https://www.ojjdp.gov/ojstatbb/crime/qa05101.asp?qa

*Figure not available. Rape estimated at 2000 for each year; estimated total arrests for 2013, 2014, and 2015 are estimated at 56500, 55800, and 52600 respectively.

In 2011 law enforcement agencies in the United States arrested nearly 1.5 million youth under the age of 18 years. Twenty-seven percent of the offenders were younger than 15 years old, and 27% of the offenses were violent. About 800 of the arrestees for murder and nonnegligent manslaughter were juvenile offenders. During the same period, the juvenile population was responsible for 2,800 forcible rapes, 23,800 robberies, and 40,700 aggravated assaults (Office of Juvenile Justice and Delinquency Prevention, 2017; Puzzanchera, 2013). Despite these figures, it is important to note that overall crime and delinquency rates, especially violent acts in general by children under the age of 18, have been decreasing, at least in the past decade.

According to the latest Office of Juvenile Justice and Delinquency Prevention (OJJDP) Statistical Briefing record, the rate of juvenile arrests in 2015 was 37% less than the rate in 2011 and 10% less than the rate in 2014. Similarly, the rate for 2013 was 48% less than the rate in 2004, 40% less than the rate in 2009, and 18% less than the rate of arrests in 2012. As reported, the rate of juveniles arrested for murder in 2012 and 2013 was 33.3% less than the rate in 2009, 27.2% less than the rate in 2004, and 38.4% less than the rate in 2005, 2006, 2007, and 2008 respectively. There were also 43% fewer juvenile arrests in 2012 than in 2003 and 42% fewer in 2012 than in 2008. Similarly, there were 53% fewer juvenile arrests in 2015 than in 2006 for aggravated assault, 30% fewer juvenile arrests in 2015 than in 2011, 40% fewer juvenile arrests for murder in 2014 than in 2005, and 25% fewer arrests for the same behaviors in 2014 than in 2010 (Office of Juvenile Justice and Delinquency Prevention, 2017). Table 6.2 illustrates the same downward trend in the rate of arrests which is observable in the number of cases juvenile courts disposed between 2005 and 2013.

TABLE 6.2 *2010–2014 Estimates of Juvenile Court Disposition by Age at Referral*

YEAR	<12	12	13	14	15	16	17	>17	TOTAL
2005	64148	81865	167244	274839	372310	393930	283605	37421	**1675361**
2006	57723	74080	154036	258938	358741	394269	284455	36139	**1618380**
2007	54680	69663	146746	252173	357181	405065	300326	38297	**1624131**
2008	51951	65174	138622	241061	349526	406088	307274	40306	**1600001**
2009	47292	59957	123635	215491	318012	377754	286859	38998	**1467997**
2010	46448	56847	115794	196688	286545	342646	260665	36234	**1341867**
2011	43995	54390	108804	179976	260491	308938	237800	32235	**1226630**
2012	43209	50854	101546	168775	238237	281479	212303	29999	**1126400**
2013	39137	46685	93015	153742	217487	253270	198930	28250	**1030514**
2014	36854	43000	87142	144519	202658	238146	194535	28095	**974950**
TOTAL	**485438**	**602515**	**1236584**	**2086202**	**2961186**	**3401584**	**2566751**	**345973**	**13686233**

Source: Puzzanchera, C., & Kang, W. (2017). Easy access to FBI arrest statistics 1994–2014. Retrieved from http://www.ojjdp.gov/ojstatbb/ezaucr/

Table 6.2 contains the number of delinquency cases processed by juvenile courts between 2005 and 2014. This table also shows that the aggregate rate of youth who made it onto the dockets of juvenile courts is falling in all age categories. Even the number of delinquent and criminal cases processed by courts involving children under the age of 12 has decreased from 64,148 in 2005 to only 36,854 in 2014, a difference of about 43%. The total number of cases for all persons under the age of 18 has also dropped from 1,675,361 in 2005 to only 974,950 in 2014, about 42% less than the figures for 2005.

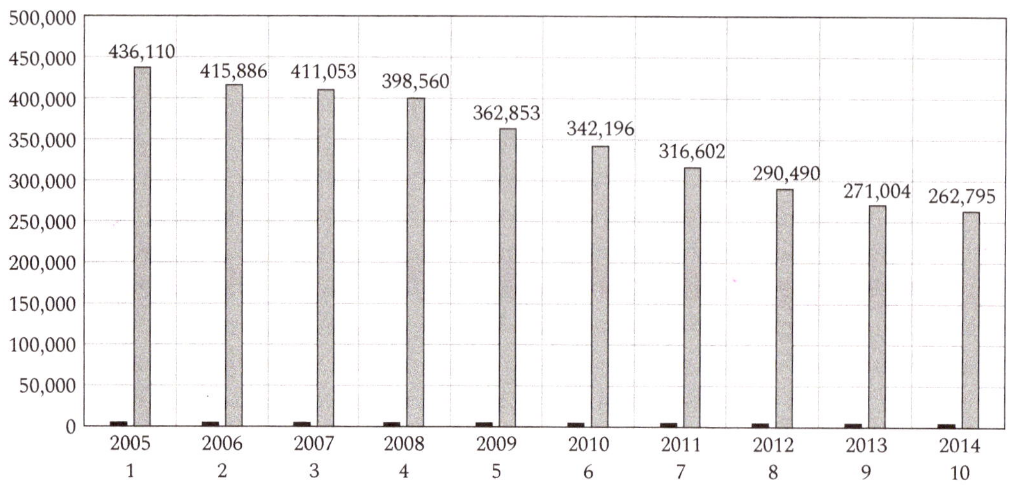

FIGURE 6.1 Referrals by Year 2005–2014 Referrals to Juvenile Courts

Source: Puzzanchera, C., & Kang, W. (2017). Easy access to FBI arrest statistics 1994–2014. Retrieved from http://www.ojjdp.gov/ojstatbb/ezaucr/

In terms of violent offenses, the overall rates of offenses against persons have also been sliding down at a healthy pace. Crimes against persons typically refers to violent crimes and thus include homicide, rape, robbery, assault and battery, armed robbery, certain categories of arson, and similar violent behavior involving persons. It is, however, to be noted that despite the decline in the number of referrals (Figure 6.1), the rates are still high given that only a fraction of crimes against persons committed by youth come to the attention of juvenile courts. What is still encouraging, however, is the fact that the rates drop as youth age, although the rate among children between the age of 14 and 17 years is the highest for all other age groups.

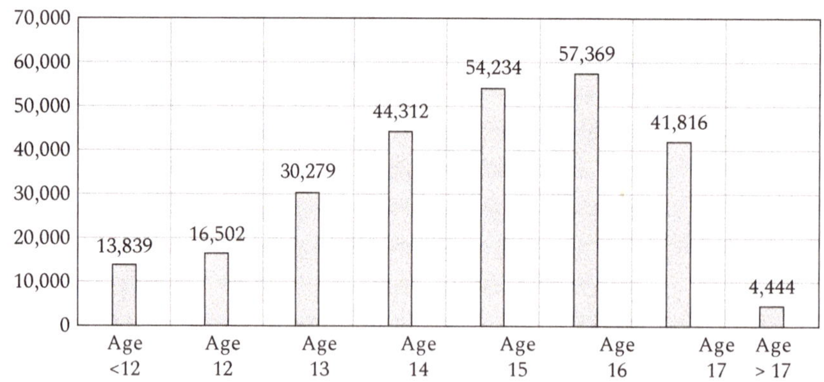

FIGURE 6.2 2014 Offenses Against Persons by Age

Source: Sickmund, M., Sladky, A., & Kang, W. (2017). *Easy access to juvenile court statistics: 1985–2014*. Retrieved from http://www.ojjdp.gov/ojstatbb/ezajcs/

Figure 6.2 shows that many of the offenses against persons were committed by youth between the ages of 14 and 17, about 75% of the 262,795 youth who were referred to the criminal justice system for crimes against persons in 2014. This pattern of offenses by children, however, is not unique to crimes against persons. Indeed, youth between the ages of 14 and 17 were responsible for a large proportion of property, drug, and public order offenses referred to the criminal justice system for processing (Sickmund et al., 2017).

Arson

Surprisingly, Table 6.3 shows that arson occurs more frequently than one might expect. In this respect, the Federal Bureau of Investigation's Uniform Crime Reporting (UCR) system treats arson primarily as a property crime. However, arson is a crime that does not always fit into one category. Under certain circumstances, the act can fall under a property, violent, or sexual offense. For example, depending on an offender's motivations, arson involving forest land or in some cases unoccupied structures may not be classified as a violent act if the offender's intention for setting the fire was not to cause death or injury to a person or animal or if the facts were such that a reasonable person would not expect direct physical harm to person or animal to result from such an act. Also, when arson is an extension of or is accompanied by a nonviolent crime such as insurance fraud, then it would be incorrect to classify such behavior as a violent crime as far as classification and assessment are concerned. Furthermore, such a classification would be particularly problematic because as much as arson can be motivated by violent tendencies, the behavior can also be motivated by lust, revulsion, or thrill.

TABLE 6.3 *2004–2015 Arrest Rates for Arson*

YEAR	TOTAL	ARSON	(%)
2004	2,064,200	7,700	.37
2005	2,039,400	8,000	.39
2006	2,098,900	8,100	.38
2007	2,061,900	7,200	.34
2008	1,991,600	6,500	.33
2009	1,812,900	5,300	.29
2010	1,642,500	4,600	.28
2011	1,47,0000	4,900	.33
2012	1,319,700	4,400	.33
2013	1,081,400	3,700	.34
2014	1,023,800	3,200	.31
2015	921,600	2,700	.29

Source: Office of Juvenile Justice and Delinquency Prevention. (2017). *OJJDP statistical briefing book: Estimated number of juvenile arrests, 2015*. Retrieved from https://www.ojjdp.gov/ojstatbb/crime/qa05101.asp?qa

As depicted in Table 6.3, arson is one of the many serious offenses committed by children under 18. As a result, the 2014 Juvenile Offenders and Victims National Report shows that about 40% of all offenders arrested for arson in 2010 were children younger than 18, and about 1 in 4 of those children was younger than 15 years old (Sickmund & Puzzanchera, 2014). Broadly speaking, arson can be motivated by distinct reasons that include violent tendencies, crime concealment, thrill, and lust. Consequently, some risk assessment tools treat arson as violent or sexual or both violent and sexual, depending on the circumstances (Anwar, Långström, Grann, & Fazel, 2011, p. 584).

Crime concealment arsons are motivated by the desire to cover up criminal activities. In such cases, the act of violence is an extension of a separate crime, such as murder, or is as an extension of an acquisitive crime, such as insurance fraud. Arsonists with violent tendencies use fire to express feelings of disgust, revulsion, distaste, or hate and thus the desire to harm a person or group of people. The thrill-seeking arsonist sets fire for the sake of watching how big the fire gets, to enjoy the reaction of other people to the fire, or to simply experiment with fire setting. Hence, this category of fire-setting behavior falls under property offenses.

The violent tendency arsonist's goal is to cause direct pain and suffering to a person or group of people. Common examples include the setting on fire of structures belonging to other individuals or groups of people. Typically, these types of arsonists may set on fire religious buildings, such as churches, mosques, or synagogues. The lust arsonist is typically motivated by desires for pyromania or sexual self-gratification and thus typically has a history or tendency to derive sexual pleasure mainly from watching the flames. Thus, while the violent tendency offenders fit the clinical profile of violent offenders, the lust offender may be classified as a sex offender.

Domestic Violence

Domestic violent acts by children are serious offenses that are highly underreported. In fact, when the phrase "domestic violence" is mentioned in most contexts, people may first think of adult offenders in part because juvenile domestic violence incidents hardly come to the attention of law enforcement agencies. After all, most victims of juvenile-perpetuated domestic violence are parents, siblings, and/or girlfriends and boyfriends, who are often less inclined to report their victimization to law enforcement. As a result, most victims conceal their victimization to protect the offenders.

About one-third (35%) of juveniles who commit domestic violence assaults are girls and two-thirds (67%) of the victims of juvenile domestic assault are females under the age of eighteen (Snyder & McCurley, 2008). Studies have also found that juvenile offenders who are violent toward their parents tend also to have more emotional problems than other juvenile offenders and nonoffenders; thus, they tend to exhibit behavioral problems in other social settings outside their homes (Ibabe, Arnoso, & Elgorriaga, 2014). Furthermore, irrespective of the type of household and the offenders' gender, mothers are often the ones who suffer the brunt of juvenile offenders' domestic violence (Contreras & Cano, 2014).

School Violence

The Centers for Disease Control and Prevention defines school violence as "youth violence that occurs on school property, [or] on the way to or from school or school-sponsored events" (Centers for Disease Control and Prevention, 2016). School violence has remained a serious concern for law enforcement agencies since the April 20, 1999, Columbine High School shooting, a massacre that took the lives of 12 students and one teacher and left 21 people injured. Since then, the number of pupil-initiated high school shootings with such a large casualty figure has been rare. In the end, however, school violence of some sort remains a part of everyday life in schools around the nation.

A survey of 9th through 12th graders in public and private schools throughout the United States shows that a sizable number of high school students constantly deal with school-based violence. These acts of violence range from possession of weapons for self-protection, involvement in physical fights, and failure to attend school due to feeling unsafe on school grounds (Youth Risk Behavior Survey, 2017). As reflected in Table 6.4, the most violent acts between 2009 and 2015 were bullying in school. The second most common acts of violence associated with interactions on school grounds between 1993 and 2015 were physical fights, and the third most common violent behaviors for the same period were being threatened with weapons or sustaining injuries as a consequence of violent victimization.

TABLE 6.4 *Prevalence of Violence on School Grounds: 1991–2015*

VIOLENCE ON SCHOOL GROUNDS	YEAR: 1991–2015											
Year	**93**	**95**	**97**	**99**	**01**	**03**	**05**	**07**	**09**	**11**	**13**	**15**
Carried a weapon to school	11.8	9.8	8.5	6.9	6.4	6.1	6.5	5.9	5.6	5.4	5.2	4.1
Felt threatened or was injured by a weapon in school	7.3	8.4	7.4	7.7	8.9	9.2	7.9	7.8	7.7	7.4	6.9	6.0
Involved in a physical fight	16.2	15.5	14.8	14.2	12.5	12.8	13.6	12.4	11.1	12.0	8.1	7.8
Did not go to school due to safety concerns	4.4	4.5	4.0	5.2	6.6	5.4	6.0	5.5	5.0	5.9	7.1	5.6
Bullied in school	na	na	na	na	na	na	na	na	19.9	20.1	19.6	20.2

Source: Youth Risk Behavior Survey. (2017). *Trends in the prevalence of behaviors that contribute to violence on school property; National YRBS: 1991–2015*. Retrieved from https://www.cdc.gov/healthyyouth/data/yrbs/pdf/trends/2015_us_violenceschool_trend_yrbs.pdf

The good news is that the results of Youth Risk Behavior Survey show that overall the rate of school violence has been declining compared to the rest of the behaviors covered by the survey. The data in Table 6.4 also show that overall the rate of violent incidents have decreased, especially with respect to youth who carry weapons on school property and incidents where juveniles refused to go to school because of a fear of victimization. There remain, however, a few trouble areas.

From July 1, 2013, through June 30, 2014, alone, there were 48 school violence-related deaths (Musu-Gillette, Zhang, Wang, Zhang, & Oudekerk, 2017). In 2015, about 2.7 million, or 0.98%, of all persons age 12 or older experienced at least one violent victimization (Truman & Morgan, 2016). About 15% of fourth graders and 7% of eighth graders in the United States experienced bullying at least once a month. Another 7% of fourth graders felt less safe in school than they do off school grounds (Musu-Gillette et al., 2017). The rate of youth who reported being bullied on school property during the 12 months that preceded the interview went from 19.9 in 2009 to 20.2 in 2015 (Youth Risk Behavior Survey, 2017).

One in every eight students in 2011 was involved in a fight, and more than three in 10 high school students were involved in one or more physical fights resulting in one in 25 being injured. Also, one-third of youth who carried one or more weapons took them to school (Sickmund & Puzzanchera, 2014). Similarly, according to the United States Department of Education, from July 2010 to July 2011 there were 31 school-related violent deaths in the United States. During the same period, 3.5% of students between the ages of 12 and 14 suffered violent victimization on school grounds.

In the same period, 17.6% of students between the ages of 12 and 18 reported being made fun of, called names, or insulted, while 18.3% were subjected to rumors and 5% were threatened by other students. In the same year, 8.9% of students in similar age groups reported being asked to do things they did not want to do, or were purposely excluded from activities or isolated by peers. Twenty-eight percent of students also reported being bullied, while 7.9% reported being pushed, shoved, tripped, or spit on by other students on school grounds (U.S. Department of Education, 2013). Given these accounts, school-based violence remains a major concern on public safety agendas and a gateway to serious and felonious acts of violence.

Gang Violence

Gang problems in the United States are prevalent and destructive and pose such a threat that almost any large police department has a specialized gang unit to deal with gang-related criminal activity. Some probation and parole departments also maintain specialized probation and parole agents who are specifically charged with the supervision of offenders whose behaviors are gang affiliated. Despite the level of attention that gangs and gang violence receive, it is, however, extremely difficult to determine the scope and breadth of youth criminal gang activities. Furthermore, there is no "consensus on what defines a gang and gang activity" (Sickmund & Puzzanchera, 2014, p. 69) nor is there consensus about the definition and membership of criminal or street gangs (O'Brien, Daffern, Chu, & Thomas, 2013).

YOUTH WHO MURDER AND ROB

United States Department of Justice reports show that youth violence is a national concern as evidenced by the rise in juvenile arrests for violence, especially murder, robbery, and aggravated assault. The most serious violent behaviors are, however, mostly associated with criminal gang members and a handful of chronic offenders. That is, only a small fraction of juvenile repeat offenders commit the majority of serious violent offenses. Chronic offenders represent less than 10% of the delinquent youth population, yet they account for more than two-thirds of all violent offenses that come to the attention of criminal justice practitioners.

The likelihood of juveniles getting arrested for serious violent offenses typically begins to increase at age 12. The arrest rate doubles between the ages of 13 and 14, peaks between the ages of 16 and 17, and drops about 50% by the time youth reach the age of 18. The rate continues to decrease more rapidly between age 18 and 27 (U.S. Department of Justice, 2019).

Source:

U.S. Department of Justice. (2019). Juvenile Crime Facts. Retrieved from https://www.justice.gov/jm/criminal-resource-manual-102-juvenile-crime-facts

The National Youth Gang Center's annual Gang Survey remains the best source of information on contemporary gangs and gang activities in the United States (Sickmund & Puzzanchera, 2014, p. 69). According to federal statute 18 USC § 521, a gang is an ongoing group of people, a club, an organization, or an association of five or more persons with a primary purpose of conspiring to commit offenses or to engage in the actual commission of felonies or that is involved in crimes of violence. Youth gangs may be described, at least for the purpose of risk assessment and classification, as a group of youth with the common goal to engage in criminal, delinquent, or deviant behaviors that are criminogenic or antisocial in nature.

Gang membership is one of the most reliable predictors of violent behaviors and, of course, of spending time in the company of high-risk youth. As such, studies show that "gang membership is a high-risk life" connected to a wide range of criminal and delinquent behaviors that include "substance abuse, unsafe sexual practices, gun carrying, illicit drug sales, arrest, nonfatal intentional injury, homicide," and a host of other antisocial problems that aggravate risk levels (O'Brien et al., 2013; Pyrooz & Sweeten, 2015, p. 414). In short, this means that most youth who make contact with the criminal justice system have some form of gang affiliation, and most youth who are active gang members are bound to make some form of contact with the criminal justice system. That is, gang membership and gang violence are almost interchangeable.

Criminologists have "consistently found that, when compared with youth who do not belong to gangs, gang members are far more involved in delinquency, especially serious and violent delinquency" (Battin-Pearson, Thornberry, Hawkins, & Krohn, 1998, p. 3). This finding is not, however, surprising because gang membership comes with the requirement to be violent, to possess weapons, to engage in self-defense activities, to acquire and hold onto territories, and to engage in violent street crimes. The need to carry guns and other forms of deadly weapons is particularly problematic because it remains the case that youth with violent propensities are more likely to own and carry guns for protection and to also use such weapons.

Juvenile males who own guns for protection are "six times more likely to carry guns, eight times more likely to commit a crime with a gun, four times more likely to sell drugs, almost five times more likely to be in a gang, and three times more likely to commit serious and violent crimes than youth who do not own guns for protection" (Howell, 1998, p. 10). That is, the possession of guns and other weapons heightens the risk for lethal conflict (Deanna, Marquette, Brice, Shelly, & Kerryn, 2009).

Other researchers have also found that youth who carry handguns are significantly more likely to have encountered violence compared with youth who did not carry handguns (Michael et al., 2012). Furthermore, once a youth becomes a gang member, the chances of being involved in delinquent, criminal, or deviant behaviors increases drastically, in part because gangs in general glamorize violent crimes; thus, street gang members use violence as means for achieving their goals in most instances (Howell, 1998). In reality, gang membership means participation in violent, delinquent, criminal, or deviant activities and spending more time with antisocial peers and thus the greater likelihood of carrying and using weapons (Hutson, Anglin, & Eckstein, 1996). Criminologists have also found consistently that youth who are gang members are at higher risk of getting into trouble with the law compared with those who are not gang members because gang members are far more involved in delinquency, especially serious and violent acts, than are non-gang members (Battin-Pearson et al., 1998; Dong & Krohn, 2016; O'Brien et al., 2013; Pyrooz & Sweeten, 2015).

Cyberviolence

Two main forms of cyberviolence are commonly associated with juveniles: cyberbullying and cyberstalking. The distinction, however, between these two behaviors, cyberstalking and cyberbullying, is not always clear, although the intention that produces each is usually unique. For instance, both behaviors may use threats of harm, may involve the spreading of false information about victims, and may involve identity theft and constant provocation. However, one of the primary goals pursued by cyberbullies is to intimidate or create fear in the minds of their victims. The main goal of cyberstalkers is to create the impression that they are in control by engaging in behaviors that demonstrate the ability to intrude upon victims' privacy at will without regard for how such behavior may impact their victims. In other words, a stalker wants their victims to recognize their presence, often in the victim's private space, while a bully wants victims to feel threatened and, in some cases, to fear for their own safety.

Cyberbullying is a serious form of violence often committed by youth against other youth through a variety of phone and Internet media. The act typically involves one youth sending mean-spirited or threatening messages to another youth, spreading hurtful rumors about another youth, or circulating sexually suggestive pictures, videos, or damaging messages about another youth on a social networking site or web page. These behaviors mostly occur on media outlets such as Facebook, Instagram, Snapchat, or Twitter, or get communicated via text message, email, or other instant messaging services.

Some studies have shown that about 5.1% of youth have perpetrated cyberbullying, another 5% have suffered cyberbullying, and 9.5% have been associated with the perpetuation of cyberbullying and have also suffered cyber victimization at the hands of other youth (Hemphill & Heerde, 2014). Other studies have found that an estimated 12.1% of all youth who bully other youth offline also engage in some form of cyberbullying, and about 7.4% of youth who are physically victimized on school grounds also fall victim to cyber victimization (Baldry, Farrington, & Sorrentino, 2016).

Cyberstalking is the use of the Internet and or phone technologies to stalk another person. Both cyberstalking and physical stalking involve a youth repeatedly intruding on another person in ways that produce fear or distress. However, unlike physical stalking that involves continuous unwanted physical communication and unwanted and sporadic physical presence in a victim's home, workplace, or school, cyberstalking involves the continuous and unwanted communication or attempt to communicate with a victim via communication technologies (Marcum, Higgins, & Ricketts, 2014).

Typically, cyberstalking is also characterized by the unwanted presence of the offender in a victim's cyberspace, including media platforms such as Facebook, Instagram, Snapchat, Twitter, text messages, emails, and other instant messaging services. The unwanted behavior ranges from bullying-like behaviors that include threats or intimidation and repeated electronic communication with the victim; impersonation of the victim; illegal possession of the victim's online information, including login credentials; and posting of unwanted messages on the victim's social medial pages, even after the offender has been asked by the victim to stop. The majority of cyberstalking and cyberbullying offenders are male (Antoniadou, Kokkinos, & Markos, 2016).

Hate Crimes

A hate crime is one of the troubling violent acts that law enforcement agencies deal with at all levels. Bias or hate crimes are generally characterized by violent acts toward one or more persons and are motivated by a victim's race, religion, ethnicity, nationality, gender, sexual orientation, gender identity, disability, or similarly protected category of persons. While most hate crimes produce a significant amount of damage for the intended victims and society at large, "studies have established that most hate crimes are committed by single or small groups of young males unaffiliated with organized hate groups" (Steinberg, Brooks, & Remtulla, 2003, p. 978).

Law enforcement agencies around the country who reported a hate crime to the Federal Bureau of Investigation's Uniform Crime Reporting program in 2015 reported 5,493 known offenders in 5,850 hate- or bias-motivated incidents. Most racially motivated offenses were committed by Whites (48.4%) while 24.3% were committed by Blacks. Individuals of other races accounted for only 9.1% of hate crimes. Of the reported 3,331 known ages of offenders, 15.3% were under the age of 18. Of the 7,173 victims of hate crimes reported in 2015, about 4,482, or 62.5%, were victims of crimes against persons; 2625, or 36.6% were victims of crimes against property; and 65, or 0.9%, were victims of crimes against society, such as a perpetrator's illegal possession of weapons and gambling offenses (Federal Bureau of Investigation, 2017).

The majority of reported hate crimes were acts of intimidation (41.3%), simple assault (37.8%), and aggravated assault (19.7%). Of the 1,440 known property-related hate crimes committed in 2015, almost 58.1% were destruction, damage, or vandalism; 15.8% were for robbery; 12.3% were for larceny-theft; and 8% of the offenses were for burglary. Table 6.5 shows that the majority of the crimes were motivated by victims' race, ethnicity, or ancestry (59.2%), while religion accounted for 19.7%, sexual orientation informed 17.7% of the offenses, and gender-related identity and characteristics accounted for about 2% of the victimization incidents (Federal Bureau of Investigation, 2017). The actual distribution of victims is reported in Table 6.5.

TABLE 6.5 *Victims of Race, Ancestry-Based Hate Crime in 2015*

CATEGORY OF RACE, ETHNICITY, OR ANCESTRY	%
Anti-Black or African American	52.2
Anti-White	18.7
Anti-Hispanic or Latino	9.3
Anti-multiple races, group	3.8
Anti-American Indian or Alaska Native	3.3
Anti-Asian	3.2
Anti-Arab	1.1
Anti-Native Hawaiian or other Pacific Islander	0.1
Anti-Other Race/Ethnicity/Ancestry	8.1

Source: Federal Bureau of Investigation. (2017). *Uniform crime report: Hate crime statistics, 2015.* Retrieved from https://ucr.fbi.gov/hate-crime/2015/topic-pages/victims_final.pdf

According to the U.S. Justice Department, on average, U.S. residents experienced 250,000 hate crime victimizations between 2004 and 2015. The most common motivating factor was racial bias, which accounted for 48% of the offenses (Masucci & Langton, 2017). In 2015, there were 4,216 victims of race, ethnicity, or ancestry-based motivated hate crimes. The majority of the victimization in Table 6.5 was motivated by anti-Black or African American sentiments (52.2%). The second racial group targeted was Whites (18.7%), and the third group was Hispanics (9.3%). The number of victims with mixed racial, ethnic, or ancestral backgrounds was also high (8.1%) compared to American Indians or Alaska Natives, Asians, Arabs, and Native Hawaiian or other Pacific Islanders combined. Black or African Americans have higher chances of being a victim of hate crime than any other racial or ethnic group.

CONCLUSION

In spite of all the promising data about the gradual drop in youth violence, offenses against persons and property must be assessed with greater attention with the understanding that the potential for violence, delinquency, and crime is always high among youth. It must always be noted that youth who make contact with the criminal justice system for any category of offense represent a small number of the actual figure for youth violence. Furthermore, victims of serious violent crimes such as aggravated and simple assault experience significant socioemotional problems. Some experience moderate to severe distress, and some have problems with work and social interaction, difficulty getting along, and an inability to trust other people who resemble their abusers. The majority (91%) of violent crime victims also experience one or more physical symptoms for a period of time after their victimization (Langton & Truman, 2014).

DISCUSSION QUESTIONS

1. To what extent do factors that explain school violence inform or actually explain non-school violence?
2. The reasons many youth engage in criminal street gang activities are numerous. What are other factors that contribute to youth gang activities besides those briefly discussed in this chapter?
3. Apart from increased treatment, what are some of the key factors that explain the consistent drop in the number of juvenile arrests in the last 10 years?
4. Comparatively, which behavior is more harmful to victims: cyberstalking or cyberbullying?
5. Cyberstalking and cyberbullying are both harmful. That said, which of the two vices has the most impact and or is more prevalent among middle school and/or high school pupils?
6. What factors might explain the drop in the number of juveniles who get arrested for violent crimes?

REFERENCES

Antoniadou, N., Kokkinos, C. M., & Markos, A. (2016). Possible common correlates between bullying and cyber-bullying among adolescents. *Psicología Educativa, 22*, 27–38.

Anwar, S., Långström, N., Grann, M., & Fazel, S. (2011). Is arson the crime most strongly associated with psychosis? A national case-control study of arson risk in schizophrenia and other psychoses. *Schizophrenia Bulletin, 37*(3), 580–586. doi: 10.1093/schbul/sbp098

Baldry, A. C., Farrington, D. P., & Sorrentino, A. (2016). Cyberbullying in youth: A pattern of disruptive behaviour. *Psicología Educativa, 22*(1), 19–26. doi.org/10.1016/j.pse.2016.02.001

Battin-Pearson, S. R., Thornberry, T. P., Hawkins, J. D., & Krohn, M. D. (1998). *Gang membership, delinquent peers, and delinquent behavior.* Retrieved from the National Criminal Justice Reference Service website: https://www.ncjrs.gov/pdffiles/171119.pdf

Centers for Disease Control and Prevention. (2016). *Understanding school violence: Fact sheet, 2016.* Retrieved from https://www.cdc.gov/violenceprevention/pdf/school_violence_fact_sheet-a.pdf

Contreras, L., & Cano, C. (2014). Family profile of young offenders who abuse their parents: A comparison with general offenders and non-offenders. *Journal of Family Violence, 29*(8), 901–910. doi: 10.1007/s10896-014-9637-y

Deanna, L. W., Marquette, S. M., Brice, W., Shelly, B., & Kerryn, B. (2009). Peers and gun use among urban adolescent males: An examination of social embeddedness. *Journal of Contemporary Criminal Justice, 25*(1), 20–44. doi: 10.1177/1043986208328449

Dong, B., & Krohn, M. D. (2016). Escape from violence: What reduces the enduring consequences of adolescent gang affiliation? *Journal of Criminal Justice, 47*, 41–50. doi.org/10.1016/j.jcrimjus.2016.07.002

Federal Bureau of Investigation. (2017). *Uniform crime report: Hate crime statistics, 2015.* Retrieved from https://ucr.fbi.gov/hate-crime/2015/topic-pages/victims_final.pdf

Hemphill, S. A., & Heerde, J. A. (2014). Adolescent predictors of young adult cyber-bullying perpetration and victimization among Australian youth. *Journal of Adolescent Health, 55*(4), 580–587. doi: 10.1016/j.jadohealth.2014.04.014

Howell, J. C. (1998). *Youth gangs: An overview.* Retrieved from https://www.ojjdp.gov/jjbulletin/9808/contents.html

Hutson, H. R., Anglin, D., & Eckstein, M. (1996). Drive-by shootings by violent street gangs in Los Angeles: A five-year review from 1989 to 1993. *Academic Emergency Medicine, 3*(4), 300–303.

Ibabe, I., Arnoso, A., & Elgorriaga, E. (2014). The clinical profile of adolescent offenders of child-to-parent violence. *Procedia-Social and Behavioral Sciences, 131*(Supplement C), 377–381. doi.org/10.1016/j.sbspro.2014.04.133

Langton, L., & Truman, J. (2014, September). *Socio-emotional impact of violent crime.* Retrieved from the Bureau of Justice Statistics website: https://www.bjs.gov/content/pub/pdf/sivc.pdf

Marcum, C. D., Higgins, G. E., & Ricketts, M. L. (2014). Juveniles and cyber stalking in the United States: An analysis of theoretical predictors of patterns of online perpetration. *International Journal of Cyber Criminology, 8*(1), 47–56.

Masucci, M., & Langton, L. (2017). *Hate crime victimization, 2004–2015.* Retrieved from the Bureau of Justice Statistics website: https://www.bjs.gov/content/pub/pdf/hcv0415.pdf

Michael, G. V., Brian, E. P., Arnelyn, A., René, O., Ralph, G., & Li-Tzy, W. (2012). Correlates of handgun carrying among adolescents in the United States. *Journal of Interpersonal Violence, 27*(10), 2003–2021. doi: 10.1177/0886260511432150

Morgan, R. E., & Truman, J. L. (2018). *Criminal victimization, 2017.* Retrieved from the Bureau of Justice Statistics website: https://www.bjs.gov/content/pub/pdf/cv17.pdf

Musu-Gillette, L., Zhang, A., Wang, K., Zhang, J., & Oudekerk, B. A. (2017). *Indicators of school crime and safety: 2016.* Retrieved from the National Center for Education Statistics website: https://nces.ed.gov/pubs2017/2017064.pdf

O'Brien, K., Daffern, M., Chu, C. M., & Thomas, S. D. M. (2013). Youth gang affiliation, violence, and criminal activities: A review of motivational, risk, and protective factors. *Aggression and Violent Behavior, 18*(4), 417–425. doi.org/10.1016/j.avb.2013.05.001

Office of Juvenile Justice and Delinquency Prevention. (2017). *OJJDP statistical briefing book: Estimated number of juvenile arrests, 2015.* Retrieved from https://www.ojjdp.gov/ojstatbb/crime/qa05101.asp?qa

Puzzanchera, C. (2013, December). *Juvenile arrests 2011.* Retrieved from the Office of Juvenile Justice and Delinquency Prevention website: https://www.ojjdp.gov/pubs/244476.pdf

Puzzanchera, C., & Kang, W. (2017). *Easy access to FBI arrest statistics 1994–2014.* Retrieved from the Office of Juvenile Justice and Delinquency Prevention website: http://www.ojjdp.gov/ojstatbb/ezaucr/

Pyrooz, D. C., & Sweeten, G. (2015). Gang membership between ages 5 and 17 years in the United States. *Journal of Adolescent Health, 56*(4), 414–419. doi.org/10.1016/j.jadohealth.2014.11.018

Sickmund, M., & Puzzanchera, C. (Eds.). (2014). *Juvenile offenders and victims: 2014 national report.* Retrieved from the Office of Juvenile Justice and Delinquency Prevention website: https://www.ojjdp.gov/ojstatbb/nr2014/downloads/NR2014.pdf

Sickmund, M., Sladky, A., & Kang, W. (2017). *Easy access to juvenile court statistics: 1985–2014.* Retrieved from the Office of Juvenile Justice and Delinquency Prevention website: http://www.ojjdp.gov/ojstatbb/ezajcs/

Snyder, H. N., & McCurley, C. (2008). *Domestic assaults by juvenile offenders.* Retreived the National Criminal Justice Reference Service website: https://www.ncjrs.gov/pdffiles1/ojjdp/219180.pdf

Steinberg, A., Brooks, J., & Remtulla, T. (2003). Youth hate crimes: Identification, prevention, and intervention. *American Journal of Psychiatry, 160*(5), 979–989.

Truman, J. L., & Morgan, R. E. (2016). *Criminal victimization, 2015.* Retrieved from the Bureau of Justice Statistics website: https://www.bjs.gov/content/pub/pdf/cv15.pdf

U.S. Department of Education. (2013). *Indicators of School Crime and Safety: 2012 (NCES 2013-036).* Retrieved from the National Center for Education Statistics website: https://nces.ed.gov/pubs2013/2013036.pdf

U.S. Department of Justice. (2019). *Juvenile Crime Facts.* Retrieved from https://www.justice.gov/jm/criminal-resource-manual-102-juvenile-crime-facts

Youth Risk Behavior Survey. (2017). *Trends in the prevalence of behaviors that contribute to violence on school property: National YRBS: 1991–2015.* Retrieved from the Centers for Disease Control and Prevention website: https://www.cdc.gov/healthyyouth/data/yrbs/pdf/trends/2015_us_violenceschool_trend_yrbs.pdf

Credits

CHAPTER SEVEN

Alcohol and Drug Abuse

ONE KEY FACTOR that facilitates unwanted contact between law enforcement agencies and at-risk youth is drug and alcohol use or abuse. This is particularly true because in the case of youth, the physical consumption, possession, transportation, or sale of controlled substances including alcohol may constitute delinquent acts. It is therefore necessary that juvenile correction officers and clinical staff develop adequate knowledge about the scope and trends of substance use and abuse among juvenile offenders. Such knowledge is vital in determining the type and level of scrutiny each offender deserves so each may fully benefit from correctional resources.

The purpose of this chapter is to provide criminal justice professionals who assist at-risk youth with brief overviews of the current scope, trends, and effects of alcohol and substance use and abuse. Special attention is paid to the different types of controlled substances, the typology of drugs and how certain categories of drugs and alcohol impact offenders and society, and related public safety and health concerns.

SCOPE AND TRENDS OF ALCOHOL AND DRUG ABUSE BEHAVIORS

The National Institute on Drug Abuse, the Office of National Drug Control Policy, and the U.S. Department of Health and Human Services and its subagencies, such as the Substance Abuse and Mental Health Services Administration and the Centers for Disease Control and Prevention, are key examples of the vast number of credible institutions devoted to the issue of substance abuse. The Office of National Drug Control Policy is concerned with the reduction and consequences of drug use and thus leads and coordinates the development, implementation, and assessment of United States' drug policies. The U.S. Department of Health and Human Services is charged with enhancing and protecting the health and well-being of people residing in the United States. Collectively, these institutions are reliable sources of up-to-date information about the trends and consequences of alcohol and drug use and abuse.

The National Survey on Drug Use and Health (NSDUH) provides national and state-level data on the use of tobacco, alcohol, and illicit drugs, including nonmedical use of prescription drugs, and its impact on mental health in the United States. NSDUH is an annual survey of noninstitutionalized civilian population in the United

States. The study does not survey residents of group shelters such as boarding houses, college dormitories, camps and halfway houses, or people without a fixed address such as homeless people, active military personnel, inmates, and residents of nursing homes, mental institutions, and long-term care hospitals. The survey generally samples about 67,500 persons aged 12 years and older. The results of the survey are thus a reliable source of information on the patterns and scope of illicit drugs and alcohol use and abuse, as well as substance and alcohol use and abuse disorders (Bose, Hedden, Lipari, & Park-Lee, 2016).

The 2015 NSDUH results show that about 27.1 million people, or 1 in 10 Americans (10.1%) aged 12 and older, used an illicit drug in the 30 days that preceded the survey (Bose et al., 2016). About 2.2 million of the 27.1 illicit drug users were adolescents between the ages of 12 and 17 years. Other studies show that about half of the 8th, 10th, and 12th graders who had used an illicit drug, even once, had also used other controlled substances, excluding marijuana. Furthermore, about one in four high school seniors (25%) or 50% of seniors who used any illicit drugs also used one or more additional illicit drug brands, excluding marijuana (Sickmund & Puzzanchera, 2014). In 2013, juvenile courts handled an estimated 1,058,500 delinquency cases, or about 2,900 a day, of which 141,700 (13%) were for drug-related offenses (Hockenberry & Puzzanchera, 2015).

MARIJUANA IS NOT MEDICINE

The label "medical marijuana" can mislead many youth. Indeed, studies show that marijuana makes youth feel silly, sleepy, relaxed, happy, nervous, and scared. Marijuana alters youth's sense of sight, hearing, and touch and makes it harder for youth to think clearly. Marijuana makes youth feel like time is slowing down and increases sound appreciation. Marijuana makes youth feel dizzy, laugh for no reason, develop red and bloodshot eyes, and easily forget things that just happened. Marijuana also causes memory problems, making it harder to learn in school or to pay attention to detail. Marijuana use makes youth feel hungry and thus increases the chance of their overeating unhealthy food.

Of course, none of these effects are a protective factor for doing well in school, being socially accepted, or being productive in controlled environments such as school and the workplace. Rather, these effects produce more risk factors that interfere with success at school and at work. Further, the additional need for money to finance marijuana use and the increased chance of making contact with other high-risk youth significantly increases the overall risk of making contact with the criminal justice system. In fact, recent studies show that youth who begin regular marijuana use during their teenage years lose an average of 6 to 8 IQ points and do not get them back even if they stop using the drug. Medical marijuana has also been linked to heart problems because it increases heart rate. Marijuana can cause coughing and breathing problems and can cause harm to the lungs in ways that are similar to the harms suffered by cigarette smokers. Marijuana prevents youth from adequately concentrating and from caring about important things in life. Hence, although in reality marijuana may have some comforting effects, the drug can make life worse for youth. In other words, marijuana is not a medicine for children.

Source:

Drug Fact. (2017, January 1, 2017). *Marijuana (weed, pot) facts*. Retrieved from https://easyread.drugabuse.gov/sites/default/files/EasyToRead_MarijuanaFacts_012017.pdf

Alcohol is also wildly abused by people under 18 or 21 years old. Out of the estimated 2.4 million respondents between the age of 12 and 17 years old who reported using alcohol in the 30 days preceding the 2015 survey, 221,000 (0.9%) and 1.4 million (5.8%) had consumed alcohol regularly and drank four or more alcoholic beverages in one sitting on a single day respectively. Additionally, about 7.7 million people between the ages of 12 and 20 engaged in underage alcohol violations. Specifically, about 5.1 million qualified as binge drinkers and 1.3 million as heavy alcohol users, although in all 50 states and the District of Columbia the consumption of alcohol was prohibited for people below age 21 (Bose et al., 2016).

CHOICES OF ALCOHOL AND DRUGS

As indicated in Table 7.1, the list of substances used and abused by youth is substantially long. Drug choices typically include alcohol, marijuana, inhalants, crack cocaine, cocaine, methamphetamine, heroin, MDMA, and PCP. Teenagers also use hallucinogens, performance-enhancing drugs, prescription and over-the-counter drugs, and just about any illicit drug on the street (Sickmund & Puzzanchera, 2014). Many of the substances can be grouped under four distinct headings: inhalants, hallucinogens, alcohol, and over-the-counter and prescription drugs.

Inhalants

Inhalant use is sometimes referred to as "huffing." The practice involves the inhalation of aerosol, gases, or solvent vapors through the nose or mouth. Aerosols include pressurized spray paint, hair spray, and similar sprays. Gases consist of materials used in medical procedures, such as chloroform, ether, and nitrous oxide. Solvents typically comprise dry cleaning fluid, paint removers and thinners, certain types of markers, gasoline, and even white-out (Bose et al., 2016).

One hundred and seventy-five thousand youth, or 0.7% of adolescents aged 12 to 17, reported abusing these substances. Inhalants are very popular among teenagers because they act almost instantly. In addition, vapors from cleaning fluids, gasoline, spray paint, computer keyboard cleaners, felt-tip pens, glue, cigarette lighter fluid, whipped cream cans, and propane tanks are common household items. It is, however, important to note that the rate of abuse of inhalants among youngsters generally decreases after age 17 (Bose et al., 2016). Thus, inhalants are more of a problem for children in the early and mid-teen age range.

Hallucinogens

In addition to pain relievers, tranquilizers, stimulants, and sedatives, juveniles are also known for abusing hallucinogens. Generally, hallucinogens include lysergic acid diethylamide (commonly known as acid or LSD), psilocybin mushrooms, MDMA ("ecstasy" or "molly"), peyote, mescaline, and PCP (phencyclidine). This group of substances cause offenders to hallucinate, or see, hear, smell, taste, or feel things that may not exist. Hallucinogens also cause dizziness and loss of control of motor skills, and weaken an individual's ability to think clearly. Medically, the use of hallucinogens leads to panic attacks, brain damage, and sometimes death. In 2015, an estimated 121,000, or 0.5% of adolescents between the age of 12 to 17 reported the use of hallucinogens. This figure is high considering all the harsh consequences associated with the use and abuse of hallucinogenic substances.

TABLE 7.1 *Common Street Drugs*

DRUGS OR ALCOHOL	STREET NAMES
Alcohol	Booze, Brew, Liquor
Anabolic Steroids	Juice, Roids
Bath Salts	Bloom, Cloud Nine, Vanilla Sky, White Lightning
Cocaine	Blow, Bump, C, Charlie, Coca, Coke, Flake, Rock, Snow, Toot
Cough and Cold Medicines	Candy, Dex, Drank, Robo, Robotripping, Skittles, Triple C, Tussin, Velvet Robotripping, Robo, Tussin, Triple C, Dex, Skittles, Candy, Velvet, Drank
Heroin	Black Tar, H, Horse, Junk, Ska, Smack
Inhalants	Bold, Laughing Gas, Poppers, Snappers, Whippets
Marijuana	Grass, Herb, Mary Jane, Pot, Reefer, Skunk, Weed
MDMA (Ecstasy or Molly)	Adam, Beans, Clarity, E, Hug, Love Drug, X, XTC
Methamphetamine (Meth)	Chalk, Crank, Crystal, Fire, Glass, Go Fast, Ice, Speed, Tina
Phencyclidine (PCP)	Angel Dust, Hog, Ozone, Rocket Fuel, Shermans, Wack, Crystal and Embalming Fluid
Prescription Depressant Medications	A-minus, Barbs, Candy, Downers, Phennies, Red Birds, Reds, Sleeping Pills, Tooies, Tranks, Yellow Jackets, Yellows, Zombie Pills
Prescription Drugs	Barbs, Candy, Oxy, Percs, Reds, Speed, Tranks, Vikes
Prescription Pain Medications (Opioids)	Happy Pills, Hillbilly Heroin, OC, Oxy, Oxycotton, Percs, Vikes
Prescription Stimulant Medications (Amphetamines)	Bennies, Black Beauties, Hearts, Roses, Skippy, Speed, The Smart Drug, Uppers, Vitamin R
Salvia	Maria Pastora, Sally-D, Salvia divinorum, Shepherdess's Herb, Ska Pastora
Spice	Fake Weed, K2, Moon Rocks, Skunk, Yucatan Fire
Tobacco, Nicotine, & E-Cigarettes	Chew, Cigs, Dip, Smokes, Snuff
Gamma-Hydroxybutyric Acid (GHB)	G, Georgia Home Boy, Goop, Grievous Bodily, Harm, Liquid Ecstasy, Liquid X, Soap, and Scoop.

Alcohol

Though alcohol use does not often raise as much concern as do other illicit substances, the abuse of alcohol is very consequential, especially when the user is a child. The 2015 NSDUH puts alcohol use into three categories: current, binge, and heavy alcohol use. Current alcohol use is defined as any use of alcohol in the past 30 days. Binge drinking is the consumption of five or more standard alcoholic drinks by male drinkers or four for females, at least 1 day within a 30 days period. Heavy drinking refers to the consumption of eight or more drinks per week for women or 15 or more drinks per week for men (Bose et al., 2016).

In 2015, there were an estimated 2.4 million alcohol users between the age of 12 and 17 in the United States. Of that number, 221,000 (0.9%) and 1.4 million (5.8%) were heavy and binge alcohol users respectively. In addition, although alcohol consumption is currently prohibited for people below age 21 in all 50 states and the District of Columbia, survey results show that 7.7 million people between age 12 and 20 are underage alcohol users, 5.1 million are binge drinkers and 1.3 million are heavy alcohol users (Bose et al., 2016). These figures are obviously very high because alcohol use affects users' ability to successfully participate in the pursuit and maintenance of important goals such as quality education and the building of a healthy employment history.

Over-the-Counter and Prescription Medication

Other than alcohol and marijuana, by far the most commonly abused substances in the United States are over-the-counter and prescription medications. As categories of substances abused by children, over-the-counter and prescription medications are major challenges for anyone charged with the supervision of a substance user or abuser. The most popular over-the-counter medications are cough and cold medicines, which generally contain DXM, or dextromethorphan. These medications can be easily bought from many different outlets. Like prescription medications, over-the-counter medications are also popular with teenagers.

Prescription drugs can be grouped under four categories: pain relievers, tranquilizers, stimulants, and sedatives. According to the United States Food and Drug Administration, prescription pain relievers include narcotics, depressants, and stimulants. Pain relievers comprise synthetic, semisynthetic, and nonsynthetic opioid medications such as fentanyl, codeine, oxycodone, and hydrocodone. These medications are safe and effective when used consistent with a medical doctor's directive. Unfortunately, however, a large number of youth, about 276,000, or 1.1%, of adolescents aged 12 to 17 abuse prescription pain relievers (Bose et al., 2016).

Tranquilizers are used by psychiatrists and anesthesiologists to induce sleep or to depress the central nervous system. This category of drugs includes barbiturates and benzodiazepines. Despite obvious potential to cause serious medical and mental harm to users, tranquilizers are abused by an estimated 162,000, or 0.7%, of adolescents age 12 to 17.

Drugs classified as stimulants heighten bodily activity and in some cases elevate the release of dopamine and increase energy and mental alertness. Cocaine and amphetamines are examples of stimulant drugs. In 2015, there were about 117,000 adolescents, representing about 0.5% of adolescents age 12 to 17 who misused these and other types of stimulants.

Sedatives are powerful prescription drugs that induce sleep or calmness. Sedative substances such as oxycontin and benzodiazepines depress the central nervous system. Unfortunately, however, the results of the 2015 survey showed that an estimated 21,000, or 0.1%, of adolescents abused sedatives (Bose et al., 2016). Similarly, 492,000 adolescents between the age of 12 and 17 (about 2%) misused prescription medications such as Xanax (alprazolam), Zoloft (sertraline), and Prozac. These and similar psychotherapy medications are used to treat major psychological disorders that impair the mental and physical function of affected persons.

CONSEQUENCES OF DRUG AND ALCOHOL ABUSE

Abuse of over-the-counter and prescription medication and the misuse of controlled substances such as alcohol and illicit drugs have severe consequences for both the individual abuser and society at large. Indeed, beyond the distortion of substance abusers' perceptions of time and space and the alteration of sensory perception, alcohol, illicit drugs, and over-the-counter and prescription medication negatively impact public safety, put pressure on public resources, and severely compromise users' physical and mental health. Consequently, substance use and abuse increase the risk for delinquent and criminal activities, lead to substance abuse disorders or addiction, and enhance a person's chance of developing other serious mental health and medical problems, including suicidal tenancy.

DRUGS ARE TEEN ENEMY NUMBER ONE

In the past 15 years, the number of youth who die each year as a result of overdoses from prescription and illicit drugs has been steadily increasing. Table 7.2 shows the rate of overdose around the country in 2006 through to 2015. The most common causes of overdose-related deaths are prescription drugs (opioid pain relievers, benzodiazepines), illicit drugs (cocaine, heroin), opioids (opioid pain relievers, opioid pain relievers other than synthetic opioids or methadone, heroin), and illicit opioids (heroin, synthetic opioids other than methadone).

TABLE 7.2 *National Overdose Deaths From Select Prescription and Illicit Drugs*

YEAR	2006	2007	2008	2009	2010	2011	2012	2013	2014	2015
TOTAL	34,425	36,010	36,450	37,004	38,329	41,340	41,502	43,982	47,055	52,404
FEMALE	12,532	13,712	13,982	14,411	15,323	16,352	16,390	17,183	18,243	19,447
MALE	21,893	22,298	22,468	22,593	23,006	24,988	25,112	26,799	28,812	32,957

To make matters worse, unlike sexual and violent offending behaviors, the warning signs or symptoms of substance abuse or use-related behavioral problems are manifested through other behavioral categories such as sexual, violent, or general offending behaviors.

Source:

National Institutes of Health. (2019). *National overdose deaths from select prescription and illicit drugs.* Retrieved from https://rockrecoverycenter.com/wp-content/uploads/2017/06/overdose_data_1999-2015.pdf

Public Safety Impacts

After following more than 1,300 serious juvenile offenders for a period of 7 years after their first conviction or adjudication, researchers found that the majority of court-involved adolescents have recent histories of illegal substance abuse (Mulvey, Schubert, & Chassin, 2010). It is also not surprising that 10% of the 921,600 persons under the age of 18 arrested by law enforcement agencies across the United States were arrested for drug abuse violations. It is equally not surprising that .7% (6,600) were arrested for driving under the influence, 4.7% (43,100) for liquor law violations, and .6% (5,500) for drunkenness (Office of Juvenile Justice and Delinquency Prevention, 2017). There is a strong link between substance use and unwanted contact with the criminal justice system. Many factors associated with substance use and abuse increase the likelihood of criminal or delinquent behaviors.

First, "adolescent substance use can produce a false sense of reality and autonomy that interferes with the development of emerging social competencies and coping skills" (Mulvey et al., 2010, p. 7). The state of "being high" also reduces youth's chances of resisting criminal or delinquent activities. Second, drugs cost money, a lot of money, hence the need to find money to finance the purchase of controlled substances using any means, including criminal or delinquent activities—as Walsh and Stohr (2010) note, "most drug related crimes are crimes committed to obtain money to buy drugs" (p. 345). Third, substance use and abuse require the possession of illegal or prohibited substances; thus, drug use is inextricably linked to lawbreaking. These and similar factors also explain why studies consistently find that substance use and abuse increase the chance of involuntary contact with law enforcement.

Public Health Impacts

Beyond the commission of crimes and participation in delinquent acts, the public health system also negatively suffers the financial effects, such as Medicaid costs and higher insurance premiums, of substance use and abuse. Take for example the Drug Enforcement Administration report that "there were an estimated 53,542 emergency department visits associated with PCP use" alone in 2013 (Drug Enforcement Administration, 2013). As also reported, out of 656,827, about 517,800, or 78.8%, of all underage alcohol misuse-related visits to emergency departments between 2010 and 2013 were for alcohol misuse only, while 139,028, or 21.2%, of the visits involved combined drug and alcohol use. In terms of age, nearly 40% of substance-related visits to emergency department were by people between the ages of 12 and 20 and involved alcohol misuse. About 5.5% of alcohol abusers were between the ages of 12 and 14, while 29% were age 15 to 17 and 65.1% of the abusers were age 12 to 20 years old. About 6.3%, 34.3%, and 59.5% were age 12 to 14, 15 to 17, and 18 to 20 years old respectively (Naeger, 2017).

Substance Use Disorders

Other consequential results of substance use are, of course, substance use disorders or addiction. Substance use disorders are medical conditions caused by repeated misuse of a substance, often characterized by clinically significant impairment that can be traced to the recurrent use of alcohol and or drugs (U.S. Department of Health and Human Services, 2016). In their most severe form, disorders are in fact addictions, the compulsive or uncontrolled use of one or more controlled substances. Hence, studies also show that serious chronic offenders are more likely than others to qualify as having substance use disorders (Mulvey et al., 2010).

In general terms "over two-thirds of incarcerated adolescents exhibit at least one substance use disorder" (Hunter, Miles, Pedersen, Ewing, & D'Amico, 2014, p. 1082). According to the 2015 NSDUH results, about 1.2 million adolescents also qualified as having one or more forms of substance abuse disorder. More specifically, 623,000 (2.5%) and 855,000 (3.4%) have alcohol and illicit drug use disorders respectively. A significant number of these youth suffer from pain reliever (0.5%), tranquilizer (0.3%), prescription stimulant (0.2%), and/or cocaine (0.1%) use disorder. About 5.1%, or 1.3 million people, have substance abuse disorders (Bose et al., 2016).

CONCLUSION

Evidence is overwhelmingly clear that most substance abusers have a high risk of making unwanted contacts with the criminal justice system, and indeed, many of those who make contact with the criminal justice system have a history of substance abuse. It is also worth remembering that each substance user or abuser is unique in terms of social, mental, and medical history that informs behavior, threat to public safety, and mental and medical health. As Walsh and Stohr note, "many offenders have substance-abuse problems, many have character disorders, a few have chemical imbalances, and some are normally responsible individuals who have succumbed to the pressures and urges of the moment" (2010, p. 325).

It is also important to note that while substance use may not be the primary cause of delinquent or criminal behavior, factors associated with substance use or abuse can "initiate or heighten the risk of offending either independently or in conjunction with other risk factors" (Mulvey et al., 2010, p. 3). It is, however, in the best interest of the child for probation, parole, or correction officers to assume, during initial contact, that the offender they are dealing with has a history of substance use or abuse. Such an attitude or approach would greatly minimize the danger of misclassification and the chance of missing the opportunity to clinically address a youth's substance use or abuse behaviors.

DISCUSSION QUESTIONS

1. What are some of the key factors that lead children to the use or abuse of intoxicants or substances such as gasoline, spray paint, felt-tip pens, glue, and cigarette lighter fluid?
2. Why is the abuse of materials such as inhalants, hallucinogens, alcohol, and over-the-counter and prescription drugs so common in the United States?
3. Discuss some of the common criminal and delinquent acts that are influenced by drugs and alcohol abuse.
4. What would be the best way to minimize the public health impacts of substance or alcohol abuse?
5. Which controlled substance is more destructive to children and why?

REFERENCES

Bose, J., Hedden, S. L., Lipari, R. N., & Park-Lee, E. (2016). *Key substance use and mental health indicators in the United States: Results from the 2015 National Survey on Drug Use and Health.* Retrieved from the Substance Abuse and Mental Health Services Administation website: https://www.samhsa.gov/

Drug Enforcement Administration. (2013). *Phencyclidine (Street names: PCP, angel dust, supergrass, boat, tic tac, zoom, Shermans).* Retrieved from https://www.deadiversion.usdoj.gov/drug_chem_info/pcp.pdf

Hockenberry, S., & Puzzanchera, C. (2015). *Juvenile court statistics 2013.* Retrieved from the National Center for Juvenile Justice website: http://www.ncjj.org/publication/juvenile-court-statistics-2013.aspx

Hunter, S. B., Miles, J. N. V., Pedersen, E. R., Ewing, B. A., & D'Amico, E. J. (2014). Temporal associations between substance use and delinquency among youth with a first time offense. *Addictive Behaviors, 39*(6), 1081–1086. doi.org/10.1016/j.addbeh.2014.03.002

Mulvey, E. P., Schubert, C. A., & Chassin, L. (2010). *Substance use and delinquent behavior among serious adolescent offenders.* Retrieved from the National Criminal Justice Reference Service website: https://www.ncjrs.gov/pdffiles1/ojjdp/232790.pdf

Naeger, S. (2017). *Emergency department visits involving underage alcohol misuse: 2010 to 2013.* Retrieved from the Substance Abuse and Mental Health Services Administation website: https://www.samhsa.gov/

National Institutes of Health. (2019). *National overdose deaths from select prescription and illicit drugs.* Retrieved from the Rock Recovery Center website: https://rockrecoverycenter.com/wp-content/uploads/2017/06/overdose_data_1999-2015.pdf

Office of Juvenile Justice and Delinquency Prevention. (2017). *Estimated number of juvenile arrests, 2015.* Retrieved from https://www.ojjdp.gov/ojstatbb/crime/qa05101.asp?qa

Sickmund, M., & Puzzanchera, C. (Eds.). (2014). *Juvenile offenders and victims: 2014 national report.* Retrieved from the Office of Juvenile Justice and Delinquency Prevention website: https://www.ojjdp.gov/ojstatbb/nr2014/downloads/NR2014.pdf

U.S. Department of Health and Human Services. (2016). Facing addiction in America: The Surgeon General's report on alcohol, drugs, and health. Retrieved from https://addiction.surgeongeneral.gov/sites/default/files/surgeon-generals-report.pdf

Walsh, A., & Stohr, M. (2010). *Correctional assessment, casework and counseling.* Alexandria, VA: American Correctional Association.

CHAPTER EIGHT

Sex Offending Behaviors

IRRESPECTIVE OF AGE, the offending group that creates and evokes more anxiety and fear in citizens and raises more concerns among criminal justice practitioners and policy and law makers is made up of sex offenders (Carter & Morris, 2007; Levenson, Brannon, & Fortney, 2007). The fear and concerns are warranted and sustained by the fact that sex offenders create more victims than any other category of offender. Furthermore, the impact of sex offending behaviors on victims and society is more intense, intrusive, and long lasting than the pain and suffering generated by substance abuse-related and most violent or general offenders. Also, the large proportion of sex offenses is committed against mainly children, many of whom are usually too young to speak about their ordeals or to seek help.

This chapter discusses juvenile sex offending behaviors. It therefore talks about the commonality of sexual offending behaviors among people under the age of 18 as well as the typologies and patterns of their sexual offending behaviors. Furthermore, this chapter provides a brief coverage of victims with the understanding that the mere history of being sexually victimized as a child does not necessarily mean that an individual will become a sex offender. Rather, juveniles who have been sexually victimized are more likely to select sexual victimization reflective of their own sexual victimization in terms of victim age, gender, and types of sexual offending behavior (Hockenberry & Puzzanchera, 2015).

Juvenile sex offenses typically involve unwanted physical or virtual sexual contact or behavior involving two or more minors or a minor and one or more adults (DeBaca, 2014; Gilligan, 2008). The definition of sexual behavior includes any type of unwanted sexual contact or action that occurs without the explicit consent of the victims or sexual behavior that involves someone who is legally, mentally, or physiological incapable of consenting. Examples of unlawful sexual behavior include child molestation, incest, sexual fondling, child pornography, peeping tom acts, sexual assault, or rape or any forced sexual intercourse, sodomy, or penetration, no matter how slight, of the victim's vagina, mouth, or anus with any body part or object.

STAYING INFORMED ABOUT SEX OFFENDERS AND OFFENDING BEHAVIORS IS ESSENTIAL

Adequate knowledge of sexual misconduct laws, patterns, causes, trends, and interventions is critically important for the correct assessment and classification of sex crimes and sexual offenders. For example, some of the factors such as laws, trends, and modes of intervention differ from one jurisdiction to another based on public attitudes and policies relating to sexual offending behaviors in each jurisdiction. Knowledge of the differences in this area is also critical because in some cases a change in law can produce different assessment and classification results and thus affects the choices of therapeutic intervention that seek to correct sexual misconduct. Luckily, however, public interest in every aspect of sexual offending behaviors consistently produces a broad range of information on this matter. The U.S. Department of Justice and its Office of Justice Programs, along with branches such as the Bureau of Justice Statistics, the National Institute of Justice, and the Office for Victims of Crime, as well as other governmental and private institutions such as the Centers for Disease Control and Prevention and the Center for Sex Offender Management, regularly publish useful and reliable information pertaining to many aspects of sexual offending behavior.

Legally, the list of above behaviors constitutes sexual offenses. Clinically, however, sexual acts involving objects or animals and similar behaviors are sexual misconduct and practices that must be considered when assessing risk and needs associated with an offender. Obviously, the ability to categorize sexual offending behaviors is vital in determining the type and level of scrutiny and treatment each juvenile sex offender deserves to fully benefit from available correctional services. It is also important to keep in mind that, in general, when assessing and classifying juveniles to ascertain the true nature of the offenders' sexual offending behaviors or lack thereof, general knowledge about the scope of juvenile sex offending behaviors is very useful.

SCOPE OF JUVENILE OFFENDING BEHAVIORS

Sex crimes are fairly common, with an estimated one in every five girls and one in every seven boys experiencing sexual abuse, while approximately 67% of all victims of reported sexual assaults are children younger than 18 years, and more than half of the victims are younger than 12 years old (Gilligan, 2008). Furthermore, there is no fixed characteristic of an adult sex offender—they come from all backgrounds. For example, some are poor, some well-educated, some are married, male, and young with strong community ties and a criminal history, while others are rich, less educated, unmarried, female, and old with weak ties to society and no prior criminal history. By all means, this is not an exhaustive list; all sorts of permutations exist.

The U.S. Office of Justice Programs (https://ojp.gov) provides rich resources on sex offending behaviors, offenders, and victims. The most relevant bureaus and offices include the Office of Sex Offender Sentencing, Monitoring, Apprehending, Registering, and Tracking (SMART), the Bureau of Justice Statistics (BJS), the Office of Juvenile Justice and Delinquency Prevention (OJJDP), and the National institutes of Justice (NIJ). In particular, the Sex Offender Management Assessment and Planning Initiative is very useful. This comprehensive report prepared by the U.S. Department of Justice covers current demographics information about adults and children who commit sex offenses.

SOME ESTABLISHED FACTS ABOUT JUVENILE SEX OFFENDERS

The most misunderstood and incorrectly talked about behavioral category is sex offending behaviors. The misunderstanding exists because public perception about sex offending behaviors and offenders is sometimes informed by myths and stereotypes that are not informed by any scientific process. In that regard, studies show that the following are accurate characterizations of juvenile sex offenders and their behaviors:

- Most juvenile sexual assaults are committed by children who are known to the victims.
- Adolescents are responsible for a significant number of both reported and unreported child molestation cases involving child victims.
- Adolescents who participate in sexual offending treatment programs are less likely to reoffend compared to those who do not receive treatment.
- Most youthful sex offenders are not deviant or violent sex offenders.
- Youth are particularly amenable to treatment interventions designed to address sex offending behaviors.
- Most child sex abusers are not pedophiles.
- Most child sex abusers do not have history of being sexually abused.
- No single risk factor explains why individual youth engage in sexual offending behaviors because sex offenses are informed by multiple factors including individual characteristics and developmental experiences.
- More than two-thirds of child sex offenders have more than one and less than nine victims, and about one-fifth of child sex offenders have between 10 and 40 victims.
- Juvenile sex offenders are responsible for more than one-third of total sex offenders known to law enforcement agencies for committing sex offenses against children.

Source:

Finkelhor, D., Ormrod, R., & Chaffin, M. (2009). *Juveniles who commit sex offenses against minors*. Retrieved from the National Criminal Justice Reference Service website: https://www.ncjrs.gov/pdffiles1/ojjdp/227763.pdf

Contrary to existing myths about sex offenders, a large percentage of child molesters are not strangers, nor do they use force, aggression, or threats in the commission of child molestation offenses. Most child molesters are family members, acquaintances, neighbors, legal custodians, or authority figures. Also, most sex offenders are not social misfits, strangers, or "dirty old men" (Levenson et al., 2007, p. 7). Juvenile sex offenders in particular come from diverse ethnic, racial, economic, and social backgrounds. They include males and females from wealthy and poor backgrounds. Some come from dysfunctional or supportive family backgrounds. Some have mental health or substance abuse issues, and others do not have such needs and risk. Some youthful offenders do well in school; other youth perform poorly. Some youth have prior delinquent histories, while others do not have any history of delinquent or criminal behaviors. Juvenile sex offenders also come from diverse social, developmental, and environmental backgrounds. Other factors that inform juvenile sexual offending behaviors range from social factors such as exposure to social messages that normalize aggression, exposure to domestic violence, easy access to victims, and extreme levels of stress.

SEX OFFENSE PERPETRATORS AND VICTIMS

The true scope of juvenile sexual offending behavior is difficult to gauge in part because most sexual offending behaviors are not reported and thus go undocumented. It is, however, well-established that a substantial number of sex offenses against children are committed by other minors (Finkelhor, Ormrod, & Chaffin, 2009). In fact, juvenile offenders account for 17% of all arrests for sex crimes, and they commit approximately 35.6% of all sex offenses against other children (Ratnayake, 2013). Offending behavior against younger victims increases at age 12 and peaks at age 14, but offenses against teenagers go up during mid- to late-adolescent years, and only about one out of eight offenders is younger than 12.

Juvenile offenders are more likely to have younger victims—about a third (31.6%) of their victims are younger than 12 years old, and more than one-fifth (23.8%) are older than 12. The majority (78.8%) of juvenile sex offenses are against females under the age of 18, and only 24.7% are against males. Further, 57.15% of victims of juvenile sex offenders are younger than 6 years, and 31.25% are 7–10 years old, while 10.9% are between the ages of 11 and 14. Among the youngest victims, about 36.6% are male while 63.4% are female (Finkelhor et al., 2009).

It is also estimated that at least one in every four girls and one in every seven boys are sexually abused by the time they reach age 18, and 61% of reported cases of rape occur before the victim reaches age 18 (Carter & Morris, 2007). In a nationally representative survey of adults in the United States, 42.2% of female rape victims suffered their first sexual victimization before age 18 and 29.9% first suffered victimization between the ages of 11 and 17; 12.3% of female victims and 27.8% of male rape victims were first raped at the age of 10 or younger (Centers for Disease Control and Prevention, 2012).

Underreported Juvenile Sex Offenses

Studies estimate that juveniles account for about one in four (25.8%) sexual offenses known to law enforcement and more than one in three (36.6%) sex offenders known to law enforcement who victimize minors (Przybylski & Lobanov-Rostovsky, 2014, p. 175). Most likely, however, these figures provide only a glimpse into the scope of juvenile sex offenses because for several reasons the degree and characteristics of juvenile sex offenders remain underdeveloped.

SEXUAL PREDATORS' HANGOUTS

One question that constantly prompts misleading answers from people not familiar with child molesters is the question about where to find child molesters. In response to this question, people typically imagine bushes, dark alleyways, malls, bus stops, arcades, school grounds, and other places frequented by children as places where child molesters strategically hang around in an effort to gain access to potential child victims. The problem with such responses, however, is that the locations are not where one should go looking for child molesters. Rather, child molesters' hangouts are in domestic places such as adjacent bedrooms, living rooms or common areas. Indeed, the majority of people who sexually exploit, abuse, or victimize children are family members and other people close to children. Those who want to protect children from sexual abuse, molestation, and victimization should therefore focus on parents, relatives, siblings, neighbors, caregivers, religious leaders, and people with whom children privately and officially interact as a result of established formal or informal relationships. These people overwhelmingly account for most child molestation cases.

Several reasons explain why the majority of juvenile sex offenders and sex offenses are not reported to authorities or are not known or reported. First, most juvenile sex offenders are known to their victims or are acquaintances, relatives, friends, or close family members. In fact, studies show that victims of juvenile sex offenders consist mainly of family (25%) and acquaintances (63.2%), and only 2.5% are strangers (Finkelhor et al., 2009). Also, in 80% of rape and sexual assault cases, the victim is known to the offender (Sinozich & Langton, 2014), and the majority of the victims are also family members and neighbors, or institutional mates or other children present with the offender in an institution. Consequently, as a result of the relationships between victims and offenders, victims are often reluctant to report their abuse. In some cases, the relationship may cause the offender to conceal their victimization, fearing that he or her will lose or weaken he or her relationship to the abuser. In instances where there is no apparent relationship, some offenders may use intimidation, including direct threats of physical or psychological harm to the victims or victims' loved ones, to prevent disclosure.

Secondly, many victims do not trust law enforcement agencies. For example, victims may assume that authority figures such as parents, guardians, and law enforcement authorities will not believe their claims of victimization, or authority figures will exaggerate the offense and take measures that have a far-reaching impact on the offenders or their dependents. In some cases, victims may fear that contact with law enforcement will expose them to other criminal allegations. Some victims simply do not want to make their victimization public, or may feel ashamed, guilty, and/or embarrassed (Sinozich & Langton, 2014).

Thirdly, sex offenders rely heavily on grooming, secrecy, and behavioral manipulation to keep their offenses secret. That is, juvenile sex offenders work very hard at grooming their victims to go along with their victimization—so much so that some victims end up willingly helping their victimizers to keep the victimization secret. Many victims of juvenile sex offenders also may not even know that they have been sexually victimized. Further, although juvenile offenders engage in aggressive sexual behavior including forced anal or vaginal intercourse (National Center on Sexual Behavior of Youth, 2003), most juvenile sex offenders are also very careful and mindful of causing physical harm to their victims and thus avoid penile penetration or vaginal and anal penetration if the victim is young enough to show signs of physical trauma. Instead, sexual victimization generally involves offenders exposing themselves to their victims, fondling, touching, rubbing, and engaging in oral sex more commonly than penile penetration. Consequently, the majority of sex offenses (88.8%) against children do not result in physical harm to victims, and only 1.6% involve major injury and 9.6% result in minor injury. Finally, some victims may not want to make public what they consider a private matter by bringing it to the attention of a third person. In some cases, victims may also worry about being blamed for their victimization or about not being believed, and they may feel ashamed, guilty, or embarrassed (Sinozich & Langton, 2014).

CHARACTERISTICS OF JUVENILE SEX OFFENDERS

The vast majority (93%) of juvenile sex offenders are males, and the majority of male juvenile offenders (85.6%) are between the age of 12 and 17 years old. Only 4.4% are 6 to 8 years old, and 10% are 9 to 11 years old. About 25.6% of their victims are 6 years old or younger, while 17.8% are between 7 and 8, about 39.2% are between 11 and 14, and 17.4% are older than 15. Comparatively, however, although female juvenile sex offenders (69.5%) offend more than male juvenile sex offenders (52.3%) prior to age 15, male juvenile sex offending is higher (47.7%) than female offending (30.4%) between ages 15 and 17 (Finkelhor et al., 2009).

Female Sex Offenders

Little is known about female sex offenders because sex offenses are usually thought of as crimes perpetrated by males against females. Consequently, the little that is known about female juvenile sex offenders comes from self-reported histories of adult female offenders and records of the few juvenile sex offenders that make contact with the criminal justice system in connection with sex offenses. The actual number of juvenile female sex offenders who do not come to the attention of law enforcement officials may be far greater than what is currently known or reported, especially considering that sex offenders in general have the tendency to minimize their offending behaviors and to claim a history of victimization among other acts to escape responsibility for their behavior.

Although in a way there is some truth to the conclusion that the majority of sex offenses are committed by men, there is "accumulating evidence that sexual abuse committed by females is not rare and can be just as traumatic as sexual abuse committed by males" (Carter & Morris, 2007, p. 698). In fact, female offenders account for 7% to 10% of juveniles whose sex offending behavior is known to authorities. Studies also reveal "that up to 63% of female victims and as many as 27% of male victims report having been sexually victimized by a female" (Carter & Morris, 2007, p. 7).

Compared to males, female juvenile sex offenders tend to be much younger. More precisely, the majority of juvenile female sex offenders (68.7%) are between the age of 12 and 17 years old. The number of female offenders between the age of 6 and 8 is of course higher (10.6%) than the number of male sex offenders (4.4%). Similarly, only 10% of male sex offenders are between the ages of 9 and 11, compared to 20.6% of female juvenile sex offenders in a similar age group. In other words, 31.2% of female sex offenders began offending between age 6 and 11, compared to only 14.4% of male juvenile sex offenders in the same group.

Female offenders are more likely to offend girls (63.4%) compared to male offenders who offend girls (78.6%) but only 21.4% of the same sex. Comparatively, girls are more likely to abuse younger victims: 39.8% are age 6 or younger, 20.2% are between 7 and 19, 26% are between 11 and 14, and only 13.9% are between 15 and 17 years old. Females are also more likely than male juvenile offenders to victimize children younger than age 11 (60% versus 43%) (Finkelhor et al., 2009). Female offenders are also slightly more likely (91%) to use force in the commission of sex offenses than boys (90.4%). Most victims (60%) of female offenders are 10 years old or younger.

Female juvenile offenders also tend to have histories of physical or emotional abuse or neglect and thus to show symptoms of depression, post-traumatic stress disorder, hyperactivity or attention deficit disorder, and or conduct disorder (Carter & Morris, 2007). For example, an analysis of court files and other criminal records of 66 female juveniles convicted or adjudicated for sexual offences in the Netherlands between 1993 and 2008 shows that the number of female sex offenders who have mental health conditions is higher than male sex offenders (Reaves, 2017). This is, however, out of bounds because unlike male offenders, female sex offenders have been "sexually victimized at almost twice the rate of men, most often by a family member" (Carter & Morris, 2007, p. 7). These accounts highlight the harmfulness of abuse in general and sexual victimization in particular.

IMPACT OF SEXUAL OFFENDING BEHAVIORS

It is always a good practice to remind sex offenders that victims of sexual assault and abuse suffer significant emotional, psychological, financial, and physical harm. That is, sexual abuse or assault in various forms can cause victims to show a wide range of short- and long-term psychological symptoms including an unjustifiable sense of guilt, shame, and distrust of others, and can severely disrupt victims' physical and psychological development. Other documented effects include moderate to severe distress, depression, unhealthy social interaction including difficulty getting along with others, loss of a relationship, and feelings of loneliness and social rejection.

History of sexual victimization is particularly impactful when the victimization occurs at a time when the victims are age 3 to 7 years old, "a sensitive period during which sexual abuse can do the most damage and place a youth at higher risk for engaging in sexually abusive behavior later in life" (Leversee, 2015, p. 186). It is also during this period between age 3 and 7 years that children start developing most of their important basic skills. As Eccles (1999) notes, during this period children start taking initiative on their own and begin to view their unacceptable deeds and actions with some sense of guilt and to show interest in undertaking many adult-like activities, sometimes overstepping the limits set by parents. Unfortunately, in many ways sexual victimization at this stage can disrupt the natural process of child development.

TYPOLOGY OF JUVENILE SEX OFFENDERS

Most juvenile sexual offending behaviors can be classified as partly a consequence of situational, exploratory, and environmental factors. A situational offense is an opportunistic misconduct. Thus, situational sex offenses refer to the presence of a circumstance that creates a perceived opportunity for an offender to think that he or she can molest their victims without any consequences. Opportunistic sex offenders can be viewed as people with a high tendency of having poor impulse control. Examples of situational sexual misconduct therefore include the presence of a potential offender and victim in an environment with less likelihood of being caught and more likelihood of successfully carrying out the desired offense. In this regard, it is the unique circumstances that trigger the offender into thinking about the sexual victimization, although the circumstance does not necessarily cause the sexual offending behavior. Another example is being alone with a vulnerable and potential victim, knowing that the victim lacks the physical or mental ability to resist or to report their victimization.

THE IDENTIFICATION OF SEX OFFENDERS IS SOMETIMES NOT EASY

Salame is a 15-year-old girl and Tony just turned 17. These two were found naked, asleep, and probably recovering from drug and alcohol use. The girl's parents had gone away on a weekend. While they were gone, the daughter invited Tony to her parents' home. At about 2:00 p.m. on the following day, the parents returned home and found both of them naked and asleep in each other's arms. In the room was evidence of alcohol and marijuana use. The father called the police and filed a criminal complaint alleging sexual misconduct by the boy. The public prosecutor filed a petition with the juvenile court alleging sexual misconduct, and accordingly the boy was adjudicated. However, although this meant that the youth became legally a sex offender as a result of the adjudication, there is no evidence that he forced the girl, and there is no evidence that he predatorily seeks out underage children. So, clinically the boy is not a sex offender. Of course, alcohol and marijuana use and participation in sexual acts with a minor are bad behaviors, but they do not make someone a sex offender.

Some sexual offending behaviors are socially driven in the sense that the child engages in the behavior after being socialized either through direct victimization by another person or by witnessing such victimization and assuming that the inappropriate behavior is normal. Sexual offending behaviors aided by environmental or sociocultural conditions happen when an offender finds himself or herself in an environment that condones the behaviors or that makes sexual misconduct appear acceptable. For instance, if a child grows up in a home where sexual behavior among siblings or family members is tolerated, that child might have less difficulty engaging in inappropriate sexual acts, thinking that the sexual misconduct is normal. Similarly, a child who is exposed to an environment that normalizes sexual victimization may engage in sexual offending behaviors in and outside that environment, thinking that such behavior is acceptable.

The impact of social factors such as the social normalization of deviant sexual acts on adolescents' sexual offending behavior is more visible among offenders who have been sexually victimized. In this case, a sexually abusive youth may use the same modus operandi learned or endured at the hands of their sexual victimizer (Leversee, 2015, p. 186). That is, some adolescents' sexual offending behaviors represent a reenactment of their own sexual victimization or something that they experienced or learned.

Finally, sexual behaviors are natural behaviors. Therefore, since most natural behaviors have to be experimented with or learned, it is expected that adolescents will engage in experimental sexual activities as their bodies begun to sexually develop. In the absence of proper guidance, or in situations where a youth lacks adequate knowledge about what are appropriate or inappropriate sexual acts, the chances of sexual misconduct are bound to increase. Of course, none of these factors (environmental, experimental, and social) provides any legitimate reason for a child to violate another child, but these factors do explain certain aspects of juvenile sexual offending behavior, and they do increase the chance of juvenile offenders' committing, particularly, child molestation, rape, and animal abuse offenses.

Rape

According to the U.S. Attorney General's newly revised definition of rape for nationwide data collection, rape refers to the "penetration, no matter how slight, of the vagina or anus with any body part or object, or oral penetration by a sex organ of another person, without the consent of the victim" (Holder, 2012). Characteristically, male rapists are more likely to victimize females and strangers in comparison to child molesters (Craissati & Beech, 2004). Rapists also tend to be younger adults, to be socially competent, to have violent histories, and/or to use excessive levels of aggression and force (Musu-Gillette, Zhang, Wang, Zhang, & Oudekerk, 2017). Offenders younger than age 18 account for about 15% of rape arrestees in the United States and may be responsible for as many as four out of every 10 sexual assaults (Przybylski & Lobanov-Rostovsky, 2014, p. 175). It is to be remembered that like all forms of sexual offending behaviors, only a fraction of rape cases come to the attention of criminal justice authorities.

Child Molestation

Child molestation is any unlawful sexual conduct or sexual exploitation of a person under the age of 18 years. Thus, generally not all juvenile child molesters are pedophiles because pedophilic behaviors are different from child molestation. While a pedophile is a person who is sexually aroused and gratified by sexual behavior involving children, generally age 13 years or younger, a child molester is simply someone who engages in a sexual act with a child under the age of 18. Most juvenile sex offenders fall into this category not because they are attracted to children but rather because they have unrestricted access to and direct control over many potential victims. Such opportunistic and circumstantial access makes it easier to sexually molest other children. It should also be noted that children spend most of their time in the company of other children and often "outside the orbit of parental control" (Eccles, 1999, p. 34). This natural condition of childhood increases the opportunity for child molestation.

Sexual Abuse of Animals

Clinical staff who have delivered sex offender treatment for a reasonable period have experienced juvenile offenders who disclose history of sexually abusing animals, especially pets. Yet, reliable sources of information on the degree and scope of sexually motivated abuse of animals by juveniles is hard to come by, if at all such information exists. The lack of information on this subject is, however, expected because victims are animals unable to complain. Second, most human interactions with animals, especially dogs and other pets, take place behind closed doors, out of the reach or sight of people who can report such abuse. Further, most sex offenses in general occur in secret, and thus knowledge of the behavior rarely comes to the attention of a third person.

Third, the medical patient confidentiality law suppresses offenders' self-disclosed information about sexual abuse of animals. The main purpose of the law is to protect communication between a patient and his or her doctor regarding their medical and mental health status as a basis for criminal prosecution. Since the doctor-patient confidentiality law extends to licensed mental health practitioners including therapists and psychologists, self-reported accounts of sexually abusing animals seldom get recorded in a youth's file. This makes it harder to assess the frequency and depth of juvenile sexual misconduct involving animals. Lastly, not all jurisdictions criminalize or prosecute sexual contact with animals. Even those jurisdictions with laws on the books that prohibit sexual conduct with animals find it extremely difficult to prove such cases.

CONCLUSION

Undoubtedly, the most difficult criminal, deviant, or delinquent behavior to assess, classify, or manage is sexual offending behavior. The complication lies in part with the fact that dealing with sex offenders generally means working with victims because most offenders have some sort of history of being sexually, violently, and or mentally victimized. Also, sex offending behavior has serious and wide-ranging effects on society as a whole. The behavior affects individual victims and more importantly poses major challenges for correctional staff charged with managing such behaviors.

Unfortunately also, a large number of sex offenders and offending behaviors cases do not come to the attention of criminal justice authorities. The little that is known about juvenile sex offenders comes from the less than 30% of juvenile offenses and offenders that get reported to law enforcement institutions and from self-reports from adult sex offenders about their childhood sex offenses. All of these factors therefore reinforce the need to stay abreast of developments relating to juvenile sexual offending behaviors.

DISCUSSION QUESTIONS

1. List and discuss some of the common myths about sex offenders' characteristics.
2. What would be the most enhanced ways to ascertain the annual number of each sexual offending behavior category discussed in this chapter?
3. Why do female sex offenders differ from male sex offenders in terms of the use of force, age of victims, and their mental health status?
4. Why are female sex offending behaviors more underreported than male sex offending behaviors?
5. There are several differences between juvenile sex offenders and adults sex offenders in terms of the patterns of behaviors. Discuss some of the key differences.
6. Why does sexual victimization of animals raise concerns about sexual victimization of humans?

REFERENCES

Carter, M. M., & Morris, L. (2007). *Enhancing the management of adult and juvenile sex offenders: A handbook for policymakers and practitioners.* Retrieved from the Center for Sex Offender Management website: https://www.csom.org/pubs/CSOM_handbook.pdf

Centers for Disease Control and Prevention. (2012). *Sexual violence: Facts at a glance.* Retrieved from http://www.cdc.gov/violenceprevention/pdf/sv-datasheet-a.pdf

Craissati, J., & Beech, A. (2004). The characteristics of a geographical sample of convicted rapists: Sexual victimization and compliance in comparison to child molesters. *Journal of Interpersonal Violence, 19*(4), 371–388. doi:10.1177/0886260503262078

DeBaca, L. C. (2014). *Sex offender management assessment and planning initiative.* Retrieved from the Office of Sex Offender Sentencing, Monitoring, Apprehending, Registering, and Tracking website: https://soortf.icjia.cloud/static/pdf/USDOJ_SOMAPI_Full%20Report.pdf

Eccles, J. S. (1999). The development of children ages 6 to 14. *The Future of Children, 9*(2), 30–44.

Finkelhor, D., Ormrod, R., & Chaffin, M. (2009). *Juveniles who commit sex offenses against minors.* Retrieved from the National Criminal Justice Reference Service website: https://www.ncjrs.gov/pdffiles1/ojjdp/227763.pdf

Gilligan, L. (2008). *Fact sheet: What you need to know about sex offenders.* Retrieved from the Center for Sex Offender Management website: http://www.csom.org/pubs/needtoknow_fs.pdf

Hockenberry, S., & Puzzanchera, C. (2015). *Juvenile court statistics 2013*. Retrieved from the National Center for Juvenile Justice website: http://www.ncjj.org/publication/juvenile-court-statistics-2013.aspx

Holder, E. (2012). *Attorney General Eric Holder announces revisions to the Uniform Crime Report's definition of rape*. Retrieved from U.S. Department of Justice website: https://www.justice.gov/opa/pr/attorney-general-eric-holder-announces-revisions-uniform-crime-report-s-definition-rape

Levenson, J. S., Brannon, Y. N., & Fortney, T. (2007). Public perceptions about sex offenders and community protection policies. *Analyses of Social Issues and Public Policy, 7*(1), 1–25.

Leversee, T. (2015). *Etiology and typologies of juveniles who have committed sexual offenses*. Retrieved from the Office of Sex Offender Sentencing, Monitoring, Apprehending, Registering, and Tracking website: https://smart.gov/pdfs/JuvenileEtiologyandTypology.pdf

Musu-Gillette, L., Zhang, A., Wang, K., Zhang, J., & Oudekerk, B. A. (2017). *Indicators of school crime and safety: 2016*. Retrieved from the National Center for Education Statistics website: https://nces.ed.gov/pubs2017/2017064.pdf

National Center on Sexual Behavior of Youth. (2003). *Adolescent sex offenders: Common misconceptions vs. current evidence*. Retrieved from http://www.ncsby.org/

Przybylski, R., & Lobanov-Rostovsky, C. (2014). Unique considerations regarding juveniles who commit sexual offenses. In *Sex offender management assessment and planning initiative*, pp. 221–226. Retreived from the Office of Sex Offender Sentencing, Monitoring, Apprehending, Registering, and Tracking website: https://www.smart.gov/SOMAPI/pdfs/SOMAPI_Full%20Report.pdf

Ratnayake, A. A. (2013). Juvenile sex offenses: Finding justice. *National Center on Domestic and Sexual Violence Update, 23*(9). Retrieved from the National Center on Domestic and Sexual Violence website: http://www.ncdsv.org/images/NCPCA_Update_JuvenileSexOffensesFindingJustice_Vol23_No9_2013.pdf

Reaves, B. A. (2017, May). *Police response to domestic violence, 2006–2015*. Retrieved from the Bureau of Justice Statistics website: https://www.bjs.gov/content/pub/pdf/prdv0615.pdf

Sinozich, S., & Langton, L. (2014, December). *Rape and sexual assault victimization among college-age females, 1995–2013*. Retrieved from the Bureau of Justice Statistics website: https://www.bjs.gov/content/pub/pdf/rsavcaf9513.pdf

CHAPTER NINE

General Criminal and Delinquent Behaviors

MOST OF THE offenses committed by youth and most of the delinquent and incorrigible behaviors engaged in by youth are not clinically or legally sexual, violent, or substance abuse-related acts. Rather, the overwhelming number of behaviors are general offenses. General behaviors are criminal, delinquent, incorrigible, and deviant behaviors that are not clinically or legally violent, sexual, or substance abuse-related. The most common general offenses that youth commonly commit are burglary, larceny, motor vehicle theft, forgery, fraud, possession of stolen property, illegal possession of guns, curfew violations, and loitering. These behaviors do not have a direct relationship to sexual, violent, or, in many cases, substance abuse behaviors.

Certain illegal behaviors such as liquor law violations, weapons offenses, crimes against family, and disorderly conduct consist of general offenses as well as specific categories of violent, sexual, and substance abuse behaviors. Indeed, while some liquor law violations such as underage drinking, public intoxication, or driving under the influence of alcohol or illicit drugs can be classified as substance abuse offenses, in some instances liquor law violations can also be assessed as general offenses, such as having an open alcohol container in vehicle, selling alcohol without a license, and selling alcohol to minors. Similarly, although the overwhelming number of property offenses are general behaviors, there are instances where certain offenses such as arson and vandalism may be classified as violence.

As far as risk and needs assessments are concerned, any history of general offending behavior is important information that can significantly impact risk and needs assessment results. This chapter therefore highlights the levels and trends of general offenses that youth commit. Further, it groups general behaviors under three sub-subcategories: crimes against property, public order crimes, and crimes against persons. It also talks about certain general offenses that can be linked to sexual, violent, and drug- and alcohol-related behaviors.

The Office of Juvenile Justice and Delinquency Prevention (OJJDP), the Bureau of Justice Statistics (BJS), and juvenile courts around the nation gather and disseminate detailed information about many aspects of juvenile offending behaviors that come to the attention of law enforcement agencies. Reports generated by OJJDP, BJS, and juvenile courts also cover activities of law enforcement agencies, trends and characteristics of specific offenses youth commit, responses of the courts, secured care and community correction institutions, and delinquent and criminal behaviors as well as the demography of the victims violated by youth.

Criminal justice agencies' official crime rates are based on data known to the police and reported to the Federal Bureau of Investigation by police agencies across the nation. The data covers arrest statistics, the number of offenses victims report, and offenders' self-reported offenses. Current figures, however, represent only 76% to 78% of the actual cases reported to authorities each year. The data are usually a few years old at the time they are published, but they are vital points of reference for discovering the trends and scope of general offenses youth commit and characteristics of juvenile offenders.

GENERAL OFFENDING BEHAVIORS

The process of identifying risk and needs requires meticulous examination of each offender's delinquent, criminal, and deviant history. This process involves the careful assessment and classification of behaviors, including general offending behaviors, which can be grouped under three behavioral categories: crimes against persons, crimes against property, and public order offenses, which also consists of crimes against government (Asscher, van der Put, & Stams, 2012).

Crimes Against Persons

Much of the public concern about crimes committed by younger children and adolescents, especially in the 1980s and early 1990s, had to do with crimes against persons, or crimes that constitute attacks or threats of an attack on a person's body. Public concern stemmed from the fact that unlike crimes against property and public order offenses, crimes against persons are designed to directly inflict pain and suffering on human victims, which produces various long-term effects for victims, those close to victims, and society as a whole. Most serious crimes against persons include homicide, manslaughter, assault, robbery, kidnapping, rape, and criminal mistreatment (Asscher et al., 2012). Thus, crimes against persons is the most serious category of the general offenses committed by children. Table 9.1 shows the distribution of crimes against persons by age.

TABLE 9.1 *2005–2014 Juvenile Court Statistics: Offenses Against Persons by Age at Referral*

AGE	<12	12	13	14	15	16	17	>17	TOTAL
2005	23,480	28,323	53,496	77,601	94,812	90,774	61,810	5,815	**436,110**
2006	21,502	25,311	48,699	72,433	91,195	90,440	60,635	5,672	**415,886**
2007	20,073	23,668	46,122	70,755	89,661	91,930	62,978	5,867	**411,053**
2008	18,681	22,492	43,358	66,971	86,779	90,840	63,145	6,294	**398,560**
2009	16,720	20,727	38,890	59,596	78,508	83,387	59,117	5,908	**362,853**
2010	16,692	20,509	37,712	55,848	72,121	78,773	54,895	5,646	**342,196**
2011	16,632	20,007	36,041	52,125	66,078	70,466	50,286	4,967	**316,602**
2012	16,079	18,427	33,520	49,263	60,823	63,849	43,995	4,534	**290,490**
2013	14,139	17,235	31,323	45,750	56,969	59,370	42,032	4,185	**271,004**
2014	13,839	16,502	30,279	44,312	54,234	57,369	41,816	4,444	**262,795**
TOTAL	**177,837**	**213,200**	**399,441**	**594,653**	**751,180**	**777,199**	**540,708**	**53,332**	**3,507,550**

Source: Sickmund, M., Sladky, A., & Kang, W. (2017). *Easy access to juvenile court statistics: 1985–2014.* Retrieved from http://www.ojjdp.gov/ojstatbb/ezajcs/

Crimes against persons cover a broad array of illegal behaviors that victimize one or more persons. Furthermore, the figures in Table 9.1 show that a significant number of referrals to juvenile courts are for crimes against persons. Most offenses against persons such as assault, armed robbery, murder, assault, sex offenses, kidnapping, and stalking fall under violence (see Table 9.2). A few such offenses against persons such as harassment, stalking, and in some cases bullying can, however, be classified as general offending behaviors. Irrespective of the subcategory of a crime against persons, those behaviors deserve all the legal and clinical attention necessary to halt future occurrences because when left unattended they can lead to serious outcomes for offenders and particularly for victims. Additionally, although they account for a relatively small proportion of all crimes, crimes against persons have the most potential for causing greater damage to individuals.

Crimes Against Property

An overwhelming number of juvenile offending behaviors are property-related offenses; hence, this subcategory of general offenses accounts for a high percentage of each year's total arrest rates for juveniles (Institute of Medicine and National Research Council, 2001). Crimes against property are offenses that affect a person's right of ownership by another person taking possession of the property, altering the condition of the property, or making use of the property without prior approval from the lawful owner. Typical examples of crimes against property include burglary, theft, robbery, criminal damage, and vandalism (see Table 9.2). As reflected in Table 9.2, undoubtedly these types of offenses are very popular among children, especially those who are 16 years old or younger.

TABLE 9.2 *2005–2014 Juvenile Court Statistics: Property-Related Offenses by Age at Referral*

YEAR	<12	12	13	14	15	16	17	>17	TOTAL
2005	27,293	32,588	64,028	103,897	137,436	141,178	96,927	10,547	**613,894**
2006	23,617	29,235	59,025	97,889	131,035	139,518	96,096	10,151	**586,567**
2007	22,778	27,892	56,755	96,521	133,558	147,294	104,129	10,866	**599,792**
2008	21,132	25,911	54,451	94,626	133,668	153,649	112,512	11,899	**607,848**
2009	19,338	23,555	48,321	84,236	123,381	145,455	105,691	11,076	**561,053**
2010	17,740	21,110	42,901	73,717	107,768	127,151	93,831	10,421	**494,639**
2011	16,136	19,855	39,830	65,570	96,433	113,276	84,210	8,759	**444,070**
2012	15,121	18,275	36,255	60,842	86,744	102,371	73,972	8,121	**401,702**
2013	12,824	16,083	32,221	53,379	76,611	88,900	67,816	7,199	**355,033**
2014	12,188	14,431	29,788	50,292	71,566	82,661	65,788	6,819	**333,533**
TOTAL	**188,168**	**228,937**	**463,575**	**780,968**	**1,098,201**	**1,241,453**	**900,973**	**95,857**	**4,998,132**

Source: Sickmund, M., Sladky, A., & Kang, W. (2017). *Easy access to juvenile court statistics: 1985–2014*. Retrieved from http://www.ojjdp.gov/ojstatbb/ezajcs/

Most arrests of persons under the age of 18 reported between 2007 and 2015 were for property offenses. Like many other types of offenses, the reported rate of crimes against property must always be read with the understanding that only a small number of the crimes committed come to the attention of law enforcement agencies. Obviously, many factors make property crimes popular among juvenile offenders. First, most property that becomes the object of offenses is replaceable, and thus juveniles may not fully grasp the consequences of such behavior. Second, offenses involving various types of property are often not reported to law enforcement agencies. Third, unlike violent or sexual crimes that are committed against persons, many of whom are capable verbalizing their victimization, property does not talk. Finally, the legal consequences of property offenses are often not as severe as those of crimes against persons. Collectively, these factors may serve as incentives for many at-risk youth to engage in property offenses.

Public Order Offenses

A healthy number of at-risk youth spend a good portion of their idle time in the company of other at-risk youth and away from their parents and people who could guide their behaviors (Monahan, Steinberg, & Cauffman, 2009; Tompsett, Veits, & Amrhein, 2016; Vásquez & Zimmerman, 2014). This means that at-risk children are likely to spend more time in environments where they can commit more public order offenses. Common offenses in this category include status offenses, which are predominantly general offenses that fall under public order offenses or offenses against government. Children commit status offenses when they engage in behaviors such as curfew violations, loitering, running away from home, or truancy. These behaviors are not offenses when exhibited by adults—certainly adults are at total liberty to attend school, leave, and return home at will, and indeed there are no standing laws that prohibit adults from roaming about the streets at any hour of the day. The figures in Table 9.3 represent the number of children who are referred to juvenile courts for public order offenses.

TABLE 9.3 *2005–2014 Juvenile Court Statistics: Public Order Offenses by Age at Referral*

YEAR	<12	12	13	14	15	16	17	>17	TOTAL
2005	12,184	17,903	39,802	71,013	100,569	107,288	76,656	16,840	**442,256**
2006	11,416	16,596	37,469	67,875	98,120	109,161	78,830	16,084	**435,550**
2007	10,744	15,483	35,285	64,690	96,472	110,041	82,026	17,001	**431,744**
2008	11,004	14,110	32,403	60,208	93,143	108,237	81,118	17,550	**417,773**
2009	10,140	12,914	28,115	53,081	82,370	99,665	75,833	17,812	**379,930**
2010	10,649	12,231	26,150	47,517	73,330	89,618	68,401	15,940	**343,838**
2011	9,881	11,480	24,113	43,838	66,323	80,041	61,917	14,699	**312,293**
2012	10,553	11,127	22,951	41,082	60,902	72,259	55,413	13,817	**288,103**
2013	10,260	10,227	21,321	38,156	56,199	66,184	51,879	13,346	**267,572**
2014	9,419	9,226	19,512	35,209	51,809	61,512	49,445	13,595	**249,727**
TOTAL	**106,250**	**131,296**	**287,123**	**522,671**	**779,238**	**904,005**	**681,518**	**156,684**	**3,568,785**

Source: Sickmund, M., Sladky, A., & Kang, W. (2017). *Easy access to juvenile court statistics: 1985–2014*. Retrieved from http://www.ojjdp.gov/ojstatbb/ezajcs/

Public order offenses are committed against society, and in some instances in public view. Public order offenses also include crimes against government such as terrorism, perjury, and obstruction as well as illegal acts that are intended to impede the smooth running of public institutions. Common types of public offenses are disorderly conduct, obstruction of justice, curfew violations, illegal sale and transportation of drugs or stolen goods, and the solicitation and proposition of prostitution (Sickmund, Sladky, & Kang, 2017).

Each of these three categories of general offenses is informed by unique sets of risk factors and needs. Obviously, some risk and needs that inform crimes against persons are different from those associated with property crimes. Some of the risks associated with public order offenses are also different from those associated with crimes against persons or property. Furthermore, the likely consequences for each category of offender are different. For example, the chance of adjudication for public order offenses is low. Even when such an act results in an adjudication, it typically results in fewer legal consequences. As a result, some youths may easily give in to the temptation of committing offenses such as loitering and curfew violations with the belief that if they are caught, the consequences will be less severe compared to other behaviors such as crimes against persons.

PATTERNS AND TRENDS OF GENERAL OFFENDING BEHAVIORS

Each year, hundreds of thousands of children younger than 18 years are arrested by law enforcement agencies across the nation. Not surprisingly, a large percentage of the children are arrested in connection with at least one or more general offenses (Puzzanchera & Kang, 2017). Consequently, a good sum of the arrests carried out between 2007 and 2015 were associated with general offenses. As indicated in Table 9.2, the most popular offenses recorded for 2014 are larceny-theft (177,100), burglary (40,500), vandalism (45,200), disorderly conduct (80,600), and curfew and loitering (53,700). It is important to note that general offenses also include motor vehicle theft, stolen property possession, and weapons violations. These offenses alone account for over one-third of the total number of general offenses for which youth were arrested and processed by American law enforcement agencies between 2007 and 2015 (Puzzanchera & Kang, 2017).

Decline in General Offense Arrest Rates

The rate of children's arrests, and hopefully the rate of offenses committed by children, has been consistently dropping since the late 1990s, and the decline is evident in all behavioral categories of offenses among all age groups. Table 9.4 shows that even the number of people in jails and prisons across the United States has been declining for nearly two decades. For example, it is estimated that each year, the number of people who serve time in local, state, and federal prisons drops by about 51,000 (Wilson, 2017). The drop is not only reflected in aggregate but also in specific behavioral categories.

In every behavioral category in Table 9.4, there is a visible difference between the numbers of youth who are arrested each year compared to the rate in later years (Puzzanchera & Kang, 2017). The drop is also evident in the number of youth who commit specific offenses. For example, previous and current National Juvenile Offenders and Victims reports show that juvenile arrest rates for burglary, property crimes, larceny, and motor vehicle crimes have all been declining substantially. The figures recorded in Table 9.5 also show that in the seven years between 2007 and 2015, the estimated number of arrests dropped from 6,196 to 3,084 per 100,000 persons. Some figures for 2014 are only half of the 2008 arrest rates.

The rate of some arrest figures in 2014 is only half that of 2008. Table 9.6 shows that during the same period, the number of burglary victims went from 246 in 2008 to only 122 in 2014. Motor vehicle theft went from 73 in 2004 to 38, stolen property from 61 to 31, and

TABLE 9.4 *Estimated Arrests of Persons Under Age 18 in the United States*

YEAR	2008	2009	2010	2011	2012	2013	2014
TOTAL ARRESTS	2,100,800	1,906,400	1,642,500	1,470,000	1,319,700	1,081,400	1,023,800
MURDER/NONNEG. MANS.	1,260	1,170	1,010	840	720	750	760
RAPE	3,320	3,110	2,870	2,800	2,530	n/a	n/a
ROBBERY	35,200	31,700	27,200	23,800	21,500	19,200	19,500
AGGRAVATED ASSAULT	55,900	49,900	44,800	40,700	36,300	30,900	30,300
BURGLARY	83,500	74,800	65,200	62,000	53,800	42,900	40,500
LARCENY-THEFT	321,500	317,700	281,100	253,800	224,200	186,000	177,100
MOTOR VEHICLE THEFT	24,900	19,900	15,800	14,000	13,100	11,600	12,700
ARSON	6,500	5,300	4,600	4,900	4,400	3,700	3,200
OTHER ASSAULTS	231,900	219,700	210,200	190,900	173,100	146,900	140,500
FORGERY	2,600	2,100	1,700	1,600	1,400	1,100	1,200
FRAUD	7,200	6,200	5,800	5,200	4,700	4,500	4,300
EMBEZZLEMENT	1,300	600	400	400	400	400	500
STOLEN PROPERTY	20,700	18,700	14,600	13,300	12,900	10,300	10,400
VANDALISM	106,800	90,500	77,100	67,900	59,900	46,700	45,200
WEAPONS	39,800	33,900	31,400	28,200	24,700	20,300	20,800
PROSTITUTION	1,500	1,400	1,000	1,000	800	800	700
SEX OFFENSES (OTHER)	14,500	13,400	13,000	12,600	12,400	n/a	n/a
DRUG ABUSE VIOLATIONS	179,400	170,300	170,600	148,700	140,000	117,100	113,600
GAMBLING	1,600	1,800	1,400	1,000	1,000	700	600
OFFENSES AGAINST FAMILY	5,800	4,500	3,800	3,600	3,300	2,800	3,400
DUI	15,900	13,500	12,000	10,100	9,400	7,600	7,000
LIQUOR LAWS	129,300	110,300	94,700	88,300	77,800	59,100	51,200
DRUNKENNESS	15,500	13,800	12,700	11,400	9,900	7,300	6,500
DISORDERLY CONDUCT	188,500	170,100	155,900	139,200	120,100	95,400	80,600
VAGRANCY	4,000	2,700	2,100	1,800	1,400	900	1,000
ALL OTHER OFFENSES	360,200	323,300	296,800	264,900	239,600	195,100	186,200
CURFEW AND LOITERING	133,100	112,600	94,800	76,900	70,200	56,400	53,700
	1,991,680	**1,812,980**	**1,642,580**	**1,469,840**	**1,319,550**	**1,068,450**	**1,011,460**

Source: Sickmund, M., Sladky, A., & Kang, W. (2017). *Easy access to juvenile court statistics: 1985–2014*. Retrieved from http://www.ojjdp.gov/ojstatbb/ezajcs/

the rate for vandalism dropped from 315 per every 100,000 persons in 2008 to only 136 in 2014 (Puzzanchera & Kang, 2017).

Table 9.6 shows that between 2007 and 2015 the total number of arrests involving juveniles dropped from 14.9% to just 9.1%, while the percentage of adults who were arrested during the same period went from 85% to 90.8%. Indeed, law enforcement agencies are not less inclined to arrest people who are below the age of 18. In fact, children are more vulnerable to unwanted contact with law enforcement agencies compared to adults because in addition to the expectation to comply with all the laws that regulate adult behaviors, children are

TABLE 9.5 *Arrest Rate of Persons Age 10 to 17 per 100,000 U.S. Residents*

YEAR	2008	2009	2010	2011	2012	2013	2014
TOTAL ARRESTS	**6,196**	**5,656**	**4,888**	**4,394**	**3,968**	**3,261**	**3,084**
PROPERTY CRIME INDEX	1,287	1,239	1,091	1,000	888	736	703
BURGLARY	246	222	194	185	162	129	122
LARCENY-THEFT	948	942	836	759	674	561	534
MOTOR VEHICLE THEFT	73	59	47	42	39	35	38
ARSON	19	16	14	15	13	11	10
OTHER ASSAULTS	684	652	626	571	520	443	423
FORGERY	8	6	5	5	4	3	4
FRAUD	21	18	17	16	14	14	13
EMBEZZLEMENT	4	2	1	1	1	1	1
STOLEN PROPERTY	61	56	44	40	39	31	31
VANDALISM	315	268	229	203	180	141	136
WEAPONS	117	100	93	84	74	61	63
PROSTITUTION	4	4	3	3	2	2	2
GAMBLING	5	5	4	3	3	2	2
OFFENSES AGAINST FAMILY	17	13	11	11	10	8	10
DISORDERLY CONDUCT	556	505	464	416	361	288	243
VAGRANCY	12	8	6	5	4	3	3
ALL OTHER OFFENSES	1,062	959	883	792	720	588	561
CURFEW AND LOITERING	392	334	282	230	211	170	162

Source: Puzzanchera, C., & Kang, W. (2017). *Easy access to FBI arrest statistics 1994–2014*. Retrieved from https://www.ojjdp.gov/ojstatbb/ezaucr/asp/ucr_display.asp

TABLE 9.6 *Change in Adult and Juveniles Arrest Rates, 2008–2014*

YEAR	2008	2009	2010	2011	2012	2013	2014
Total all arrests	**14,005,600**	**13,687,200**	**13,120,900**	**12,408,900**	**12,197,000**	**11,302,100**	**11,205,800**
Adult %	85.0	86.0	87.4	88.1	89.1	90.4	90.8
Juveniles %	14.9	13.9	12.5	11.8	10.8	9.5	9.1

Source: Sickmund, M., Sladky, A., & Kang, W. (2017). *Easy access to juvenile court statistics: 1985–2014*. Retrieved from http://www.ojjdp.gov/ojstatbb/ezajcs/

additionally required to obey status laws that do not apply to adults. It is nonetheless not surprising that the group of offenders that comparatively shows the most visible and constant decline in the rates of arrests over the past two decades are children. Indeed, the arrest rates for offenders in this age group have been trending downwards since the mid-1990s.

Even by age, the declining rate is encouraging. In fact, as indicated in Table 9.7, in some age groups, such as children below the age of 12 and those who are 13 years old, the rate for 2014 is half of the 2005 rate. Table 9.7 also shows that as children age, the risk of arrest increases but then drops sharply as they approach adulthood. Even among the most active offending age group, age 13 to 17, the change in rate for each year clearly suggests a downward trend. In other words, as children progress toward age 18, the rate of arrest by law enforcement agencies for various categories of behaviors spikes but then sharply drops as children approach age 18. These spikes and declines are, however, expected because adolescent brains are understandably underdeveloped, and children's behaviors at this age are largely influenced by immediate gratification and intense peer influence (Carson, 2013; Esiri, 2016; Monahan et al., 2009; Thomas, 2015). Despite this well-established knowledge about adolescent brain development and at-risk behaviors, the number of youth in detention and on probation also shows a continuous decline.

TABLE 9.7 *2005–2014 Juvenile Court Statistics: Number of Arrest by Age at Referral*

YEAR	<12	12	13	14	15	16	17	>17	TOTAL
2005	64,148	81,865	167,244	274,839	372,310	393,930	283,605	37,421	1,675,361
2006	57,723	74,080	154,036	258,938	358,741	394,269	284,455	36,139	1,618,380
2007	54,680	69,663	146,746	252,173	357,181	405,065	300,326	38,297	1,624,131
2008	51,951	65,174	138,622	241,061	349,526	406,088	307,274	40,306	1,600,001
2009	47,292	59,957	123,635	215,491	318,012	377,754	286,859	38,998	1,467,997
2010	46,448	56,847	115,794	196,688	286,545	342,646	260,665	36,234	1,341,867
2011	43,995	54,390	108,804	179,976	260,491	308,938	237,800	32,235	1,226,630
2012	43,209	50,854	101,546	168,775	238,237	281,479	212,303	29,999	1,126,400
2013	39,137	46,685	93,015	153,742	217,487	253,270	198,930	28,250	1,030,514
2014	36,854	43,000	87,142	144,519	202,658	238,146	194,535	28,095	974,950
Total	**485,438**	**602,515**	**1,236,584**	**2,086,202**	**2,961,186**	**3,401,584**	**2,566,751**	**345,973**	**13,686,233**

Source: Sickmund, M., Sladky, A., & Kang, W. (2017). *Easy access to juvenile court statistics: 1985–2014*. Retrieved from http://www.ojjdp.gov/ojstatbb/ezajcs/

Decline in Detention Rate

The rate of youth who end up in detention or in secured care, as reported in Table 9.8, has been on the decline for over a decade. For example, OJJDP records show that the rate of children in detention dropped significantly in the period between 2004 and 2015. In fact, the number of children in detention has been steadily dropping since the 1990s. The drop may imply that since most juvenile offenders are medium or minimum risk offenders, the majority of such offenders end up on probation or are diverted to other forms of community correction and antisocial behavioral modification and prevention programs or services. The drop in the arrest rate is also reflected in the rate of youth who end up in detention or in a secured care facility.

In Table 9.8, for instance, the total number of youth who were detained in 2005 was 358,978 but in 2010 that number dropped to only 272,696, and in 2014 the number of youth who were detained was only 212,914 compared to the figure for 2005. A similar pattern of drops in the number of youth detained by juvenile courts is observed for each age group, with the most significant drops associated with children below the age of 14.

Evidently, the drop in detention rates must be celebrated with caution. First, presence in detention means spending time in the company of other high-risk and high-needs offenders with established history of serious antisocial behaviors and all the knowledge or skill for engaging in prohibited acts. Secondly, while these figures continue to drop, juvenile

TABLE 9.8 *2005–2014 Juvenile Court Statistics: Offenses by Detained/in Detention*

AGE	<12	12	13	14	15	16	17	>17	TOTAL
2005	5,070	11,901	30,575	58,180	86,333	92,107	67,486	7,326	**358,978**
2006	4,673	10,019	28,397	54,933	85,500	94,191	69,289	7,446	**354,448**
2007	4,309	9,462	26,685	53,923	82,933	94,000	70,274	7,662	**349,247**
2008	3,639	8,522	24,179	48,512	76,466	90,922	67,280	7,749	**327,270**
2009	3,538	7,799	20,564	43,330	68,068	82,828	62,047	7,440	**295,614**
2010	3,060	6,992	19,106	38,779	62,358	76,179	58,663	7,559	**272,696**
2011	2,772	6,702	18,549	35,955	57,374	69,138	55,055	6,852	**252,397**
2012	2,707	6,435	18,031	35,523	57,244	66,842	54,032	6,514	**247,329**
2013	2,923	6,418	17,393	34,294	53,438	63,297	50,561	5,949	**234,274**
2014	2,557	5,592	16,313	31,103	47,168	56,526	47,553	6,102	**212,914**
TOTAL	**35,247**	**79,842**	**219,792**	**434,533**	**676,882**	**786,030**	**602,240**	**70,599**	**2,905,166**

Source: Sickmund, M., Sladky, A., & Kang, W. (2017). *Easy access to juvenile court statistics: 1985–2014*. Retrieved from http://www.ojjdp.gov/ojstatbb/ezajcs/

detention rates in countries around the world are much smaller compared to the United States. Obviously, from a classification standpoint, any unwanted contacts with law enforcement, especially those that end with arrest, are strong risk factors that increase the chances of future acts of delinquency or criminality. That said, it is important to note that youth who end up in detention tend to have higher risks than those who are placed on probation.

Probation Rates

It is encouraging that the majority of youth who get arrested, as indicated in Table 9.9, end up on probation instead of in detention. Clearly, youth who are placed in detention tend to have higher risk and needs levels than those on probation because the mere physical presence of any youth in detention means interaction with many other at-risk youths from diverse delinquent and criminal backgrounds. There are a number of sociological and criminological theories, such as social learning theory and differential association theory, that also support the premise that increased close association and interaction with multiple high-risk and needs offenders are likely to increase the likelihood of future delinquent and criminal behaviors or thinking. Hence, the high number of youth on probation, compared to those in detention, is very promising, especially in light of the fact that the rate of youth on probation is also dropping, suggesting that perhaps the use of diversion programs to remove low-risk youths from formal criminal justice processing is on the rise.

Table 9.9 shows that in every age group, the rate of juveniles who annually end up on probation has been shrinking, at least in the past decade. For example, the rate of children under the age of 12 on probation in 2005 dropped from 17,941 to 9,679 in 2014, which is about 46% less than the 2005 figures. For children between the age of 12 and 13, the rate of probation shrank about 45% between 2004 and 2015. Similarly, the rate of 17-year-olds who were on probation in 2004 dropped 26% from 85,895 to only 63,454 in a 10-year period.

In the end, there is no single factor responsible for changes in the rates of arrest, detention, and probation for general offenses, or any other category of criminal or delinquent behavior for that matter. In fact, many competing explanations further cloud the possibility of pinning

TABLE 9.9 *2005–2014 Juvenile Court Statistics: On Probation by Age*

AGE	<12	12	13	14	15	16	17	>17	TOTAL
2005	17,941	28,386	60,740	99,967	133,988	141,158	85,895	10,373	**578,447**
2006	15,950	26,086	56,544	95,660	131,554	142,440	88,380	10,473	**567,087**
2007	15,060	24,366	53,574	93,470	131,067	147,973	94,015	11,089	**570,615**
2008	14,518	22,526	51,674	90,564	130,052	149,606	98,259	11,483	**568,682**
2009	12,800	20,830	45,624	80,868	119,505	139,303	91,159	10,757	**520,847**
2010	12,130	19,454	42,560	74,144	107,882	128,186	83,018	10,062	**477,435**
2011	11,852	18,975	40,322	68,159	98,253	115,190	77,115	8,812	**438,679**
2012	11,197	18,018	38,546	64,585	89,563	105,118	68,657	7,872	**403,557**
2013	10,319	16,539	35,787	59,429	84,068	96,508	64,586	7,488	**374,724**
2014	9,679	15,635	34,010	57,111	79,139	92,034	63,454	7,666	**358,729**
TOTAL	**131,447**	**210,816**	**459,381**	**783,958**	**1,105,071**	**1,257,515**	**814,540**	**96,075**	**4,858,802**

Source: Sickmund, M., Sladky, A., & Kang, W. (2017). *Easy access to juvenile court statistics: 1985–2014*. Retrieved from http://www.ojjdp.gov/ojstatbb/ezajcs/

the drops on one factor. Obviously, one possible explanation would be that the lack of one single factor reaffirms that crime and arrest rates are never constant and that consequently the changes in arrest, detention, and probation rates occur as a result of various factors. These include the sustained effort to promote programs that seek to reduce crimes and arrest rates, the gradual movement away from punishment to rehabilitation, and the introduction of risk and needs assessment and classification as critical functions of detention, probation, and parole institutions.

It is also well-established that therapeutic responses to at-risk youth's behaviors in the last two decades have positively contributed to the decline in juvenile offending behaviors or rates of arrest, detention, and probation. Other explanations are that early intervention programs and improved parenting skills have had an impact. It must also be noted that all of these changes took place around the time when the so-called millennials were populating the prime age bracket for criminal activities, which is said to be between age 15 to 24, or more conservatively from 15 to 19 years old. Further, while the adult system is still struggling to fully embrace positivist responses to crime, for decades the juvenile justice system has been steadily careening toward therapeutic interventions that value rehabilitation (National Institute of Justice, 2018). It is also true that there has been a gradual rise in the amount of time and resources the criminal justice system devotes to the prevention of juvenile delinquency and crime.

TECHNOLOGIES AND GENERAL OFFENSES

Slowly but surely, cybercrimes are becoming a main source of several general offending behaviors and indeed represent a major challenge for most criminal justice professionals charged with legally or clinically responding to youth delinquency. Every advancement in Internet and phone technologies increases youth's ability to commit more general offenses from the comfort of their homes (Bossler, Holt, & May, 2012; McCuddy & Esbensen, 2017).

Examples of this are youth's ability to engage in gambling, stalking, criminal harassment, selling and buying drugs, and engaging in other cyber-mediated offenses that were once very difficult for youth to successfully pull off.

Without the aid of the Internet or cell phone technologies, it would be extremely difficult for many children to have the resources, time, physical ability, and knowledge required for successful commission of general crimes such as forgery, fraud, embezzlement, and similar general offenses that were once only common among adult offenders. Internet and cell phone technologies mask many natural limitations, such as the lack of resources such as a getaway car or the lack of knowledge or skill to commit crimes. Technology also removes legal, social, and physiological barriers that naturally make it difficult for youth to engage in certain criminal behaviors.

CONCLUSION

Some important facts that come to light after careful examination of the general offenses juveniles commit are that this category of behaviors is less recognized by the public and is also underreported by victims. Similarly, unlike sexual, violent, and substance abuse offending behaviors, which receive targeted interventions and treatment, general offending behaviors are more likely to go clinically untreated. It is, however, the case that most general offenders tend to fall into one or more other categories of criminal or delinquent behaviors (sexual, violence, or substance abuse-related).

Children are active general offenders, especially when one considers that only a fraction of the actual offenses they commit come to the attention of law enforcement authorities. The plurality of general offenders and offending behaviors also shows that the job of assessing and classifying juveniles is as complex as classifying adult offenders because each juvenile offender has a unique background and pattern of offending behaviors. Further, each juvenile offender has individualized behavioral history and patterns, thus unique needs and risk scores.

DISCUSSION QUESTIONS

1. Why are public reactions to general offenses less visible compared to reactions to violent or sexual offending behaviors?
2. Why should general offenses receive less or more attention during risk and needs assessment?
3. What are some factors that comparatively explain the increase in adult arrest rates and the decrease in juvenile arrest rates?
4. How might the increased use of the Internet and cell phone technologies to engage in criminal, delinquent, and incorrigible behaviors explain some aspects of the decline in juvenile arrest rates?
5. Why does the risk of arrest increase as children grow but then drop sharply as they approach adulthood?

REFERENCES

Asscher, J. J., van der Put, C. E., & Stams, G. J. J. M. (2012). Differences between juvenile offenders with and without intellectual disability in offense type and risk factors. *Research in Developmental Disabilities, 33*(6), 1905–1913. doi: https://doi.org/10.1016/j.ridd.2012.05.022

Bossler, A. M., Holt, T. J., & May, D. C. (2012). Predicting online harassment victimization among a juvenile population. *Youth and Society, 44*(4), 500–523. doi: 10.1177/0044118x11407525

Carson, D. C. (2013). Perceptions of prosocial and delinquent peer behavior and the effect on delinquent attitudes: A longitudinal study. *Journal of Criminal Justice, 41*(3), 151–161. https://doi.org/10.1016/j.jcrimjus.2013.01.005

Esiri, M. O. (2016). The influence of peer pressure on criminal behaviour. *IOSR Journal of Humanities and Social Science, 21*(1), 08–14.

Institute of Medicine and National Research Council. (2001). *Juvenile crime, Juvenile justice*. Washington, DC: National Academies Press. Retrieved from https://doi.org/10.17226/9747

McCuddy, T., & Esbensen, F-A. (2017). After the bell and into the night: The link between delinquency and traditional, cyber-, and dual-bullying victimization. *Journal of Research in Crime and Delinquency, 54*(3), 409–441. doi: 10.1177/0022427816683515

Monahan, K. C., Steinberg, L., & Cauffman, E. (2009). Affiliation with antisocial peers, susceptibility to peer influence, and antisocial behavior during the transition to adulthood. *Developmental Psychology, 45*(6), 1520–1530. doi: 10.1037/a0017417

National Institute of Justice. (2018). *From juvenile delinquency to young adult offending*. Retrieved from https://www.nij.gov/topics/crime/Pages/delinquency-to-adult-offending.aspx

Puzzanchera, C., & Kang, W. (2017). *Easy access to FBI arrest statistics 1994–2014*. Retrieved from the Office of Juvenile Justice and Delinquency Prevention webiste: https://www.ojjdp.gov/ojstatbb/ezaucr/asp/ucr_display.asp

Sickmund, M., Sladky, A., & Kang, W. (2017). *Easy access to juvenile court statistics: 1985–2014*. Retrieved from the Office of Juvenile Justice and Delinquency Prevention webiste:http://www.ojjdp.gov/ojstatbb/ezajcs/

Thomas, K. J. (2015). Delinquent peer influence on offending versatility: Can peers promote specialized delinquency? *Criminology, 53*(2), 280–308. doi: 10.1111/1745-9125.12069

Tompsett, C. J., Veits, G. M., & Amrhein, K. E. (2016). Peer delinquency and where adolescents spend time with peers: Mediation and moderation of home neighborhood effects on self-reported delinquency. *Journal of Community Psychology, 44*(2), 263–270. doi: 10.1002/jcop.21759

Vásquez, B. E., & Zimmerman, G. M. (2014). An investigation into the empirical relationship between time with peers, friendship, and delinquency. *Journal of Criminal Justice, 42*(3), 24–256. doi: 10.1016/j.jcrimjus.2014.03.001

Wilson, R. (2017, January 3). U.S. prison population falling as crime rates stay low. *The Hill*. Retrieved from https://thehill.com/homenews/news/312480-us-prison-population-falling-as-crime-rates-stay-low

SECTION III

Assessment and Classification of Thoughts and Behaviors

CHAPTER TEN

Ethical Obligations

JUVENILE OFFENDERS FALL under the description of a vulnerable population, a group of people unable to protect their own rights and welfare (Fisher, 1993; Fouka & Mantzorou, 2011, p. 7). Therefore, given the importance of the decisions correctional staff have to make during every minute of their interactions with youthful offenders, correctional staff take an oath to uphold all ethical conditions as part of their professional training or as a condition of employment. Correctional staff include pretrial, correction, probation, and parole officers as well as educational, medical, and mental health personnel. Each of these people work directly with youth who enter the criminal justice system, and in the process, those staff members make critical decisions that affect various aspects of the lives of such youth. Hence, there are codes of conduct for pretrial officers, probation officers, correctional officers, and parole officers, as well as medical and clinical staff.

This chapter provides a concise discussion of some important ethical issues and obligations that inform the day-to-day operations of correctional staff with a particular emphasis on pretrial, probation, correction, and parole officers as well as other correctional and clinical staff. Indeed, every contact with juvenile offenders by criminal justice practitioners creates unavoidable opportunities to engage in unethical behaviors. It is obviously impossible to cover all the possible ethical issues that arise out of each interaction with a juvenile offender. It is, however, hoped that the discussion of ethical questions that arise out of or that are associated with the use of force, personal boundaries, equal treatment, respect for rules and law, communication with offenders, and information gathering and reporting will provide a responsible guide for dealing with most of the critical and challenging ethical questions that criminal justice practitioners face when dealing with juvenile offenders.

DEFINING PROFESSIONAL ETHICAL BEHAVIOR

Criminal justice practitioners' ethical rules are generally known as codes of conduct, professional standards, or codes of ethics. Irrespective of the title of these documents, they provide the marching orders for criminal justice practitioners who work with juvenile offenders. Criminal justice practitioners, like most noncriminal justice professional staff, subscribe to these codified ethical standards—the written codes of conduct that must be respected and that are used to assess competency and professionalism. Like dentists, judges, lawyers, medical doctors, nurses, teachers, and similar professionals who are guided by ethical codes, criminal justice practitioners too have codes of ethics that must be followed regardless of which employer or population they serve (Fowler, 2015).

Despite the existence of numerous code of conduct documents for various professions, including correction and law enforcement, there is, however, no universal definition of what is ethical or not ethical because many ethical questions arise out of dilemmas or in situations where the legitimate options available to the decision maker are equally convincing or compelling. Notwithstanding this fact, ethics, broadly speaking, is a system of principles that regulates the dynamics of decision-making regarding what is right and wrong (Fouka & Mantzorou, 2011). A correctional code of ethics is therefore a set of rules designed to protect practitioners from violating the pledge they make to faithfully serve their employers, the people for whom they care, and the public at large.

Generally speaking also, codes of ethics provide correctional staff with guidelines for preventing ethical violations and serve as guidelines for dealing with ethical dilemmas. These documents help correctional staff navigate many of the ethical dilemmas that they encounter on a regular basis. An ethical dilemma refers to a situation in which the choices of decisions available to a decision maker consist of at least one or more favorable results and one or more undesirable outcomes. Ethical violations could be as simple as failing to return phone calls or to answer emails within a reasonable time or a more serious violation of agency policy or procedure and even a grave violation such as the breach of federal or state penal law. Each correctional code of ethics therefore covers specific agency values, responsibilities, and obligations correctional staff must demonstrate to their stakeholders. These code of ethics documents are particularly helpful to pretrial, correction, probation, and parole officers as well as other correctional staff.

PROFESSIONALISM AND ETHICAL COMPLIANCES

Most professional codes of ethics, and particularly those applicable to correctional settings, emphasize integrity, honesty, and impartiality when dealing with the recipients of the services offered. The oath taken by correctional staff also demands that they faithfully serve offenders, victims, the criminal justice system, and the public at large who employ their services. Each correctional staff member must therefore uphold these and other principles such as, for example, those that are embedded in the American Probation and Parole Association's code of ethics in Box 10.1 and 10.2.

BOX 10.1: AMERICAN PROBATION AND PAROLE ASSOCIATION CODE OF ETHICS

I will render professional service to the justice system and the community at large in effecting the social adjustment of the offender.

I will uphold the law with dignity, displaying an awareness of my responsibility to offenders while recognizing the right of the public to be safeguarded from criminal activity.

I will strive to be objective in the performance of my duties, recognizing the inalienable rights of all persons, appreciating the inherent worth of the individual, and respecting those confidences which can be reposed in me.

I will conduct my personal life with decorum, neither accepting nor granting favors in connection with my office.

I will cooperate with my co-workers and related agencies and will continually strive to improve my professional competence through the seeking and sharing of knowledge and understanding.

I will distinguish clearly, in public, between my statements and actions as an individual and as a representative of my profession.

I will encourage policy, procedures and personnel practices which will enable others to conduct themselves in accordance with the values, goals and objectives of the American Probation and Parole Association.

I recognize my office as a symbol of public faith and I accept it as a public trust to be held as long as I am true to the ethics of the American Probation and Parole Association.

I will constantly strive to achieve these objectives and ideals, dedicating myself to my chosen profession.

Source:

Federal Probation and Pretrial Officers Association. (2019). *Code of ethics*. Retrieved from https://www.fppoa.org/page/code-ethics

The obligations expressed in this document, and by the Federal Probation and Pretrial Officers Association and the American Probation and Parole Association code of ethics, represent the ethical values for pretrial, probation, correction, and parole agencies' standards for correctional staff and all those who make contact with juvenile offenders. The American Probation and Parole Association (APPA) is one of the largest professional national criminal justice systems. Its members are bound by the American Probation and Parole Association code of ethics.

The APPA documents state that pretrial and probation officers are ethically required to render professional service and to uphold all laws with dignity, especially criminal and constitutional laws and institutional policies and procedures. The APPA code of ethics also requires probation and parole officers to exercise respect for the worth of the individuals they serve and with whom they interact and to demonstrate professional competence at all times (American Probation and Parole Association, 2018).

BOX 10.2: FEDERAL PROBATION AND PRETRIAL OFFICERS ASSOCIATION CODE OF ETHICS

As a federal probation/pretrial services officer,

I am dedicated to rendering professional service to the courts, the parole authorities and the community at large in effecting the social adjustment of the offender and assuring the compliance of defendants with their legal responsibilities.

I will conduct my personal life with decorum, will neither accept nor grant favors in connection with my office, and will put loyalty to moral principles above personal consideration.

I will uphold the law with dignity and with complete awareness of the prestige and stature of the judicial system of which I am a part. I will be ever cognizant of my responsibility to the community which I serve.

I will strive to be objective in the performance of my duties, respect the inalienable rights of all persons, appreciate the inherent worth of the individual, and inviolate those confidences which can be reposed in me.

I will cooperate with my fellow workers and related agencies and will continually attempt to improve my professional standards through the seeking of knowledge and understanding.

I recognize my office as a symbol of public faith and I accept it as a public trust to be held as long as I am true to the ethics of the federal probation and pretrial services system. I will constantly strive to achieve these objectives and ideals, dedicating myself to my chosen profession.

Source:

Federal Probation and Pretrial Officers Association. (2019). *Code of ethics*. Retrieved from https://www.fppoa.org/

The principles and values expressed in the APPA are similar to those of the Federal Probation and Pretrial Officers Association (FPPOA), shown in Box 10.2. Specifically, the FPPOA obligates pretrial and probation officers to render professional service to courts; to remain faithful to their duties; to show respect for the law, policies, and procedures; to serve the criminal justice system with dignity; and to uphold the moral principles and values enshrined in the FPPOA code of ethics (Federal Probation and Pretrial Officers Association, 2019).

PROBATION AND PAROLE OFFICERS

The job of juvenile probation and parole officers is quite broad. The main tasks they perform include assessment and classification as well as the supervision of offenders. In addition, probation officers appear in court and speak to treatment teams about the qualifications of offenders for probation and other correctional interventions. Parole officers appear before parole boards and before treatment teams to talk about offender readiness for parole and to recommend specific correctional actions. In their supervisory and management roles, probation and parole officers make field visits to offenders' work places, schools, or homes. In addition, probation and parole officers are also required to investigate allegations pertaining to probation and parole violations and to prepare and submit investigative reports to juvenile courts. Probation and parole officers also have a duty to screen and classify offenders in order to determine appropriate therapeutic interventions. In order to adequately perform these important tasks, probation and parole officers must collect, interpret, and analyze information; talk to a range of people including offenders, witnesses, victims, and arresting officers; and read various reports pertaining to each offender.

The successful performance of each of these obligations means probation and parole officers have to constantly deal with challenging ethical issues. For example, probation officers have to decide on a regular basis about which information should be collected, which information should be disclosed to a third party, and which decisions should be made in response to a particular behavior or action by an offender. Thus, in order to prevent ethical violations, probation and parole officers are guided by established ethical standards such as those in Box 10.3 and 10.4.

BOX 10.3: AMERICAN CORRECTIONAL ASSOCIATION CODE OF ETHICS

The American Correctional Association expects of its members unfailing honesty, respect for the dignity and individuality of human beings and a commitment to professional and compassionate service. To this end, we subscribe to the following principles.

Members shall respect and protect the civil and legal rights of all individuals.

Members shall treat every professional situation with concern for the welfare of the individuals involved and with no intent to personal gain.

Members shall maintain relationships with colleagues to promote mutual respect within the profession and improve the quality of service.

Members shall make public criticism of their colleagues or their agencies only when warranted, verifiable, and constructive.

Members shall respect the importance of all disciplines within the criminal justice system and work to improve cooperation with each segment.

Members shall honor the public's right to information and share information with the public to the extent permitted by law subject to individuals' right to privacy.

Members shall respect and protect the right of the public to be safeguarded from criminal activity.

Members shall refrain from using their positions to secure personal privileges or advantages.

Members shall refrain from allowing personal interest to impair objectivity in the performance of duty while acting in an official capacity.

Members shall refrain from entering into any formal or informal activity or agreement which presents a conflict of interest or is inconsistent with the conscientious performance of duties.

Members shall refrain from accepting any gifts, services, or favors that is or appears to be improper or implies an obligation inconsistent with the free and objective exercise of professional duties.

Members shall clearly differentiate between personal views/statements and views/statements/positions made on behalf of the agency or Association.

Members shall report to appropriate authorities any corrupt or unethical behaviors in which there is sufficient evidence to justify review.

Members shall refrain from discriminating against any individual because of race, gender, creed, national origin, religious affiliation, age, disability, or any other type of prohibited discrimination.

Members shall preserve the integrity of private information; they shall refrain from seeking information on individuals beyond that which is necessary to implement responsibilities and perform their duties; members shall refrain from revealing nonpublic information unless expressly authorized to do so.

Members shall make all appointments, promotions, and dismissals in accordance with established civil service rules, applicable contract agreements, and individual merit, rather than furtherance of personal interests.

Members shall respect, promote, and contribute to a work place that is safe, healthy, and free of harassment in any form.

Source:
The American Correctional Association, *ACA Code Of Ethics*.

Specifically, the American Probation and Parole Association (APPA) and the American Correctional Association (ACA) unambiguously demand from their members (probation and parole officers) honesty, respect for the dignity and individuality of human beings, and commitment to professional and compassionate service including demonstration of trustworthiness, selflessness, and integrity. For example, the case reported in Box 10.3, demands that correctional staff professionally execute their official duties and asks that correctional staff to refrain from using their positions for personal gain and taking part in activities that present a conflict of interest.

Additionally, probation officers are officials of the court, and thus they are also subject to a code of judicial conduct, generally adopted by state supreme courts. Of course, there are variations of judicial codes of ethics, but such documents commonly emphasize judicial independence, impartiality, integrity, confidentiality, diligence, good public communication and association, prosocial extra-judicial behaviors that minimize the risk of conflict with judicial obligations, and compliance with the code of judicial conduct.

Detention Officers

The primary duties of detention officers consist of three important tasks: to detain offenders and keep them from escaping, to maintain security and peace within correctional institutions, and to offer treatment or rehabilitation to offenders. That is, detention officers must effectively and professionally maintain the safety of each detained youth and to ensure order within correctional facilities by ensuring the protection of offenders, correctional staff, visitors to correctional facilities, and property situated on correctional grounds.

The prevention of escape demands that offenders be kept safely guarded to ensure, in part, their availability for treatment and court proceedings (Palmer, 2010). These functions require a variety of official functions that demand frequent use of force consisting of any physical force directed toward an offender, either by direct physical contact; by the use of a weapon, including the use of chemicals such as teargas; and the use of verbal commands or warnings that threaten punishment. Excessive use of force, however, is unconstitutional. In addition, corrections officers house and supervised juvenile offenders for various offenses—serious breaches of penal law such as felony violence as well as minor offenses and nonviolent felonies such as illegal drug possession. The nature of these tasks, and the fact that detention officers are required to regularly interact with family members of each offender and that juvenile offenders constitute a vulnerable population because of their ages and their presence in secured facilities, means that detention officers have to abide by strict agency codes of ethics in addition to the general code of ethics for corrections officers.

Generally, agency codes of ethics for corrections officers demand that every correctional activity be informed by a legitimate therapeutic purpose. That is, offenders must be afforded evidence-based therapeutic services designed to prevent recidivism and to increase the success of the offenders both within and outside correctional facilities. The ACA also orders that officers attend to the welfare of the individuals, to respect and protect the rights of all individuals, to avoid any corrupt or unethical behavior, and to treat all individuals fairly without reference to race, gender, creed, national origin, religious affiliation, age, or disability.

Clinical Staff

The main function, at least in theory, of the juvenile justice system is to give each juvenile offender the tools, resources, and opportunities needed to reform their behaviors.

However, since judges and indeed most detention officers do not generally possess the required training or knowledge to effectively execute therapeutic goals, detention employees include a host of qualified mental health practitioners. The title *clinical staff* therefore covers any and all correctional staff that are directly responsible for the mental and medical needs and behavioral treatment of juvenile offenders within a correctional facility. The list therefore includes psychiatrists, psychologists, medical personnel, and caseworkers and managers. Among many other ethical challenges, these criminal justice practitioners regularly deal with whether to disclose to third parties some of the information they gather from offenders.

BOX 10.4: TO REPORT OR NOT REPORT SERIOUS THREATS: OBLIGATION OF CONFIDENTIALITY VERSUS THE DUTY TO WARN

Occasionally, criminal justice practitioners who work with youth at more intimate levels encounter offenders who threaten to inflict harm on other persons. Such incidents create ethical dilemmas for criminal justice practitioners, as happened for Dr. Lawrence Moore, who found himself having to deal with the murder of a young lady and a lawsuit in the late 1960s. In the case of *Tarasoff v. Regents of University of California* (1976), the California Supreme Court ruled that therapists, or indeed criminal justice practitioners, have a duty to warn potential victims about credible threats made by offenders.

Tatiana Tarasoff was a student at the University of California, Berkeley. She engaged in brief romantic activity with another student, Prosenjit Poddar, on New Year's Eve in 1968. Shortly after the encounter, she started dating other men. The move aggravated Mr. Poddar. During one of his sessions with Dr. Moore, a psychologist employed by the Cowell Memorial Hospital at the University of California, Berkeley, Poddar confessed that he intended to kill Ms. Tarasoff. Dr. Moore diagnosed Poddar with a mental disorder and consequently ordered him to be involuntarily committed to inpatient care for mental health needs. Dr. Moore did not, however, warn Tarasoff or her parents that Poddar had confessed to wanting to kill her. On October 27, 1969, Poddar killed Tarasoff in her home. Tarasoff's parents sued Dr. Moore and his employer, the Regents of the University of California, for negligence in failing to warn Tarasoff or her parents of the peril Poddar posed. During the legal proceeding, the university and Dr. Moore argued that they had no duty to inform Tarasoff or her parents and that they were also immune from legal liability under the California Tort Claims Act of 1963 (Gov. Code, § 810 ff.). The court rejected the defense and held that Dr. Moore had a duty to warn the victim.

Source:

Tarasoff v. Regents of University of California, Supreme Court of California, 551 P.2d 334 (Cal. 1976)

These groups of correctional staff perform functions that typically include the collection of information from various sources—detention, probation and parole officers, schools, parents, juvenile courts, victims, and indeed the offenders—and use all such information to assess and classify juvenile offenders and to prescribe evidence-based interventions in relation to particular behaviors. These important tasks are guided by standard professional as well as agency-specific codes of ethics relevant to the performance of such clinical duties.

CRITICAL ETHICAL ISSUES IN CORRECTIONAL FUNCTIONS

The wide range of roles played by each correctional staff member creates reasons for various categories of ethical violations, hence the need to understand common violations and critical ethical challenges. Obviously, there are many such critical issues, but those dealt with by every correctional staff member, irrespective of experience and character, in their contact with juvenile offenders are ethical issues relating to the use of force, personal boundaries, report writing and submission, information gathering, treatment of offenders, information management, and off-duty behavior as well as the ethical issues associated with the assessment and classification of offenders' risk and needs.

Off-Duty Ethical Issues

In most professions, life outside work is considered private and thus has little to do with professional obligations. In the correctional field, however, correctional staff are expected to conduct their private lives in ways that reflect well upon the employer. In addition, correctional staff are peace officers, and as such, they are required by law to uphold and obey all federal, state, and county laws as well as municipal ordinances. In addition, correctional staff are also required to comply with their agencies' policies, procedures, rules, regulations, and directives. Most of these expectations do not change even while staff are off duty. Accordingly, living a personal life that reflects dignity, respect for law, and exemplary citizenry is ethically required of every correctional staff member both on and off duty.

Off-duty ethical challenges come in various forms. For example, periodically, correctional staff accidentally run into offenders that they have come to know during the performance of their official duties. This is especially common in places where the chances of running into past clients is greater. In such encounters, a number of ethical problems emerge. For instance, the need or opportunity may arise to use the behavioral history of an offender as a point of reference for certain adverse actions, such as not renting to a past client because of his or her criminal or delinquent history. The need may also arise to initiate contact with the offender as a correctional officer, which may violate the privacy of the offender. Obviously, only ex-detainees may run into their former detention officers, or only ex-parolees or probationers may run into their old probation or parole officer. Certainly, any third person who is made aware that a person has a former probation or parole officer would easily conclude that such person has had an unwanted dealing with the criminal justice system. Of course, such knowledge can, among other factors, affect a person's employability and social relationships with severe consequences.

Information Gathering and Report Writing

At most levels of interaction with juvenile offenders, some documentation is required to support, explain, or justify decisions that affect offenders. Consequently, most offender interactions with clinical staff, including probation and parole officers, result in report writing. Also, probation and parole officers in particular rely on the information they gather from reviewing offenders' field files and criminal records, trial courts documents, and other reports that make their way into each offender's file. Such reports generally cover offenders' mental ability to adequately comply with court orders, prior civil records or ties to society, and social standing, plus the seriousness of alleged offenses and whether the offenses involved physical violence against persons. Offenders' field files also contain statements made by defendants, victims, and co-defendants to arresting officers, as well as offenders' medical, psychiatric, or psychological reports. A number of computing interests arise out of the process of writing reports.

Common ethical challenges include questions regarding the ethical necessity to conceal a source of information from a defendant, especially when doing so would raise questions about reliability, and the right of the defendant to challenge allegations made by the pretrial service or probation officer or the third party who provided the information. Furthermore, third-party access to information may also raise ethical questions.

Certainly, the Freedom of Information Act gives the public access to government documents. The law is intended to prevent governments from secretively taking actions that are designed to adversely affect a person without that person's knowledge and to allow the public to question or scrutinize the actions of public agencies (Cate, Fields, & McBain, 1994; Launay, 1988). The act also protects individual privacy, or more accurately, protects "personnel and medical files and similar files the disclosure of which would constitute a clearly unwarranted invasion of personal privacy." In short, the Act protects private information, generated by or in possession of the government that can be used to identify the legitimate owners of the information (Cateet al., 1994). However, the rights of the public and even the rights of correctional staff to information pertaining to offenders compete with the rights of the offenders to privacy.

Again, as with most ethical questions and dilemmas in working with juvenile offenders, there is no one-size-fits-all response to the ethical questions raised by report writing. In general, however, officers are expected to include only factual information in the reports they write, not to intentionally misrepresent any information, and to respect the anonymity of sources and the confidentiality of information that can be potentially linked to the identity of the sources, especially in situations where correctional staff promise the source complete confidentiality and anonymity in an attempt to gather such information. The ACA code of ethics specifically requests that correctional staff "preserve the integrity of private information" and "refrain from seeking information on individuals beyond that which is necessary to implement responsibilities" and from revealing nonpublic information without express authorization (American Correctional Association, 2018). These codes of ethics do not, however, solve the problem, although collectively these and existing federal and other agencies' policies, like the America Bar Association's, provide a basis for making ethical decisions.

The federal criminal justice system, in some states, allows the contents of the pretrial service officers to be disclosed to the defendants; other states give trial judges the discretion to disclose or conceal certain sources or content of the reports. Also, the American Bar Association has argued the importance of disclosing certain information, even when the disclosure of such information may create safety issues for the source and may force some witnesses to withhold important information, because the failure to disclose sources denies defendants the right to challenge inaccurate claims or allegations.

Excessive Use of Force

Sometimes working with offenders requires the use of force. In particular, correctional officers and clinical staff have to use force in certain situations in order to secure offenders' cooperation. Infliction of any pain without penological justification, however, constitutes an excessive use of force and thus a cruel and unusual act. The use of force is only permissible when all nonforceful options have failed and force is reasonably necessary to control an offender. Ethical questions arise around such contact when a particular use of force goes from being reasonable to unreasonable and in some cases to excessive and untherapeutic. That is, the proportionality of force as a legitimate response to a genuine threat presented by an offender is a critical determining factor as to what is ethical and what is not ethical.

The question of whether an action is reasonable or ethical depends on whether the officers' actions are "objectively reasonable" in light of the circumstances being confronted. In the end, however, what makes a particular use of force ethical or unethical is well-established, but what constitutes reasonable is debatable because it is the officer who determines the appropriateness of certain force under a given circumstance, that is, whether the level of force is appropriate given the degree of force against which the officer's force is directed. Indeed, the courts have argued that the "reasonableness" of a particular use of force must be judged from the perspective of a reasonable officer dealing with the situation, and the calculation must account for the fact that officers are often forced to make split-second decisions about the amount of force necessary in a particular situation (Palmer, 2010).

Need and Right to Know

Criminal justice practitioners are granted access to a wide range of personal information. The ethical challenge is whether accessing such information is justifiable. A justifiable need to know or not know something depends on whether knowledge of the information is reasonably related or beneficial to official and lawful functions.

The right to know and the need to know raise two separate questions: the right of correctional staff to access a particular fact and the need to know that fact. The right to know and the need to know also deal with the right of a third person to access a piece of information and the need to know such a fact. Ethical questions arise when an officer accesses an offender's personal information for purposes unrelated to the performance of that officer's official duty.

Unfortunately, as with all other ethical matters, the need to know something about an offender depends on the situation and the motivation informing the effort to know a particular piece of information (Cate et al., 1994; Hunter & Lexier, 1998; Reilly, 2014). In this regard, the right to know a particular piece of information does not mean that an officer needs to know such information under all conditions. For example, a probation officer has the right to access a juvenile offender's home address, but the officer does not have a need to know such information if the purpose for accessing such information is to avoid living in the same area as the juvenile offender.

Professional Training and Scope

Simply put, it is unethical for an unqualified person to perform a function that requires specialized training because if a person isn't properly trained, then the chances of hurting someone else get significantly higher than when a person is qualified to perform the same task. In this case, it is unethical to play psychologist if one is not a licensed mental health professional. It is also unethical to play judge if one is not wearing a robe and sitting as a judge or to play detective unless one has a badge to show the offender legitimate credentials. Also, medical training and a state-approved license are required for practicing medicine or diagnosing disease and for prescribing and administering medication. When an officer acts without qualifications, he or she may be violating the law as well as engaging in unethical practices. To avoid this unethical pitfall, correctional staff are required to act only within the scope of their prescribed authority and professional training.

Professionalism can prevent the occurrence of many ethical violations. For example, professionalism demands that correctional staff maintain self-control regardless of provocation to do otherwise and to show respect and care for all juvenile offenders without regard to race, age, religion, national origin, sexual orientation, gender, or disability. Professionalism demands that officers respect mutual trust, avoid verbal and physical altercations, maintain a courteous and professional demeanor at all times, be less an authoritative figure in interactions, and to refrain from any act that would contribute to the delinquency of a minor. It is also unprofessional and indeed unethical to emotionally, financially, or physically abuse or exploit offenders and to share with youth, or expose youth to, drugs, alcohol, or sexually explicit materials. Professionalism also means that corrections officers will report all conflict of interest cases to their immediate supervisors and will refrain from acting as the key decision maker in matters involving conflicts of interest (Chaplan, 1996).

CONSEQUENCES AND PREVENTION OF UNETHICAL CONDUCT

Ethical violations incur a variety of consequences, including verbal reprimand, written reprimand, suspension without pay, demotion, dismissal, and criminal prosecution. Beyond these consequences, most ethical violations produce victims. Most violations also increase the chance of unfair treatment, misuse of public resources, or violations of a penal law. To avoid these pitfalls, some established guidelines are applicable to all correctional staff who work with juvenile offenders, such as the principle to not cause harm to offenders.

Cause No Harm!

Although there is no such thing as a universal ethical norm applicable to all ethical problems, the phrase "first do no harm" is considered a standard principle that applies to all social workers, including correctional staff, psychologists, psychiatrists, other medical doctors, and social workers.

BOX 10.5: MANY PRACTITIONERS VICTIMIZE INNOCENT PEOPLE

One of the most disturbing statistics about the American criminal justice system is the fact that the Innocence Project, founded in 1992 by Peter Neufeld and Barry Scheck at Cardozo School of Law, has as of April 2019, helped secure the exoneration of 362 innocent persons wrongfully convicted and sentenced to long-term imprisonment. Some exonerated victims were sentenced to death or to life imprisonment without the possibility of parole. In fact, 20 of the 362 people who have been exonerated by postconviction DNA testing were on death row. On average, the wrongly convicted victims served 14 years in prison before exoneration.

Of course, wrongful adjudication is not common within the juvenile justice system, but the fact is that each wrongful conviction represents one or more criminal justice practitioners who either unethically failed to perform their due diligence or wrongfully prosecuted persons for offenses that they did not commit. In the end, one of the ways to minimize the victimization of youth who enter the juvenile justice system is to collect all necessary information that proves or disproves delinquent tendencies and behaviors and to make sure that reports are written accurately and decisions are informed by strong consideration of all the information available about each offender and his or her thoughts and behaviors.

Source:

Innocence Project (2019). *Exonerate the innocent*. Retrieved from https://www.innocenceproject.org/exonerate/

Unfortunately, as Sokol notes, "clinicians inflict harm all the time, whether it is by inserting a cannula, administering chemotherapy, performing a tracheotomy, opening an abdomen, or drilling into the skull" (Sokol, 2013). However, it is helpful for officers to operate within this frame of mind because although harm in its simplest form is unavoidable, a goal to harm no one can minimize harm to offenders. Indeed, at an individual level, correctional staff can "balance their obligation to benefit the patient (the principle beneficence) against their obligation not to cause harm (the principle of non-maleficence)" (Sokol, 2013, p. 23). Obviously, being aware of conflicts of interest and taking steps to avoid them can minimize the chances of causing harm to offenders.

Interpersonal Boundaries

Most people who have worked with juvenile offenders, especially in correctional facilities, recognize that staff-offender interaction frequently creates ethical situations that can easily lead to interpersonal boundary violations by staff. Interpersonal boundaries refer to ethical and legal lines between behavior that is acceptable, legal, or ethical, and what is not acceptable, legal, or ethical during staff interactions outside the narrow scope of professional duties. In the absence of good preemployment and in-service training, it is relatively easy for a correctional staff member to cross ethical and even legal boundaries that must be preserved during social interactions with juvenile offenders.

Interactions with both well-behaved and poorly behaved juvenile offenders can raise ethical problems under certain conditions. For example, when juvenile offenders are in a state of distress for reasons such as bad news or failure and/or disappointment over progress toward goals can create opportunities for a correctional staff member to lower expectations, at least to empathize, and can also emotionally push a correctional staff member to cross interpersonal boundaries. Examples of ethical violations that may arise out of these and other interpersonal interactions include harmful self-disclosure, preferential treatment, and, most commonly, the development of nonprofessional relationships.

Harmful self-disclosure involves a correctional staff member telling an offender personal information that may either increase the risk of delinquent and deviant behaviors or compromise correctional staff's ability to perform official duties. There are, however, situations where it is not easy to classify certain disclosures as harmful or harmless. For example, an officer who tells a substance abuser that he or she was once a substance abuser raises the possibility of either harming or helping such youth. The offender is helped if he or she receives such information as an assurance that substance abuse behavior can be rehabilitated. At the same time, if the offender takes the information as a guarantee that they can continue using the controlled substance and quit in the future just like the correctional staff member did, then the disclosure is of course harmful. At the same time, such disclosures can also be maliciously used against the officer in ways such as spreading rumors that the officer is a substance abuser.

Exploitation of relationships such as trading with youth; over-identifying with an offender; horse-playing with offenders; interaction with sexual overtones between staff and offenders; and giving offenders access to personal effects such as letters, photos, and phone numbers or home addresses is of course not criminal and in most institutions may not be explicitly prohibited, but these sorts of behaviors may open the door to serious ethical or legal violations. Many institutions, however, recognize that chances of unethical or illegal behaviors increase when staff spend an unexplainable amount of time with an offender, when staff are overly concerned about an offender, when staff work in a secluded area with offenders, when staff take juvenile detainees out of their cells at unusual times, or when staff delegate duties such as supervisory roles, cleaning, or other assignments to particular offenders. Similarly, the risk of a serious ethical or legal violation drastically increases when staff start bringing food items including soda and snacks to work, conversing with offenders in manners that are sexual in nature, including talking about the officer or the offender's physical attributes, and/or granting special requests or showing favoritism to a particular youth.

While it is important to recognize and appreciate diversity, differences, and similarities, the use of such markers as a basis for adverse or even favorable treatment is also both unethical and illegal in many cases. In fact, characteristics and attributes such as language, ethnic grouping, nationality, and gender are legally protected against discrimination. Also, while shared values, traditions, norms, and customs are not legally protected, it is unethical to use these attributes as a basis for adverse or discriminatory treatment or favoritism. Similarly, the use of racial remarks, sexual remarks, or stereotypes opens the door to unethical behaviors.

CONCLUSION

It is critically important to remember that codes of ethics regulate correctional staff behavior, not juvenile offenders' behavior. Hence, staff and not juvenile offenders are the ones who violate ethical codes. Broadly speaking, compliance with professional, legal, and ethical guidelines is generally enough to keep criminal justice practitioners from the pitfall of ethical violations. Recognizing the frequent occurrences of ethical violations and the fact that there are legitimate reasons for correctional staff to get frustrated, disgusted, or even angry in the performance of their official duties justifies the creation of and compliance with codes of ethics. Fortunately, however, these possibilities push correctional agencies to invest heavily in preemployment and postemployment training, and those correctional staff who take advantage of such training stand a better chance of avoiding ethical violations.

It is also important to keep in mind that the central goal for every code of ethics and for enforcement of ethical rules is to first and foremost prevent juvenile offenders from suffering unjustifiable pain and consequences that extend beyond the natural consequences of their own behaviors. Compliance with codes of ethics can also save correctional staff from the many harmful consequences guaranteed to befall those who engage in ethical violations. After all, codes of ethics in general require correctional staff to serve their clients with high degrees of courteousness, impartiality, civility, and respect for laws, rules, and humanity. They are instructed to respect the public faith entrusted to them and to live an honorable private life that shows respect for human dignity.

CRITICAL QUESTIONS

1. Do certain people have individual characteristics, attributes, or attitudes that make them likely to obey the ethical standards and conduct discussed in this chapter? If yes, why, and if no, why?
2. To what extent can ethical violations be completely avoided?

3. Should correctional agencies develop and enforce a juvenile-specific code of conduct, either as a therapeutic move or to safely guide correctional staff from falling victim to ethical violations, especially where the violation is a product of interpersonal interaction?
4. If a detention officer chooses to weep alongside a weeping offender in her cell after the offender has received depressing news, should the officer be disciplined for violating ethical expectations, and if so, what is the ethical violation?
5. Should all criminal justice practitioners have access to each offender's medical records? If yes, why, and if no why?

REFERENCES

American Correctional Association. (2018). *Code of ethics*. Retrieved from http://www.aca.org/ACA_Prod_IMIS/ACA_Member/Home/ACA_Member/Home.aspx

Federal Probation and Pretrial Officers Association. (2019). *Code of ethics*. Retrieved from https://www.fppoa.org/page/code-ethics

Cate, F. H., Fields, D. A., & McBain, J. K. (1994). The right to privacy and the public's right to know: The "central purpose" of the Freedom of Information Act. *Administrative Law Review, 46*(1), 41–74.

Chaplan, J. A. (1996). Youth perspectives on lawyers' ethics: A report on seven interviews. *Fordham Law Review, 64*(4), 1763–1784.

Federal Probation and Pretrial Officers Association. (2019). *Code of ethics*. Retrieved from https://www.fppoa.org/

Fisher, C. B. (1993). Integrating science and ethics in research with high-risk children and youth. *Social Policy Report, 7*(4), 1–27.

Fouka, G., & Mantzorou, M. (2011). What are the major ethical issues in conducting research? Is there a conflict between the research ethics and the nature of nursing? *Health Science Journal*, 5(5), 3–14.

Fowler, M. (2015). *Guide to the code of ethics for nurses with interpretive statements: Development, interpretation, and application*. Silver Spring, MD: American Nurses Association.

Hunter, J. A., & Lexier, L. J. (1998). Ethical and legal issues in the assessment and treatment of juvenile sex offenders. *Child Maltreatment, 3*(4), 339–348. doi:10.1177/1077559598003004006

Innocence Project. (2019). *Exonerate the innocent*. Retrieved from https://www.innocenceproject.org/exonerate/

Launay, R. (1988). Warriors and traders: The political organization of a West African chiefdom (Guerriers et commerçants: l'organisation politique d'une chefferie ouest-africaine). *Cahiers d'Études Africaines, 28*(111/112), 355–373.

Palmer, J. W. (2010). *Constitutional rights of prisoners* (9th ed.). New Providence, NJ: Mathew Bender.

Reilly, B. (2014). The public right-to-know on a need-to-know basis: Striking the balance between national security and environmental protection. *Boston College Environmental Affairs Law Review, 41*(2), 515–539.

Sokol, D. K. (2013). "First do no harm" revisited: Following the dictum means balacing moral principles. *British Medical Journal, 347*(7932), 23–23.

Tarasoff v. Regents of University of California, Supreme Court of California, 551 P.2d 334 (Cal. 1976).

CHAPTER ELEVEN

Crimes Against Children Domain

KEY FACTORS THAT influence delinquent and criminal behaviors include histories of sexual, physical, or emotional victimization; early aggressive behaviors; deficits in social, cognitive, or information-processing abilities; high emotional distress; exposure to violence and conflict in the family; and antisocial beliefs and attitudes (Centers for Disease Control and Prevention, 2017). Studies also show that in general over two-fifths of child offenders who are adjudicated or convicted of criminal wrongdoing in the United States have histories of being abused sexually, physically, or psychologically (Holder, Leary, & Hanes, 2011). Knowledge about these and other domains enhances criminal justice professionals' ability to explain past and present behaviors and to predict future criminal or delinquent activities.

This chapter discusses some of the measurable effects of sexual, physical, and psychological abuse on delinquency, incorrigibility, and criminality as well as ways that such abuse impacts mental health disorders and distorted thinking, attitudes, and behaviors, and informs criminal justice assessment and classification of risk and needs levels. In other words, this chapter explains the likely impact of abuse on offenders' past, present, and future thinking and behaviors.

Psychological, physical, and sexual abuse often lead to various forms of drugs and alcohol abuse, deviant acting out, and overt displays of incorrigibility, criminality, and delinquency. Unfortunately, however, national surveys of adolescents aimed at assessing the level of sexual, physical, and psychological abuse children suffer and how such acts subsequently affect children's mental health, and substance use, delinquent, incorrigible, and criminal behaviors show that a high number of youth 12 to 17 years old have indeed suffered sexual, physical, and psychological abuse at the hands of someone they know well. More precisely, about three-quarters (74.4%) of the 22.3 million 12- to 17-year-old youth in the United States have suffered one or more forms of abuse that have been linked to mental health disorders, criminality, and delinquency (Kilpatrick, Saunders, & Smith, 2003).

PHYSICAL VICTIMIZATION

National Survey of Adolescents (NSA) was conducted in 1995, when information about child abuse was held in many quarters as family secrets and viewed as a social normality and thus hardly came to the attention of authorities. The survey shows that at that time, approximately 3.9 million children age 12 to 17 suffered severe physical abuse each year (Kilpatrick et al., 2003). Later studies show that 18% of all aggravated assault cases reported to law enforcement agencies concerned male victims under age 18, and 16% of similar cases involved female victims under age 18 (Snyder & Sickmund, 2006). These numbers are important for criminal justice assessment and classification because a history of physical abuse is associated with alcohol and drug abuse, physical and sexual acting out, and long-lasting mental reenactments of trauma (Felson & Lane, 2009, p. 498).

Children who have suffered physical abuse are at higher risk of developing various forms of social, cognitive, emotional, and behavioral problems, including cognitive deficits and poor emotional competence, than those without such histories (Cipriano, Skowron, & Gatzke-Kopp, 2011; Holder et al., 2011; Kilpatrick et al., 2003; Starzyk & Marshall, 2003). Physical abuse takes many forms, but the most common form includes physical beatings and threats with weapons (including guns or knives) with the intent to kill or cause physical pain to the victim. According to the National Institute of Justice's youth victimization report, approximately six million, or 27%, of American children are subjected to these sorts of physical assaults each year, and about three-quarters (74.4%) of the 22.3 million youth age 12 to 17 years old in the United States suffer one or more forms of such abuse (Kilpatrick et al., 2003).

CHILDHOOD PHYSICAL ABUSE IS VERY DESTRUCTIVE

In a study examining how childhood physical abuse by parents impacts mid-life mental and physical health, Springer, Sheridan, Kuo, and Carnes (2007) found that 11.4% of respondents (10.6% of males and 12.1% of females) in their sample of 2,000 middle-aged men and women reported being physically abused by parents. After controlling for age, sex, childhood adversities, and family background, they also found that "childhood physical abuse predicted a graded increase in depression, anxiety, anger, physical symptoms, and medical diagnoses. Childhood physical abuse also predicted severe ill health and an array of specific medical diagnoses and physical symptoms. … [Further] childhood physical abuse predicted worse mental and physical health decades after the abuse" (Springer et al., 2007, p. 1).

Physical abuse seriously impacts the thinking and behavior of child victims. It is often a contributing factor behind mental health disorders, aggressive behaviors, substance abuse, sexual offending behaviors, and other forms of criminality, delinquency, and incorrigibility. For example, Felson and Lane (2009) studied nationally representative samples of inmates from state and federal facilities, finding that "offenders who have experienced physical abuse are more likely to commit violent offenses than nonviolent offenses" (p. 495), in part because "physically abused offenders learn a lesson about the use of violence generally" as a tool for solving social and personal problems (p. 498).

Research also shows that physical abuse and exposure to high degrees of violence at home, especially during childhood, increases the likelihood of future violent offending behaviors, particularly for boys. For instance, male children who are subjected to physical abuse during childhood are more likely than those who are not abused to use physical force against their dating partners (Starzyk & Marshall, 2003), and they tend to be more prone to physical aggression compared to girls (Evans, Davies, & DiLillo, 2008). Studies also show that "early onset of violence and delinquency is associated with more serious and chronic violence" (Hawkins et al., 2000, p. 3); although the level of intensity (minimum, medium, or high) of risk and needs levels for violence as a result of past physical abuse depends on factors such as history of aggressiveness, early shows of violent tendencies, access to firearms, and exposure to violence.

PSYCHOLOGICAL VICTIMIZATION

Each year, approximately 2.1 million children age 12 to 17 are subjected to a combination of physical and psychological abuse (Kilpatrick et al., 2003). This number is troubling because relationships between mental illnesses and histories of physical, sexual, and psychological abuse and criminal and delinquent behaviors have been well-documented (Springer et al., 2007). Emotional or psychological abuse refers to the humiliation of children and withholding of love, care, information, rights, and material goods from children for the sole purpose of subjecting them to some form of suffering. Other examples include isolation of victims from friends or other family members; denial of access to basic needs and resources; and messages of worthlessness, stupidity, ugliness, and unworthiness of protection from physical, sexual, financial, or psychological harm.

Overwhelming evidence shows that juveniles' sexual, physical, and psychological offending is in some cases partly informed by past sexual, physical, and psychological abuse. In particular, relationships exist between mental disorders and delinquent and criminal behaviors, undeveloped problem-solving skills, distorted thinking, and poor attitudes and behaviors, which in turn lead to substance abuse and other forms of antisocial behaviors (Cuevas, Finkelhor, Shattuck, Turner, & Hamby, 2013; Felson & Lane, 2009; Schubert, Mulvey, & Glasheen, 2011). Also, youth who make contact with the criminal justice system have disproportionately high rates of mental health disorders, between 50% and 70%, compared with nonoffenders, who account for about 9% to 21% of the general adolescent population (Schubert et al., 2011).

Children who are psychologically abused are at higher risk of developing various forms of social, emotional and behavioral problems as well as cognitive deficits that collectively weaken their ability to display healthy emotional competence (Cipriano et al., 2011; Holder et al., 2011; Kilpatrick et al., 2003; Starzyk & Marshall, 2003). That is, emotional or psychological abuse can lead to the development of serious mental health problems with serious consequences such as alcohol and drug abuse, physical and sexual acting out, and self-harm, including suicide, suicidal attempts, or suicidal ideation. Studies have found that compared to youth without mental disorders, youth with mental problems are also at higher risk of making unwanted contact with the criminal justice system and that those with co-occurring disorders are at even higher risk than those with no such history (Schubert et al., 2011).

Certain categories of childhood trauma, such as subjection to prolonged psychological victimization or extreme physical and/or sexual violence, have also been linked to abnormal thinking and behaviors such as "low self-worth and a profound feeling of powerlessness that can be relieved, if only temporarily, by the experience of total control over the fate of another person" (DeFronzo, Ditta, Hannon, & Prochnow, 2007, p. 5). Other repercussions of psychological abuse include doubting one's ability to remember events, questioning one's experience, feeling anger, feeling fear of sexual behaviors that would otherwise be considered normal by people without histories of abuse, feeling a sense of powerlessness, feeling unloved and undesirable, and feeling a sense of guilt, shame, and hatred toward self or those that appear to look or behave like them.

Psychological abuse can also lead to depression, low self-esteem, emotional incompetency, suicidal ideation, and lack of trust. In fact, some researchers have argued that "psychopathic and sexual sadist mental disorders" among serial killers can be traced to mistreatment during childhood, experience of childhood trauma, and psychological and physical abuse, which collectively impede the "conscience development" of children and halt their "psychosocial maturation" as well as imprint in their minds "perverse sexual inclinations" or "hatred for the person perceived as responsible for the maltreatment," all of which are later projected onto other persons who end up paying the ultimate price (DeFronzo et al., 2007, p. 5).

There are no scientifically credible estimates of the number of children who suffer psychological or emotional violence in part because data for emotional victimization of children are often combined with physical and sexual abuse figures. However, much can be deduced from what is known about the socioemotional impact of violent crimes on victims. For example, data from the National Crime Victimization Survey shows that about 68% of victims of serious violence suffer socioemotional problems as a consequence of their victimization. When the offender is an intimate partner, the victim suffers severe distress and socioemotional problems, especially when she is female, as female victims experience greater socioemotional problems than do male victims, regardless of the victim-offender relationship. About 91% of victims of violent crimes also exhibit socioemotional symptoms for a month or more, and 61% experience one or more physical symptoms for a month or more (Langton & Truman, 2014). Further, a total of 8.8 million, or 40%, of children are mentally traumatized by exposure to acts of violence involving other people, including close family members being shot, stabbed, sexually or physically assaulted, or verbally threatened with weapons, including guns (Kilpatrick et al., 2003).

SEXUAL VICTIMIZATION

One of the most common and devastating forms of abuse suffered by children is sexual abuse and exploitation in various forms. This form of victimization is also one of the key sources of mental health problems and delinquent, criminal, and incorrigible behaviors (Kilpatrick et al., 2003). Unfortunately, the number of children who suffer sexual abuse is alarmingly high. According to a 1995 national survey on child abuse, each year approximately 1.8 million children age 12 to 17 suffer sexual abuse (Kilpatrick et al., 2003). Recent studies show that about 67% of female victims of sexual assaults reported to law enforcement tend to be children under the age of 18, and 88% of male victims of sexual assaults tend to be under the age of 18 (Snyder & Sickmund, 2006).

The Center for Sex Offender Management, in collaboration with the U.S. Department of Justice, Office of Justice Programs; the National Institute of Corrections; the State Justice Institute; and the American Probation and Parole Association, defines sexual abuse as unwanted sexual contact between two or more minors, or any sexual contact between an adult and a minor or any unwanted sexual contact initiated by a youth toward an adult. The actual act of abuse may involve physical contact, such as deviant sexual touching, or virtual contact through Internet and cell phone communication technologies (Center for Sex

Offender Management, 2017). Generally, the legal definition of sexual abuse includes physical and sexual penetration of a child victim's vagina, mouth, or anus by an offender using a penis, finger, or object as well as the physical touching of the victims' sexual organs, the forcing of victims to touch offenders' sexual parts, or the forcing of child victims to perform sexual acts on the offenders. Sexual abuse also includes child pornography production, child sex tourism, and the commercial sexual exploitation of children.

According to the U.S. Department of Justice's National Sex Offender Public Website (NSOPW), 9.3% of all cases of maltreatment of children reported to law enforcement authorities in 2012 were classified as sexual abuse, and a total of 62,939 cases of child sexual abuse were reported in the same year (National Sex Offender Public Website, 2017). NSOPW also reports that 26% of the children who were sexually abused were in the age group of 12–14 years and 34% were younger than 9 years. Approximately one in six boys and one in four girls are sexually abused before the age of 18, and 35.8% of sexual assaults occur when the victim is between the ages of 12 and 17. Further, children between the ages of 16 and 19 are 3½ times more likely than people in the general population to be victims of rape, attempted rape, or sexual assault. These figures must also be read with the understanding that most sexual abuse cases are not reported to authorities. In fact, only 30% of all sexual assault cases are reported, many long after the fact. Child sexual victims are often too afraid to speak to anyone about their victimization because of perceived negative reactions from their parents or because they are terrified of being harmed by their abusers (National Sex Offender Public Website, 2017).

Sexual abuse produces a long list of negative effects that significantly impact the well-being and behavior of a child (Kilpatrick et al., 2003). The experience of sexual abuse can lead to the development of mental health disorders, abuse of alcohol and drugs, and victimization of others physically and sexually. Studies also show that children who are sexually abused are at higher risk of developing various problems such as precocious sexual behavior, poor social skills, inability to form and maintain healthy friendships, weakened capacity to demonstrate adequate understanding of interpersonal dynamics, and the inability to display cognitive and emotional competence (Cipriano et al., 2011; Holder et al., 2011; Kilpatrick et al., 2003; Starzyk & Marshall, 2003).

Sexual abuse has also been linked to mental health disorders, aggressive behaviors, substance abuse, and sexual victimization of others (Black et al., 2011). This broad effect is not, however, surprising because sexual abuse involves psychological and physical violence beyond the sexual violation of child victims. For example, the commercial exploitation of children physically and psychologically renders a great deal of damage to the childhood experience of victims, and in addition to the physical abuse children suffer at the hands of pimps, clients, and police, commercial sexual exploitation also leads "to low self-esteem, shame, guilt and a loss of self-respect," which are consequentially followed by "post-traumatic stress syndrome (PTSD), drug and alcohol abuse, and 'maladjustment' in adult life" (Kropiwnicki, 2012, pp. 235–236).

Similarly, beyond the physical and psychological harm associated with the production of child pornography, child pornography victims experience pain and suffering associated with flashbacks, sleeplessness, emotional isolation, anxiety, fear, feelings of shame and despair, worthlessness, hopelessness, disassociation, and difficulties in establishing and maintaining healthy emotional and sexual relationships (Wortley & Smallbone, 2006). Also, in addition to the pain associated with rape and sodomy most sexually abused children experience, the production of graphic child pornography images is also particularly damaging and painful because the mucosal lining of a child's vagina, anus, and rectum are very thin and thus easily rupture and result in painful tissue tears during sexual abuse (Fraley, 2012).

The impact of child sex tourism also includes physical and psychological problems, including the contraction of diseases such as HIV/AIDS and other STD infections, unwanted pregnancy at an early age, introduction and addiction to drug use, social stigmatization, and a host of psychological problems such as depression, post-traumatic stress disorder, and flashbacks of past sexual abuse (Youth Advocate Program International, n.d.). Even some of the child pornography production methods such as voyeurism that do not include physical interaction with child victims can have lasting psychological impact. As Wolak, Liberatore, and Levine (2014) note, for example, "victims who realize their images are trafficked online may suffer from knowing their images are viewed for sexual purposes" by strangers and possibly acquaintances alike (p. 348).

That is, in addition to the physical violence and psychological coercion, such as the threat of exposing images of victims to friends and family to force child victims to engage in sexually graphic or compromising activities (U.S. Department of Justice, 2010), and the physical and psychological pain and suffering victims experience during the production of child pornography, child victims also suffer from "additional psychological distress and harm through wondering whether they will be identified and whether viewers will believe they were complicit with their own abuse, drawing (incorrect) conclusions" (Gillespie, 2012). Indeed, a child's knowledge of his or her image being paraded around the world by pedophiles for the purpose of others' achieving deviant sexual pleasure is psychologically harmful. In the end, these sorts of thoughts can physically and psychologically brutalize the child victim further beyond the moment of the physical sexual abuse. The consequences of such pain manifest themselves in many ways including desensitization to sexual and physical abuse, involvement with drugs and alcohol, and the adoption of violence as a tool for negotiating social conflict.

Physical and psychological effects of sexual abuse manifest themselves in ways that commonly include the heightening of instinctive and sensory responses to any behaviors or events that contain characteristic resemblance to those associated with memories of past abusive events in ways that make it difficult for the abused child to live a normal life. Child victims may also feel ashamed, humiliated, and confused. Victims' inability to control such feelings and memories may then lead to anger and frustration directed at themselves or rage against their victims or a sense of confusion about what they might have done or not done. Sexual abuse also introduces victims to nonnormative sexual behaviors and experiences and further leaves the impression that the behavior they experience is normal, hence the likelihood that they will grow to engage in similar behavior.

THE PROCESS OF BECOMING SEX OFFENDER IS NOT STRAIGHTFORWARD

It is not always the case that victims of sexual, physical, and emotional abuse grow up to be sexual, psychological, and emotional abusers because many other factors explain sexual, violent, substance abuse, and other categories of offending behaviors beyond the history of past victimization. For example, studies show that physiological and biological differences, including sexual attraction to children, exposure to broader social messages supportive of aggression, exposure to domestic violence, easy access to victims, and high levels of stress, increase a person's chances of sexual offending behave or (Center for Sex Offender Management,

2017). There is, however, a close relationship between physical, sexual, psychological, or emotional abuse and a host of adverse effects including compromised physical health. It is therefore logical to expect that juvenile offenders with a history of sexual, physical, or emotional abuse would manifest a greater degree of risk than those with no such history of co-occurring risk and needs—meaning offenders having medium or higher risk and needs in at least two or more domains (substance, sexual, aggression, and/or mental health disorders).

Sexual abuse has been linked to the commission of sexual offenses by victims both as adolescents and adults. For example, Felson and Lane's (2009) study of nationally representative samples of inmates from state and federal facilities shows that sexual abuse against children has strong associations with violent sexual offenses by abused children, in part because abused offenders learn from their abusers that the behavior is acceptable (p. 498). For these reasons, any mention of an offender suffering sexual abuse in the past should therefore be thoroughly investigated so as to ascertain the correct level of risk and needs associated with sexual abuse. Of particular clinical value in the process is the number of sexual activities, ages of victims and the offenders, types of sexual abuse, degrees of physical pain, and gravity of sexual exposure. Collectively, the ages of the victims, the number and types of sexual acts, and the degree of exposure and pain suffered by victims create a better clinical picture of the extent to which the victim suffered and continues to suffer as a result of the sexual abuse—which is a measurement of the needs—and a good assessment of the extent to which the experience will influence the victim's future decision-making and criminal and delinquent behaviors.

EXPOSURE TO VIOLENCE

Certain acts of violence, although not directed at children, may have adverse effects on the thinking and behavior of youth. Among the most commonly cited and researched as having effects on children are exposure to violence in a domestic setting and through mass media. In support of the latter, a well-documented UNICEF study shows that "children who live with and are aware of violence in the home face many challenges and risks that can last throughout their lives" and thus there is "significant risk of ever-increasing harm to the child's physical, emotional and social development" and "a strong likelihood that this will become a continuing cycle of violence for the next generation" (UNICEF, 2017, p. 7). However, although exposure to violence, particularly in domestic and interpersonal settings, impacts future violent behaviors of offenders (Fantuzzo & Mohr, 1999; UNICEF, 2017), the extent to which the media or nondomestic or interpersonal violence impacts future behaviors of children remains debatable.

Indeed, much of the argument about the role played by media in youth violence revolves around the violent behaviors of American children. The debate about media influence gained steam in the period immediately following Eric Harris and Dylan Klebold's 1999 Columbine High School massacre. The two high school seniors shot dead 12 students and one teacher and injured more than two dozen (Moore, 2003). The problem with the media-blaming argument, however, is that in the era of technologically aided global interconnectedness and interdependence, children in particularly advanced countries are exposed to as much violence on television and the Internet and in movies and video games as are American children. Yet, the number of violent incidents perpetrated by youth in these places falls far below the rate in the United States.

Children born and raised in violent regions of the world do not necessarily turn out more violent than American children. That is, there is no evidence that children in Europe, where some of the world's most peaceful countries are located, are less delinquent in terms of sexual, violent, substance abuse, and other crimes than are children from some of the world's most violent territories in places such as the Middle East, Latin America, and Africa. Similarly, European American children are not more or less delinquent than Middle Eastern, Latin, or African American children, nor are children from Sudan, Central African Republic, Honduras, Guatemala, El Salvador, Somalia, Syria, Iraq, or Yemen at a greater chance of committing violent crimes because of their exposure to violence in those countries.

CONCLUSION

Evidently, not all children who are abused (physically, sexually, or psychologically) go on to become offenders or emotional wrecks, but there is solid empirical evidence in sociolegal, criminological, psychological, and medical literature that child abuse of any kind—sexual, physical, or psychological—increases the likelihood of future criminal and deviant behaviors, particularly in the area of sexual offending, violence, and substance abuse (Cuevas et al., 2013). Histories of physical, sexual, and psychological abuse are therefore some of the well-established measurements of risk and needs levels, as many child offenders engaging in delinquent and criminal behaviors were at some point in their lives physically, sexually and or psychologically victimized.

DISCUSSION QUESTIONS

1. Which theory clearly explains why some abused children become abusers?
2. What are some of the main distinctions between physical abuse and psychological abuse?
3. When addressing an offender's delinquent or criminal behaviors, how much attention should be paid to the offender's history of victimization?
4. Children who are sexually abused are at higher risk than victims of psychological abuse to sexually offend other children, during their childhood and/or as adults. Why?
5. How can one avoid pushing a child offender to believe that the person who victimized them is responsible for their delinquent and criminal behaviors?
6. Should probation or parole officers concern themselves more with the victimization a child offender suffered or with the child offender's own behaviors?
7. Is one form of victimization (violent, sexual, or psychological) more harmful than the others?
8. Why do some victims of sexual, violent, and psychological abuse become offenders while other take the complete opposite path?

REFERENCES

Black, M. C., Basile, K. C., Breiding, M. J., Smith, S. G., Walters, M. L., Merrick, M. T., ... Stevens, M. R. (2011). *National intimate partner and sexual violence survey: 2010 summary report.* Retrieved from the Centers for Disease Control and Prevention website: http://www.cdc.gov/violenceprevention/pdf/nisvs_report2010-a.pdf

Center for Sex Offender Management. (2017). *Fact sheet: What you need to know about sex offenders.* Retrieved from http://www.csom.org/pubs/needtoknow_fs.pdf

Centers for Disease Control and Prevention. (2017). *Risk and protective factors.* Retrieved from https://www.cdc.gov/violenceprevention/youthviolence/riskprotectivefactors.html

Cipriano, E. A., Skowron, E. A., & Gatzke-Kopp, L. M. (2011). Preschool children's cardiac reactivity moderates relations between exposure to family violence and emotional adjustment. *Child Maltreatment, 16*(3), 205–215.

Cuevas, C. A., Finkelhor, D., Shattuck, A., Turner, H., & Hamby, S. (2013). *Children's exposure to violence and the intersection between delinquency and victimization.* Retrieved from the Office of Juvenile Justice and Deliquency Prevention website: http://www.ojjdp.gov/pubs/240555.pdf

DeFronzo, J., Ditta, A., Hannon, L., & Prochnow, J. (2007). Male serial homicide: The influence of cultural and structural variables. *Homicide Studies, 11*(1), 3–14.

Evans, S. E., Davies, C., & DiLillo, D. (2008). Exposure to domestic violence: A meta-analysis of child and adolescent outcomes. *Aggression and Violent Behavior, 13*(2), 131–140.

Fantuzzo, J. W., & Mohr, W. K. (1999). Prevalence and effects of child exposure to domestic violence. *The Future of Children, 9*(3), 21–32. doi:10.2307/1602779

Felson, R. B., & Lane, K. J. (2009). Social learning, sexual and physical abuse, and adult crime. *Aggressive Behavior, 35*(6), 489–501.

Fraley, A. (2012). Child sex tourism legislation under the PROTECT Act: Does it really protect? *St. John's Law Review, 79*(2), 445–483.

Gillespie, A. A. (2012). Jurisdictional issues concerning online child pornography. *International Journal of Law and Information Technology, 20*(3), 151 177.

Hawkins, J. D., Herrenkohl, T. I., Farrington, D. P., Brewer, D., Catalano, R. F., Harachi, T. W., & Cothern, L. (2000). *Predictors of youth violence.* Retrieved from the National Criminal Justice Reference Service website: https://www.ncjrs.gov/pdffiles1/ojjdp/179065.pdf

Holder, E. H., Leary, M. L., & Hanes, M. (2011). *How OJJDP is working for youth justice and safety: 2011 annual report.* Retrieved from the Office of Juvenile Justice and Deliquency Prevention website: https://www.ojjdp.gov/pubs/238638.pdf

Kilpatrick, D. G., Saunders, B. E., & Smith, D. W. (2003). *Youth victimization: Prevalence and implications.* Retieved from the National Criminal Justice Reference Service website: https://www.ncjrs.gov/pdffiles1/nij/194972.pdf

Kropiwnicki, Z. O. D. S. (2012). The politics of child prostitution in South Africa. *Journal of Contemporary African Studies, 30*(2), 235–265.

Langton, L., & Truman, J. (2014). *Socio-emotional impact of violent crime.* Retrieved from the Bureau of Justice Statistics website: https://www.bjs.gov/content/pub/pdf/sivc.pdf

Moore, M. (Producer). (2003). *Bowling for Columbine* [Documentary film]. United States of America, MGM Home Entertainment.

National Sex Offender Public Website. (2017). *Raising awareness about sexual abuse: Facts and statistics.* Retrieved from https://www.nsopw.gov/en-US/Education/FactsStatistics

Schubert, C. A., Mulvey, E. P., & Glasheen, C. (2011). Influence of mental health and substance use problems and criminogenic risk on outcomes in serious juvenile offenders. *Journal of the American Academy of Child & Adolescent Psychiatry, 50*(9), 925–937.

Snyder, H. N., & Sickmund, M. (2006). *Juvenile offenders and victims: 2006 national report.* Retrieved from the Office of Juvenile Justice and Deliquency Prevention website: https://www.ojjdp.gov/ojstatbb/nr2006/downloads/nr2006.pdf

Springer, K. W., Sheridan, J., Kuo, D., & Carnes, M. (2007). Long-term physical and mental health consequences of childhood physical abuse: Results from a large population-based sample of men and women. *Child Abuse and Neglect 31*(5), 517–530. doi:10.1016/j.chiabu.2007.01.003

Starzyk, K. B., & Marshall, W. L. (2003). Childhood family and personological risk factors for sexual offending. *Aggression and Violent Behavior, 8*(1), 93–105.

UNICEF. (2017). *Behind closed doors: The impact of domestic violence on children.* Retrieved from https://www.unicef.org/media/files/BehindClosedDoors.pdf

U.S. Department of Justice. (2010). *The national strategy for child exploitation prevention and interdiction.* Retrieved from https://www.justice.gov/psc/docs/natstrategyreport.pdf

Wolak, J., Liberatore, M., & Levine, B. N. (2014). Measuring a year of child pornography trafficking by U.S. computers on a peer-to-peer network. *Child Abuse & Neglect, 38*(2), 347–356.

Wortley, R., & Smallbone, S. (2006). *Child pornography on the Internet: Guide No. 41.* Retrieved from the Center for Problem-Oriented Policing website: https://popcenter.asu.edu/content/child-pornography-internet-0

Youth Advocate Program International. (n.d.). *CSEC and child trafficking: Issue summary.* Retrieved from http://yapi.org/csec-and-child-trafficking/

CHAPTER TWELVE

Prosocial and Antisocial Domains

MULTITUDES OF FACTORS explain delinquent and criminal behavior. However, an overwhelming number of studies show that family history and behavior, peer social influence, use of structured and unstructured leisure time, educational achievement and potential, and employment history and potential have strong predictive values. Hence, knowledge about these factors and how they actually inform delinquent and criminal behaviors enhances criminal justice professionals' ability to explain past and present behaviors and to predict future criminal or delinquent activities. Understanding the likely impact on behaviors and thinking of an offender's peer associations, family dynamics, use of free time, academic achievement, and employment history also enables criminal justice practitioners to more accurately assess and predict the manner in which an offender's social history may inform recidivism.

This chapter discusses the impact of the offenders' family dynamics, and social interaction with family members, friends, and prosocial institutions as well as how such interactions inform offenders' thinking and behavior. It specifically covers how offenders relate to the external world and how those relationships interact with offenders' thinking and behaviors. Educational preparedness, family dynamics, peer relationships, leisure time, and social interaction, skills, and control are discussed as factors that can influence delinquent and criminal behaviors and are thus critical for predicting future behavioral outcomes.

By educational preparedness, this chapter is referring to the acquisition of minimal education and the readiness of the offender to seek and maintain gainful employment using the acquired education. Family dynamics refers to the relevant family history, social functions, beliefs, and attitudes that studies show have the potential to shape offenders' thinking and behavior. Peer relationships covers the types of friends (antisocial or prosocial) an offender entertains and how the thinking and behaviors of those friends may influence the offender's thinking and behavior. Leisure time means the types of structured or unstructured social activities an offender engages in during free time. Social interaction, skills, and control covers an offender's attachment or lack thereof to key prosocial institutions such as an offender's family and school community.

EMPLOYMENT PREPAREDNESS

Socioeconomic factors inform a high number of particular survival-type crimes and delinquent activities; therefore, a youth's potential for gainful employment is a good predictor of future criminal and delinquent behavior. Employment potential does not necessarily mean having past employment history, but it does include willingness and readiness to take up employment. Legitimate employment history can be used to measure employability and the offender's ability to maintain stable sources of legitimate income, the willingness to follow instructions, and the motivation to excel in a chosen field. Motivation in this process may be hard to gauge, but it is obvious that youth who ask about legitimate career paths show lower risk than those who argue that formal employment or a career path is irrelevant.

The employment risk level for those who do not have employment history can be calculated using acquired employment skills, short- and long-term employment goals, and the type of future job the offender desires. For example, the youth who shows interest in becoming a nurse, police officer, fire fighter, teacher, medical doctor, professor, lawyer, or politician is at high likelihood of achieving occupational goals because genuine interest in any of these jobs represents a certain level of courage needed to achieve such academic outcomes. Furthermore, professed interest in civil service shows that the offender has some healthy prosocial attitudes toward the responsibilities that come with the holding of each office. Employment risk can also be calculated by measuring the level of a child's commitment to the pursuit of goals that are related to future prosocial careers.

EDUCATIONAL PREPAREDNESS

A strong consensus among researchers holds that poor academic achievement is a good predictor of future criminal and delinquent behavior in part because strong academic achievement often opens doors to postsecondary education, which ultimately increases the chance of gainful employment (Mallaney, 2014). There is also a well-established relationship between school attachment and academic achievement because attachment to school is positively related to academic achievement, and higher grades strengthen individuals' attachment to schools (Hoffmann, Erickson, & Spence, 2013). Achievement here refers to an offender's love, care, and respect for all that for which a school stands. Attachment is, of course, a factor that enhances the chance of getting a good grade, and good grades increase the possibility of living a prosocial life.

Research on the relationship between academic achievement and delinquency has shown that children who perform poorly in school for reasons such as not paying attention in class, not trying hard enough, failing to identify with school, finding school unpleasant, and placing less value on success in school-related activities are more likely to drop out of school and thus generally tend to have higher risk of engaging in delinquent and criminal activities than children who engage in school-related activities and tasks. The connection between poor school performance and prosocial lifestyles can also be cued from the fact that poor grades place youth at a high risk of dropping out of school, and poor grades can also easily pave the way for a bleak future with regard to gainful employment and economic prosperity. Similarly, studies show that bonding to school is a protective factor against criminal and delinquent activities (Akers, Sellers, & Jennings, 2017; Williams & McShane, 2018).

Bonding to school means attachment to and interaction with teachers and participation in school-sponsored activities. Relationship between bonding to school and educational achievement is positive because as the degree of bonding goes up, so does academic achievement. However, the relationship between bonding to school and criminal and delinquent behaviors is negative—meaning as attachment to school increases the chances of criminal or delinquent activity drops significantly (Hawkins et al., 2000).

Active ties to or engagement in school promotes "competencies and values that allow adolescents to successfully transition into adulthood" (Wang & Fredricks, 2014, p. 722). The absence of ties to school may therefore signifies a lack of reasonable motivation that could generally shape the youth's "capacity to deal with difficulties and obstacles in school"; therefore, adolescents "who are emotionally attached and connected to school may show less risky behavior because they generally strive to meet society's expectations and are more likely to form supportive relations with teachers and other engaged peers" (p. 723).

Academic failure and success are, however, radically dynamic factors compared to other factors because transition from high academic achievement to failure can be dramatically effected within a very short period. Criminal justice assessment and classification therefore focuses on how well a youth is tied to school, history of academic performance, and academic motivation level. Additionally, bonding to school can be measured by calculating the level of a youth's participation in extra curriculum activities and an offender's academic strength and weakness. The risk can be assessed by measuring factors such as academic goals, grades, and school-related behaviors and problems. The extent to which a child is attached to school depends on a number of factors, such as membership in a student club, shows of respect and admiration for high educational expectations, school performance, history of school suspensions, level of educational aspirations, and degree of commitment to academic excellence.

FAMILY DYNAMICS

The techniques and attitudes needed to sustain criminal or delinquent behaviors are more easily learned through interactions with antisocial family members, and delinquency and criminal activities flourish more easily in a socially disorganized environment. On the contrary, prosocial family members are good sources of protective factors that can insulate youth from many risk and criminogenic factors. Family members are therefore good sources of information for understanding an offender's past, present, and future behaviors as well as an offender's risk level. This premise is supported by many criminological and sociological theories, such as social control, social learning, social bond, and differential association theories, which collectively pay special tribute to the important roles family members play in shaping children's behaviors as well as their physical and psychological development.

Theories such as social learning, social bond, differential association, and social control argue that the extent to which a child is emotionally and physically attached to his or her family can provide a good idea about the degree to which family members negatively or positively impact a child's prosocial and antisocial behaviors and thoughts (Akers et al., 2017). This idea is consistent with many studies which show that antisocial families are more likely than prosocial families to produce high-risk children because children learn both criminal and noncriminal or delinquent behaviors as well as the rationalization, beliefs, and values that inform good and bad behaviors through social interactions with close family members

(Smith & Stern, 1997; Simons, Simons, & Wallace, 2004; Staff, Whichard, Siennick, & Maggs, 2015; Evans, Simons, & Simons, 2016). As such, families that promote antisocial attitudes and beliefs or engage in criminogenic behaviors place children at greater risk of internalizing those negative beliefs and attitudes, and such children are therefore more likely to view antisocial behaviors favorably.

Indeed, "one of the most significant systems in child and adolescent development is the family. Families are considered to be a frontline defense against delinquency" (Smith & Stern, 1997, p. 382). The nature of relationships between a child and his or her family is therefore a critical source of information for predicting a child's beliefs, values, and prosocial and antisocial behaviors and tendencies.

SOME WAYS FAMILIES MAKE AT-RISK YOUTH

A family's attitudes and beliefs that portray physical, physiological, psychological, or socioeconomic and political limitations—whether caused by legitimate gender disadvantage, mental deficiency, or socioeconomic and political obstacles—as grounds for working extra hard are likely to produce a well-prepared child. Indeed, it is true that an economically depressed or underprivileged person would benefit most from a value that teaches hard work and perseverance, and any child would benefit from a family that imparts in their children the value of seeing limitations as reasons for increased prosocial efforts. Inevitably, children who are exposed to such values and beliefs are more likely to take firm ownership of their circumstances and are therefore likely to emerge victorious.

The children at risk of becoming victims of their own limitations are those who are taught to use their unfavorable conditions as reasons for hopelessness and explanations for their own failures. Those children's families inculcate in them values and beliefs that push them to view their limitations as sources of constraint, and those children are therefore unlikely to overcome their limitations. Equally, families that encourage or tolerate antisocial attitudes and activities as a normal way of life can drastically increase their children's likelihood of engaging in delinquent and criminal activities. The children cared for by such families may also be at greater risk of viewing crimes and delinquency as a legitimate or normal social or domestic endeavor.

The function of the family is important with regard to physical parental control. Indeed, studies show that ineffective parental control increases youth's risk of delinquency or criminality (Piquero et al., 2016). Therefore, the degree of parental supervision a youth receives can be a good source of information about a youth's likely risk of acting on delinquent or criminal urges or engaging in behaviors that would potentially increase the risk of committing criminal or delinquent acts. Hence, information about the level of parental supervision a youth receives can tell a lot about a youth's risk level.

The relationship between parental ties, juvenile delinquency, and criminality is an inverse one in that children who are attached to their parents are less likely to engage in delinquent and criminal behaviors. This also means that children who come from dysfunctional families are at higher risk of adopting criminal and delinquent life styles than children who come from prosocial families (Hawkins et al., 2000; Brannigan, Gemmell, Pevalin, & Wade, 2002). A dysfunctional family in this context is one that physically, sexually, or psychologically abuses children, exposes children to antisocial thoughts and behaviors, or deprives children of love and care, which in turn leads children to think that antisocial behavior is a legitimate means for achieving compliance, gaining control over others, and settling social disputes and disagreements.

Dysfunctional family environments impact children in many ways. For instance, studies have consistently shown that children whose parents are unloving or abusive are at high risk of behaving in accordance with the distorted perception of the causes of their rejection and abusive history (Skrapec, 2001, p. 52). It is therefore not surprising that children from families with a high history of violence tend to show "poorer emotional adjustment" than children from families with no such history (Cipriano, Skowron, & Gatzke-Kopp, 2011, p. 207). As Wooditch, Tang, and Taxman (2013) note, "strong family relations are important to reducing offending behavior" in part because prosocial families provide emotional support, facilitate the change processes children go through as they transition from childhood to adulthood, and insulate youth from criminal and delinquent influences and behavior, including illicit substance use (p. 279).

SOME CORE FACTORS ASSOCIATED WITH FAMILY

The impact of each family on a child's behaviors, beliefs, and attitudes depends largely on factors such as (1) how emotionally and physically attached a child is to the family, (2) the level of antisocial and prosocial attitudes and activities to which the family exposes a child, (3) the amount of control a family exercises over a child, and (4) how much protection against physical and psychological harm a family provides for a child. The risk and needs levels associated with an offender's family domain can also be assessed by measuring the degree and level of criminality associated with an offender's family; the presence or absence of conflict at home; the level of delinquency and criminality associated with an offender's family members; the level of supervision the offender receives from parents and guardians; the history of physical, sexual, and mental abuse; the family's prosocial and antisocial thinking, beliefs, attitudes, and behaviors; the strength of the link between the offender's behaviors and the family's antisocial thoughts and behaviors; and the view of the offender regarding the importance of the family to the offender's life.

Unquestionably, the family is usually the first social institution with which children make contact, and as such, the institution of family is a key source of basic knowledge about many important factors, such as attitudes, beliefs, thinking processes, and behaviors. Families play leading roles in cementing in the minds of children what is right and wrong, moral and immoral, important and less important, and the correct or wrong way to attend to most social, physiological, and psychological needs.

PEER RELATIONSHIPS

Children learn criminal and delinquent behaviors, techniques, and motivation through interactions with those who are close to them (Burgess & Akers, 1966; Akers et al. 2017; Williams & McShane, 2018). For children this means peer relationships are a critical part of the equation because peers are arguably the most important factor when discussing causes of delinquency. Of course, the extent of the impact of the relationship on both the offender and the offender's risk level depends largely on the strength of the relationship, the views and actions of the friends, and how frequently and effectively peers directly and indirectly reinforce delinquent and criminal thinking and behaviors (Burgess & Akers, 1966; Payne & Cornwell, 2007).

Friends have a strong impact on the behaviors of their peers, and for that reason children who befriend antisocial peers have a high chance of engaging in criminal and delinquent behaviors due to factors such as direct and indirect pressure (Hawkins et al., 2000). Direct peer pressure takes place when youth directly ask one or more of their peers to participate in antisocial acts. Indirect pressure occurs through observing the social rewards and consequences that are dished out by peers to other friends for participating or not participating in illegal or deviant acts and through exposure to antisocial behaviors including criminogenic activities that by nature directly increase the chances of more delinquent and criminal behaviors and thus involuntary contact with the criminal justice system. Additionally, the presence of negative peers makes antisocial acts more rewarding because such behaviors tend to be rewarded with praise, admiration, and physical rewards by friends.

At-risk youth surround themselves with antisocial peers because such relationships help them feel fearless when engaging in delinquent and criminal behavior, because their peers literally are on the lookout while they engage in delinquent and criminal acts, and because of the reassurances that, when needed, the peers will zealously collaborate any defensive stance that might be needed in order to escape the negative ramifications of their behaviors. Collectively, the negative effect of associating with negative peers makes it hard for troubled youth to fully understand the extent to which they are drifting away from a prosocial life style.

According to Sutherland's (1947) differential association theory, offenders master the techniques and motives of crime and delinquency in the company of peers and associates who are equally delinquent (Burgess & Akers, 1966; Williams & McShane, 2018). As a result, negative peers rationalize and reinforce criminal and delinquent thinking and behavior, including some of the most harmful and risky behaviors that have been linked to negative peer influence such as substance abuse, violence, and illegal sexual activities (Burgess & Akers, 1966; Payne & Cornwell, 2007; Augustyn & McGloin, 2013; Boisvert, Boutwell, Vaske, & Newsome, 2014; Hughes & Short, 2014). This is particularly problematic because increased association with negative peers often takes place in unstructured and unsupervised environments where antisocial behaviors including substance abuse and violence among adolescents are glorified and socially rewarded. As a result, in such environments antisocial acts will be a lot easier and more rewarding. For example, the "absence of authority figures reduces the potential for social control responses to deviance; and the lack of structure leaves time available for deviant behavior" (Hughes & Short, 2014).

Friendships among at risk youth are formed out of self-selection; therefore, friends generally resemble each other in the sense that they tend to have similar characteristics and attributes including race or ethnicity, attitudes and beliefs, school performance and educational aspirations, behavioral problems, and delinquent and criminal behaviors (Augustyn & McGloin, 2013). Association with deviant peers is therefore a strong predictor of criminal and delinquent conduct because outside the immediate circles of a youth's family, peers are important models from whom youth learn delinquent behavior and receive approval for and reinforcement of their delinquent and criminal behaviors (Payne & Cornwell, 2007; Kretschmer, Oliver, & Maughan, 2014).

Consequently, the assessment and classification of the peer relationship domain examines the impact of peer relationships on offenders' behaviors by assessing the history of drugs and alcohol use by the offender's peers, the offender's ability to resist antisocial influence and behaviors, the offender's attachment to responsible adult figures, and whether the offender engages in delinquency or criminal activities in the company of antisocial friends. The risk and needs levels in this domain can also be measured by looking at the age at which the youth initiated contact with negative peers, the extent to which the offender's friends or peers participate in the offender's delinquent or criminal behaviors, how the offender impacts peers' views, the extent to which the offender is influenced by antisocial peers, the offender's willingness to resist antisocial influences, and the offender's respect and admiration for prosocial peers. The assessment must also take note of the intensity of friendships, the number of friends who use controlled substances, the number of peers with criminal and delinquent histories, and the length and depth of friendships with the most troubled peers.

LEISURE TIME

Activities that people engage in during their leisure time are often representative of their normal behaviors, and thus teenagers' most delinquent and criminal acts, especially substance abuse use, sexual offending behaviors, and violent activities, take place during leisure time (Hirschi, 1969; Caldwell & Smith, 2006; Liebregts et al., 2015). Assessment and classification of leisure time is therefore about "what youth do with their time, where they do it, with whom they do it, and the social controls on their time use" as well as whether or not the leisure time is dominated by structured or unstructured activities (Caldwell & Smith, 2006, p. 399).

Unstructured use of free time typically lacks direct and indirect social control from authority figures, while structured activities tend to offer fewer opportunities to engage in antisocial behaviors. Unstructured activities are therefore major sources of risk factors that involve socializing with antisocial peers in a manner that generally "provides inherent situational inducements for deviance" (Augustyn & McGloin, 2013, p. 118). Unstructured use of free time oftentimes leads to antisocial activities because at-risk children, particularly teenagers, are not generally known for gathering together to discuss ongoing community projects, how to improve grades, plans for their futures, and/or the consequences of their behaviors.

On the contrary, structured leisure activities tend to generate protective factors because increased guidance and prosocial goal-oriented activities reduce delinquent and criminal behavior. Furthermore, structured activities during leisure time are less likely to lead to antisocial activities because leisure time is often organized in ways that are likely to produce positive results such as the acquisition of useful skills and knowledge and the improvement of health and cognition. In most cases, structured use of free time also involves prosocial peers and activities that take place in prosocial environments that are less likely to get youth into trouble (Caldwell & Smith, 2006; Wooditch et al., 2013).

Children who are well attached, committed, and involved with their families, schools, communities and other positive social institutions are less likely to be involved in antisocial activities during their free time. For instance, girls are significantly limited when it comes to the number of high-risk public locations that they are socially expected or allowed to frequent compared to male. Hence research shows "that at all levels of unstructured and unsupervised time with peers, girls engage in less predatory delinquency than boys do" (Augustyn & McGloin, 2013, p. 131).

PREDICTION OF LIKELIHOOD OF PARTICIPATING IN STRUCTURED ACTIVITIES WITH PROSOCIAL PEERS

An offender's leisure risks can be partly calculated through the measurement of the offender's ability to (1) resolve simple social problems, (2) to lodge complaints and reconcile differences, (3) to recognize and appropriately react to external feelings, (4) to respond appropriately to allegations, (5) to deal with frustration, (6) to engage in consequential thinking, (7) to avoid, cope with, or escape high-risk social confrontations, and finally (8) his or her types of structured and unstructured activities. These factors can predict the likelihood of a youth's participation in structured activities with prosocial peers.

Spending time with delinquent friends may increase the risk of engaging in delinquent and criminal acts because it makes it easier for the youth to offend and to be rewarded by their peers. Therefore, the degree to which an offender uses leisure time to engage in productive behaviors can significantly explain future criminal or delinquent behaviors and tendencies. The assumptions are that the more structured a leisure activity, the more productive, prosocial, and protective the end results tend to be.

SOCIAL INTERACTION AND SKILLS

Delinquent, criminal, and antisocial propensity and behaviors are partly influenced by individual social history in terms of the types of people with whom one interacts at both personal and professional levels and the kinds of beliefs, thoughts, and behaviors that define social interactions. In the case of youth, the impact of social interactions is usually very strong, of course depending on the types of thoughts, beliefs, and attitudes of the peers and family members with whom the youth interacts on a regular basis.

Indeed, social interactions help offenders develop social skills, enhance their coping skills, and learn how to deal with individual and collective social needs. Further, social interactions are a good mechanism through which youth learn to deal with getting offended by others and learn to face the consequences of offending others. Social skills are also important tools for developing and maintaining positive relationships with social institutions such as family and schools, and with other forms of public institutions, such as churches and work places, where social interaction and social skills are needed to independently and collectively function.

The logic behind the importance of social interaction is that the level of a youth's problem-solving skills, such as the ability to lodge complaints, reconcile contradictions, respond to allegations, deal with frustration, read facial expressions and feelings, communicate and respond to affection, and socially interact with others can improve individual socioeconomic standing in terms of school, employment, and relationships because good standing in each of these areas is inversely related to antisocial behaviors. Key assumptions are that weakened social and familial bonds to prosocial institutions, families, and friends increase the risk of delinquent and criminal behaviors. The criminal justice assessment and classification process therefore takes into account the thoughts, beliefs, attitudes, and behaviors of the offender's family members and friends and ways that the offender spends free time.

CONCLUSION

As with all risk and protective factors, the factors of educational preparedness, family dynamics, peer relationships, leisure time, social interaction and control do not guarantee even a single prosocial behavior, nor does the presence of "bad" or "good" educational preparedness, family dynamics, peer relationships, leisure time, or social interaction and skills mean an offender will engage in prosocial or antisocial behavior. The conclusion, however, is that the juvenile justice system is dominated by offenders who tend to have weak educational preparedness, poor family dynamics, negative peer relationships, unstructured leisure time, antisocial social interaction, and weak social control ties to critical institutions such as family and schools.

It is also deducible from this chapter that the possibility of living a successfully crime- and delinquent-free life requires deliberate effort. In particular, one has to invest in the pursuit of quality education and maintenance of good relationships with a healthy family. Further, one has to associate with prosocial peers and use leisure time wisely and in ways that further enhances a prosocial lifestyle. The good news, however, is that with the exception of family dynamics, the pursuit and achievement of these protective factors are within the reach of each offender who is willing to put forth the effort.

DISCUSSION QUESTIONS

1. Which domain has the strongest influence on future delinquent behaviors?
2. How does gainful employment affect the risk of participating in delinquent activities?
3. Which of the domains discussed in this chapter has the least impact on delinquent thinking and behaviors?
4. To what extent do the impacts of negative family relationships and interaction outweigh negative peer relationships and interaction?
5. Which domain has the weakest influence on recidivism?
6. Which is more harmful, negative family interactions or negative peer interactions?

REFERENCES

Akers, R. L., Sellers, C. S., & Jennings, W. G. (2017). *Criminological theories: Introduction, evaluation, and application*. New York, NY: Oxford University Press.

Augustyn, M. B., & McGloin, J. M. (2013). The risk of informal socializing with peers: Considering gender differences across predatory delinquency and substance use. *Justice Quarterly, 30*(1), 117–143.

Boisvert, D., Boutwell, B. B., Vaske, J., & Newsome, J. (2014). Genetic and environmental overlap between delinquent peer association and delinquency in adolescence. *Criminal Justice and Behavior, 41*(1), 58–74.

Brannigan, A., Gemmell, W., Pevalin, D. J., & Wade, T. J. (2002). Self-control and social control in childhood misconduct and aggression: The role of family structure, hyperactivity, and hostile parenting. *Canadian Journal of Criminology and Criminal Justice, 44*(2), 119–142.

Burgess, R. L., & Akers, R. L. (1966). A differential association-reinforcement theory of criminal behavior. *Social Problems, 14*(2), 128–147.

Caldwell, L. L., & Smith, E. A. (2006). Leisure as a context for youth development and delinquency prevention. *Australian and New Zealand Journal of Criminology, 39*(3), 398–418.

Cipriano, E. A., Skowron, E. A., & Gatzke-Kopp, L. M. (2011). Preschool children's cardiac reactivity moderates relations between exposure to family violence and emotional adjustment. *Child Maltreatment, 16*(3), 205–215.

Evans, S. Z., Simons, L. G., & Simons, R. L. (2016). Factors that influence trajectories of delinquency throughout adolescence. *Journal of Youth and Adolescence, 45*(1), 156–171.

Hawkins, J. D., Herrenkohl, T. I., Farrington, D. P., Brewer, D., Catalano, R. F., Harachi, T. W., & Cothern, L. (2000). *Predictors of youth violence.* Retrieved from the National Criminal Justice Reference Service website: https://www.ncjrs.gov/pdffiles1/ojjdp/179065.pdf

Hirschi, T. (1969). *Causes of delinquency.* Berkeley: University of California Press.

Hoffmann, J. P., Erickson, L. D., & Spence, K. R. (2013). Modeling the association between academic achievement and delinquency: An application of interactional theory. *Criminology, 51*(3), 629–660.

Hughes, L. A., & Short, J. F. (2014). Partying, cruising, and hanging in the streets: Gangs, routine activities, and delinquency and violence in Chicago, 1959–1962. *Journal of Quantitative Criminology, 30*(3), 415–451.

Kretschmer, T., Oliver, B. R., & Maughan, B. (2014). Pubertal development, spare time activities, and adolescent delinquency: Testing the contextual amplification hypothesis. *Journal of Youth and Adolescence, 43*(8), 1346–1360.

Liebregts, N., van der Pol, P., van Laar, M., de Graff, R., van den Brink, W., & Korf, D. J. (2015). The role of leisure and delinquency in frequent cannabis use and dependence trajectories among young adults. *International Journal of Drug Policy, 26*(2), 143–152.

Mallaney, S. (2014, January 3). Cause or effect: The relationship between academic achievement and delinquency in America. *Chicago Policy Review.* Retrieved from http://chicagopolicyreview.org/

Payne, D. C., & Cornwell, B. (2007). Reconsidering peer influences on delinquency: Do less proximate contacts matter? *Journal of Quantitative Criminology, 23*(2), 127–149.

Piquero, A. R., Jennings, W. G., Diamond, B., Farrington, D. P., Tremblay, R. E., Welsh, B. C., & Reingle Gonzalez, J. M. (2016). A meta-analysis update on the effects of early family/parent training programs on antisocial behavior and delinquency. *Journal of Experimental Criminology, 12*(2), 229–248.

Simons, R. L., Simons, L. G., & Wallace, L. E. (2004). *Families, delinquency, and crime: Linking society's most basic institution to antisocial behavior.* Los Angeles, CA: Oxford University Press.

Skrapec, C. A. (2001). Phenomenology and serial murder: Asking different questions. *Homicide Studies, 1*(5), 46–63.

Smith, C. A., & Stern, S. B. (1997). Delinquency and antisocial behavior: A review of family processes and intervention research. *Social Service Review, 71*(3), 382–420.

Staff, J., Whichard, C., Siennick, S., & Maggs, J. (2015). Early life risks, antisocial tendencies, and preteen delinquency. *Criminology, 53*(4), 677–701.

Sutherland, E. H. (1947). *Principles of criminology.* Chicago, IL: J. B. Lippincott.

Wang, M.-T., & Fredricks, J. A. (2014). The reciprocal links between school engagement, youth problem behaviors, and school dropout during adolescence. *Child Development, 85*(2), 722–737.

Williams, F. P., & McShane, M. D. (2018). *Criminological theory* (7th ed.). New York, NY: Pearson.

Wooditch, A., Tang, L. L., & Taxman, F. S. (2013). Which criminogenic need changes are most important in promoting desistance from crime and substance use? *Criminal Justice and Behavior, 41*(3), 276–299.

CHAPTER THIRTEEN

Cognitive Domain

ADVANCEMENT IN THE fields of criminology, psychology, and psychiatry have led to increased understanding of how certain mental disorders and mental health challenges may inform certain delinquent and criminal behaviors, including substance abuse, aggressive, and sexual offending behaviors. As a result, the criminal justice assessment and classification process weighs mental health diagnoses, distorted thinking, and suicidal ideation when predicting risk and needs levels. Obviously, none of these factors represents criminal or delinquent behaviors, and they are certainly not by any means deviant in nature. Rather, mental deficiency represents a crucial manifestation of offenders' thinking and behavior, and thus is a good source of information for proper criminal justice assessment and classification.

Offenders' cognitive functions are by far one of the key factors that drive criminal and delinquent behaviors. This chapter therefore talks about how mental health diagnosis, suicidal ideation, antisocial beliefs and attitudes, and criminal and distorted thinking influence criminal behaviors, as well as how these cognitive domains inform criminal justice risk assessment and classification process. The chapter concludes with a brief explanation of common thinking errors that facilitate delinquent thinking and behaviors: blaming, confusion, entitlement, justification, fronting, minimization, "poor me" and victim stance, mindreading, and vagueness.

MENTAL HEALTH DIAGNOSIS

Having a mental health condition does not necessarily make any person an offender, but certain mental health conditions can create opportunities for increased antisocial behaviors as well as elevate a person's chance of making involuntary contact with law enforcement agencies (Morgan, Fisher, Duan, Mandracchia, & Murray, 2010; Schubert, Mulvey, & Glasheen, 2011; Wilson, Farkas, Ishler, Gearhart, & Morgan, 2014). For example, studies show that about 50% to 70% of delinquent youth within and outside the criminal justice system have at least one mental health or psychiatric diagnosis (Schubert et al., 2011). Studies have also found that "6.4 to 14.5% of men and 12.2 to 31.0% of women in jails" have one or more serious mental health diagnoses (Wilson et al., 2014, p. 592). Serious mental health illnesses such as controlled substance dependency, oppositional defiant disorder, and conduct disorder are strong risk factors for criminal and delinquent behavior. It is therefore not surprising that people with serious mental illnesses are substantially overrepresented in the criminal justice system.

As noted by Ruchkin, Schwab-Stone, Koposov, Vermeiren, & King (2003), conduct disorder, which is usually shown by aggression toward people and animals, destruction of property, and deceitful behaviors such as stealing and lying, is a strong risk factor. Similarly, substance dependence increases the chance of arrest for possession of illegal substances and elevates offenders' likelihood of engaging in serious and minor crimes acts such as burglary, armed robbery, fraud, theft, and even murder in pursuit of a substance (Caudy et al., 2015). Substance use and abuse as a coping tool by offenders also affects recidivism by increasing "the odds of criminal involvement" to "nearly 3 times higher," although the "likelihood of offending may be mediated by the type of drug" being abused (Wooditch et al., 2013, p. 281).

SUICIDAL IDEATION

Suicide attempts and self-abusive behaviors including cutting, intentional drug overdose, and other forms of attempts to commit suicide as well as thoughts about suicide are powerful predictors of future suicidal ideation and attempts (Abram et al., 2008, p. 297). Therefore, as the third leading cause of death for persons between the age of 10 and 24 in the United States, suicide and its prevention is an important chapter in the criminal justice assessment and classification process. Clinical interest in preventing suicide is also heightened by the fact that detention and other forms of involuntary removal of children away from their habitual place of residence significantly increase their risk of suicidal ideation, attempts, and suicidal acts.

Other reasons why suicide prevention is treated with seriousness is that around one-third of adolescents experience suicidal ideation at some time in their lives, and 1 in 10 youth attempt suicide (Schilling, Aseltine, Glanovsky, James, & Jacobs, 2009). The risk of suicide, suicidal ideation, and suicidal attempts are higher among detained youths than youths in the general population (Abram et al., 2008, p. 297). In fact, suicide is the leading cause of death among incarcerated youth, and the risk is said to be between 3 and 18 times higher than it is for children in the community (Casiano, Katz, Globerman, & Sareen, 2013, p. 120). This means that incarceration sometimes "serves as an additional stressor" that adversely influences offenders' mental health and potentially exacerbates existing psychopathology (Ruchkin et al., 2003, p. 1063). Unfortunately, most youth who end up in detention already have a history of mental health needs such as depression, oppositional defiant disorder, alcohol use disorder, borderline personality disorder, post-traumatic stress disorder, bipolar disorder, schizophrenia, or attention-deficit hyperactivity disorder, each of which has been found to significantly increase the risk of suicidal behavior, particularly among incarcerated youth (Casiano et al., 2013; Schilling et al., 2009).

Connections between serious psychopathology, incarceration, and suicidal behaviors are obvious because "youthful suicidal behavior entails significant psychological distress" (Ruchkin et al., 2003, p. 1058). Also, the pain of separation from friends and loved ones in the community, the discomfort of sleeping in crowded rooms, and the sense of isolation and loneliness associated with sleeping in locked cells can create psychological conditions that easily increase incarcerated youth's likelihood of committing suicide (Abram et al., 2008). Thus, irrespective of the absence of a mental health diagnosis, an offender with suicidal ideation may be classified as high risk because of the apparent high tendencies for such an offender to engage in self-abusive behavior.

SUICIDE PREVENTION IS A SERIOUS MATTER

Fourteen known facts about suicidal behaviors in the United States, especially among persons below the age of 18, as reported by the National Institute of Mental Health, Office of Juvenile Justice and Delinquency Prevention, and the Centers for Disease Control and Prevention (Abram et al., 2014; Centers for Disease Control and Prevention, 2019; National Institutes of Health, 2019).

1. One out of every 25 suicide attempts succeeds.
2. About 1 in 10 juvenile detainees (10.3%) think about committing suicide.
3. About 11% of juvenile detainees attempt suicide.
4. More than 33% of male juvenile detainees and nearly 50% of female juvenile detainees feel hopeless, think a lot about death, or think a lot about dying in the 6 months prior to their detention.
5. Female detainees with anxiety disorders are at high risk of attempting suicide.
6. Each year, 1 in 100,000 children age 10 to 14 die by suicide.
7. Each year, 7 in 100,000 youth age 15 to 19 die by suicide.
8. Each year, 12.7 in 100,000 young adults age 20 to 24 die by suicide.
9. Adults age 18 to 29 are at greater risk of developing suicidal thoughts, engaging in suicidal planning, and attempting suicide than adults age 30 and above.
10. Suicide is the third leading cause of death for Americans age 15 to 24 years old.
11. Suicide is the 10th leading cause of death in the United States for all ages.
12. There is one death by suicide in the United States every 12 minutes.
13. Each year, suicide takes the lives of over 44,965 Americans.
14. Whites, American Indians, and Alaska Natives are more likely to commit suicide compared to Blacks and Hispanics.

Sources:

Abram, K. M., Choe, J. Y., Washburn, J. J., Teplin, L. A., King, D. C., Dulcan, M. K., & Bassett, E. D. (2014). *Suicidal thoughts and behaviors among detained youth*. Retrieved from https://www.ojjdp.gov/pubs/243891.pdf

Centers for Disease Control and Prevention. (2019). *Leading causes of death reports, 1981–2017*. Retrieved from https://webappa.cdc.gov/sasweb/ncipc/leadcause.html

National Institute of Mental Health. (2019). *Suicide*. Retrieved from https://www.nimh.nih.gov/health/statistics/suicide.shtml

The likelihood of future suicidal behavior can be assessed by measuring current and previous suicidal ideation, suicidal attempts, and any history of self-abusive behaviors (Schilling et al., 2009). In many cases, the race and gender of the offender are also important because statistics show that Caucasian youth generally manifest suicidal ideation, engage in suicidal attempts, and commit suicidal acts more often than all non-White groups. Thus, Caucasian youth are generally at greater risk of engaging in suicidal behaviors than non-Whites (Casiano et al., 2013). This implies that while all suicidal histories and symptoms must be treated seriously, history of suicidal behaviors, suicidal attempts, and suicidal ideation associated with Caucasian youth must be treated with additional seriousness.

ANTISOCIAL BELIEFS AND ATTITUDES

Behaviors are products of complex thought processes, and when a thought process is structurally and functionally antisocial in nature, the behavior that falls from it tends to be substantively criminal in nature. The category of attitudes and beliefs is therefore "one of the most robust predictors of recidivism among dynamic risk factors" (Caudy et al., 2015, p. 12). The criminal justice assessment and classification process therefore logically assumes that antisocial beliefs and attitudes that favor delinquent and criminal behaviors have a high likelihood of influencing delinquent and criminal behaviors (Hawkins et al., 2000).

While some individuals hold negative attitudes about many entities including people, objects, behaviors, laws, social issues, and ideals and beliefs, the criminal justice assessment is primarily concerned with attitudes toward matters that have been linked to antisocial behaviors—chiefly, an offender's attitudes about specific and general public laws, academic achievement, employment, substance abuse, public policies, and punishable antisocial behaviors. In short, attitude is a person's belief in matters as having the likelihood of producing protective or negative outcomes. Criminological studies have concluded that antisocial attitudes are good predictors of criminal and delinquent behaviors. Studies also show that attitudes and beliefs toward delinquent and criminal behaviors are important predictors of offending. In fact, attitudes toward crime are "more strongly associated" with crime and delinquency than is self-control, and even those who generally hold negative attitudes toward crime neutralize "those attitudes before committing crime" (Rebellon, Manasse, Gundy, & Cohn, 2014, p. 363).

The impact of beliefs and attitudes on criminality is, of course, not surprising because working against one's beliefs means in most cases acting against one's own sense of truth and interest regarding specific behavioral outcomes. An individual's attitudes toward risk can therefore reasonably "influence the likelihood of offending by shaping the perceived (and actual) rewards of the process of crime" (Burt & Simons, 2013, p. 1327). As Wikström and Svensson (2010) further note, "acts of crime (and human action more generally) are ultimately an outcome of how individuals perceive their action alternatives and, on this basis, make their choices when confronted with the particulars of a social setting in which they are taking part" (p. 396).

Antisocial attitudes are antisocial reactions that are informed by antisocial beliefs. An antisocial belief is a held knowledge about particular behaviors, social phenomena, and expectations that logically and empirically conflict with shared public norms, laws, policies, and views. For instance, an offender may harbor the antisocial idea that "education is not important" or "substance abuse is not all that harmful." Obviously in each of these cases, the held belief conflicts with the established logical views and empirical evidence in existence as well as public laws and policies pertaining to education and substance abuse. Furthermore, the offender holding these views is likely to respond to a failing grade with an "I don't care" attitude and is also likely to show an antisocial response to substance abuse. As a result, the offender is less likely to pursue academic achievement or stop the abuse of substances.

An antisocial attitude toward education can include an offender's professed beliefs along the lines that education has no practical benefit in life, that the pursuit of education is a waste of time, or that it is impossible to achieve a particular level of education. To the contrary, an offender with prosocial attitudes toward education would express faith in the power of education to gradually enhance the ability to fight off harsh social conditions such as unemployment and to prevent gravitation toward criminal activities. Similarly, antisocial attitudes toward substance abuse will generate antisocial attitude statements that show a failure to recognize the risks associated with substance use or the numerous psychological and physical harms the behavior produces.

Since antisocial beliefs generate antisocial attitudes that promote impactful risk factors and criminogenic behaviors, the best way to assess beliefs and attitudes is to ask offenders to speak about how they felt about engaging in delinquent and criminal acts, how they felt during the acts, how they felt after the acts, and how they retrospectively view their acts at the time of the assessment and classification. The expectation is that offenders with low-risk beliefs and attitudes will usually confess to being nervous about engaging in the prohibited act, speak of being scared during the act, express regret after the act, show genuine remorse for engaging in the behavior, and articulate the true impact of the behavior. The latter responses point to the offender's ability to engage in consequential thinking, recognize differences between right and wrong, and appropriately develop and express remorse. Offenders with high-risk attitudes will show no fear and will be unlikely to speak of being nervous during the act or to show a genuine sense of remorse.

CRIMINAL AND DISTORTED THINKING

At the core of every antisocial belief and attitude is at least one distorted thought that provides the rationalization needed to engage in criminal and deviant behaviors and to keep the antisocial beliefs and attitudes alive (Bartholomew & Simpson, 2005; Caudy et al., 2015). That is, "criminal thinking is a core feature of antisocial cognition, in that it constitutes the attitudes, beliefs, and rationalizations offenders use to justify and support their criminal behavior" (Walters, 2012, p. 272). For instance, studies found that in an attempt to create circumstances to excuse their behaviors, many sex offenders advanced thinking errors such as "being drunk, lacking in mental control," or that their victims enjoyed the act of victimization, or the act of victimization did not cause their victims any significant harms (Hatch-Maillette, Scalora, Huss, & Baumgartner, 2001, p. 103).

THINKING ERRORS CAN PREDICT FUTURE RISK OF ANTISOCIAL BEHAVIORS

Frequent use of thinking errors in connection with criminal and antisocial attitudes in general are critical factors that must be calculated in order to adequately predict future behaviors and to match behaviors with appropriate interventions. Of course, symptoms of serious mental health conditions always require additional specialized clinical assessment and classification by qualified mental health practitioners. A mental health condition is serious when the mental abnormality begins to interfere with a child's ability to perform normal social functions such as the ability to follow instructions and perform socially acceptable tasks.

Understanding the criminal mind that informs criminal acts is critical, and in order to fully appreciate the process of how a criminal or delinquent mind operates, one must understand the stages of thought that make antisocial and prosocial behaviors possible. That is how offenders move from noncriminal activities to criminal activities and why some offenders easily gravitate toward antisocial behaviors.

COMMON PATTERN OF ANTISOCIAL THINKING AND BEHAVIORS

Most behaviors begin with one or more trigger events—stimuli that come to the attention of the offender through one or more of the five senses: touch, smell, taste, sight, and hearing. For example, an offender may be triggered to think about marijuana use if he or she smells or sees marijuana or hears something about marijuana. The crucial stage after a trigger event is the decision-making point. At this level in the behavior process, the offender either makes a decision to engage in logical thinking that would lead to prosocial activities or to engage in distorted thinking that ultimately leads to antisocial behaviors.

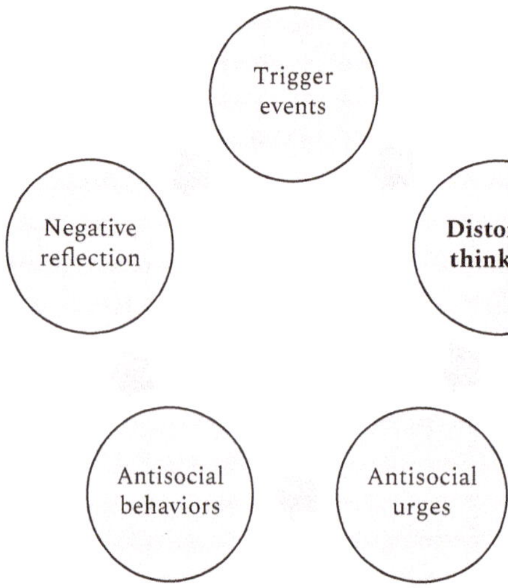

FIGURE 13.1 Thinking Patterns

Distorted thinking generates urges that push an offender to engage in criminal or delinquent behaviors, which in turn are likely to end with antisocial reflections. Similarly, logical thinking is more likely to generate prosocial urges to undertake prosocial behaviors and is likely to lead to prosocial reflection. For example, thinking about the pleasure of smoking marijuana (antisocial urge) increases the likelihood of marijuana use, and thinking about the harms associated with marijuana use (prosocial urge) reduces likelihood of marijuana use. Unlike antisocial reflection, prosocial reflection allows offenders to recognize the mental and physical benefits that good behaviors generate. On the contrary, however, antisocial reflection is a product of thinking errors that allow offenders to sharpen their delinquent and criminal skills.

The phrase "thinking errors" means delinquent and criminal rationalizations, criminal thinking, criminal cognition, distorted cognition, and distorted thinking (Mandracchia, Morgan, Garos, & Garland, 2007). In the context of antisocial behavior, each label refers to a wide range of verbal attempts to provide a rationale for antisocial behavior in order to avoid being held accountable or in order to normalize an antisocial thought or behavior (Caudy et al., 2015; Wooditch et al., 2013). Offenders develop these thinking errors over a long period of time, and the process can be attributed to a history of prolonged delinquent or criminal behavior, developmental deficiencies, environmental and social conditioning, psychological disorders, and criminal subcultural conditioning (Paulauskas, 2013).

There are many kinds of thinking errors (Hatch-Maillette et al., 2001; Walters, Deming, & Casbon, 2015); however, the ones that are of most interest to the criminal justice assessment and classification system are those that more directly reinforce criminality and delinquency by deflecting responsibility, thus making it harder for the offender to recognize the actual impact of their behaviors. Such distorted thinking includes (1) blaming, (2) confusion, (3) fronting, (4) "poor me," (5) justification, (6) mindreading, (7) minimization, and (8) victim stance. These thinking errors allow offenders to blame other people, thus helping offenders avoid responsibility for their behaviors and providing offenders with reasons to continue to engage in antisocial behaviors.

Blaming

Offenders typically use blaming when they are compelled to face the consequences of their prohibited behaviors by arguing that their bad behaviors are intentionally or unintentionally caused by another person and that person must therefore be held responsible (Bartholomew & Simpson, 2005). Thus, the use of this thinking error is usually characterized by attempts to make the case that someone else caused the antisocial behavior. By pointing fingers at the actions of others, either to justify or minimize the antisocial behaviors or to find fault in another person's actions, the offender tries to free himself or herself from any sense of guilt and responsibility.

AT EVEN A NATIONAL LEVEL, THE THINKING ERROR "BLAMING" OCCURS

Even at the national level there is evidence of distorted or illogical thinking being used to legitimize national policies. A good example is President Donald J. Trump's January 2019 speech to the nation from the Oval Office on the crisis at the border. As noted from the excerpt, the president blames drug dealers and specifically Mexican nationals for the high number of Americans who die from or who are addicted to methamphetamine, heroin, cocaine, and fentanyl. He claims: "Our southern border is a pipeline for vast quantities of illegal drugs, including meth, heroin, cocaine, and fentanyl. Every week, 300 of our citizens are killed by heroin alone, 90 percent of which floods across from our southern border. More Americans will die from drugs this year than were killed in the entire Vietnam War" (White House, 2019). The problem is that this is distorted thinking, equating deaths with the drug supply and solely blaming suppliers. There is no evidence that drug dealers force-feed any controlled substance user with drugs. Most drug users make their first contact with drug sellers only after learning about or being exposed to drugs by friends, acquaintances, family members, or relatives.

Source:

White House. (2019). *President Donald J. Trump's address to the nation on the crisis at the border*. Retrieved from https://www.whitehouse.gov/

Examples of the thinking error "blaming" may sound like "he called me names—that's why I punched him," or "I failed the class because the teacher didn't clearly explain the assignment," or "drug dealers are responsible for my son's death as a result overdose." In the first instance, the offender's illogical argument is that the only reason the victim was punched was because of the victim's alleged insult. This statement is distorted because the appropriate response to name calling is not throwing a punch at someone. Furthermore, punching another person can seriously hurt someone and can also lead to a felony charge for aggravated assault, manslaughter, or even murder.

In the second example, the offender attempts to make the case that the teacher is responsible for the failure. However, the offender failed to note that he or she did not make any tangible attempt to get further clarification or let the teacher know before the fact that the assignments were still unclear. Even if the offender made the required effort, the failure to realize that seeking external help could have averted the negative outcome shows that the offender is at risk of repeating the behavior. In the third case, the goal is to blame the drug dealer for the choices drug users make. In all of these cases, the use of the thinking error "blaming" is also a serious risk factor because the offender spent more time "pointing fingers" without providing evidence to show that any significant time was devoted to thinking about the cause of the antisocial behavior and on finding a realistic solution.

Confusion

The use of the thinking error "confusion" is often motivated by the desire to project innocence and is characterized by the offender's being puzzled and confused about the wrongfulness and impact of the behavior so as to win sympathy and to go unblamed for the bad behavior (Bartholomew & Simpson, 2005). The problem, however, is that in most cases, offenders choose confusion only after they have failed to follow a sanctioned rule, complete a task, or carry out an obligation. This thinking error is therefore characterized by the offender's claim of being puzzled, baffled, or confused about a behavior that most people would clearly consider undesirable. Yet, the offender uses confusion with the hope that the unfavorable consequences of the undesirable behavior will suddenly vanish through his or her simply denying that the alleged antisocial behavior took place or by claiming to have little or no knowledge about whether the behavior was appropriate.

Offenders may pretend to be confused about the very rule that they have violated and that they were expected to obey. As a result, offenders may try to argue that they lack the ability to understand rules, expectations, or obligations. For instance, the offender may ask about whether the behavior is prohibited. The goal is that by pretending to be totally ignorant and unaware of the wrongfulness of the behavior, the offender will make the consequences disappear or significantly shrink. Similarly, a less-hardworking student may use confusion by arguing that the assignments were unclear, even after strenuous efforts are made to provide clarification. Offenders may also use confusion by claiming that they are unsure about the expectation or rule that has already been violated. In these examples, the offender acts as though no knowledge existed about the rules, expectations, and assignments. Obviously, what qualifies these statements as products of thinking errors is the fact that the offender failed to account for the lack of effort to ask for clarification before the fact, although the offender obviously had ample time to ask for clarification in order to avoid the negative outcome.

Entitlement

Offenders who use the thinking error "entitlement" do so with the mindset that they are somehow "better than" others, and thus they are more deserving of certain favorable treatments than other people in the same circumstance. Therefore, the offender will repeatedly insinuate that the rules do not and should not apply to them, that things should be made easier for them, and that they should not pay for the consequences of their antisocial behaviors or lack of effort. The offenders feel more deserving of better outcomes even though they might be unwilling to earn such outcomes. Of course, the goal of entitlement is to ultimately establish an uncontested right to engage in antisocial behaviors and reap the benefits.

As Hatch-Maillette et al. (2001) observe, for instance, "sex offenders approach their victims from a perspective of entitlement in which the offenders' needs are placed above those of the victims" (p. 104). Offenders in other criminal and delinquent categories may victimize with the attitude that their victim(s) deserve to suffer the consequences of their antisocial behaviors because something special about them sets them apart from everyone else or gives them some legal rights that are not available to other people in a similar situation.

Justification

In some instances, when offenders learn that their antisocial behaviors have been detected, they use "justification" as a reactive thinking error to mitigate the impact and severity of their prohibited actions. These efforts are generally designed to make a bad behavior look as though it was not, after all, that bad. Thus, justification is generally characterized by the offender's repeated attempts to make the behavior seem normal (Bartholomew & Simpson, 2005). When offenders justify their behaviors, they are therefore not arguing that somebody else engaged in the behavior or that the behavior is not wrong. Rather, justification implies that the offender recognizes the wrongfulness of the behaviors, but in most cases the argument is that the negative behavior was the best response given the circumstance under which the offender acted and that the action taken was in good faith aimed at providing the best outcome.

The tactic of justifying involves a number of verbal tricks, which include sidetracking the main issue, controlling the conversation, shifting the focus away from the actual behavior, and admitting that the behavior was undesirable while at the same time attempting to make the behavior look desirable under the circumstances. For instance, an offender may argue that shoplifting at department stores is okay because department stores are very wealthy. In another instance, the offender may claim that boredom led to the antisocial behavior. In both cases, the goal is to make the antisocial behaviors appear acceptable and justified under a given condition. The flaws, however, are that the offender failed to explain why boredom did not provide a reason for volunteering at the community center and did not lead to a productive activity such as reading, exercising, or finding gainful employment. The offender also failed to explain how the size of a business' wealth justified individual dishonesty and stealing habits.

Fronting

The thinking error "fronting" is sometimes referred to as "Mr. or Ms. Good Guy," meaning the offenders attempt to present themselves in a positive manner so as to gain trust and to minimize the consequences of their antisocial behaviors. The offenders feel as though they are the only persons doing the right thing and thus demand to be viewed and treated as faultless persons unlikely to engage in antisocial behavior. The obvious intention behind the projection of self as a good citizen that is incapable of engaging in antisocial behavior is to create the illusion that it is impossible for the offender to engage in the depicted antisocial behavior.

Some skilled offenders use fronting by simply admitting to their behaviors and then moving on to express sympathy for their victims, sounding respectful of the victims' suffering and showing remorse for the harm caused. The hope is to minimize and in some cases to completely escape the prescribed consequences for the antisocial action. For instance, while many offenders genuinely change while in detention by embracing religion and by "finding

Jesus," many use religion as a front for getting by in detention, including winning the minds of correctional practitioners with power over their fates. Thus, offenders trying to secure parole release or any sort of reduction in the consequences of their crimes or delinquent behaviors generally manifest fronting as a thinking error.

Minimization

The act of making a delinquent or criminal behavior seem less serious than the behavior actually looks like to others is an act of minimization and therefore a thinking error in which the offender downplays the importance and impact of the antisocial behavior with the intention of making the antisocial behavior less important and thus warranting less blame and consequence. Obviously, in the process of minimizing the behavior, offenders may make an otherwise significant behavior appear smaller than it is in order to create grounds for reduced consequences. The offender achieves such goals by reducing the impact of their behaviors and by attacking the victim's projection of the consequential suffering.

The use of minimization can be characterized by phrases such as "not a big deal," "not even serious," "it was just a tiny scratch," and "it was not even a push—my finger barely touched her." In each of these statements, the offender is attempting to speak for the victim although the offender has no way of knowing the exact feeling the antisocial behaviors caused the victim to suffer. Furthermore, in the first and second instances, the offender is trying to minimize the response of the victim or authority by arguing that the undesirable action is not serious enough to warrant any harsh response. In the third example, the offender is attempting to minimize the behavior by suggesting that the action is very minimal. In the final example, the offender suggests that the victim or authority misinterpreted the undesirable behavior by making it look worse than it was.

"Poor Me" and Victim Stance

When offenders use the thinking error "poor me," they assume that no matter how much effort they exert, things always go against their interests; therefore, the best action is to stop trying. "Poor me" invokes self-pity; therefore, it is characterized by offenders' attempts to win the sorrow of others in an attempt to avoid consequence. As a result, offenders may present themselves as being unable to follow rules or meet expectations because of certain abnormalities beyond their control.

The use of "poor me" as a thinking error can therefore be exemplified by an offender's attempt to present herself or himself as helpless, not because of the action of another person but because of the offender's perceived circumstances. A typical example of the use of "poor me" may therefore sound like "I'm a slow learner," and "I get easily irritated because of my limitation." Obviously, none of these circumstances provides a logical reason for failure, in part because millions of people with similar backgrounds do not use their condition as a source of pity and reason for failure.

To the contrary, the offender in this case is arguing that it is not his or her fault but the fault of his or her "slow learner" status, therefore they should not be held responsible for their own failure. In the second instance, the offender argues that they should not be held responsible for their agitation. Instead, they should be pitted for having to deal with their agitation.

When offenders use their natural physiological makeup and social circumstances in statements such as "my family is poor" or "I got fired because the boss doesn't like my voice," they are in most cases using the thinking error "victim stance" by blaming the consequences of their actions on their status. In such instances, offenders present themselves as victims of their own circumstances, although they may have had the chance to correct their adverse circumstances.

Even in situations where the means for correcting the behaviors might not have existed, society holds that the offender still has the responsibility to bear the consequences of their actions just like billions of people who have found themselves in similar situations. The obvious goal of the victim stance is to deflect attention away from the actual antisocial behavior, win sympathy from victims, and escape the consequences of the behavior. The fact remains that full compliance with job requirements minimizes the chance of getting fired. The fact is that being born into poverty is perhaps more of a reason to work harder and engage in prosocial activities than a legitimate excuse for an antisocial life style.

Offenders also use the victim stance when they act like victims of the whole world, and indeed their own actions. Hence, the victim stance is sometimes displayed in statements of the offender's inability to engage in prosocial behaviors due to traits that are naturally entrenched in an offender's being. Such a mindset can generally be detected from statements about the offender being a total failure who can never do anything right. Examples of victim stance also include attempts to make the case that irrespective of whatever effort is exerted, the offender always ends up with the same undesirable outcomes. One can also easily detect the use of victim stance when offenders act as though the only reasons for their predicament are the alleged unfortunate circumstances in which they find themselves; therefore, it is unfair to hold them accountable for their delinquent or criminal behaviors.

Mind Reading

Offenders who use mind reading can be easily identified by their claim to know victims' or authority figures' thought processes and by their frequent citing of authorities' and victims' alleged thoughts that make the offenders' antisocial behaviors appear acceptable. That is, a mind reader would claim to have knowledge about what a victim or an authority figure was thinking at the time the condemned act took place. Typically, offenders who use this thinking error do so with the hope of establishing grounds for arguing that the undesirable actions were undertaken in good faith; therefore, the antisocial behaviors were purely accidental, and the only harm that ought to be the focus of condemnation is the fact that the good-faith behaviors ended up producing undesirable results.

Mind reading gives an offender the right to jump to conclusions without any tangible or logical evidence or reasoning. This thought process is also known as "assuming" because it involves the offender presumptuously concluding, without bothering to ask the true thoughts and feelings of others, that what other people think and feel about a particular antisocial behavior is similar to the thoughts and feelings of the offender. For instance, a child molester may interpret a child victim's passive resistance during an act of victimization as a manifestation of that child's willingness to participate in the act. Other offenders may arbitrarily assume that they are objects of everyone's hate; therefore, there is no reason to try to obey any particular rule.

Vagueness

Offenders use vagueness as a thinking error with the aim to redefine their antisocial behavior using words and phrases that make their behaviors appear less serious and also as a means for escaping the negative social labels and consequences of their behaviors. For instance, a child molester may refer to his or her behavior as "doing inappropriate things to a child victim" instead of admitting to "sexually molesting a child." A thief may avoid the word "stealing" and instead argue that he "took something that belonged to another person." In the first case, the goal for describing child molestation as "doing inappropriate things to a child" is designed to make the behavior appear less harmful and impactful. In the second example, the offender attempts to make the behavior appear less deviant by referring to it as "taking something that belongs to another person," totally avoiding the word "stealing" and the label "thief." In both cases, the goals are to create a vague sense of their own action by redirecting the focus to what they might view as a lesser form of the actual behavior.

CONCLUSION

Greater caution must always be utilized when calculating risks that are primarily based on antisocial beliefs and attitudes, suicidal ideation, mental health diagnosis, and criminal and distorted thinking. Indeed, misclassification in this section tends to have severe consequences that can include death or serious harm to the offender or innocent victims. Consequently, in order to avoid such mishaps, most criminal justice agencies have policies and procedures in place that call for multiple layers of assessment and classification by qualified mental health practitioners and secure care and community correction staff. In addition, anyone tasked with supervising offenders generally takes interest in ensuring their safety and in correcting and redirecting their thinking and behaviors, irrespective of the offenders' mental health classification.

DISCUSSION QUESTIONS

1. What steps could be taken to minimize self-abusive behaviors, especially suicidal attempts or ideation among juveniles who end up in the criminal justice system?
2. Some thinking errors are more commonly used than others. Which of the thinking errors discussed in this chapter do typical offenders more frequently use?
3. Which of these thinking errors are more frequently used by sex offenders, violent offenders, or substance abusers?
4. Why are thinking errors are used in risk calculation?
5. What is the difference between thinking errors and mental health illness such as schizophrenia and obsessive-compulsive disorder?

REFERENCES

Abram, K. M., Choe, J. Y., Washburn, J. J., Teplin, L. A., King, D. C., & Dulcan, M. K. (2008). Suicidal ideation and behaviors among youths in juvenile detention. *Journal of the American Academy of Child & Adolescent Psychiatry, 47*(3), 291–300.

Abram, K. M., Choe, J. Y., Washburn, J. J., Teplin, L. A., King, D. C., Dulcan, M. K., & Bassett, E. D. (2014). *Suicidal thoughts and behaviors among detained youth*. Retrieved from the Office of Juvenile Justice and Delinquency Prevention website: https://www.ojjdp.gov/pubs/243891.pdf

Bartholomew, N. G., & Simpson, D. D. (2005). *Unlock your thinking, open your mind: A collection of materials for leading counseling sessions that address thinking patterns that can hamper behavior change*. Retrieved from Texas Christian University, Institute of Behavioral Research website: http://ibr.tcu.edu/wp-content/uploads/2013/09/TMA05Aug-mind.pdf

Burt, C. H., & Simons, R. L. (2013). Self-control, thrill seeking, and crime motivation matters. *Criminal Justice and Behavior, 40*(11), 1326–1348. doi:10.1177/0093854813485575

Casiano, H., Katz, L. Y., Globerman, D., & Sareen, J. (2013). Suicide and deliberate self-injurious behavior in juvenile correctional facilities: A review. *Journal of the Canadian Academy of Child and Adolescent Psychiatry, 22*(2), 118–124.

Caudy, M. S., Folk, J. B., Stuewig, J. B., Wooditch, A., Martinez, A., Maass, S., ... Taxman, F. S. (2015). Does substance misuse moderate the relationship between criminal thinking and recidivism? *Journal of Criminal Justice, 43*(1), 12–19.

Centers for Disease Control and Prevention. (2019). *Leading causes of death reports, 1981–2017*. Retrieved from https://webappa.cdc.gov/sasweb/ncipc/leadcause.html

Hatch-Maillette, M. A., Scalora, M. J., Huss, M. T., & Baumgartner, J. V. (2001). Criminal thinking patterns: Are child molesters unique? *International Journal of Offender Therapy and Comparative Criminology, 45*(1), 102–117.

Hawkins, J. D., Herrenkohl, T. I., Farrington, D. P., Brewer, D., Catalano, R. F., Harachi, T. W., & Cothern, L. (2000). *Predictors of youth violence*. Retrieved from University of Cambridge, Institute of Criminology website: http://www.crim.cam.ac.uk/people/academic_research/david_farrington/predviol.pdf

Mandracchia, J. T., Morgan, R. D., Garos, S., & Garland, J. T. (2007). Inmate Thinking Patterns: An Empirical Investigation. *Criminal Justice and Behavior, 34*(8), 1029–1043. doi: 10.1177/0093854807301788

Morgan, R. D., Fisher, W. H., Duan, N., Mandracchia, J. T., & Murray, D. (2010). Prevalence of criminal thinking among state prison inmates with serious mental illness. *Law and Human Behavior, 34*(4), 324–336. doi:10.1007/s10979-009-9182-z

National Institute of Mental Health. (2019). *Suicide*. Retrieved from https://www.nimh.nih.gov/health/statistics/suicide.shtml

Paulauskas, R. (2013). Is causal attribution of sexual deviance the source of thinking errors? *International Education Studies, 6*(4), 20–28. doi:0.5539/ies.v6n4p20

Rebellon, C. J., Manasse, M. E., Gundy, K. T. V., & Cohn, E. S. (2014). Rationalizing delinquency: A longitudinal test of the reciprocal relationship between delinquent attitudes and behavior. *Social Psychology Quarterly, 77*(4), 361–386. doi:10.1177/0190272514546066

Ruchkin, V. V., Schwab-Stone, M., Koposov, R. A., Vermeiren, R., & King, R. A. (2003). Suicidal ideations and attempts in juvenile delinquents. *Journal of Child Psychology and Psychiatry, 44*(7), 1058–1066. doi:10.1111/1469-7610.00190

Schilling, E. A., Aseltine, R. H., Glanovsky, J. L., James, A., & Jacobs, D. (2009). Adolescent alcohol use, suicidal ideation, and suicide attempts. *Journal of Adolescent Health, 44*(4), 335–341. doi:10.1016/j.jadohealth.2008.08.006

Schubert, C. A., Mulvey, E. P., & Glasheen, C. (2011). Influence of mental health and substance use problems and criminogenic risk on outcomes in serious juvenile offenders. *Journal of the American Academy of Child and Adolescent Psychiatry, 50*(9), 925–937.

Walters, G. D. (2012). Criminal thinking and recidivism: Meta-analytic evidence on the predictive and incremental validity of the Psychological Inventory of Criminal Thinking Styles (PICTS). *Aggression and Violent Behavior, 17*(3), 272–278. doi:10.1016/j.avb.2012.02.010

Walters, G. D., Deming, A., & Casbon, T. (2015). Predicting recidivism in sex offenders with the Psychological Inventory of Criminal Thinking Styles (PICTS). *Assessment, 22*(2), 167–177. doi:10.1177/1073191114539384

White House. (2019). *President Donald J. Trump's address to the nation on the crisis at the border.* Retrieved from https://www.whitehouse.gov/

Wikström, P.-O. H., & Svensson, R. (2010). When does self-control matter? The interaction between morality and self-control in crime causation. *European Journal of Criminology, 7*(5), 395–410. doi:10.1177/1477370810372132

Wilson, A. B., Farkas, K., Ishler, K. J., Gearhart, M., & Morgan, R. (2014). Criminal thinking styles among people with serious mental illness in jail. *Law and Human Behavior, 38*(6), 592–601. doi:10.1037/lhb0000084

Wooditch, A., Tang, L. L., & Taxman, F. S. (2013). Which criminogenic need changes are most important in promoting desistance from crime and substance use? *Criminal Justice and Behavior, 41*(3), 276–299. doi:10.1177/0093854813503543

CHAPTER FOURTEEN

Other Predictive and Nonpredictive Domains

RECENT DEBATES ABOUT race, nationality, and religion indicate that some segments of the American public still entertain a belief that race, nationality, religion, and sexual orientation accurately predict thinking, attitudes, and behaviors. More specifically, some people share the belief that (1) certain nationalities are rapists and murderers, (2) a particular sexual orientation is a risk factor for deviance, (3) members of specific religions are terrorists, (4) certain racial groups are predators, unproductive and violent, and (5) particular racial groups are racists that long for a society where people of different races could be treated as subhuman. These baseless and in most cases illogical claims are examples of how race, religion, gender differences, nationality, and other social and biological characteristics are talked about, presented, and viewed by segments of the American public. The danger, therefore, is that the treatment of race, nationality, gender, or religion as factors that shape thinking, attitudes, and behaviors maximizes the potential for a tainted risk and needs assessment and classification result.

This chapter discusses the importance of gender, race, nationality, religion, and physical characteristics in relation to the prediction of antisocial attitudes, thinking, and behaviors. Specifically, this chapter talks about why the best explanation for any behavioral statistic, and indeed any risk and needs assessment and classification process, is not gender, age, nationality, religion, or physical characteristic. Rather, the factors to pay attention to are an offender's environment, attitudes, behaviors, and history coupled with individual family history and the makeup of friends and peer groups, schools, and neighborhood (see, for example, Shader, 2001; Wasserman et al., 2003). These factors are discussed under two headings: other predictive domains and nonpredictive domains.

OTHER PREDICTIVE DOMAINS

Most criminal justice risk and needs assessment tools capture age and gender. These two characteristics, however, do not directly form part of the calculation of risk and needs levels in detention centers, in probation and parole departments, or in the court system. The questions, therefore, are whether gender and age should be viewed as useful sources of information for the purpose of risk or needs assessment and classification. The answer to this question is not straightforward, especially when those answers come from people with narrow or limited points of reference about relationships between gender, age, and delinquency.

One of the main sources of misunderstanding of girls' delinquency, for example, is the misreading and interpretation of unique female reactions to certain risk factors and the effects of certain risk factors on girls as a consequence of social conditioning and environmental constraints. Further, contemporary criminological, sociological, and psychological theories that explain antisocial thinking and behavior—for example, differential association, social learning, social bonding, labelling, and social disorganization theories—were developed primarily in response to male delinquency (Agnew, 2009; Akers, Sellers, & Jennings, 2017). The few theorists who devoted their works to understanding women's behaviors stereotypically and erroneously presented female offenders as inferior and biologically different from the "normal" female population (Flowers, 1995; Lombroso & Ferrero, 1898). This section therefore discusses the relationship between gender, age, and antisocial thinking, attitudes, and behaviors specifically as they apply to furthering the best interests of youth at risk of making initial or future contact with the criminal justice system.

Gender Differences

Although both girls and boys respond to many known risk and protective factors in the same way without any significant difference (Zahn et al., 2010), there are a few gender-specific risk or protective factors and patterns of behavior (Cauffman, 2008; Flowers, 1995). Girls are less likely than boys to become chronic offenders, especially in terms of serious criminal behaviors such as violence, drug trade, and even gang-related crimes. Certain social conditions such as poverty, neighborhood disorganization, and family disruption affect girls slightly more negatively than boys. Girls tend to have tighter connections to their families than boys do, and thus they are at greater risk of suffering more negative consequences from violence, sexual abuse, or substance use, or from a dysfunctional family history or a family with poor parental supervision, or one that encourages antisocial thinking, attitudes, and behaviors.

Girls face limitations that are more social, and they tend to deal with certain biologically based risk factors that create opportunities for delinquent or criminal behavior more than boys do. For instance, mentally, biologically, and socially, teen parenthood affects girls more negatively than boys. Girls are also more likely to be sexually victimized or traumatized than boys. Girls experience and respond to known risk and protective factors in the same way as boys, but girls tend to differ in terms of the rate at which they are exposed to certain risks such as sexual abuse, trauma, and assault. Consequently, girls are more likely to have a history of serious psychological and violent abuse and to suffer more from emotional and cognitive risk factors that contribute to delinquency and criminality as a consequence of their abuse. For example, delinquent girls are diagnosed at much higher rates with mental health problems such as depression, anxiety, and post-traumatic stress disorder that are linked to experiences of victimization than boys (Zahn et al., 2010).

In the same vein, studies show that boys make more unwanted contact with the criminal justice system than do girls. Male juvenile offenders dominate almost all categories of criminal and delinquent behaviors, including violent offenses, sex offending, substance abuse, and general offending behaviors. While girls tend to commit minor offenses, boys engage in more violent and serious crimes. Boys are more likely than girls, by a ratio of 3:1, to be diagnosed with attention-deficit and or hyperactivity disorder (ADD and ADHD) and conduct disorders, which influence more boy-related delinquent behaviors than delinquency among girls (Cauffman, 2008; Zahn et al., 2010).

Efforts to explain gender variation in crime and delinquency using frameworks that view female offenders as different from males in terms of criminal tendencies have been at work for more than two centuries. However, many of the early results of such undertakings are colored with "age-old stereotypes" and "notions of female inferiority" and sexism (Flowers, 1995, p. 65). In 1898, for example, Caesar Lombroso and William Ferrero argued that "the criminal woman" was a "monster" who lacked the virtues of maternity, piety, and weakness, which they argue cause many non-antisocial women to live crime-free lives (Lombroso & Ferrero, 1898, p. 152). The authors contended that criminal women possessed the characteristics of men. Accordingly, most female crimes could be attributed to women with visible masculinity.

Obviously, Lombroso and Ferrero's theory and other claims of psychological difference, as well as outright statements of women's psychological inferiority to men, have been long disproved and heavily criticized (Flowers, 1995). Instead, framing female antisocial thinking and behavior and viewing the trajectories of female criminal careers through the lenses of biological predisposition, mental health needs, and the liberation of women seem to be informative, particularly for needs assessment (Cauffman, 2008, p. 131). On the question of male offending behavior, biological theorists argue that testosterone arouses the part of the brain that coordinates aggression. Therefore, increased testosterone elevates the risk of aggressive behavior, and since men have higher testosterone levels than women, they are at higher risk of committing violent offenses than females (Batrinos, 2012, p. 564).

Contemporary feminist theories, such as the liberation hypothesis, link female criminality to the liberation of women and to women's lack of social, economic, and political resources as compared to males. The theories hold that economic marginalization, disparity in gender accesses to meaningful opportunities, and under-compensation for domestic labor increase women's risk for antisocial activities. Consequently, some girls are pushed into committing survival crimes, mostly crimes such as property crime, prostitution, and theft (Akers et al., 2017; Flowers, 1995; Williams & McShane, 2014).

The liberation hypothesis argues that the equalization of gender rights means that women compete with men in all spheres of life, including in the criminal world, and thus the increase in the number of women or girls in the criminal justice system is a direct consequence of that liberation. Hence, these theories attribute female criminality to the exposure of women to the same harsh social pressures that push men to provide for themselves and their families (Chesney-Lind, 1986; Williams & McShane, 2014). In that regard, as the degree of liberation rises, so does the rate of female crime, hence the rise in the proportion of female offenders making initial or repeat contacts with the criminal justice system since the 1980s. Since that time, female crime has risen from 17% in 1980 to 29% in 2010 with the majority of the increase occurring in the 1990s (Sickmund & Puzzanchera, 2014).

Despite the fact that some of these explanations of female criminality may sound plausible, the reality is that none of the psychological and biological frameworks explain the difference between boys' and girls' delinquency rates or explain why boys outnumber girls in almost all categories of delinquent and criminal behaviors. It is therefore not surprising that criminal justice assessment and classification instruments fail to score offenders as high or low simply on the basis of being too masculine or too feminine, or because an offender is a male or a female. That is, there is no definitive biological difference that precisely predicts how girls or boys think and behave in relation to lawful and unlawful behaviors. Rather, the key contributing factors to girls' delinquency are economic and social conditions as well as psychosocial histories—in particular, histories of dysfunctional home environment, emotional, physical, or sexual abuse, and poor means of sustenance (Cauffman, 2008). The difference between male and female crime rates are therefore calculated using individual histories that capture factors such as degree of exposure to certain risk factors, development and manifestation of antisocial thoughts and behaviors, and social conditioning including gender-specific public policies.

Age and Criminality

At a quick glance, age might be seen as a reliable predictor of criminal or delinquent behavior. For example, ample evidence suggests that after childhood, age is inversely related to criminality—that is, the older people get, the lower their risk of committing crimes. People who are at least 35 years old are less likely to engage in criminal behaviors than those who are 13 to 17 years old. The question, therefore, is whether recorded changes in behavior as people get older are direct consequences of the physiological and biological changes that typically accompany a change in age. Furthermore, what effect do social expectation and limitation, inability or ability to fully comprehend the consequences of one's behavior and thinking, and change in socioeconomic condition and means have on the frequency and typology of delinquent and criminal acts?

Indeed, if behaviors are informed by what is happening to and around an individual, then age is not the key source for predicting thoughts and behaviors. For example, if age is a key factor, then most 10-year-old youth would think and behave in a uniform manner, and most 40-year-old would behave in similar fashion. Furthermore, youth do not suddenly stop committing offenses by simply going from age 17 to 18, nor do adults stop committing crimes once they reach a certain age; rather, the means, desire, and need for certain behaviors change not necessarily as consequences of change in age but as a result of changes in individual circumstances, experiences, responsibilities, and goals. It is the case that some youth engage in delinquent or criminal behaviors. Some children desist from criminal and delinquent behaviors irrespective of their age. For each behavior and child, multiple sociological and psychological elucidations using the frameworks of differential association, social learning, routine activity, labelling, social organization, subcultural, and social control and bond theories explain why certain age groups behave in a particular manner, including participating in deviant, criminal, and delinquent activities.

Although age is not a reliable predictor of future behaviors, early involvement in delinquent, deviant, or antisocial behavior does predict criminal behavior. As noted by a group of 39 experts on child delinquency convened by the Office of Juvenile Justice and Delinquency Prevention, most juveniles who commit serious and violent crimes or who exhibit persistent disruptive behaviors tend to have histories of engagement in minor delinquent acts at an early age (Wasserman et al., 2003). The report shows that children who exhibit delinquent behaviors at an older age are less at risk than children who do so at age 13 or younger. Children who experience delinquent behaviors at earlier ages are at particular risk of becoming serious and chronic juvenile offenders. Children who are age 12 and younger are at even greater risk, with some studies suggesting that they are two to three times more likely to become future serious and violent offenders (Burns et al., 2003).

In the final analysis, it might seem logical to assume that age predicts criminal or delinquent thinking and behaviors, but the more accepted conclusion is that age is not a good predictor of thoughts and behavior, especially for the purpose of criminal justice assessment and classification. Indeed, the inverse relationship between age and criminality—that is, that older people are at lower risk of committing crimes—is not some direct consequence of the mere ticking of the clock. To the contrary, quite often the social conditioning, personal opportunities, and demands that come with increasing age are some of the core contributing factors that shape individual thoughts and behaviors.

NONPREDICTIVE DOMAINS

Unlike the questions of gender and age, there is no reliable result known to social scientists that supports the notion that a person's nationality, physical appearance, race, or religion predicts criminal and delinquent thinking and behavior. Yet American criminal justice practitioners live in a society where some people constantly claim that certain nationalities, physical characteristics, races, and religions can correlate with individual criminality, delinquency, and deviance. Consequently, in the absence of discussion about relationships between race, nationality, religion, and biological or physical characteristics, one may unconsciously or even knowingly treat these factors as predictive variables when calculating risk and needs levels.

Race

Approximately 12% of the U.S population is African American, and Black youth accounted for 17% of the juvenile population in 2010. However, 31.3% of adults who involuntarily make contact with the criminal justice system are Black. In 2010, 31% of the estimated 1,642,500 persons under age 18 detained by law enforcement agencies in the United States was also Black. During the same period, 11% of Whites and 13% of Blacks arrested were juveniles, but Black youth accounted for a greater proportion of certain offenses for which juveniles were arrested: murder (56%), motor vehicle theft (42%), and aggravated assault (41%), for example. In the same period, White youth accounted for 31% of juvenile arrests for robbery, 43% for murder, 55% for motor vehicle theft, and 56% for aggravated assault—note that the Uniformed Crime Report (UCR) data do not treat Hispanic as a separate ethnic group. However, in 2010, 89% of Hispanics age 10–17 were classified racially as White (Sickmund & Puzzanchera, 2014).

Hispanics and Blacks have consistently dominated gang membership and, of course, gang-related offenses. For example, according to the National Gang Center, 39% of gang members nationally are Black, or African American, and 45% are Hispanic, or Latino, which means 84.5% of all street gang members are either Black or Hispanic, with Whites registering 9.7% in larger cities and 14.9% in rural counties (National Gang Center, 2017). These numbers for non-White gang membership are very high given that, according to the Juvenile Offenders and Victims 2014 National Report, Blacks accounted for 15% of the juvenile population in the United States, Hispanics represented 23%, while 56% were White juveniles under the age of 18 (Sickmund & Puzzanchera, 2014). Although based on these figures one could assume that race predicts antisocial thinking and behavior, there is no scientific evidence to back up a conclusion that says skin color predicts any behavior.

RACE IS A MADE-UP CONCEPT

Race is a new idea. In fact, the word *race* did not exist in the English language until in 1508. The Public Broadcasting Service publishes these informed conclusions about race:

1. Race is a modern idea. Ancient societies, like the Greeks, did not divide people according to physical distinctions, but according to religion, status, gender, class, even language.
2. Race has no genetic basis. Not one characteristic, trait or even one gene distinguishes all the members of one so-called race from all the members of another so-called race.
3. Human subspecies don't exist. Unlike many animals, modern humans simply haven't been around long enough or populations isolated enough to evolve into separate subspecies or races. Despite surface appearances, we are among the most similar of all species.
4. Skin color really is only skin deep. Most traits are inherited independently from one another. The genes influencing skin color have nothing to do with the genes influencing hair form, height, blood type, musical talent, athletic ability or forms of intelligence. Knowing one trait, like skin color, doesn't necessarily tell you anything else about a person's other traits.
5. Most variation is within, not between, "races." Of the small amount of total human genetic variation, 85% exists within any local population, be they Italians, Kurds, Koreans or Cherokees. About 94% can be found within any continent. That means two random Koreans may be as genetically different as a Korean and an Italian.
6. Slavery predates race. Throughout much of human history, societies have enslaved others, often as a result of conquest or war, even debt, but not because of physical characteristics or a belief in natural inferiority. Due to a unique set of historical circumstances, ours was the first slave system where all the slaves shared similar physical characteristics.
7. Race and freedom evolved together. The U.S. was founded on the radical new idea that "All men are created equal." But our early economy was based largely on slavery. How could this anomaly be rationalized? The new idea of race helped explain why some people could be denied the rights and freedoms that others took for granted.
8. Race justified social inequalities as natural. As the idea of race took hold, white superiority became "common sense" in white America. It rationalized not only slavery but also the extermination of Indians, exclusion of Asian immigrants, and the taking of Mexican lands by a nation that otherwise professed a deep belief in liberty and equality. Racialized practices became institutionalized within American government, laws, and society and persist even though de jure segregation ended.
9. Race isn't biological, but racism is still real. Racism is a powerful social force that gives people different access to opportunities and resources. Our government and social institutions disproportionately, albeit often invisibly, channel wealth, power, and resources to the "unmarked" race—white people. This affects everyone, whether we are aware of it or not.
10. Colorblindness will not end racism. Pretending race doesn't exist is not the same as creating equality. Racism is more than stereotypes and individual prejudice. To tackle racism, we need to identify and remedy social policies and institutional practices that advantage some groups at the expense of others.

Source:

Public Broadcasting Service. (2019). *What is race?* Retrieved from http://www.pbs.org/race/001_WhatIs-Race/001_00-home.htm

Many reasons explain why skin color is useless when it comes to risk assessment and classification. First, the so-called racial groups come from a variety of geographic locations and socioeconomic, political, and cultural backgrounds. For example, there are 21 Spanish-speaking countries, including Ecuador (South America), Equatorial Guinea (Africa), Mexico (North America), and Spain (Europe). The geographical diversity of Hispanic ancestry is very similar to those of Blacks and Whites. As Sickmund and Puzzanchera note, "the idea of presenting crime and justice statistics that distinguish among juveniles with Irish, Italian, and German ancestry seems nonsensical" (2014, p. 3). People of each of these countries can trace their individual traditions and behaviors to unique cultures, traditions, norms, and laws in other countries or on other continents.

Without careful consideration, these figures can also lead a criminal justice practitioner to assume that race elevates or changes risk or needs scores. However, again, a close examination of why, for example, Blacks and Hispanics gravitate toward street gangs would easily reveal that at the end of the day, race does not explain or predict future thinking or behaviors. In fact, studies show "that 20 percent of the racial disparity [in crime rate] could not be accounted for after controlling for racial differences in criminal activity," particularly in relation to the numbers of Blacks who make involuntary contact with the American criminal justice system (Free & Ruesink, 2012, p. 13). Concisely, there is no evidence to suggest that race predicts criminal thinking or behaviors.

Race has no genetic basis, there are no human subspecies, most variations are within and not outside race, race is not biological, and race exists in the United States because it has historically served as justification for discriminatory practices such as slavery, segregation, and similar policies that seek to elevate one group of people at the expense of another group (Ngai, 1999; Public Broadcasting Service, 2017). Skin colors of offenders are therefore completely useless for the purpose of behavioral classification and prediction. If Black people were biologically predisposed to engage in activities that are criminal, then the whole of Sub-Saharan Africa would contain immense numbers of murderers, serial killers, drugs users and dealers, rapists, armed robbers, and other categories of criminals.

The same would be true about certain crime rates in Western Europe or Latin America, where the concentration of Whites and Latinos are respectively large. Just as it would be incorrect to assume that Whites are more likely to sexually victimize children than others based on the U.S. Department of Justice reports that "nearly 70% of those serving time for violent crimes against children were white," it would also be incorrect to assume that Whites are less likely to commit violent crimes against adults because "whites accounted for 40% of those imprisoned for violent crimes against adults" (Greenfeld, 1996). Indeed, if the source of violent victimization is race, similar or higher statistics would be found in Western Europe, where the concentration of White males is far greater.

Nationality

Increasingly, claims about a relationship between nationality and criminality seem to be visible as a national policy, so the possibility exists of such beliefs influencing the way probation and parole officers and other criminal justice practitioners treat offenders. For example, in January 2017, President Donald J. Trump issued an executive order temporarily banning all Iraqi, Syrian, Iranian, Libyan, Somalian, Sudanese, and Yemeni nationals from entering the United States and permanently banning the resettlement of any Syrian refugee in the United States. The president argued that the ban would prevent future terrorist and criminal activities in the United States (Bier, 2017). Not surprisingly, the policy is similar to past U.S. government actions informed by the desire to discriminate against people based on national origin in the name of safety, claiming that a person's nationality is a known risk factor for certain criminal behavior and thinking (National Archives, 2017; Ngai, 1999).

As the U.S. Court of Appeals for the Ninth Circuit notes, the United States in the past detained and restricted the movement of "law-abiding and loyal Americans of Japanese ancestry during World War II" based purely on national origin (*State of Washington; State of Minnesota, v. Donald J. Trump*, 2017). In addition, according to the U.S. National Archives and Records Administration, during World War II the United States rounded up and interned over 31 thousand people of specific nationalities—Germans, Japanese, Italians, and other nationals from Latin American countries in the name of national security. In those cases too, the U.S. government argued that people with these national origins were "potentially dangerous enemy aliens" (National Archives, 2017).

THE POLITICS OF USING RACE AS A COVER

A number of flaws directly highlight the contradictions inherent in the argument that restricting people based on national origin furthers crime control objectives. In terms of the recent ban on five Muslim-dominated countries in January 2017 by President Donald J. Trump, for example, the government failed to recognize that radicalization has no national border, racial makeup, or geographic marker. Secondly, in the era of technologically aided global interconnectivity and interdependency, the physical movement of people is not needed to recruit participants or carry out criminal acts in other countries. Radical Islamists are very good at radicalizing vulnerable young men and women via social media outlets, including YouTube, Twitter, LinkedIn, Pinterest, Google, Tumblr, Instagram, and many other means of cross-border interactions.

Source:

In the end, no evidence suggests that a person's nationality can predict his or her ability or willingness to participate in antisocial behaviors under any given circumstance. It is therefore not surprising that often when nationality is invoked as a basis for preventing crime, the justification for such policies tends to be the politics of fear and emotional arousal rather than facts or scientific calculation. The lack of evidence supporting links between nationality and behavior is even evident in the case of the recent immigration ban on seven nationalities (Iraqi, Syrian, Iranian, Libyan, Somalian, Sudanese, and Yemeni). As the *New York Times* editorial board noted, the use of "the attacks of Sept. 11 as a rationale, while exempting the countries of origin of all the hijackers who carried out that plot" does not support the notion that the nationality of the people banned serves as serious predictor of terrorist acts on American soil (Editorial, 2017). Notwithstanding these facts, merely labelling the nationals of the banned countries as potential terrorists who are at high risk of committing terrorist acts on American soil reinforces the unsubstantiated claim that nationality predicts behaviors.

Religion

Quite frequently, and particularly in some cases, religion and nationality are used interchangeably, in that people from certain countries are automatically viewed as belonging to a particular religion. For example, some people think that being Middle Eastern or belonging to any of the Middle Eastern countries except Israel means being a Muslim and means being at risk of engaging in terrorist acts. This state of mind feeds on the assumption that certain nationals such as Saudi Arabians, Iranians, and Indians subscribe to certain religions while discounting the fact that in any country there are religious minorities, and in every religion not all members act in accordance with the teachings and practices of the religion to which they subscribe, especially when the behavior calls for the commission of crimes.

Currently, a myth exists that "Islam is inherently violent"; therefore, "all Muslims should face heightened scrutiny" because being a Muslim is a risk factor for at least terrorist-related crimes (Ladd, 2014). To support these claims, people point to instances such as recent terrorist attacks carried out by elements of certain radical Islamic groups such as the Islamic State and Al Qaeda. Again, while terrorists tend to use religious beliefs and political grievances to legitimize their actions, religion does not predict individual criminality or delinquency. That is, being a Muslim, Jew, Christian, or Hindu does not increase one's chance of substance abuse, or committing sex offenses, violent crimes, or any general category of crimes such as fraud or thefts.

In fact, on the contrary, what is more plausible is that religiosity, although different from belonging to a religion, minimizes the chance of certain criminal behaviors. Most religions, and indeed Judaism, Christianity, Islam, Hinduism, and Buddhism, preach compassion, humility, and humanity. They condemn antisocial behaviors and promote prosocial behavior. For example, based on 1990–1991 data from 13 industrial nations, studies show that overall, "more religious countries have lower crime rates than less religious countries," and further, any relationship between religious practice and low crime rates "was more pronounced" in the case of overt religiosity, especially one that is symbolized by active participation in religious activities (Ellis & Peterson, 1996).

Physical Characteristics

Claims about physical characteristics being indicative of patterns of thinking and behavior is one of the oldest myths in circulation. In fact, the so-called biological interpretation of human behavior draws on the notion that certain individuals are born with biological markers that make it difficult for them to live a crime-free life. For example, in their widely read and cited work *The Female Offender*, Lombroso and Ferrero (1898) argued that certain humans are born criminal; therefore, certain criminal behaviors and degrees of deviance can be predicted based on the size of certain biological and physiologic characteristics such as skull size, weight of jaw, and biological and pathological anomalies. Since then, there have been scholarly attempts to lend support to the notion that physical characteristics such as "low physical attractiveness" make one more prone to commit crimes (Bull, 1982). Of course, there is no scientific backing for these claims.

A child's physical appearance, including weight, eye color, height, shape of nose, size of skull, physical "attractiveness" and the like do not predict criminal or delinquent behaviors. The danger, however, is that "though modern criminologists do not believe that criminals belong to a single physical type, it is possible that the general public, the police, juries, and so forth, may believe in such relationships and act accordingly" (Bull, 1982, p. 269), hence the possibility to include one or more physical characteristics into the calculation of risk and needs scores. Indeed, modern "criminologists do not believe that criminals belong to a single physical type" (Bull & Green, 1980, p. 269), and certainly, physical characteristics do not make up one of the predictive variables.

CONCLUSION

The general conclusions of experts on child delinquency and child psychopathology are that no single risk factor leads a young child to delinquency. Instead, "risk factors for child delinquency operate in several domains," including the individual child, the child's family and peer group, the child's school, the child's neighborhood, and in general the social conditions under which the child lives (Wasserman et al., 2003). The physical world created by social conditions and the social reality that comes with those worlds have greater influence on each child's specific thinking, attitudes, and behaviors than the child's gender, age, nationality, or religion.

Social conditions compel certain age groups to behave in certain ways. For example, children generally live with their parents, associate with peers, and follow their elders' instruction. Consequently, in the fulfillment or absence of such conditions, some children are exposed to deviant and antisocial life styles, which in turn increase their chance of making initial or repeat contacts with the criminal justice system. In such cases, the problem is not, however, the child's age, nationality, race, gender, or physical characteristics but the child's association with a dysfunctional family, antisocial peers, and other negative social conditions.

DISCUSSION QUESTIONS

1. Under what conditions or circumstances will the use of age or gender to calculate risk or needs serve the best interest of a child?
2. Is gender a good predictive variable for measuring the needs of a delinquent child?
3. How does the use of gender or age in the assessment of needs and the creation of a treatment plan as well as the delivery of services serve the best interests of a child?
4. List and discuss ways to minimize the adverse use of race, nationality, religion, or physical characteristic as predicative variable.
5. Why do males dominate almost every category of criminal behaviors, especially sexual, substance abuse, and violent behaviors?

REFERENCES

Agnew, R. (2009). The contribution of "mainstream" theories to the explanation of female delinquency. In M. A. Zahn (Ed.), *The Delinquent Girl*. Philadelphia, PA: Temple University Press.

Akers, R. L., Sellers, C. S., & Jennings, W. G. (2017). *Criminological theories: Introduction, evaluation, and application*. New York, NY: Oxford University Press.

Batrinos, M. L. (2012). Testosterone and aggressive behavior in man. *International Journal of Endocrinology and Metabolism, 10*(3), 563–568. doi:10.5812/ijem.3661

Bier, D. J. (2017, January 27). Trump's immigration ban is illegal. *The New York Times*. Retrieved from https://www.nytimes.com/2017/01/27/opinion/trumps-immigration-ban-is-illegal.html

Bull, R. (1982). Physical appearance and criminality. *Current Psychological Reviews, 2*(3), 269–281. doi:10.1007/bf02684461

Bull, R. H. C., & Green, J. (1980). The relationship between physical appearance and criminality. *Medicine, Science and the Law, 20*(2), 79–83.

Burns, B. J., Howell, J. C., Wiig, J. K., Augimeri, L. K., Welsh, B. C., Loeber, R., & Petechuk, D. (2003). *Treatment, services, and intervention programs for child delinquents*. Retrieved from https://files.eric.ed.gov/fulltext/ED474859.pdf

Cauffman, E. (2008). Understanding the female offender. *The Future of Children, 18*(2), 119–142.

Chesney-Lind, M. (1986). "Women and Crime": The female offender. *Signs, 12*(1), 78–96. Retrieved from http://www.jstor.org/stable/3174358

Editorial: Donald Trump's Muslim ban is cowardly and dangerous. [Editorial]. (2017, January 28). *New York Times*. Retrieved from https://www.nytimes.com/2017/01/28/opinion/donald-trumps-muslim-ban-is-cowardly-and-dangerous.html

Ellis, L., & Peterson, J. (1996). Crime and religion: An international comparison among thirteen industrial nations. *Personality and Individual Differences, 20*(6), 761–768. doi:10.1016/0191-8869(96)00023-2

Flowers, B. R. (1995). *Female crime, criminals, and cellmates: An exploration of female criminality and delinquency*. Jefferson, NC: McFarland.

Free, M. D., & Ruesink, M. (2012). *Race and justice: Wrongful convictions of African American men*. Boulder, CO: Lynne Rienner.

Greenfeld, L. A. (1996). *Child victimizers: Violent offenders and their victims*. Retrieved from the Bureau of Justice Statistics website: https://www.bjs.gov/content/pub/pdf/CVVOATV.PDF

Ladd, C. (2014, December 31). Which religion is the most violent? *The Washington Times*. Retrieved from http://www.washingtontimes.com/news/2014/dec/31/which-religion-most-violent/

Lombroso, C., & Ferrero, W. (1898). *The Female Offender*. New York, NY: Appleton and Company.

National Archives. (2017). *World War II Enemy Alien Control Program overview*. Retrieved from https://www.archives.gov/research/immigration/enemy-aliens-overview.html

National Gang Center. (2017). *National Youth Gang Survey analysis*. Retrieved https://www.nationalgangcenter.gov/Survey-Analysis/Demographics

Ngai, M. M. (1999). The architecture of race in American immigration law: A reexamination of the Immigration Act of 1924. *Journal of American History, 86*(1), 67–92. doi:10.2307/2567407

Public Broadcasting Service. (2019). *What is race?* Retrieved from http://www.pbs.org/race/001_WhatIsRace/001_00-home.htm

Shader, M. (2001). *Risk factors for delinquency: An overview*. Retrieved from the National Criminal Justice Reference Service website: https://www.ncjrs.gov/pdffiles1/ojjdp/frd030127.pdf

Sickmund, M., & Puzzanchera, C. (Eds.). (2014). *Juvenile offenders and victims: 2014 national report*. Retrieved from the Office of Juvenile Justice and Delinquency Prevention website: https://www.ojjdp.gov/ojstatbb/nr2014/downloads/NR2014.pdf

State of Washington; State of Minnesota, v. Donald J. Trump, 847 F.3d 1151 (9th Cir. 2017).

Wasserman, G. A., Keenan, K., Tremblay, R. E., Coie, J. D., Herrenkohl, T. I., Loeber, R., & Petechuk, D. (2003). *Risk and protective factors of child delinquency*. Retrieved from the National Criminal Justice Reference Service website: https://www.ncjrs.gov/pdffiles1/ojjdp/193409.pdf

Williams, F. P., & McShane, M. D. (2014). *Criminological theory* (6th ed.). Boston, MA: Pearson.

Zahn, M. A., Agnew, R., Fishbein, D., Miller, S., Winn, D.-M., Dakoff, G., … Chesney-Lind, M. (2010). *Causes and correlates of girls' delinquency*. Retrieved from the National Criminal Justice Reference Service website: https://www.ncjrs.gov/pdffiles1/ojjdp/226358.pdf

SECTION IV

Risk Assessment Tools

CHAPTER FIFTEEN

Historical Background of Risk Assessment

THE HISTORY OF juvenile justice risk assessment and classification is a history of a long struggle to move away from punitive responses to juvenile delinquency and criminality to therapeutic responses that focus on rehabilitating offenders who make contact with the criminal justice system (Kehl, Guo, & Kessler, 2017). As Hannah-Moffat and Maurutto (2003) note, the risk and needs assessment instruments currently in use "evolved out of an influential professional ideology—and now deeply embedded practitioner-driven research agenda that embraced the rehabilitative ideal" and "out of a long-standing organizational commitment to intervention and programs" (p, 2).

The history of risk and needs assessment is also a story of one group of people arguing that children who commit crimes must be punitively rewarded for their poor choices and another group who argues that there is a fundamental difference between the ways adults think and behave and the ways children do. The former group advocates for the selective incarceration of a subset of individuals who are identified as "career criminals" or as being prone to violence (Kehl et al., 2017). The former group views delinquent and criminal behaviors as symptoms of biological, psychological, or social pathology. This idea gained popularity in the 1980s and is now one of the main forces behind the current push for the use of risk assessment and classification as a tool for responding to delinquent and criminal behaviors.

Risk assessment and classification play crucial roles in the decision-making process associated with sanctions, referrals, or rehabilitation and for almost every major decision that affects a juvenile offender. Consequently, these instruments use science to impact recidivism by helping determine what strategies work, what factors should be strategically targeted, and what results should be the focus of a correctional intervention.

Risk assessment tools are used at various levels of juvenile justice operations, including juvenile court intake, probation, pre-detention, and disposition, and at correctional facilities and by correction or detention officers and clinical staff. The needs as well as the risk and protective factors assessed by risk assessment instruments are identified through rigorous research. That is, risk and needs assessment tools assess behaviors and attitudes that research shows are related to recidivism. Generally, only items or factors that have been identified through multiple prior studies or that one or more criminological, sociological, or psychological theories of criminal or deviant behavior support as having strong relationships to juvenile delinquency, criminality, or deviance that are included in risk assessment instruments (Development Services Group, 2015).

The history of risk assessment instruments is described in terms of waves (Burman, Armstrong, Batchelor, McNeill, & Nicholson, 2007; Schwalbe, 2007). This chapter therefore offers brief discussions of the progress made thus far by the juvenile justice system in regard to the development and use of risk assessment and classification in the past 100 years. In doing so, this chapter also discusses the critical developmental stages of current American juvenile justice risk assessment tools as well as weaknesses of the existing risk and needs assessment instruments.

RISK ASSESSMENT INSTRUMENTS

The very existence of risk assessment instruments is predicated on the principle that delinquency is a symptom of some form of biological, psychological, or social pathology, and therefore criminal justice responses to such behaviors should focus on offenders and not their offenses. Of course, this position rejects the classical view that delinquency is an act of free will and that the best way to deter such behavior is to subject offenders to sanctions commensurate with the offense. Risk assessment tools are therefore key elements of the supervision, management, and rehabilitation of juvenile offenders as well as the prevention of recidivism in general (Hempel, Buck, Cima, & van Marie, 2013).

More specifically, risk assessment tools are typically used in secured care and community correction decision-making processes, including intake, placement, treatment, case planning, release, and referrals. That is, risk assessment instruments play critical roles in the identification of treatment goals, programs, supervision levels, and commitment or custody decisions (Andrews, Bonta, & Wormith, 2006; Burman et al., 2007; Baird et al., 2013). Risk assessment instruments are also used to classify offenders and to target those juveniles who need intensive supervision and services (Pew Center on the States, 2011). These processes, however, have long histories, some of which are informed by developments in the juvenile justice system, including those initiated by *Kent v. United States.*

KENT V. UNITED STATES

The construction of risk assessment instruments and the requirement that risk assessment tools be used to guide decisions that affect every offender have taken a long period to develop, incrementally, both within the courts and detention facilities and in the field of social science. In the case of developments within the courts, *Kent v. United States* is a good example. Indeed, there is an argument to be made that the United States Supreme Court's ruling in *Kent v. United States* (1966) represents one of the earliest recognitions of the important roles risk assessment and classification play within the juvenile justice system.

Kent v. United States recognized that mental health and a history of abuse, like most risk factors, ought to be looked at when deciding the fate of a juvenile offender in the care of the state. The case also recognized that juvenile offenders ought to be thoroughly investigated in part because some extrajudicial histories are relevant and thus should be considered when making decisions that affect an offender.

The facts of the case are that the offender, Mr. Morris A. Kent, was on probation at the time of detention for previous adjudication for several housebreakings and an attempted purse snatching offense. He was arrested on September 2, 1961, for allegedly entering the home of a woman in the District of Columbia. Mr. Kent, aged 16, allegedly stole the victim's wallet and then raped her. He was subsequently identified because he left his fingerprint at the crime scene. Mr. Kent was interrogated by police officers for a prolonged period—one interview session lasted from about 3:00 p.m. to 10:00 p.m. The following day, he was also interrogated from morning hours until 5:00 p.m. the next day. Eventually, he admitted his involvement in the alleged offenses on the second day. Mr. Kent was subsequently detained for almost a week without arraignment or a determination of probable cause for his apprehension by a judicial officer. When the juvenile court judge scheduled a hearing to determine whether Mr. Kent should be waived to the adult courts, counsel for Mr. Kent challenged the move.

According to the U.S. Supreme Court, counsel for Mr. Kent challenged the juvenile court's waiver proceeding, claiming Mr. Kent was "a victim of severe psychopathology." The court explains:

> During this period of detention and interrogation, petitioner's counsel arranged for examination of petitioner by two psychiatrists and a psychologist. He thereafter filed with the Juvenile Court a motion for a hearing on the question of waiver of Juvenile Court jurisdiction, together with an affidavit of a psychiatrist certifying that petitioner "is a victim of severe psychopathology" and recommending hospitalization for psychiatric observation. Petitioner's counsel, in support of his motion to the effect that the Juvenile Court should retain jurisdiction of petitioner, offered to prove that if petitioner were given adequate treatment in a hospital under the aegis of the Juvenile Court, he would be a suitable subject for rehabilitation. (*Kent v. United States*, 1966)

The juvenile court judge rejected the motion and waived the offender over to adult jurisdiction for prosecution. Mr. Kent was subsequently indicted for housebreaking, robbery, and rape. At trial as an adult, the defense again argued that Mr. Kent was not criminally responsible because "his unlawful act was the product of mental disease or mental defect" consistent with the decision in Durham v. United States, 1954. Mr. Kent was, however, tried and found guilty on six counts of housebreaking and robbery, but the jury found him "not guilty by reason of insanity" for the rape case.

Under the law in the District of Columbia, a "not guilty by reason of insanity" verdict qualified Mr. Kent for mandatory transfer to a mental hospital or institution until his sanity was restored. Mr. Kent was, however, sentenced to serve 5 to 15 years in prison for each count, totaling 30 to 90 years. Upon appeal, the U.S. Supreme Court held that "the Juvenile Court's order waiving jurisdiction of petitioner was entered without compliance with required procedures" and hence remanded the case to the trial court for further processing. The court further argued that

> the theory of the District's Juvenile Court Act, like that of other jurisdictions, is rooted in social welfare philosophy rather than in the corpus juris. Its proceedings are designated as civil rather than criminal. The Juvenile Court is theoretically engaged in determining the

> needs of the child and of society rather than adjudicating criminal conduct. The objectives are to provide measures of guidance and rehabilitation for the child and protection for society, not to fix criminal responsibility, guilt and punishment. The State is *parens patriae* rather than prosecuting attorney and judge. But the admonition to function in a "parental" relationship is not an invitation to procedural arbitrariness. (*Kent v. United States*, 1966)

In essence, the decision of the U.S. Supreme Court in this case recognized that the juvenile justice system must take into account all necessary information, including extrajudicial matters that are relevant to the thinking and behaviors of offenders as well as matters that affect the mental status of the juvenile offender. The only problem, however, is that in the 1960s, risk assessment instruments were still in their first stage of development.

CRITICAL STAGES OF THE DEVELOPMENT OF RISK ASSESSMENT TOOLS

The drive to develop reliable and accurate actuarial risk and needs assessment instruments has taken almost a century. At the beginning, progress was slow. For example, although actuarial risk assessment methods were used by social service agencies in the United States as early as 1928, and calls to move away from the intuitive classification system began in that period, juvenile risk instruments did not materialize until the 1970s (Baird et al., 2013).

STAGES OF DEVELOPMENT OF RISK ASSESSMENT INSTRUMENTS

First Wave

Criminal justice practitioners relied on their individual professional judgment or gut feelings to separate low-risk offenders from high-risk offenders.

Second Wave

Criminal justice practitioners assigned numerical values to static factors and used aggregate scores to separate low-risk offenders from high-risk offenders.

Third Wave

Criminal justice practitioners assigned numerical values to both static and dynamic factors and used aggregate scores to separate low-risk offenders from high-risk offenders.

Fourth Wave

Criminal justice practitioners used improved third-wave risk assessment instruments to assess offenders' risk level, identify needs, and measure offenders' readiness for rehabilitation.

Current Wave

Criminal justice practitioners use multiple risk assessment instruments to produce a more accurate risk assessment and classification result.

Current risk and needs assessments and processes have therefore gone through four distinct generations: first, second, third, and fourth waves (Schwalbe, 2007; Baird et al., 2013; Kehl et al., 2017). Each of these four stages represents a critical development in the continuous scientific and criminal justice efforts to develop standardized instruments to assess individual risk and needs as well as to help with the identification of appropriate interventions that fit the needs of low-, moderate-, and high-risk youth offenders.

First Wave Assessments

The first wave or generation of risk assessment instruments covers the period during which risk levels were assigned by criminal justice practitioners without the aid of actuarial instruments (Baird et al., 2013). This first generation of risk assessments therefore consisted of mainly "unstructured clinical judgements of the probability of offending behavior" (Burman et al., 2007, p. 24). Typically, professional clinicians and correctional officers "would generally rely on their own professional judgment when making decisions for individuals about sentencing, supervision, and treatment" (Kehl et al., 2017, p. 8).

The process of assessing and assigning risk levels to juvenile offenders based on the gut feelings of the clinicians or criminal justice practitioners began informally at the beginning of the 20th century. In this period, the process was entirely a matter of professional judgement—criminal justice practitioners, particularly pretrial service departments, and probation, detention, prison, parole, and other clinical staff such as psychologists, psychiatrists, and social workers basically relied on their professional training and experiences to intuitively determine the fate of each offender (Bonta & Andrews, 2007).

In this first-generation era, criminal justice professionals basically reviewed reports generated by other criminal justice professionals and agencies and used what they made of such reports to form intuitive opinions and make judgments about offenders' thinking, behavioral patterns, and risk of reoffending and to develop appropriate intuitional responses. This meant that final risk assessment results and recommendations varied depending on the training and experience of the correctional professionals making the assessments. Consequently, under this scheme an offender could go from being classified as a low-risk offender to a high-risk offender instantly without any significant change in thinking, behavior, or history simply because of a change in the criminal justice practitioners performing the assessment and classification. Results of the assessments were therefore simply professional opinions, and the conclusions had no citable, empirical support, although in most instances the processes were informed by legitimate scientific procedures.

Second Wave Assessments

Obviously, the intuitive classification system during the first wave of risk assessment tool development could not pass empirical scrutiny. For example, the approach had no documented, positive impact on recidivism rates. The call to move away from the intuitive classification system that began in the late 1920s to a risk assessment system that emphasized empirical-based ways of assessing and classifying offenders quickly gained the backing of research. The lack of documented effectiveness coupled with the cost of running detention facilities and the need to deliver targeted treatment using reliable methods that could separate low-risk offenders from higher-risk offenders prompted the move away from intuition-based assessment methods to a more scientifically validated method. That process gained ground and popularity in the early 1970s, paving the way for the actuarial risk assessment tools in the mid-1970s (Bonta & Andrews, 2007).

Certainly, actuarial risk assessment methods were used by social service agencies in the United States as early as 1928 (Baird et al., 2013), the period during which a stronger scientific conclusion emerged that actuarial and structured risk assessment instruments were superior to unstructured clinical judgments (Singh, Grann, & Fazel, 2011; Hempel et al., 2013). That is, principle parties concluded that as a basis for "decisions about sanctions, referrals, or rehabilitation, actuarial and structured risk assessment instruments are superior to unstructured clinical judgments" (Viljoen et al., 2015). Consistent with this finding, the second generation of actuarial risk assessment adopted instruments that were statistically derived and empirically based, and that stressed static and historical risk factors, such as the number and types of convictions (Burman et al., 2007, p. 24; Campbell, French, & Gendreau, 2009).

Studies also found that the second generation of risk assessment tools "focused on identifying groups of offenders with distinctly different risks of future offending" (Baird et al., 2013). This wave of risk assessment instruments aimed to measure the probability of reoffending within a certain time frame after release into the community or after the risk assessment was complete (Nafekh, 2002). Thus, unlike the intuitive model, tools in this era assigned numerical values to factors such as criminal history and social history that were individually associated with repeat offending, substance abuse, family problems, peer delinquency, school-related problems, family dynamics and history, history of being victimized, peers' relationship and influence, educational achievements, and intellectual ability. The second-generation instruments also used the aggregate of assigned values to separate low-risk offenders from high-risk offenders—those who scored high on the scale were classified as high risk, and those who scored low were labeled as low risk (Hoffman, Stone-Meierhoefer, & Beck, 1978; Towberman, 1992; Schwalbe, 2007).

Again, studies looking at the effects on recidivism of risk assessment and classification supported the conclusion that evidence-based risk assessment and classification outcomes were far superior to the informal assessment and classification results that emerged out of the intuitive method of assessing offenders' thoughts, behaviors, and risk and needs levels. That is, the "actuarial approaches yield more accurate estimates than the unstructured clinical judgments approach" (Johnson, Lowenkamp, & VanBenschoten, 2011; Murrie, 2012, p. 162; Luallen, Radakrishnan, & Rhodes, 2016). However, the instruments primarily measured static risk factors such as history of arrest and convictions, history of substance abuse, unemployment, and past violent behaviors (Hoffman et al., 1978).

The use of static risk factors also meant that each offender's risk level rarely changed because although the effect of static risk factors could be minimized, many factors such as criminal, clinical, and social history did not change. For example, offenders who scored highly for not completing high school or having prior involuntary contact with the criminal justice system, or for having mental health diagnoses or histories of taking psychotropic medication had to be classified as having elevated risk or needs even if they could take or had taken steps to mitigate the effects of such risks.

Undoubtedly, focusing on static factors alone does not produce meaningful change in an offender's overall thinking and behavior. Thus, studies looking at the effects of risk assessment instruments and indeed the processes, overwhelmingly have confirmed that focusing on static risk factors alone while disregarding dynamic risk factors is not an effective way to predict future thinking and behavior, in part because static factors are not good measurements of behavioral changes over time. In order words, static factors do not explain or capture behavioral change over time because static factors by definition do not change. The solution, therefore, is to assess both static and dynamic risk factors, such as thinking and attitudes, as evidence-based manipulation or programing can alter their effects on future behaviors.

As the second wave of assessment development waned, these shortcomings prompted the demand for a more effective system of assessment that looks at both static and dynamic risk and protective factors.

Third Wave Assessments

Third-generation risk assessment instruments utilized both clinical and actuarial methods and aimed at objectively and systematically measuring static and dynamic risk or criminogenic factors (Burman et al., 2007, p. 26). The main distinction between the second and third wave of risk assessment, therefore, is that the latter captured both static and dynamic risk factors, while the former captured only static risk factors. The capturing of dynamic factors such as lack of interest in gainful employment or educational pursuits and association with negative friends meant that instruments could capture the daily behavioral and thought process each offender engaged in.

The assessment of dynamic risk factors also gives offenders specific guidance for mitigating their individual risk levels. For example, offenders with no high school diploma could go from high-risk for academic achievement to low-risk by simply completing general education diploma (GED) programs within a short period. Indeed, the invention of actuarial risk assessment provided probation and parole officers with the option of conditioning offenders, for instance, who did not graduate from high school to procure a GED with the promise of a change in risk level and ultimately a change in other restrictions associated with high risk levels.

Obviously, the invention of risk assessment tools that measure both static and dynamic risk assessment represented a major development because this method gave criminal justice practitioners new and rather more effective tools for not only calculating offenders' risk levels based on history but also on what they were doing in response to such behaviors. The third-wave instruments therefore significantly improved the way parole, probation, and other correctional officers and staff as a whole assessed, classified, and supervised antisocial thinking and behaviors

Fourth Wave Assessments

The fourth stage of the development of risk assessment instruments brought three important functions: assessment of risk level, identification of needs, and measurement of each offender's readiness for correcting antisocial thoughts or behaviors. That is, the fourth-generation instruments calculate static or unvarying risk factors, dynamic or modifiable risk factors, and protective factors, and thus assess risk, needs, and responsivity while allowing for the use of professional discretion where necessary to correct for individual factors. Hence, the tools produce results that can be used for the purpose of planning and delivering treatment as well as managing caseloads and guiding the supervision of offenders. These tools aim at systematically bringing together information about offenders' history and needs in order to develop individualized plans for treatment and supervision (Burman et al., 2007, p. 26).

The risk principle is that criminal and delinquent behaviors can be predicted; therefore, treatment should target the risk level of the offender, with high-risk offenders needing programs that provide more intensive treatment and services and low-risk offenders receiving minimal intervention (James, 2015). The needs principle also holds that effective treatment should focus on individual offenders' needs and dynamic risk factors (James, 2015, p. 6).

Needs assessment items identify changes that offenders must make to prevent recidivism, which include what each offender needs to learn, what behaviors ought to be changed, and what goals must be achieved as well as what resources are needed to achieve the overall therapeutic goals. Assumptions are that attendance to needs decreases the offender's likelihood of engaging in future criminal and delinquent activities. Failure to address needs increases the potential for future delinquent and criminal activities.

The principle of responsivity requires that therapeutic interventions "be delivered in a style and mode that is consistent with the ability and learning style of the offender," and thus the treatment of offenders should take into account the relevant characteristics of the offender, such as age, gender, ethnicity, and cultural identification as well as the offender's motivation levels, preferences, and personality (James, 2015, p. 6). Responsivity items therefore measure offenders' likelihood of benefiting from specific treatment interventions by assessing variables such as the offenders' cognitive abilities, attitudes and beliefs, and motivation to change (Johnson et al., 2011). Responsivity also assesses individual offenders' ability to respond to particular therapeutic interventions or to specific methods, as well as how long it will take and how difficult it will be for an offender to reduce an existing risk level.

The risk-needs-responsivity approach of the fourth-generation risk assessment instrument is therefore the current dominant paradigm. Broadly, this approach argues that "high-risk offenders need to be placed in programs that provide more intensive treatment and services while low-risk offenders should receive minimal or even no intervention" because effective treatment should focus on addressing needs that inform delinquent and criminal behaviors (James, 2015, p. i). Obviously, the inclusion in actuarial risk assessment scales of how an offender will respond to treatment is an important contribution because it makes it possible to identify the most appropriate interventions for each offender and thus has the potential to more effectively minimize recidivism (Bonta & Andrews, 2007). The measurement of needs is also particularly useful for separating offenders with high needs from offenders with low needs and thus allows for the allocation of resources to those who require intensive supervision and programming. In theory, those with high needs qualify for additional resources and those with low needs gets fewer resources allocated them. In this regard, fourth-stage risk assessment instruments are more useful than the first, second, and third brands of risk assessment tools.

CURRENT ASSESSMENT SYSTEMS

Despite the advancement made regarding the assessment of risk, needs, and responsivity, the possibility of a single risk assessment tool is far from reality. To compensate for this lack of a universal tool, agencies use multiple risk assessment tools when calculating risk and needs levels for youth (Baird et al., 2013). Agencies use unique risk assessment tools for assessing sexual offending behaviors, violent offending behaviors, substance abuse offending behaviors, mental health-related behaviors, and several offending behaviors. There is therefore a long list of risk assessment instruments that measure a variety of psychological or cognitive factors that might be relevant to particular juvenile offenders depending on their histories and typology of offending behaviors. Table 15.1 shows a list of risk assessment tools that are commonly used in the United States.

TABLE 15.1 ***Common Risk Assessment Instruments in Use***

Examples of some of the most popular instruments in use for sex offenses, violent behaviors, substance abuse, and mental health and general offending behaviors.

AGENCY	STATE	RISK INSTRUMENT
Arkansas Department of Human Services, Division of Youth Services	Arkansas	YLS/CMI: The Youth Level of Service/Case Management Inventory
Florida Department of Juvenile Justice	Florida	PACT instrument
Georgia Department of Juvenile Justice	Georgia	Comprehensive Risk/Needs (CRN) CRN instrument (COMPAS Youth)
Virginia Department of Juvenile Justice	Virginia	Youth Assessment and Screening Instrument (YASI)
Nebraska Office of Probation Administration	Nebraska	YLS/CMI: The Youth Level of Service/Case Management Inventory
Nebraska Department of Health and Human Services, Office of Juvenile Services	Nebraska	YLS/CMI: The Youth Level of Service/Case Management Inventory
Solano County, California, Probation Department, Youth Division	Solano County, CA	JSC risk assessment for boys Girls Link instrument for girls
Arizona Department of Juvenile Corrections	Arizona	Recidivism Risk Instrument
All county-based juvenile justice departments in Oregon	Oregon	Juvenile Crime Prevention (JCP). The JCP risk assessment instrument was developed specifically for Oregon.

Dozens of risk and needs assessments instruments are available to juvenile justice practitioners. Of course, different assessments target general offending behaviors while others focus on violence, sex offender behaviors, substance abuse, or mental health-related behaviors. Similarly, different states use different tools. For example, the Arizona Administrative Office of the Courts is responsible for setting policies relating to youth referred to juvenile court and youth on probation. This office uses a risk assessment instrument specifically developed and validated for cases referred to juvenile courts in Arizona.

Risk assessment tools are designed to measure specific thoughts and behaviors. For example, the Youth Level of Services/Case Management Inventory (YLS/CMI) was developed specifically for youth. This instrument measures youth's risk of recidivating and youth's need for services based on a variety of factors. The Youth Assessment and Screening Instrument (YASI) can identify moderate- or high-risk youth and is helpful in deciding which youth should receive full assessments. The Structure Assessment of Violence Risk in Youth (SAVRY) estimates youth's risk of committing specific offending behaviors such as violence. SAVRY also assesses juvenile offenders' risk levels and identifies needs that can be targeted by treatment and informs decisions regarding probation and parole supervision and case management (Baird et al., 2013). As well, SAVRY assesses violent or aggressive behaviors in both young males and young females between the age of 12 and 18 years (Burman et al., 2007, p. 51).

The Structured Clinical Judgement (SCJ) combines the systematic, evidence-based features of an actuarial approach with elements of the first generation combined with clinical judgement informed by empirically established approaches and empirical focus on established risk factors including both static and dynamic factors (Andrews et al., 2006; Burman et al., 2007, p. 23).

IDEAL INSTRUMENTS

Current risk assessment instruments still have some room for improvement (Douglas, Pugh, Singh, Savulescu, & Fazel, 2017). First, there are too many risk assessment tools, with each category of behaviors (substance abuse, violent, and general or sex offender behaviors) having multiple risk assessment instruments in use. Another area of concern is gender-sensitivity tools. Certainly, there are many areas where boys and girls may differ both in terms of how they respond to certain risk and protective factors as well as how they benefit from certain services. For example, risks associated with peer delinquency, substance abuse, violent behaviors, and family dysfunction are common items on risk assessment tools. However, current actuarial risk assessment instruments do not adequately account for documented variation between male and female offenders with regard to such items (Schwalbe, 2007, p. 1369).

Undeniably, males commit most violent offences; most research on violent behaviors, and indeed on the risk of violence that informs violent behaviors and the risk assessment instruments that come out of such research processes, continues to concentrate on males and male behaviors (Burman et al., 2007). Some have also argued that "risk and needs assessment are two distinct procedures" and therefore should be conducted separately (James, 2015, p. i). There is also a call for risk assessment instruments to address "racial disparities and disproportionate minority contact (DMC) observed in the juvenile justice system" (Development Services Group, 2015, p. 2).

Another area of concern is the fact that "despite the apparent importance of protective factors, few of the instruments commonly used with juveniles incorporate protective factors, and those that do either have no empirical support or are in development and have not yet been empirically validated" (Rich, 2014, p. 2012). One can therefore argue that the fourth generation does not contain ideal risk assessment instruments. The ideal instrument would be one that can be easily individualized and one that covers a broader list of factors that exceeds the current list of factors. Factors such as offenders' environments, social and economic status, and social needs as well as cognitive abilities could provide a broader context and understanding of each offender's behaviors. The ideal instrument would also provide a more comprehensive and accurate assessment of changes in dynamic risk and protective factors.

A long-held goal of the juvenile justice system in general and for clinical and correctional staff in particular is the existence of a risk assessment instrument that can accurately pinpoint the highest-risk cases of juvenile delinquency and criminality, identify the most critical service needs, and provide guidance for the selection and application of services that target such risk factors and needs. Such a risk assessment instrument would have the capacity to provide accurate estimates of risk that serve offenders of all sexual orientations and from all racial and socioeconomic backgrounds, and would be simple, easily understood, administered, and interpreted, and produce risk and needs scores informed by each individual offender's risk and needs (Baird et al., 2013). An ideal instrument would also account for gender, racial, and socioeconomic disparities and accurately serve a diverse population of juvenile offenders (Schwalbe, 2007).

CONCLUSION

None of the instruments in use has demonstrated strong or consistent predictive validity, and there is no single "best" risk assessment instrument in use, in part because although offenders share some elements in common, each offending behavior and offender is unique. The actual factors that inform any set of behaviors, the risk assessment instruments that are used to assess recidivism, and the very processes that produce risk scores are therefore far from certain because "there are so many determinants of human behavior that it is impossible to reason through all of the possible outcomes" (James, 2015, p. 9). However, the science of observation has identified certain factors that tend to be common among certain categories or groups of juvenile offenders. There is, therefore, a good reason to use instruments and tools capable of accurately placing a youth in the right group or category of juvenile offenders.

QUESTIONS

1. What are the major advantages or disadvantages associated with the use of or reliance on clinical judgement or intuition?
2. Youth that live in poor and underprivileged environments are expected to have more risk factors than those who live in well-to-do environments. Should these environmental factors be taken into account when assessing the risk and needs of juvenile offenders?
3. Why did it take so long for the American juvenile justice system to fully recognize the importance of assessing offenders' risk, needs, and responsivity?
4. What are the advantages and disadvantages of having gender-neutral or male-specific and female-specific risk assessment instruments?
5. In terms of positive impact on an offender's behaviors, which stage is more critical, the assessment and classification stage or the post-assessment intervention stage?

REFERENCES

Andrews, D. A., Bonta, J., & Wormith, J. S. (2006). The recent past and near future of risk and/or need assessment. *Crime and Delinquency, 52*(1), 7–27.

Baird, C., Healy, T., Johnson, K., Bogie, A., Wicke Dankert, E., & Scharenbroch, C. (2013). *A comparison of risk assessment instruments in juvenile justice.* Retrieved from the National Criminal Justice Reference Service website: https://www.ncjrs.gov/pdffiles1/ojjdp/grants/244477.pdf

Bonta, J., & Andrews, D. A. (2007). *Risk-need-responsivity model for offender assessment and rehabilitation 2006–07.* Retrieved from the Pennsylvania Board of Probation and Parole website: https://www.pbpp.pa.gov/

Burman, M., Armstrong, S., Batchelor, S., McNeill, F., & Nicholson, J. (2007). *Research and practice in risk assessment and risk management of children and young people engaging in offending behaviours: A literature review.* Retrieved from the Scottish Centre for Crime and Justice Research website: https://www.sccjr.ac.uk/

Campbell, M. A., French, S., & Gendreau, P. (2009). The prediction of violence in adult offenders: A meta-analytic comparison of instruments and methods of assessment. *Criminal Justice and Behavior, 36*(6), 567–590.

Development Services Group, 2015. Risk and Needs Assessment for Youths. Retrieved from the Office of Juvenile Justice and Delinquency Prevention website: https://www.ojjdp.gov/mpg/litreviews/RiskandNeeds.pdf

Douglas, T., Pugh, J., Singh, I., Savulescu, J., & Fazel, S. (2017). Risk assessment tools in criminal justice and forensic psychiatry: The need for better data. *European Psychiatry, 42*, 134–137. doi:10.1016/j.eurpsy.2016.12.009

Hannah-Moffat, K., & Maurutto, P. (2003). *Youth risk/need assessment: An overview of issues andpractices.* Retrieved from the Government of Canada, Department of Justice website: https://www.justice.gc.ca/eng/index.html

Hempel, I., Buck, N., Cima, M., & van Marie, H. J. C. (2013). Review of risk assessment instruments for juvenile sex offenders: What is next. *International Journal of Offender Therapy and Comparative Criminology, 57*(2), 208–228.

Hoffman, P. B., Stone-Meierhoefer, B., & Beck, J. L. (1978). Salient factor score and releasee behavior: Three validation samples. *Law and Human Behavior, 2*(1), 47–62.

James, N. (2015). *Risk and needs sssessment in the criminal justice system* (Accession No. 030113). Washington, DC: Congressional Research Service.

Johnson, J. L., Lowenkamp, C. T., VanBenschoten, S. W. (2011). The construction and validation of the federal Post Conviction Risk Assessment (PCRA). *Federal Probation Journal, 75*(2).

Kehl, D., Guo, P., & Kessler, S. (2017). *Algorithms in the criminal justice system: Assessing the use of risk assessments in sentencing.* Retrieved from the Harvard Law School, Berkman Klein Center for Internet and Society, Responsive Communities Initiative website: http://nrs.harvard.edu/urn-3:HUL.InstRepos:33746041

Kent v. United States, 383 U.S. 541, No. 104, Supreme Court of United States (1966).

Luallen, J., Radakrishnan, S., & Rhodes, W. (2016). The predictive validity of the post-conviction risk assessment among federal offenders. *Criminal Justice and Behavior, 43*(9), 1173–1189. doi:10.1177/0093854816650481

Murrie, D. C. (2012). Assessment instruments for juveniles who sexually offend. In E. P. Ryan, J., A. Hunter, & D. C. Murrie (Eds.), *Juvenile sex offenders: A guide to evaluation and treatment for mental health professionals.* New York, NY: Oxford University Press.

Nafekh, M., & Motiuk, L. L. (2002). Statistical Information on Recidivism Scale—Revised 1 (SIR-R1) Scale: A psychometric examination. Retrieved from the Correctional Service of Canada website: https://www.csc-scc.gc.ca/research/092/r126_e.pdf

Pew Center on the States. (2011). State of Recidivism: The Revolving Door of America's Prisons. Retrieved from https://www.pewtrusts.org/~/media/legacy/uploadedfiles/pcs_assets/2011/pewstateofrecidivismpdf.pdf

Rich, P. (2014). *Assessment of risk for sexual reoffense in juveniles who commit sexual offenses.* Retrieved from the Sex Offenders Management Assessment and Planning Initiative website: https://www.smart.gov/SOMAPI/sec2/ch4_risk.html

Schwalbe, C. S. (2007). Risk assessment for juvenile justice: A meta-nalysis. *Law and Human Behavior, 31*(5), 449–462.

Singh, J. P., Grann, M., & Fazel, S. (2011). A comparative study of violence risk assessment tools: A systematic review and metaregression analysis of 68 studies involving 25,980 participants. *Clinical Psychology Review, 31*(3), 499–513.

Towberman, D. B. (1992). National Survey of Juvenile Needs Assessment. *Crime and Delinquency, 38*(2), 230–238.

Viljoen, J. L., Gray, A. L., Shaffer, C., Latzman, N. E., Scalora, M. J., & Ullman, D. (2015). Changes in J-SOAP-II and SAVRY scores over the course of residential, cognitive-behavioral treatment for adolescent sexual offending. *Sexual Abuse, 29*(4), 342–374. doi:10.1177/1079063215595404

CHAPTER SIXTEEN

Logic of Risk and Needs Assessment

DESPITE THE STRUGGLE some youth have with criminal law and law enforcement agencies, most children transition into adulthood without any unwanted contact with the criminal justice system. The question, therefore, is *why* most youth reach adulthood without delinquency or contact with the criminal justice system. Most social scientists who work with children, and indeed theorists in the fields of criminal justice, sociology, psychology, and criminology, would readily say that the handful of youth who make involuntary contact with law enforcement agencies do so partly because of the absence of certain protective factors and the presence of specific risk factors as well as needs in their lives.

Social scientists believe, and many studies have shown, that criminal and delinquent behaviors are significantly influenced by certain risk and protective factors (Bonta & Andrews, 2007; Taxman, 2017). Additionally, individual offenders' responsivity and needs can predict the likelihood of recidivism. The roles these factors play in relation to delinquent, criminal, and antisocial behaviors in general are a critical focus of the assessment and classification of each juvenile offender's past, present, and future criminal and delinquent behaviors. Thus, an understanding of how risk, protective, needs, and responsivity factors can improve criminal justice professionals' ability to assess and predict future criminal and delinquent behaviors and tendencies can help professionals prescribe appropriate therapeutic interventions to minimize the adverse impact of delinquent behaviors and tendencies (Shader, 2004; Bartol & Bartol, 2012).

This chapter explains risk, protective and needs factors, as well as responsivity and the roles each factor plays when assessing and classifying delinquent and criminal behaviors and when measuring the likelihood of recidivism within a particular behavioral domain—violent, sexual, substance abuse, general, and mental health-related behaviors—and the various roles these factors collectively play in the development of therapeutic interventions to prevent future acts of delinquency and criminality. This chapter also explains the logic and assumptions that make risk, protective, needs, and responsivity factors important parts of the process of accurately identifying, assessing, and classifying behaviors and tendencies. This chapter concludes with a brief discussion of core assumptions and limitations that inform how risks are identified, assessed, and classified and how results are utilized by criminal justice practitioners to guide critical decision.

ASSESSMENT AND CLASSIFICATION OF RISK AND NEEDS

Although there are variety of risk and needs assessment tools in use by different agencies, risk assessment instruments typically measure certain impacts of various risk, protective, needs, and responsivity factors, as well as how these factors have influenced past and current deviant, criminal, or delinquent behaviors and how they will influence future ones. Consequently, criminal justice practitioners use risk and needs assessment to figure out individuals' risk of engaging in future acts of delinquency and criminality because practitioners, and indeed the public too, want fewer rates of delinquency, criminality, and deviancy.

By all means, the practice of relying on the results of risk assessment is not restricted to the juvenile justice system. Indeed, individuals and even noncriminal justice institutions such as insurance companies and universities use risk assessment. For example, insurance companies like to insure more drivers because more insurance policies mean more returns on investment. However, insurance companies certainly do not like drivers who file insurance claims or who get involved in at-fault accidents because more claims mean more financial settlements and payouts, which may significantly reduce profit margins. With this in mind, insurance companies use risk to calculate their applicants' likelihood of filing insurance claims.

In other words, insurance companies use a standard rating system that calculates risk based on answers that are provided in response to questions that have been identified by researchers as having value for predicting the likelihood of a potential applicant engaging in at-fault accidents, filing insurance claims, or failing to pay premiums. The questions insurance companies ask revolve around factors such as commuting miles and residential locations, and whether an applicant owns a home, has a full-time job and satisfactory credit history, has a recent history of filing insurance claims, or has been cited for moving violations within a given period. The answers to such questions are used by insurance companies to calculate applicants' risk of engaging in at-fault accidents, filling insurance claims, or failing to pay a premium.

The assumptions are that those who have good driving records and good credit histories, and those who own homes and who commute shorter distances, are less likely to have accidents or file insurance claims. Those who do not own homes, who have received traffic tickets, and who have filed insurance claims in the past are more likely to cause accidents or file insurance claims. Applicants who fall into the high-risk category pay higher premiums to offset the likely costs of claims they are likely to generate. Those applicants who fall into the low-risk level pay lower premiums because their chances of filing claims are lower.

LAW ENFORCEMENT PREEMPLOYMENT BACKGROUND INVESTIGATION IS ALSO A RISK ASSESSMENT EXERCISE

Table 16.1 contains common risk and protective factors law enforcement agencies look for during pre-employment background investigation include the following factors. The assumptions are that any negative or unfavorable conclusion associated with any of these factors increases an applicant's chance of becoming a criminal or civil liability for the agency, or increases the applicant's chances of not being a dependable or responsible law enforcement employee.

TABLE 16.1 *Risk and Protective Factors*

FELONY CONVICTION	ANY PAST FELONY CONVICTION.
Misdemeanor conviction	Any past serious misdemeanor conviction.
Controlled substance	Current drug use or past drug abuse.
Military service	History of military service is a strong protective factor. However, dishonorable discharge from the military is a very strong risk factor.
Domestic violence	Any history of domestic violence.
Driving records	History of traffic-rule violations. Background investigators look for evidence of character flaws, antisocial thoughts and attitudes, and or evidence of disregard for laws.
Past crimes	Felonies and misdemeanors for which applicant was not caught.
Gang affiliation	Past or current membership in a criminal gang.
Friends and family	The knowledge of friends and family members about the applicant, and the connection, if any, family members have to the criminal world and criminal justice system.
Education	Academic standing and level of acquired knowledge.
Employment history	Poor employment record. History of being terminated or fired from prior job.
Credit history	Bad credit history including whether the applicant is financially compromised. Investigators also want to know if the applicant has been meeting his or her financial obligations, and if the applicant will continue to do so.
Sexual behaviors	Any sexual act involving one or more animals or underage persons.
Honesty	Investigators place a premium on truthfulness. Thus, investigators want to know if the applicant is honest or if the applicant truthfully completed the application package and answered all questions. Investigators look for discrepancy between applicant records and applicant statements at all levels of the application process.

Most universities also use risk assessment processes to evaluate applicants for admission. Universities use college admission tests, reference letters, personal statements, and grade-point average to predict each student's likelihood of graduating within a reasonable time and their likelihood of succeeding in certain programs. At an individual level, most people use common risk assessment processes to explain how a person likely will behave in the future. Individual level risk assessment is particularly common during first-time dating encounters and typically involves each party assessing their potential romantic partner by gathering information that they believe will help them predict their potential suitors' future behaviors—note, however, that individual-level assessment is assumed to be logically less reliable because factors change from one person to another, and in all cases, the factors may have no predictive values or may be totally unrelated to the intended prediction.

LOGIC AND ASSUMPTIONS OF RISK ASSESSMENT AND CLASSIFICATION

The process of assessing and classifying risk, needs, and responsivity is grounded in a concept known as the medical model. That is, at the core of every criminal justice risk, needs, and responsivity assessment process is the belief that juvenile offenders are physically, mentally, and or socially sick, and that delinquent, criminal, and deviant thoughts and behaviors are symptoms of such illnesses. Therefore, an accurate assessment, classification, and diagnosis followed by appropriate clinical interventions can minimize the effect and continuous reoccurrence of such thoughts and behaviors (Macnamara, 1977). The adoption of this scientific approach to dealing with juvenile offenders explains criminal justice practitioners' common use of terms such as *symptoms*, *assessment*, *evaluations*, *examination*, *diagnosis*, *risk and needs*, *continuous assessment*, *follow-up*, *admitted* and *discharged*, *inpatient* and *outpatient*, *treatment plan and case plan*, *therapeutic*, and *rehabilitation*.

Risk assessment and classification in general involves the careful calculation of the presence, absence, and impact of risk, protective, needs, and responsivity factors. The calculation of these scores is known as risk-need-responsivity, meaning an offender's level of risk to reoffend and level of treatment needs and readiness for treatment in order to prevent relapse or recidivism (Bonta & Andrews, 2007; Casey et al., 2014; Walters, 2018). In this respect, the underlying assumptions are that risk and needs factors increase the chances of crime and delinquency, protective factors reduce the odds of crime and delinquency, and healthy responsivity decreases the chances of recidivism. Therefore, interventions that target the reduction of risk and needs factors can reduce the possibility of future delinquent and criminal behavior and deviance, while increasing protective factors and improving responsivity significantly lowers the risk of criminal and delinquent behaviors. Table 16.2 contain core criminogenic risk and protective factors.

The list of risk, protective, needs, and responsivity elements that are assessed come from research findings—the majority of such studies use theories such as social bond, social control, social learning, differential association, labelling, social disorganization, and similar sociological, psychological, criminal justice, general personality, cognitive social, and other criminological theories to study various aspects of human thinking and behavior in general and, specifically, factors that inform juvenile delinquency, criminality, and deviance (Bonta & Andrews, 2007). Collectively, these theories argue that environmental, biological, psychological, and social factors generate certain risk and protective factors as well as needs and responsivity that explain why some youth engage in delinquent and criminal behaviors, why others are drawn to prosocial behaviors, and why certain youth manage to stay out of the criminal justice system (Akers, Sellers, & Jennings, 2017; Bartol & Bartol, 2017; Williams & McShane, 2018).

Criminal justice practitioners assign values to the protective and risk factors that result from various studies and use those values in addition to values they assign to responsivity and needs to predict future thinking and behavior. The assumptions are that those with the highest risk and needs scores are deemed to be at high risk of engaging in criminal and delinquent behaviors. Those with medium-range scores are classified as medium risk for engaging in delinquent and criminal behaviors, and those with low risk and needs scores as well as high responsivity and protective factors are considered low risk and are thus less likely to engage in criminal or delinquent behaviors. It is also now well-established that thinking leads to behavior and that most behaviors are symptoms of individual thought processes. Consequently, a distorted or abnormal thought process leads to delinquency, criminality, deviance, and antisocial behavior in general, while a healthy thought process generates prosocial or law-abiding behaviors. As a result, mental health status is one of the factors that gets assessed most frequently by criminal justice practitioners.

CHAPTER 16.2 *Core Criminogenic Risk and Protective Factors*

	SOURCES OF RISKS	RISK	TREATMENT TARGET
1.	Antisocial Behaviors	History of criminality and delinquency including substance use, violent, sexual, and general offending behaviors. Antisocial thoughts, belief, and attitudes.	Develop prosocial thinking and behaviors and minimize support for specific risk and antisocial thinking and behaviors.
2.	Antisocial Personality	History of acting impulsively, adventurously, pleasure-seeking, restlessly being aggressive, and showing callous disregard for other human beings.	Increase ability to improve self-control, reduce impulsivity, relentless aggression, and poor problem-solving skills.
3.	Antisocial Cognition	History of antisocial attitudes, beliefs, values, and use of distorted thinking.	Reduce or eradicate antisocial thinking and behaviors and develop prosocial thinking, attitudes, beliefs, values, and use of non-distorted thinking.
4.	Antisocial Peers	History of associating with peers who engage in antisocial thinking and behaviors or who have antisocial attitudes, beliefs, values and use and use distorted thinking.	Reduce association with antisocial peers and increase interaction with peers with prosocial thinking and behaviors or who have prosocial attitudes, beliefs, and values and who use non-distorted thinking.
5.	Antisocial Family History	Parents tolerate and reward antisocial thoughts, behaviors and attitudes. Parents do not maintain strong involvement in child's life. Parents are abusive (sexually, verbally, physically, or emotionally). Parents have history of poor parent-child relationship, and harsh, lax, or inconsistent disciplinary practices.	Parents do not tolerate antisocial thoughts and behaviors. Parents provide adequate supervision, maintain strong involvement in child's life and takes steps to sexual, verbal, physical, or emotional abuse of child. Family begins to create history of healthy parent-child relationship, and consistently and appropriately discipline child.
6.	Educational achievement	Poor academic performance, not committed to school or the values the school represents. Have antisocial attitudes toward education in general and having history of behavioral problem at school.	Enhance prosocial thinking about the importance of education, improve academic performance. Strong academic performance, commitment to school and the values the school represents, and avoidance of school related behavioral problems.
7.	Leisure activities	Participation in antisocial behaviors or in unproductive activities during free or leisure time.	Participation in prosocial behaviors or in productive activities during free or leisure time.
8.	Substance use, abuse, and dependence	History of controlled substance use, abuse, or dependence.	Reduce controlled substance use, abuse or dependence, eliminate source of controlled substance use, abuse, and dependence and enhance alternatives to controlled substance use, abuse, and dependence.

RISK, PROTECTIVE, NEEDS, AND RESPONSIVITY

Criminal justice-related risk assessment and classification processes typically examine the degree to which factors such as risk, protective, needs, and responsivity are associated with each offender and how each factor informs the offender's thinking and behavior.

Understanding the critical role each factor plays in the commission of delinquent or criminal behavior, how each factor shapes future antisocial behaviors, and how to effectively eliminate or minimize the potential reoccurrence of such antisocial behaviors is vital. These concepts have influenced the development of a long list of offender risk assessment instruments, rehabilitation programs, and strategies that studies show can impact future behavior in a good way (Bonta & Andrews, 2007; Casey et al., 2014; James, 2018).

The concept and logic of risk, protective, needs, and responsivity is not unique to the criminal justice system. Rather, many practitioners, especially those in the medical and psychological fields, use many of the same factors when talking about the patients they serve. In other words, medical professionals talk about factors that increase the chances of acquiring certain diseases and illness. Medical professionals also talk about protective factors such as vitamins and how to best minimize risk, and they recognize certain risks such as cigarette smoking and lack of physical exercise as being more impactful than other risk factors. Medical professionals also talk about needs, or services that are required to revise or prevent an adverse medical condition. That said, in the field of criminal justice, especially in the area of juvenile justice systems, risk, protective, needs, and responsivity stand for specific factors and thus have specific meanings as they relate to specific risk assessment and classification functions.

Delinquent and Criminal Protective Factors

Strong protective factors are useful to any efforts that seek to prevent criminality, delinquency, and recidivism or to reduce the chances of reckless and habitual criminal or delinquent behaviors. Protective factors are generally social, environmental, psychological, and biological characteristics and experiences that are associated with at-risk youth and that studies suggest have the potential to significantly decrease the likelihood of engaging in delinquent, criminal, or deviant behaviors. Every aspect of a youth's life can therefore be a potential source of social, environmental, and psychological protective factors that support, guide, and inform prosocial behaviors in general, specifically noncriminal and nondelinquent actions.

Psychological and mental health protective factors include a healthy mental condition, feeling psychologically safe at home, and the ability to engage in prosocial thoughts. Examples of environmental protective factors include living in a crime free, drug free, or sex abuse free environment that encourages and rewards respect for laws, authorities, and prosocial achievements such as academics. Impactful protective social factors include a history of nonviolent behavior, good academic achievement, strong family ties, positive communal ties, respect for authority, clean criminal or delinquent records, no history of substance abuse, and prosocial peer association. Protective factors such as academic achievement, good coping skills, problem-solving skills, religious activities, and supportive relationships with family members are also good examples.

Delinquent and Criminal Risk Factors

Delinquent and criminal risk factors are individual characteristics and experiences as well as social, environmental, psychological, and biological factors that studies show have the potential to significantly increase a youth's likelihood of engaging in delinquent, criminal, or deviant behaviors. Research shows that some of the most impactful psychological risk factors include mental health diagnoses and antisocial thoughts and beliefs (Casey et al., 2014; James, 2018). Other examples of impactful risk factors are poor interpersonal skills, a history of violent behavior, substance abuse, poor academic achievement, being the recipient of physical or sexual victimization, association with a dysfunctional family, having criminal or delinquent records, and association with antisocial peers, especially those who engage in or who reinforce delinquent and or criminal behaviors. Similar risk factors include poor social skills including communication and problem-solving skills, negative family environments such as parental abuse of controlled substances, and a history of physical, sexual, and/or psychological abuse (Bartol & Bartol, 2012).

SOME RISK FACTORS ARE PARTICULARLY CRIMINOGENIC

Certain risk factors are criminogenic because of their potential to significantly increase a youth's risk of making contact with the criminal justice system. Criminogenic factors mainly cover factors that are either criminal or delinquent in nature or that are connected to criminal or delinquent behaviors. Criminogenic risks are therefore distinct social, psychological and behavioral factors with a strong ability to produce criminal or delinquent behaviors that easily lead to criminal and delinquent acts or because the factor itself is prohibited by law. Therefore, common criminogenic factors typically include behaviors that are unlawful or highly supportive of criminal or delinquent activities. Examples of criminogenic factors include habitual possession of controlled substances, reckless driving, selling drugs, membership in criminal gangs, shoplifting, abuse of controlled substances, and driving under the influence of alcohol or drugs. This logically means that criminogenic factors increase the chance of making unwanted contact with law enforcement agencies. It also means that criminogenic factors demand more urgent clinical interventions.

Successful responses to risk factors demand that the level of intervention be matched to the offender's level of risk and needs for treatment and services. In other words, high-risk offenders need programs that provide intensive treatment and services such as intensive supervision, frequent drug screening, contact with probation or parole officers, or constant supervision by a corrections officer. Low-risk offenders deserve programs that provide non-intensive services (James, 2018). In secured facilities, too, policies demand specific services for high-risk offenders. In fact, in most cases every contact with high-risk offenders is regulated by that offender's risk of harming himself or herself or hurting other offenders, staff, or visitors, and by the level of responsivity or receptiveness to treatment.

Delinquent and Criminal Needs

The needs score dictates the level of treatment as well as services required to address any type and level of criminogenic and noncriminogenic risk factors and to enhance protective and responsivity factors, which studies show correlate with criminal and delinquent conduct (James, 2018). Hence, needs can be described as the thinking, behaviors, resources, and services a person needs in order to break the cycle of at least the antisocial thoughts and behaviors that landed the person in the criminal justice system. In this respect, examples of needs may include the clinical need for the offenders to participate in specific treatment, the need to obtain a high school diploma, and the need for placement in a secured care facility in order to benefit from treatment in a controlled or structured environment and where factors such as controlled substances are less accessible than they are in local neighborhoods.

Responsivity Factors

After successfully completing risk and needs assessments and identifying suitable interventions, the issue of responsivity often emerges as an important factor in any move that is intended to correct an offender's thinking and behaviors. Hence, responsivity refers to the healthiness of an offender's cognitive and physical ability to reasonably benefit from clinical interventions and how well treatment is tailored to the individual's strengths. Responsivity variables therefore demand that treatment interventions should consider the personal strengths and sociobiological personality as well as the physical ability of the offender. When designing and delivering treatment interventions, policies also demand that such undertakings ensure that treatment is tailored to the risk, needs, and ability of the offender (Bonta & Andrews, 2007).

Critical elements of responsivity include the strength of individual offenders' learning skills, motivation to alter delinquent and criminal behaviors, abilities and strengths with regard to carrying out treatment expectations, and resources needed and available to facilitate offenders' activities. The principle of responsivity also demands "that treatment interventions for offenders should use cognitive social learning strategies" that are tailored to individual offenders' specific characteristics such as cognitive abilities and level of personal motivation, which are vital ingredients of any effort that seeks successful therapeutic outcomes (Casey et al., 2014, p. 5).

MANIPULABILITY EFFECTS OF PREDICTIVE FACTORS

Criminal justice professionals perform risk assessment to create some understanding of the risks or likelihood of an offender engaging in criminal or delinquent behavior and more importantly to prescribe preventive actions to reduce such likelihood. The possibility of achieving such a goal, however, depends largely on the ability of criminal justice practitioners to manipulate risk or protective factors, which means the ability to therapeutically change or alter certain behaviors and thought patterns in the offender. Hence, the ability to distinguish between dynamic and static risk or protective factors is vital to the successful completion of risk and needs assessment and classification as well as the treatment and intervention that follow. At a minimum, it is important to direct available therapeutic resources to factors that are likely to generate results.

Static Factors

It is absolutely understandable that sometimes mishaps occur at the command of nature or as a result of another person's action or inaction with little or no fault of the person being assessed. In other instances, however, poor decisions lead to unpleasant results such as arrests, which then become permanent criminal records or static risk factors. The status "static" can be applied to both risk and protective factors because in both cases "static" means factors that cannot be altered, although their effects can be minimized, maximized, or counterbalanced with other factors. For instance, getting fired from a job, growing up in a single parent home, and getting adjudicated or prosecuted are examples of static risk factors that cannot be revised.

Once a person is fired from a job, that record will exist unchanged. Even if the person is rehired by the same employer, the fact remains that the individual "got fired" for likely doing something unacceptable. The impact of such a risk factor, however, gradually drops each month the offender remains employed. Similarly, the effects of growing up in a single-parent home cannot be erased. The same can be said about a criminal conviction, unless of course a sitting U.S. president, state governor, legislative body or judge erases such adjudication or criminal conviction. Even if a presidential or gubernatorial pardon were to come through, the fact that the offender was convicted will never change; hence, records of adjudication or conviction remain static or unchanged.

Although static factors are stagnant factors, in some cases the negative effects of such risk or protective factors can be minimized or weakened by certain protective factors. For example, the adverse effects of getting fired from a job can be offset by protective factors such as a long history of gainful employment and the offenders' articulation of the negative effects of getting fired from a job. Similarly, certain criminal records can be counterbalanced by living a crime-free life for a reasonable period and by clinically correcting factors that influenced the initial criminal act. In this regard, an offender who generates a criminal record as a consequence of gang membership is unlikely to erase the criminal record but may reduce the potential impact of the criminal record by ceasing to be a gang member. A drug dealer can similarly weaken the impact of' dealing drugs by simply abandoning the act of selling drugs.

Dynamic Factors

Dynamic risk factors are far better than static risk factors because human behaviors, particularly those associated with youth, do change through interactions with other people and through contact with vital social institutions such as schools, families, and religious institutions. Dynamic risk factors are variable risk or protective factors that can be clinically or therapeutically manipulated, changed, altered, reshaped, enhanced, or weakened. It is therefore fortunate that the majority of risk and protective factors that inform delinquent and criminal behaviors are dynamic.

Examples of dynamic risk factors are befriending antisocial peers, lack of interest in school work, poor social skills, and poor academic performance. For example, a student may start off doing poorly in a math and social science classes at the beginning of a semester, and for that reason the student is at high risk of failing both classes. However, if the student takes advantage of afterschool tutoring services and increases the amount of time that is usually devoted to math and social science assignments, he or she may end up doing excellently in the two subject areas because the additional tutoring and increased study time are protective factors that can lower the student's likelihood of failing both classes.

LIMITATION OF PREDICTABILITY AND EFFECTS

The results of trying to understand the patterns of juvenile offending behaviors and what to do with juvenile offenders who make contact with the criminal justice system have generated a lot of academic activities in the last 40 years or so. The broad list of areas that have benefited from the academic interest in juvenile offending behaviors include the identification of limitations that guide how risk assessment and classification results should be interpreted or used. The limitations cover risk, protective, needs, and responsivity factors in terms of how they impact individual offenders' thinking and behaviors differently depending on (1) who is the offender in terms of age, gender, socioeconomic background, and similar characteristics, (2) the precise nature of risk, protective, needs, and responsivity factors that are associated with the offender, (3) where the offender resides, (4) the mental capacity of the offender, (5) resources available to the offender, and (6) the offender's motivation level with regard to ending the cycle of delinquency, criminality, and deviance.

Variability of Risk and Needs Levels

In the world of risk assessment, no risk or protective level is permanent. Indeed, a youth with no history of violent behaviors can go from having the protective factor of being a nonviolent offender to being a violent person by simply assaulting another person or by using violent means to respond to situations that do not warrant the use of violence. In both cases, the change from protective to risk or from risk to protective factor is made possible by the fact that learned behaviors can be unlearned, suppressed, or controlled. Of course, the degree to which changes occur depends entirely on how individual circumstances influence the decision to learn or unlearn certain behaviors. Also, offenders who are better positioned to benefit from unlearning or learning certain behaviors, and who stand to benefit most from unlearning or learning a particular behavior, may find it more compelling to invest in such an undertaking.

Aggregate Effects

The presence of multiple risk factors increases an at-risk youth's chances of offending. Indeed, there is no single risk factor that can explain a youth's delinquent or criminal behavior; therefore, criminal justice professionals are concerned with the aggregate effects of multiple risk, protective, needs, and responsivity factors (Shader, 2004, p. 1). In fact, most risk and protective factors lead to additional factors, and the aggregate effect of all the factors ultimately produce a thought process or behavior. Having a criminal history, for instance, may have no impact until such history is used as a basis for denying employment. In such a case, the denial may lead to lack of unemployment, which may lead to lack of income, not being able to afford a home, home, or not being able to comply with certain social and legal regulations—note that a single risk factor, criminal history, has generated multiple risk factors (lack of employment, lack of home or place to sleep, lack of money, and increased stress or mental anguish). Collectively, these risk factors increase the chances of illegal activity.

Not Always the Case

Risks do not always lead to antisocial thoughts or behaviors, and protective factors certainly do not always produce prosocial thoughts or behaviors. Furthermore, risk and protective factors do occasionally lead to opposite outcomes or no outcome. For instance, poor academic performance increases the risk of dropping out of high school, which in turn increases the risk of unemployment, low wages, and chances of acquisitive offenses and an increased likelihood of making contact with the criminal justice system. However, many high school dropouts live their lives without any legal problems. That is, the hypothesis that people who drop out of high school or college may end up in poverty do not always come through—obviously it did not financially apply to successful people like David Karp, Richard Branson, Kirk Kerkorian, Quentin Tarantino, Joe Lewis, and many other prosperous millionaires and billionaires who accommodate their wealth after dropping out of school. Although these people are arguably outliers, they ended up doing much better financially than most people who completed high school or college.

Relativity of Results

The effect of each protective and risk factor on criminal or delinquent behavior may differ from person to person and from situation to situation (Thompson & McGrath, 2012; Walters, 2018). That is, risk and needs factors are relative to the offender's characteristics, environment, mental capacity, and similar conditions. For example, there are societies outside the United States where formal education does not play any vital role in individual members' ability to live law-abiding lives. In fact, in many developing countries the mere lack of formal education or formal employment does not propel a person into criminality or delinquency. Furthermore, what constitutes poverty or education may have dissimilar definitions and understanding in different localities.

Variability and Predictability of Protective, Risk, and Needs Factors

Some risk, protective, needs, and responsivity factors are more impactful than others, and the cumulative effects of risk factors vary depending on each offender's circumstances and the context in which a particular behavior takes place. The issue of subjectivity is therefore highly important when working with at-risk youth because risk, protective, and needs factors in general develop and form meaning within specific social, environmental, and cognitive contexts that are unique to each offender. In this regard, what is a risk factor for one offender might be a completely different thing for another offender.

Opposite Factors

Risk and protective factors are not necessarily opposite each other because the impact of risk factors on thoughts and behaviors tends to be much stronger than the typical impact of protective factors on thoughts and behaviors. For example, the negative effect of not graduating from high school is much greater and immediate than the positive effect of graduating. The effects of being abused sexually, physically, or psychologically are easy to calculate and are far more destructive than the effects of not graduating from school or than the effects of not having a history of being sexually, physically, or psychologically abused.

CONCLUSION

Risk assessment and classification as a function of the criminal justice systems is now a core function of any criminal justice professional who is charged with managing or supervising juvenile offenders within secured facilities and in the community. Hence, there is a strong need for becoming familiar with all the intricate relationships between risk, protective, and needs levels as well as future acts of delinquency and criminality, and for knowing how to successfully measure those relationships so as to develop strategies that will enhance the possibility of treatment.

The accurate assessment and classification of offenders' risk levels and the development and delivery of treatment interventions that best address the clinical and legal needs of offenders are now the core requirements for correctional, probation, and parole officers as well as clinical and administrative staff who work with at-risk youth. In fact, many agencies now hire applicants who have the skills to administer and interpret risk assessment instruments and to deliver services that are dictated by the results of such assessments. Obviously, emphasis on risk assessment is partly prompted by the national call for a more therapeutic or positivist approach to juvenile delinquency, criminality, and deviance. In many ways, this push for a risk-needs-responsivity approach directly conflicts with the principle of the so-called zero tolerance or classical push for punishment as an effective form of response to delinquency, which obviously has remarkably failed to lower the rate of delinquency and criminality.

CRITICAL QUESTIONS

1. Which should be prioritized for treatment: all risk factors in general, or criminogenic factors specifically?
2. Which are more important when rehabilitating offenders: needs or responsivity factors?
3. What are the similarities and dissimilarities between how medical professionals assess and classify patients and how criminal justice practitioners assess and classify offenders?
4. To what extent might children living in the United States be impacted by risk and needs differently than children in other countries, and to what extent might such differences be similar to differences in risk and needs between urban and rural American children?
5. Which of the core sources of risk and protective factors (individual, family, school, peer group, and community) is most impactful?

REFERENCES

Akers, R. L., Sellers, C. S., & Jennings, W. G. (2017). *Criminological theories: Introduction, evaluation, and application*. New York, NY: Oxford University Press.

Bartol, C. R., & Bartol, A. M. (2012). *Criminal behavior: A psychological approach* (10th ed.). Upper Saddle River, NJ: Pearson.

Bartol, C. R., & Bartol A. M. (2017). *Criminal behavior: A psychological approach* (11th ed.). Boston, MA: Pearson.

Bonta, J., & Andrews, D. A. (2007). *Risk-need-responsivity model for offender assessment and rehabilitation 2007-06*. Retrieved from the Pennsylvania Board of Probation and Parole website: https://www.pbpp.pa.gov/

Casey, P. M., Elek, J. K., Warren, R. K., Cheesman, F., Kleiman, M., & Ostrom, B. (2014). *Offender risk & needs assessment instruments: A primer for courts*. Williamsburg, VA: National Center for State Courts.

James, N. (2018) *Risk and needs assessment in the federal prison system* (Congressional Research Service Report No. R44087). Retrieved from the Homeland Security Digital Library website: https://www.hsdl.org/?abstract&did=813480

MacNamara, D. E. J. (1977). The medical model in corrections requiescat in pace: Requiescat in pace. *Criminology*, *14*(4), 439–448.

Shader, M. (2004). *Risk factors for delinquency: An overview*. Retrieved from https://www.ncjrs.gov/pdffiles1/ojjdp/frd030127.pdf

Taxman, F. S. (Ed.). (2017). *Handbook on risk and need assessment: Theory and practice*. New York, NY: Taylor & Francis.

Thompson, A. P., & McGrath, A. (2012). Subgroup differences and implications for contemporary risk-need assessment with juvenile offenders. *Law and Human Behavior, 36*(4), 345–355.

Walters, G. D. (2018). Risk, need, and responsivity in a criminal lifestyle. In F. S. Taxman (Ed.), *Handbook on risk and need assessment: Theory and practice*. New York, NY: Taylor & Francis.

Williams, F. P., & McShane, M. D. (2018). *Criminological theory* (7th ed.). New York, NY: Pearson.

CHAPTER SEVENTEEN

Risk Assessment Instruments

THE USE OF risk assessment instruments to aid in decision-making regarding juvenile offenders is now well-accepted and a required practice within every juvenile justice agency and institution in the United States. In this respect, juvenile justice practitioners are expected to assess offenders and to provide evidence-based therapeutic services to each offender, guided by risk and needs assessment and classification results. Risk and needs assessment instruments contain measurable items (risk and protective factors) that come from multiple studies that collectively concluded that each item has predictive value or has the potential to significantly inform antisocial or prosocial behaviors (Savignac, 2010). Risk assessment instruments are therefore designed to identify the likely cause of a particular offending behavior and to predict the likelihood of delinquent behaviors by an offender if appropriate therapeutic steps are not taken to revise the risk level (Vincent & Guy, 2013).

In addition to other functions, risk assessment and classification instruments also gather relevant information about offenders' offending behaviors, risk, needs, and in some cases offenders' responsivity (Vincent, Guy, & Grisso, 2012, p. 6). It is therefore essential for criminal justice practitioners to acquire basic knowledge about existing risk and needs assessment tools in use as well as the very process of risk and needs assessment and classification (Douglas, Pugh, Singh, Savulescu, & Fazel, 2017). In this regard, this chapter highlights some of the validated risk assessment tools that are commonly used and provides examples of common risk assessment items that assess and classify juvenile offenders who commit violent offenses and sex-, general-, and substance abuse-related offenses as well as youth with mental health issues that significantly inform their delinquent and criminal behaviors.

CONTENT AND FUNCTIONS OF RISK ASSESSMENT INSTRUMENTS

Criminal justice risk assessment instruments and the concept of risk, needs, protective factors, screening, assessment, classification, and intervention as used in particularly the juvenile justice systems are similar to the medical model—the methods by which medical personnel treat patients. The process starts with a patient showing up at a health center with a specific ailment or a collection of symptoms. Medical personnel first screen the patient by measuring body temperature, blood pressure, and weight, and asking the patient a few relevant questions. In serious cases, the patient is sent to a lab to undergo additional assessment based on the results of the initial screening. Medical personnel use the results of the assessment to either prescribe a required treatment or to refer the patient to an expert for further evaluation.

In the juvenile justice system, too, an offender shows up due to a particular criminal behavior that is considered a symptom of antisocial tendencies. The intake officer performs the initial screening, at which point the offender may be discharged or subjected to further assessment by a member of the clinical team. The results of that process are used to guide decisions regarding further criminal justice processing that typically involve a comprehensive and individualized examination of the risk and needs of the offender identified during the initial screening process.

Despite the similarities, however, between the way medical personnel treat patients and the manner in which offenders are treated in the juvenile justice system, risk assessment in the juvenile justice system is primarily concerned with the risk of reoffending, the risk of harm to others, the risk of harm to self, the identification of at-risk youth, the identification of the specific offense the youth is at risk of committing, and the offender's mental ability to participate in court proceedings (Grisso & Underwood, 2004; Savignac, 2010).

RISK ASSESSMENT TOOLS

The list of validated risk assessment and classification instruments in use within various juvenile justice institutions is very long (Baird et al., 2013; Klein et al., 2012; Murrie, 2012; Schwalbe, 2007; Singh, Grann, & Fazel, 2011). However, despite the diversity, instruments have common structures and features in terms of the factors they assess and the scientific process that informs their operation. For example, many specialized risk assessment instruments, such as those for violent, sexual, and substance abuse offending behaviors, assess common risk factors and needs and thus have certain common variables such as family history, history of prior offending behaviors, and history of past victimization by other offenders.

Existing instruments are also similar in the sense that none of the tools produce definitive results, and "to date, no single risk assessment tool has been consistently shown to have superior ability to predict offending behavior" (Singh et al., 2011, p. 500). Consequently, although some instruments such as those discussed in this chapter are more commonly used than others, there is no uniformity with regard to the specific instruments used by different agencies (McKeown, 2015; Singh et al., 2011). Indeed, the majority of correctional clinicians simply take advantage of the "potential value of using more than one instrument during the assessment process" (Baldwin, 2015, p. 3).

The purpose of completing a risk assessment also varies depending on the stage of the juvenile justice processing and the goals of the agency completing the risk assessment (Vincent & Guy, 2013). For instance, juvenile courts use risk assessment results as a guide to make decisions about sentencing. Correctional institutions use assessment results to make decisions about treatment types and intensity, housing arrangements, and supervisory restrictions. Parole and probation officers use risk assessment to guide their decisions about community risk and needs as well as to determine specialized parole or probation conditions (Hannah-Moffat & Maurutto, 2003). Multidisciplinary teams use risk assessment results for identifying behavioral risk factors that should be targeted in order to reduce the risk of recidivism.

The content of risk assessment and classification instruments, including the items in tables 50, 51, 52, 53, and 54, are also designed with the understanding that risk and protective factors are negatively correlated and that psychopathologies are positively correlated with risk factors but negatively correlated with protective factors (Klein et al., 2012). Most instruments, including the samples in table 50, 51, 52, 53, and 54, also use averages to calculate the final risk and needs scores. Finally, most risk assessment instruments, including the samples in Tables 50, 51, 52, 53, and 54, contain items that research has found to be related to criminal, delinquent, and other forms of antisocial behaviors among both children and adults (Baird et al., 2013; Klein et al., 2012; Murrie, 2012; Schwalbe, 2007).

VIOLENT BEHAVIORS

The assessment and classification instruments used to evaluate violent offenders and behaviors are designed primarily to identify youth at high risk of committing violent offenses and to guide interventions that can prevent future violent behaviors. The Structured Assessment for Violence Risk in Youth (SAVRY) and the State-Trait Anger Expression Inventory (STAXI) are good examples of common risk assessment instruments used to assess violent behaviors among youth (Grisso & Underwood, 2004; Savignac, 2010). The STAXI is used in the assessment of offenders who are at least 13 years old. The instrument's 44 items measure several types of anger-related behaviors, including suppressed anger and anger directed at self (Grisso & Underwood, 2004).

Studies show that the SAVRY produces the highest rates of predictive validity (Singh et al., 2011; Vincent & Guy, 2013). This instrument is a structured professional judgment instrument designed to assess violent risk and to supplement other instruments that assesses risk among juvenile offenders (Viljoen et al., 2015). The SAVRY identifies risk factors that can be targeted in order to mitigate the chances of future violent behaviors, and thus it is designed for use as a guide in planning and implementing evidence-based interventions that address violent or aggressive behaviors (Savignac, 2010) among both males and females between the age of 12 and 18 years (Burman, Armstrong, Batchelor, McNeill, & Nicholson, 2007, p. 51). Tables 17.1 contains samples of items that are used to assess the likelihood of future violent behaviors.

Risk assessment tools that evaluate violent offenders and their behaviors look at offenders' histories of violent behaviors, past violent victimization, anxiety levels during stressful situations, frequent displays of anger, involvement with firearms or weapons, homicidal ideation, and offenders' understandings of the seriousness of their behaviors. Most instruments also measure offenders' ability to control anger, physical possession or ownership of weapons with possible intent to use, and past histories of violence. Instruments and items in this domain assess histories of past violent behaviors, exposure to trauma, and histories of being violently victimized, including a history of suffering from emotional abuse as a child.

MENTAL HEALTH

Criminal justice institutions have ethical, moral, and legal duties to conduct mental health risk assessments because the process plays important roles in identifying offenders with mental health disorders and in ascertaining the level of risk each offender poses to society and to himself or herself (Grisso & Underwood, 2004). Mental health risk assessments are also helpful for identifying critical interventions that may ultimately enhance the welfare and

TABLE 17.1 ***Violent Behaviors***

This sample risk assessment instrument contains common items found in most risk assessment instruments that are used by criminal justice practitioners to assess violent offenders and their risk and needs levels.

	COMMON PREDICTIVE ITEMS	0–8
1.	*Offender has committed one or more violent crimes	0
2.	Offender suffered violent victimization on one or more occasions	0
3.	Offender shows excessive level of anxiety during stressful situations	4
4.	Offender shows overt and intense displays of sudden frustration	2
5.	Offender frequently displays anger	1
6.	Offender reacts with inappropriate force in ordinary situations	0
7.	Offender frequently uses intimidation in stressful situations	0
8.	When feeling frustrated or angry, offender strikes objects or furniture	0
9.	Offender is involved with firearms or weapons	0
10.	Offender exhibits homicidal ideation	0
11.	Offender minimizes violent behaviors	0
12.	Offender blames violent behaviors on victims or others	0
13.	Offender did not show significant anxiety *before* violent behaviors	0
14.	Offender did not show significant anxiety *during* violent behaviors	0
15.	Offender did not show significant anxiety immediately *after* violent behaviors	0
16.	Offender does not show remorse for violent behaviors	0
17.	Offender does not have a realistic plan to correct violent behaviors	0
18.	Offender is not motivated to alter violent behaviors	0
	*Score 8 for "yes" to item 1. For all other items, score 0 for a "no" and 1 to 8 for a "yes" answer. Do not compute items that have no answers.	**Total**
		Average

Key

0 = low-low, **1** = low, **2** = high low, **3** = low-medium, **4** = medium, **5** = high medium, **6** = low high, **7** = high, **8** = high-high

safety of both youth and staff. This important clinical task is performed by court-appointed or correctional-based psychologists or other qualified mental health practitioners.

The main concerns of the juvenile justice mental health assessment by courts is to determine an offender's state of mind at the time of the offense and an offender's current mental ability to adequately participate in court proceedings. In correctional facilities, including group homes, the focus of mental health risk assessment tends to be on identifying violent tendencies and self-abusive behaviors, protecting the offender from himself or herself, protecting staff and property from the offenders, and on understanding the contributions of mental health-related conditions such as ADHD, depression, and bipolar disorder to an offender's unwanted behaviors (Briner & Manser, 2013).

The recognition of mental health as something that explains certain criminal and delinquent behaviors and as a condition that qualifies certain offenders for specific therapeutic interventions has a long history. The case of Daniel M'Naghten represents a critical point in that history. In this case, Mr. M'Naghten shot and killed Edward Drummond, the private secretary of the British prime minister, Sir Robert Pell, while attempting to kill the prime minister. At trial, Mr. M'Naghten was found not guilty by reason of insanity. The English courts provided guidelines for distinguishing between who was or was not legally liable for their criminal and delinquent behaviors. The relevant part of that guideline reads as follows:

> Jurors ought to be told in all cases that every man is to be presumed to be sane, and to possess a sufficient degree of reason to be responsible for his crimes, until the contrary be proven to their satisfaction; and that to establish a defense on the ground of insanity, it must be clearly proved that, at the time of committing the act, the party accused was laboring under such a defect of reason, from disease of the mind, as not to know the nature and quality of the act he was doing, or, if he did know it, that he did not know he was doing what was wrong.

In 1871, the New Hampshire Supreme Court also recognized "mental disease" as a legitimate criminal defense. In 1954, the U.S. Court of Appeals for the District of Columbia also ruled in *Durham v. United States* that "an accused is not criminally responsible if his unlawful act was the product of mental disease or mental defect." In contemporary times, courts have also distinguished between mental illness (or insanity) at the time of the offense and competency, which refers to the ability of the offender to understand the charges brought against him or her (Durham v. United States, 1954).

In recent decades, the recognition of mental health as a risk factor for delinquent and criminal behavior has also gained significant support within probation and parole departments and in secured care facilities, in part because increasingly high numbers of children who make contact with the juvenile justice system have mental health disorders, most commonly depression, bipolar disorder, anxiety disorders, and, most importantly, suicide risk (Grisso, Vincent, & Seagrave, 2005). In fact, it has been found that at least one in every five youth who enters the juvenile justice system meets the criteria for at least one or more serious mental disorders, often in addition to a co-occurring substance use disorder (Grisso & Underwood, 2004, p. 1).

The actual process of putting offenders through mental health risk assessment is usually brief because the screening process is typically not intended to "provide an accurate psychiatric diagnosis, but rather to distinguish a set of exceptionally troubled youth for whom some special and relatively immediate response is necessary" (Grisso & Underwood, 2004, p. 2). Hence, mental health risk assessment generally focuses on factors such as self-abusive behaviors, including a history of self-harm, suicidal ideation, feelings of hopelessness, and social isolation. Tables 17.2 contains samples of factors that are used to assess mental health status.

TABLE 17.2 *Mental Health-Related Offending Behaviors*

This box contains items found in common mental health risk assessment instruments that are used by criminal justice practitioners to assess all offenders, and particularly offenders with severe mental health needs.

	COMMON PREDICTIVE ITEMS	0–8
1.	*Offender has attempted suicide in the past	
2.	Offender engages in self-abusive behavior such as cutting	
3.	Offender currently has suicidal ideation	
4.	Offender is not motivated to stop self-abusive behaviors	
5.	Offender refuses to take psychotropic medication as prescribed	
6.	Offender has a relevant mental health diagnosis	
7.	Offender hears voices that command him or her	
8.	Offender thinks he or she has no mental health needs	
	*Score 8 for "yes" to item 1. For all other items, score 0 for a "no" and 1 to 8 for a "yes" answer. Do not compute items that have no answers.	**Total** **Average**

Key

0 = low-low, **1** = low, **2** = high-low, **3** = low medium, **4** = medium, **5** = high medium, **6** = low high, **7** = high, **8** = high-high

Various instruments are used to assess an offender's mental health status and the effects of that status on his or her behavior. Examples include the (1) Carlson Psychological Survey (CPS), (2) Posttraumatic Stress Diagnostic Scale (PDS), (3) Brief Psychiatric Rating Scale–Children (BPRS–C), (4) Suicide Ideation Questionnaire (SIQ), (5) Devereux Scales of Mental Disorders (DSMD), (6) Inventory of Suicide Orientation–30 (ISO–30), and the (7) Massachusetts Youth Screening Instrument-Second Version (MAYSI–2).

The CPS is considered a reliable instrument for assessing a variety of mental health issues, including thought disturbances and antisocial tendencies among youth age 14 and above. The PDS is used to assess offenders between the age of 17 and 65 years old. The instrument is a brief self-reporting tool that measures stressful and past traumatic events that interfere with the offender's current social and psychological function. It specifically looks at the severity of stressful and past traumatic events as well as the duration of the symptoms.

The MAYSI–2 is a self-report instrument. The 52-item assessment is designed to identify potential mental health and substance use needs of youth between 12 and 17 years old. The instrument also assesses alcohol and drug use, depressed/anxiousness, suicidal thoughts or ideation, traumatic experiences, and angry outbursts or irritability. It is typically administered to juveniles on probation as part of the intake process and within 24 to 48 hours after admission into juvenile secured facilities (Grisso & Underwood, 2004).

The BPRS–C assesses the severity of a variety of mental health conditions, including depressive mood, hostility, hyperactivity, disorientation, and suicidal ideation. The SIQ instrument is a 25-item and self-report instrument designed to measure suicidal ideation among youth age 12 to 18 years. The DSMD is designed to measure behaviors informed by psychopathology in children and adolescents. It also measures delinquency, anxiety, depression, and other critical pathologies associated with children between 5 and 18 years old. The ISO–30 is a self-report assessment of youth between the age of 13 and 18. It is specifically designed to identify youth at risk for suicide by assessing offenders' sense of hopelessness and suicidal ideation.

SEX OFFENDING BEHAVIORS

The risk assessment process for juveniles is a core part of the prevention of recidivism among juvenile sex offenders (Hempel, Buck, Cima, & van Marle, 2013; Vincent & Guy, 2013). Consequently, sex offender assessment is a highly specialized field that relies on empirically based assessment instruments (Center for Sex Offender Management, 2009). Many such juvenile sex offending risk assessment tools guide comprehensive interventions for juvenile sex offenders (Musu-Gillette, Zhang, Wang, Zhang, & Oudekerk, 2017). However, although "no instrument is 100% accurate nor does any single tool include the full range of risk factors" (Center for Sex Offender Management, 2009, p. 8), there are many scientifically validated instruments "that can reliably determine if an adolescent will commit a subsequent sex offense" (National Center on the Sexual Behavior of Youth, 2003, p. 3). Moreover, "empirically based sex offense-specific assessment tools are fairly reliable" (Center for Sex Offender Management, 2009, p. 8). Thus, there are well-defined items, including those listed in Table 17.3, that are generally assessed by most juvenile sex offender assessment instruments.

TABLE 17.3 ***Sex Offending Behaviors***

The items listed in this sample risk assessment instrument represent common items found in most risk assessment instruments that are used by criminal justice practitioners to assess juvenile sex offenders and their risk and needs levels.

	COMMON PREDICTIVE ITEMS	0–8
1.	*Offender has committed one or more sexual offenses	
2.	Offender has suffered sexual victimization on one or more occasions	
3.	Offender gets sexually aroused by deviant sexual images or acts	
4.	Offender has attempted/completed more than two deviant sexual acts	
5.	Offender has used violence to commit at least one deviant sexual act	
6.	Offender started sexually offending at a young age (<16)	
7.	Offender has a history of physically hurting animals	
8.	Offender has a history of sexually abusing animals	
9.	Offender has a history of intentional fire setting	
10.	Offender uses elaborate planning to groom victims	
11.	Offender uses elaborate methods to conceal sexual offending behaviors	
12.	Offender blames sexual behaviors on victim or others	
13.	Offender did not show significant anxiety *before* sexual behaviors	
14.	Offender did not show significant anxiety *during* sexual behaviors	
15.	Offender did not show significant anxiety immediately *after* sexual behaviors	
16.	Offender does not show remorse for his or her sexual offending behaviors	
17.	Offender does not have a realistic plan to correct behaviors	
18.	Offender is not motivated to alter sexual offending behaviors	
	*Score 8 for "yes" to item 1. For all other items, score 0 for a "no" and 1 to 8	**Total**
	for a "yes" answer. Do not compute items that have no answers.	**Average**

Key

0 = low-low, **1** = low, **2** = high-low, **3** = low medium, **4** = medium, **5** = high medium, **6** = low high, **7** = high, **8** = high-high

The overall purpose of juvenile sex offender assessment and classification is to estimate the risk of future sexual offending and to identify the most effective interventions to mitigate or eradicate the source of the risk itself. Sex offender risk assessment tools therefore generally assess sexual interest in children, history of prior sexual offenses, the age at which the offending behaviors started, patterns of offending behaviors, and the degree of sexual offending as well as specific skills such as grooming and justification of sexual offending behaviors. The items in Table 17.3 are representative of the specific items used to evaluate sex offender-specific behaviors.

Six commonly used risk assessment instruments are employed by clinicians to assess and classify juvenile sex offenders: (1) the Juvenile Sex Offender Assessment Protocol-II (J-SOAP-II), (2) the Juvenile Sexual Offence Recidivism Risk Assessment Tool-II (J-SOR-RAT-II), (3) the Estimate of Risk of Adolescent Sexual Offence Recidivism (ERASOR), (4) the Juvenile Risk Assessment Scale (JRAS), (5) the Structured Assessment of Violent Risk in Youth (SAVRY), and (6) the Hare Psychopathy Checklist: Youth Version (PCL:YV) (Hempel et al., 2013; Holoyda & Newman, 2016; Viljoen et al., 2015).

The J-SOAP-II, the ERASOR, and the SAVRY are among the most commonly used adolescent risk assessment tools for assessing and evaluating juvenile sex offenders, although the SAVRY is not designed specifically for juvenile sex offenders (Viljoen et al., 2015). Both the J-SOAP-II and the ERASOR are also the instruments most used in North America for clinical assessment of juvenile sex offenders (Murrie, 2012, p. 164).

The ERASOR assesses the risk of sexual offending among youth with a history of sexual offending behaviors. The J-SOAP-II is a structured actuarial risk assessment instrument that measures static and dynamic factors associated with sexual offending behavior among boys age 12 to 18. Studies show that juvenile sex offenders tend to have fewer "criminal histories, fewer antisocial peers, and fewer substance abuse problems compared with nonsexual offenders" (Leversee, 2015, p. 181). Hence, the J-SOAP-II assesses the quality of an offender's peer relationships, evidence of the offender's thinking errors or cognitive distortion, whether the offender shows remorse and guilt or accepts responsibility for offense(s), and whether an offender understands his or her risk factors and is able to apply risk management skills (Murrie, 2012; Prentky & Righthand, 2003)

Questions about past sexual offending behavior and offenders' histories of being sexually victimized are among the items that appear on almost every sex offender-specific risk assessment tool because such a history significantly increases the risk of a juvenile sex offender engaging in future sexual offending behaviors. As Leversee (2015) notes, some juvenile sexual offending behaviors are the result of imitating the offender's own sexual victimization by other persons, as sexual aggression can also be a learned behavior, mainly by imitating behaviors that have been observed or experienced in the offender's environment.

Also important is the age at which the offender was victimized, the number of people who victimized the offender, the age difference between the offender and the victim(s), the duration of the offending history, the duration of each act of victimization, the level of violence and degree of deviance the offender deployed, and the number and types of sex offenses the offender suffered. The length of time between the offender's first known sexual-contact offense and the last known illegal or inappropriate sexual contact, including both legally charged sex offenses and those reported by the offender or not reported to authorities, is relevant and thus is commonly assessed.

GENERAL OFFENDING BEHAVIORS

Typically, general risk assessment tools measure whether an offender has committed one or more nonsexual offenses, substance-related acts, or violent offenses, and the extent to which an offender accepts responsibility for his or her own criminal or delinquent behavior. Most risk assessment instruments that evaluate general behaviors also examine offenders' association with deviant peers, participation in alcohol or drug use and abuse, academic achievement, ability to secure or maintain gainful employment, and histories of engaging in delinquent and criminal activities. Tables 17.4 contains samples of items that are used to assess the likelihood of future general behaviors.

Some risk assessment instruments assess multiple behavioral domains (substance abuse, violence, sex offending, and general offending behaviors). The (1) Child and Adolescent Needs and Strengths-Juvenile Justice (CANS-JJ), (2) the Child and Adolescent Needs and Strengths-Mental Health (CANS-MH), (3) the Youth Level of Service/Case Management Inventory

TABLE 17.4 *General Offending Behaviors*

The predictive items in this box are samples of items that are usually found on risk assessment instruments used by criminal justice practitioners to assess juvenile offenders and their risk and needs levels.

	COMMON PREDICTIVE ITEMS	0–8
1.	*Offender has committed one or more nonsexual, substance, or violent offenses	
2.	Offender cannot easily secure employment	
3.	Offender does not currently have a job	
4.	Offender blames criminal behaviors on others	
5.	Offender did not show significant anxiety *before* offending behaviors	
6.	Offender did not show significant anxiety *during* offending behaviors	
7.	Offender did not show significant remorse immediately *after* offending behaviors	
8.	Offender does not currently show remorse for illegal behaviors	
9.	Offender does not have a realistic plan to correct offender behaviors	
10.	Offender is not motivated to alter offending behaviors	
	*Score 8 for "yes" to item 1. For all other items, score 0 for a "no" and 1 to 8 for a "yes" answer. Do not compute items that have no answers.	**Total** **Average**

Key

0 = low-low, **1** = low, **2** = high-low, **3** = low medium, **4** = medium, **5** = high medium, **6** = low high, **7** = high, **8** = high-high

(YLS/CMI), and (4) the Child Behavior Checklist (CBCL) are examples of instruments that assess multiple behavioral domains (Grisso & Underwood, 2004; Savignac, 2010; Vincent & Guy, 2013).

The CANS-JJ is usually used by multidisciplinary treatment teams, probation officers, child welfare caseworkers, and mental health professionals to assess general criminal and delinquent behavior, substance abuse, mental health complications, juvenile offenders' safety, caregiver needs, and the strength and intensity of services for youth between the age of 4 and 21. The CANS-MH instrument also assesses mental health challenges, including psychosis, attention deficit disorder, impulse control, depression and anxiety, oppositional behavior, antisocial behavior, and substance abuse. The CANS-MH measures the level of danger posed by youth to themselves and others, sexually abusive behavior, intellectual development, physical and medical condition, the intensity of needed care, and general criminal and delinquent behaviors associated with children.

Some probation officers, parole officers, and/or correctional officers use the YLS/CMI to measure the appropriate level of supervision and treatment. The instrument measures prior and current offenses, family circumstances, educational achievement, employment history or potential, peer relations, substance abuse history, how leisure and recreational time are spent, and personality, behaviors, and attitudes of youth offenders age 12 to 16. The CBCL is used for children between the age of 4 and 18 years. The instrument measures youth's overall mental and emotional well-being as well as their ability to adapt to therapeutic changes. Specifically, the CBCL measures a host of mental and social problems, including anxiety and depression, attention problems, general delinquent behavior, social problems, and aggressive behaviors.

DRUGS AND ALCOHOL ABUSE

Alcohol-influenced behaviors can include, in the short and long term, unintentional injuries, death, suicidal ideation, unplanned pregnancy, unprotected sexual behaviors, poor academic performance, and other social problems (National Institute on Alcohol Abuse and Alcoholism, 2015). Unfortunately, most juveniles have co-occurring disorders or have substance use disorders in addition to one or more mental health disorders. The diagnosis and treatment of alcohol and drug-related problems and behaviors are, however, made possible by a number of well-researched instruments used to screen and assess juvenile offenders' substance abuse risk and needs.

The initial screening of offenders with substance use and abuse problems is a relatively easy process because admission of the use of alcohol or controlled substances indicates the presence of risk or some foreseeable likelihood of abusing alcohol or drugs. What is not an easy task, however, is determining the likelihood of future use or abuse of alcohol or drugs. Tables 17.2 contains samples of items that are used to assess the likelihood of future abuse or use of drugs or alcohol.

TABLE 17.5 *Drugs and Alcohol Abuse*

The existing risk assessment instruments that assess substance abuse-related risk contain items like those listed in this sample box. These and similar items are used by criminal justice practitioners to assess juvenile offenders and their substance abuse and use risk and needs levels.

	COMMON PREDICTIVE ITEMS	0–8
1.	*Offender has been charged with one or more drug abuse-related offenses	0
2.	Offender currently uses marijuana	8
3.	Offender currently uses cocaine, acid, or similar controlled substance	0
4.	Offender currently abuses prescription drugs	7
5.	Offender currently abuses alcohol or other drugs	4
6.	Offender has committed crimes to support substance abuse habit	8
7.	Offender has committed crimes while under the influence of a substance	1
8.	Offender did not show adequate anxiety *before* substance abuse behaviors	0
9.	Offender did not show adequate anxiety *during* substance abuse behaviors	0
10.	Offender did not show adequate anxiety immediately *after* substance abuse behaviors	0
11.	Offender currently has no remorse about the substance abuse behavior	3
12.	Offender does not have a realistic and achievable plan to correct behaviors	5
13.	Offender is not motivated to change substance abuse behaviors	5
14.	Offender has had at least one blackout as a result of substance abuse	8
15.	Offender felt sick when he or she stopped abusing one or more substances	2
16.	Offender's family member or friend has complained about offender's drug use	2
17.	A family member has sought help for offender regarding substance abuse	8
18.	Offender has unsuccessfully attended at least one substance abuse treatment program	
19.	Offender has friends who drink beer, wine, or alcoholic beverage and use other controlled substances, including marijuana, cocaine, and prescription pills.	1

*Score 8 for "yes" to item 1. For all other items, score 0 for a "no" and 1 to 8 for a "yes" answer. Do not compute items that have no answers. **Total**

Key

0 = low-low, **1** = low, **2** = high-low, **3** = low medium, **4** = medium, **5** = high medium, **6** = low high, **7** = high, **8** = high-high **Average**

Examples of substance abuse risk assessment instruments include (1) the American Drug and Alcohol Survey (ADAS), (2) the Drug Use Screening Inventory-Revised (DUSI-R), (3) the Comprehensive Addiction Severity Index for Adolescents (CASI-A), and (4) the Substance Abuse Subtle Screening Inventory—Adolescent (SASSI-A2) (Grisso & Underwood, 2004). These and other instruments are used for screening and assessing substance use and dependency or disorders. The ADAS is a 57-item self-report instrument that assesses more than 36 types of abusable substances and their frequency of use. It is designed for children between age 9 and 12 and between age 12 and 18.

The DUSI-R addresses the health, behavior, and psychosocial adjustment of offenders between the age of 12 and 17. It is reported as being helpful for assessing offenders with alcohol and drug problems, psychosocial issues including substance abuse, plus peer relations and the use of leisure and recreational time (Grisso & Underwood, 2004). The CASI-A measures the severity of addiction, consequences of adolescent alcohol and drug use, and youth's awareness of their own behavioral problems. Like the DUSI-R, the CASI-A also measures alcohol and drug use, offenders' use of free time, and peer relationships among youth between the age of 12 and 18. The SASSI-A2 is used to detect youth who have substance abuse and substance dependence problems. The instrument targets both boys and girls between the age of 12 and 18 (Savignac, 2010).

It is important to note that the quantity, frequency, and intensity of drug and alcohol use or abuse are critical determining factors with regard to the seriousness of substance abuse disorders. For instance, the National Institute on Alcohol Abuse and Alcoholism (2015) and its Alcohol Screening and Brief Intervention for Youth recommend that the number of drinks an offender usually consumes on an occasion and the level of the youth's drinking can predict future likelihood of substance use or abuse.

CONCLUSION

Irrespective of the risk and needs assessment instrument, risk and needs scores should be read with the understanding that each individual is unique, each risk factor is unique, each risk has a unique level of seriousness, and that the predictability of each factor depends on the extent to which such factors are related to the offender's delinquent and criminal thinking and behavior. Each offender is also unique. For example, sex offenders vary in terms of offending behaviors and patterns and the motivations that inform the behaviors as well as the risk of future offending. Furthermore, the effect or actual clinical relevance of a particular risk or need depends on each offender's current social and contextual circumstances.

It is also important to remember that risk and needs assessment instruments are still in the developmental stage, and thus they can be misleading in some cases (Douglas et al., 2017). Furthermore, criminal justice practitioners administering a particular risk assessment instrument may have different interpretations of individual risk and needs, although adherence to specific standards may minimize the effect of individual professional biases or lack of training.

QUESTIONS

1. Is the plurality of risk assessment instruments a good thing, knowing that for each category of behaviors there is a long list of risk assessment instruments to pick from?

2. Which of the domains in this chapter is likely to produce the weakest and the strongest risk assessment results?
3. Which behavioral domain (violent, general, mental health, sex, or substance abuse) could be better served by an instrument with a more diverse content that accounted for, for example, gender and ethnic differences?
4. Each of the sample scales presented in this chapter contains questions or statements about offenders' frames of mind relating to specific delinquent or criminal behaviors. How important are offender attitudes about their behaviors before, during, and after the unwanted act?
5. How important is screening juvenile offenders for underage alcohol use or abuse compared to screening juvenile offenders for illicit drug use or abuse?

REFERENCES

Baird, C., Healy, T., Johnson, K., Bogie, A., Dankert, E. W., & Scharenbroch, C. (2013). *A comparison of risk assessment instruments in juvenile justice.* Retrieved from the National Criminal Justice Reference Service website: https://www.ncjrs.gov/pdffiles1/ojjdp/grants/244477.pdf

Baldwin, K. (2015). *Sex offender risk assessment.* Retrieved from the National Criminal Justice Reference Service website: https://www.ncjrs.gov/sexoffenders/treatment.html

Briner, M., & Manser, T. (2013). Clinical risk management in mental health: A qualitative study of main risks and related organizational management practices. *BMC Health Services Research, 13,* 44–44. doi:10.1186/1472-6963-13-44

Burman, M., Armstrong, S., Batchelor, S., McNeill, F., & Nicholson, J. (2007). *Research and practice in risk assessment and risk management of children and young people engaging in offending behaviours: A literature review.* Retrieved from the Scottish Centre for Crime and Justice Research website: https://www.sccjr.ac.uk/

Center for Sex Offender Management. (2009). *Twenty strategies for advancing sex offender management in your jurisdiction.* Silver Spring, MD: Center for Effective Public Policy. Retrieved from https://www.csom.org/pubs/twenty_strategies.pdf

Douglas, T., Pugh, J., Singh, I., Savulescu, J., & Fazel, S. (2017). Risk assessment tools in criminal justice and forensic psychiatry: The need for better data. *European Psychiatry, 42,* 134–137. doi:10.1016/j.eurpsy.2016.12.009

Durham v. United States, 214 F.2d 862 (1954).

Grisso, T., & Underwood, L. A. (2004). *Screening and assessing mental health and substance use disorders among youth in the juvenile justice system: A resource guide for practitioners.* Retreived from the National Criminal Justice Reference Service website: https://www.ncjrs.gov/pdffiles1/ojjdp/204956.pdf

Grisso, T., Vincent, G., & Seagrave, D. (2005). *Mental health screening and assessment in juvenile justice.* New York, NY: Guilford Press.

Hannah-Moffat, K., & Maurutto, P. (2003). *Youth risk/need assessment: An overview of issues andpractices.* Retrieved from the Government of Canada, Department of Justice website: https://www.justice.gc.ca/eng/index.html

Hempel, I., Buck, N., Cima, M., & van Marle, H. (2013). Review of risk assessment instruments for juvenile sex offenders: What is next? *International Journal of Offender Therapy and Comparative Criminology, 57*(2), 208–228. doi:10.1177/0306624X11428315

Holoyda, B. J., & Newman, W. J. (2016). Recidivism risk assessment for adult sexual offenders. *Current Psychiatry Reports, 18*(2), 1–7. doi:10.1007/s11920-015-0650-5

Klein, V., Yoon, D., Briken, P., Turner, D., Spehr, A., & Rettenberger, M. (2012). Assessment of accused juvenile sex offenders in Germany: A comparison of five different measures. *Behavioral Sciences and the Law, 30*(2), 181–195. doi.org/10.1002/bsl.2006

Leversee, T. (2015). *Etiology and typologies of juveniles who have committed sexual offenses.* Retrieved from the Office of Sex Offender Sentencing, Monitoring, Apprehending, Registering, and Tracking website: https://www.smart.gov/SOMAPI/sec2/ch2_etiology.html

McKeown, A. (2015). Female offenders: Assessment of risk in forensic settings. *Aggression and Violent Behavior, 15*(6), 422–429. doi:10.1016/j.avb.2010.07.004

Murrie, D. C. (2012). Assessment instruments for juveniles who sexually offend. In E. P. Ryan, J. A. Hunter, & D. C. Murrie (Eds.), *Juvenile sex offenders: A guide to evaluation and treatment for mental health professionals.* New York, NY: Oxford University Press.

Musu-Gillette, L., Zhang, A., Wang, K., Zhang, J., & Oudekerk, B. A. (2017). *Indicators of school crime and safety: 2016.* Retrieved from the National Center for Education Statistics website: https://nces.ed.gov/pubs2017/2017064.pdf

National Center on Sexual Behavior of Youth. (2003). *Adolescent sex offenders: Common misconceptions vs. current evidence.* Retrieved from http://www.ncsby.org/

National Institute on Alcohol Abuse and Alcoholism. (2015). *Alcohol screening and brief intervention for youth: A practitioner's guide.* Retrieved from https://www.niaaa.nih.gov/

Prentky, R., & Righthand, S. (2003). *Juvenile Sex Offender Assessment Protocol-II (J-SOAP-II).* Retrieved from the Commonwealth of Kentucky Department of Juvenile Justice website: https://djj.ky.gov/800%20Policy%20Manual/JSOAP%20II.pdf

Savignac, J. (2010). *Tools to identify and assess the risk of offending among youth.* Retrieved from the Public Safety Canada website: https://www.publicsafety.gc.ca/cnt/rsrcs/pblctns/tls-dntf-rsk-rprt/tls-dntf-rsk-rprt-eng.pdf

Schwalbe, C. S. (2007). Risk assessment for juvenile justice: A meta-analysis. *Law and Human Behavior, 31*(5), 449–462.

Singh, J. P., Grann, M., & Fazel, S. (2011). A comparative study of violence risk assessment tools: A systematic review and metaregression analysis of 68 studies involving 25,980 participants. *Clinical Psychology Review, 31*, 499–513.

Viljoen, J. L., Gray, A. L., Shaffer, C., Latzman, N. E., Scalora, M. J., & Ullman, D. (2015). Changes in J-SOAP-II and SAVRY scores over the course of residential, cognitive-behavioral treatment for adolescent sexual offending. *Sexual Abuse: A Journal of Research and Treatment, 1*(33). doi:10.1177/1079063215595404

Vincent, G. M., & Guy, L. S. (2013). How to get the most out of risk assessment in juvenile justice. *Perspectives.* Retrieved from https://www.researchgate.net/

Vincent, G. M., Guy, L. S., & Grisso, T. (2012). *Risk assessment in juvenile justice: A guidebook for implementation.* Retrieved from the National Juvenile Justice Network website: http://njjn.org/

SECTION V

Supervision and Management of Offenders

CHAPTER EIGHTEEN

Correctional Team

ULTIMATELY, EVERY YOUTH is in some way responsible for his or her own actions, and indeed it is very important for youth to recognize that they are responsible for the consequences of the good or bad behavioral choices they make. It is, however, important to remember that delinquent tendencies and behaviors do not develop overnight, and accordingly, delinquency and criminality are not the result of a child's actions alone. Rather, delinquency is a symptom of many contributing factors and persons including family members, acquaintances, peers, other people with whom a youth interacts at various levels, and the conditions under which a youth lives. Thus, it takes many people to correct a youth's thinking and behaviors, and the treatment or correctional team plays important roles in that process. Specifically, the treatment team plays a very critical function in how the criminal justice system responds to an at-risk youth, especially in terms of how that youth benefits from every interaction with every member of the treatment team.

The treatment team is composed of people whose works are motivated by the beliefs that every child needs special care and that future acts of victimization by any child can be prevented or minimized through collective and individual actions in the best interest of a child. This means that all members of the treatment team are guided by the common goal to advance the child's best interest, attend to the child's mental and medical health needs, and to promote the overall physical health, security, and development of the child. This chapter therefore discusses the different functions each member of the treatment team performs and the relevancy of such functions to the offender's criminal and delinquent behaviors, as well as the offender's physical health and development.

MULTIDISCIPLINARY CLINICAL TEAM

The multidisciplinary team meets monthly to share information and to discuss comprehensive assessment and classification results for at-risk youth in detention, on probation, or on parole. The team's other key responsibilities are to develop a treatment plan for the youth, coordinate the youth's reentry services, provide feedback to youth about behavioral records, and brief all members about the youth's progress. The correctional treatment team is therefore composed of individuals who work collaboratively to develop and to maintain a comprehensive and individualized treatment plan that specifically addresses an offender's risk and needs.

The correctional team is sometimes referred to as clinical team, treatment team, rehabilitation team, or multidisciplinary team. Irrespective of the name, however, the team ideally consists of the youth, the juvenile court, the youth's case manager, a close family member, youth correctional staff, a youth advocate, a correctional administrator, mental health and medical teams, child welfare agencies, the educational team, the public prosecutor, and the public defender. Each team member makes important contributions to the overall welfare of the child.

The work and functions of the correctional treatment team, as a whole and individually, are informed by beliefs and policies that promote the best interest of the child, the belief that it is best for children to grow up in their natural homes with their individual biological or otherwise-constructed families, the belief that treatment must be provided in the safest and least restrictive environment as needed, and, most importantly, the belief that children can be rehabilitated and or in most cases outgrow their criminal and delinquent habits. Of course, the commonly circulated beliefs about American detention institutions of any kind in the United States are not in line with the goals and objectives of these correctional treatment team beliefs about juvenile offenders in general.

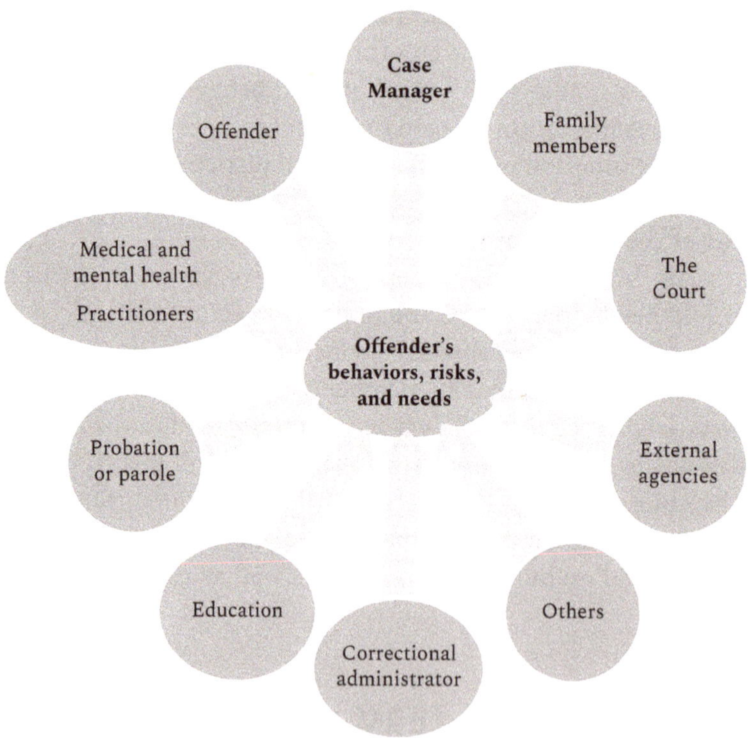

FIGURE 18.1 Essential and Nonessential Members of the Correctional Treatment Team

American correctional facilities are built with security in mind rather than therapy. As a result, correctional facilities are more likely to expose children to criminogenic risk factors, which are the strongest predictors of future criminal and delinquent behaviors, instead of protective factors that mitigate future delinquency and criminality (Smith & Schweitze, 2014; Steiner & Meade, 2014). The treatment team's core tasks are therefore to mitigate some of the common consequences of detention and the effects of risk that explain each offender's presence in a correctional facility. Additionally, the correctional treatment team also supports the prevention of future crimes and delinquency and the provision of physical, emotional, and financial support to the at-risk offender and, in some cases, the offender's family. The correctional treatment team is also responsible for all of the offender's therapeutic and safety needs including making sure that each child has a discharge plan and a safe place to return. That is, the treatment team sets the agenda and provides the means and resources required for the achievement of each offender's goals.

Essential members of correctional treatment teams generally include the youth, case manager, parole or probation officers, family members, correctional staff, correctional administrators, the educational team, and the medical and mental health teams. Noncore members of the correctional treatment team typically consist of prosecutors and public defenders, victims, the tribal team, the courts, and youth advocates. The legal and clinical functions and responsibility of each treatment team member are further assessed.

MENTAL HEALTH AND MEDICAL TEAM

Correctional treatment teams rely on the behavioral, medical, and mental health assessment and classification system that identifies appropriate risk and needs. Obviously, many youth who show up in correctional institutions tend to have some history of mental health disorders and medical needs that require professional attention. The task of assessing and classifying the levels of mental or medical defects and the extent to which such defects impact delinquent and criminal choices made by the youth falls on the shoulders of the clinical and mental health personnel—precisely, a psychologist, psychiatrist, or other medical doctor. In the overwhelming majority of cases, however, the mental and medical team are represented at the treatment team meeting by registered nurses and master's level, qualified mental health professionals.

Qualified mental health practitioners and medical staff are responsible for setting and reviewing the youth's mental health and medical goals, evaluating the youth's compliance with mental and medical goals, and for informing the team about how the youth's mental health or medical health inform his or her antisocial or prosocial choices and how to meaningfully reverse such behaviors or thinking. During the meeting, these team members report and assess mental and medical health screenings and record a summary of discussions that focus on the youth's mental and medical health needs. The mental and medical health practitioners help the rest of the team members understand the relationships among the youth's day-to-day thinking and behaviors, his or her mental and medical health, and how the offender's compliance with mental and medical health goals can enhance the offender's thinking and behavior.

CORRECTIONAL CASE MANAGERS

At all times, youth in detention facilities come into physical contact with various members of the juvenile correctional institutions. In particular, at any given time, each youth is in direct physical contact with line staff who carry the keys to each youth's room and who control their movements from one location to another. However, contact with the courts, prosecutors, public defenders, and pre-adjudication service providers are coordinated by the pre-adjudication or intake case managers. Youth interaction with line staff, medical and mental health staff, educators, institutional administrators, and even contact with family and service providers are also coordinated by case managers. For youth on probation and parole, contact with family members, school personnel, and service providers are coordinated by community case managers or probation and parole officers.

The intake case manager works directly with or for the juvenile courts and thus is essentially an information gatherer and analyzer or an assessment and classification officer, whose job is to help the courts make the right decisions about whether a youth should be committed to a secured facility, be placed on probation, or be diverted to a noninstitutional program. In the institutional settings, the correctional treatment team is headed by the institutional case manager who coordinates all matters relating to the offenders' mental health, medical health, and thinking and behaviors. In the community, the probation or parole officers oversee everything pertaining to the youth's mental and medical health, and educational and other service needs.

Intake Case Managers

The juvenile justice intake officer manages the cases of all youth who make contact with the juvenile justice system as a consequence of police apprehension or referral by a school official, a parent, or a guardian for any statutory violation. Upon referral to juvenile justice institutions, the intake officers or case managers evaluate all matters pertaining to the alleged behaviors and make one of three decisions: referral to a diversion program, dismissal of the complaint, or detention of the youth in a juvenile correction facility pending a formal hearing by the juvenile court. The court in turn may (1) refer the youth to the district or county attorney for possible consideration for prosecution as an adult, (2) commit the youth to a secured facility to receive inpatient treatment for the alleged behavior, (3) place the youth on probation to receive treatment in the community, or (4) dismiss the case if the state fails to satisfactorily prove the allegations.

The role played by the intake case manager is crucial because this is the body that initiates all the major documentations that are later used by institutional case managers as well as community case managers to assess and classify the youth's behaviors, needs, and risk. Intake case managers who act on behalf of the juvenile court judges gather all the social, behavioral, and mental and medical health information and document the youth's needs. Generally, youth who are considered less dangerous end up on probation with orders to participate in some form of community programing such as attending school. Those youth whom the court considers as threats to the public are committed to secured facilities for inpatient treatment.

Institutional Case Managers

Within the first 30 to 45 days after a youth is placed in a secured care facility, a treatment team is formed to review the offender's progress and to help the youth develop and pursue prosocial goals. The composition of the institutional-based correctional treatment usually includes some or all of the essential and nonessential team members, headed by the institutional case managers, who are typically well-experienced staff and familiar with each youth's behaviors, social history, potential for change, and risk and needs levels. Precisely, the correctional case manager is responsible for coordinating all treatment team members' compliance with the active treatment team case plan.

Correctional case managers also serve as liaisons between the youth, the institution, and all other treatment team members. As core members of the correctional treatment team, correctional case managers coordinate all matters relating to the offender's risk and needs and are also responsible for reviewing each youth's file, conducting intake interviews and screenings, and developing and implementing case plans that detail short- and long-term behavioral, educational, career, and mental and medical health goals and objectives. Institutional case managers are responsible for recording treatment team meetings' minutes and for making sure that members of the teams are fully briefed about treatment team goals and objectives for each offender. Finally, the correctional case manager is also responsible for the implementation of the behavioral and mental and medical health goals and objectives, as well as for evaluating and keeping track of the youth's progress and keeping other members of the treatment team abreast of the offender's progress or lack thereof.

Community Case Managers

Community-based treatment teams are formed when the behaviors that brought the offender into contact with the juvenile justice system or the intake case manager are not serious enough to warrant detention in secured facilities but are serious enough to qualify the offender for informal or intensive probation or parole. The head of the community treatment team is therefore either the youth's probation or parole officer, depending on whether the youth is on probation or has adequately demonstrated to the correctional treatment team that the youth is not a serious threat to himself or herself or to the public and thus has merited parole.

Duties and responsibilities of community case managers are almost identical to those of the institutional case managers. For example, community case managers are responsible for interviewing youth, their family members, and prior supervising agents or agencies, for securing schools and medical and mental health services, and for making community placement (home or group home) recommendations to the team in collaboration with all other community-based agencies and personnel.

Through their actions, community treatment team members review risk and needs assessment results, learn about a youth's history, collectively develop a case plan for the youth, assess and approve placement facilities, identify and implement behavior-specific programing activities for substance abuse, violence, and sexual offending behavior, and hold offenders accountable for the poor choices they make. Hence, probation and parole officers work with many types of community partners that offer mental health, family, school, employment, medical, and other programs and services that target specific behaviors, such as substance abuse, violence, and sexual offending behaviors.

Irrespective of the location and category, case managers, in general, work collaboratively with community partners as well as with the youth and their family representatives to develop and execute monthly case plans. Important functions of community case managers are therefore to develop a youth's case or formal reformation plan that contains precise interventions for particular behaviors or thinking. Case plans detail the exact course of action youth must take to correct a particular antisocial, criminal, or delinquent behavior. The community case manager or the probation or parole officer also coordinates the contributions of other treatment team members, community agencies, and government entities in pursuit of a successful implementation of a youth's case plan.

FAMILY REPRESENTATIVE(S)

As Garfinkel (2010) notes, if "rehabilitation and behavioral change are the primary goals of the courts, approaches that are family centered are likely to have greater impacts. Therefore, both the youth and his or her family (guardian, surrogate, or other family stand-in) should be included in the process" (p. 52). Indeed, irrespective of whether a family representative is a biological parent, surrogate, foster parent, guardian, or simply a person designated as a family member, the roles such family representatives play in the planning and execution of treatment are critically important. That is, with regard to prevention, intervention, and aftercare services, family involvement in the rehabilitation process is crucial.

Of course, juvenile correctional agencies recognize that the parents or family members of an at-risk youth have greater potential to positively influence therapeutic processes and change in youth's delinquency and criminality (Burke, Mulvey, Schubert, & Garbin, 2014). Consequently, juvenile justice institutions make strong efforts to increase positive family involvement in every troubled youth's life and operate with the belief that supportive parental involvements are helpful to the overall effort to correct a youth's thinking and behaviors. Obviously, the contributions of family are valuable in terms of who has the most influence on a youth's overall thinking and behaviors and who are closer to the youth. Unquestionably, family members spend more time with the offender than any other member of the correctional treatment team.

CORRECTIONAL LINE STAFF

The achievement of treatment goals in secured care facilities heavily depends on how safe and closely offenders are monitored as well as the how committed the people tasked with such responsibility are. Naturally, that crucial responsibility falls on the shoulders of the correctional staff, who are sometimes referred to as line staff. For example, correctional staff are responsible for recording each youth's day-to-day behaviors as well as each youth's compliance with the expectation set by the correctional treatment team. Line staff update the correctional treatment team about each offender's observed behavioral and thought patterns.

Additionally, correctional staff teach youth problem-solving skills, organize and supervise behavioral management activities, and document youth's day-to-day behavioral progress. Correctional staff provide safety and security for the youth in their care and act as therapeutic group leaders, tasked with facilitating group discussion sessions that are designed to teach offenders basic social skills that boost therapeutic progress. Correctional line staff document the extent to which a youth complies with overall treatment goals and objectives.

EDUCATIONAL TEAMS

States demand that offenders without high school diplomas who are committed to secure care facilities regularly participate in prescribed educational activities commensurate with their grade level and consistent with their educational needs. The role of the education representative therefore includes the duty to document and assess each offender's educational achievement and to educate the treatment team on matters relating to the youth's academic career and technical needs, as well as to develop ways to enhance the youth's overall academic performance. In cases where the offender is a youth with special education needs, the teacher helps the team understand the relationship between the youth's needs and behaviors both in and outside the classroom or educational setting. It therefore makes sense that the educational representative is typically the offender's primary teacher or someone familiar with the youth's classroom behavior and academic performance.

During the treatment team meetings, the educational representative serves as the leading expert on all educational matters and related behaviors, including the youth's classroom behavior, academic output, and similar matters. Hence, educational representatives play important roles and are extremely useful, especially in matters regarding youth with special educational needs and behaviors that are observed in and outside the educational settings. Note that "statistically students in a correctional facility are more than three times more likely to have a learning disability than their counterparts in general education" and that their conditions qualify them under the Individuals with Disabilities Education Act to receive free and appropriate public education carefully tailored to their individual needs (Weissman et al., 2008, p. 8).

NONCORE MEMBERS OF CORRECTIONAL TREATMENT TEAM

Given the long list of people who are expected to attend correctional treatment meetings, and the requirement that treatment teams meet at least once every 30 to 45 days to review youth's progress and to discuss future treatment plans, one would logically expect that not all members can make it to every treatment meeting. Obviously, the reality is that most victims can't make it to such meetings. In addition, there are not enough court employees or youth rights advocates available to attend every meeting that potentially impacts an offender's status. Similarly, there are not enough child protective service employees to attend every treatment team meeting and the same can be said about public defenders, prosecutors, and tribal representatives. However, to mitigate the effects of such absences, treatment teams allow victims, public defenders, and service providers who can't attend the regular treatment team to express their concerns, comments, or feedback in writing to the respective correctional treatment team.

The Juvenile Courts

Comparatively, juvenile courts are different from adult courts in the sense that they rely heavily on experts' participation, which includes the contributions of child protective caseworkers, probation officers, psychologists, mental health professionals, physicians, behavioral specialists, educators, child development specialists, and family representatives including foster parents, relatives, caretakers, and legal guardians. Juvenile courts work with these people to better understand offenders' behaviors and to identify the best responses to delinquent or criminal behaviors.

Orders issued by juvenile courts in response to an offender's behaviors stay in force until they are rescinded or when the affected youth is permanently discharged from the jurisdiction of the juvenile justice system either as a result of the youth reaching age 18 or as a consequence of the youth being discharged from the jurisdiction of the court for good behavior. Obviously, the juvenile court as the primary authority with jurisdiction over the youth gets involved and stays active in many matters that directly affect the status of the youth, including matters relating to education, criminal or delinquent behavior, and commitment to a secured facility or placement on probation or parole. Hence, in some cases the court may order additional supervisory functions such as ordering correctional institutions to furnish the court with monthly progress reports. Through its involvement, the juvenile court can help youth and those who work with them, including their parent or family representative, to increase their capacity to effectively support, supervise, and guide at-risk youth (Davies & Davidson, 2001).

In cases where a court orders that a particular youth participate in special behavioral programs to mitigate the risk of future offending behaviors, or as a condition of post adjudication release or a relief from any particular adverse treatment by the court, the correctional treatment team becomes the key authority to assess and report youth's compliance with the specific court order. That is, it is the treatment team that decides whether a youth is making progress or not, whether a youth is ready for parole release from a secured facility, and if a youth should be spared an adverse decision by the court.

Another function of the juvenile court as a critical member of the treatment team is the ability to enhance the capacity of those who are in direct contact with the youth on a regular basis. Indeed, studies encourage both juvenile court judges and probation officers or case managers in general to "be more active in expressing to parents the importance of their becoming more involved in their child's life" because studies recognize that the roles the family plays in the rehabilitative process are valuable (Davies & Davidson, 2001, p. 10). For example, the courts can encourage both custodial and noncustodial parental participation and involvement at all stages of the juvenile justice process. Such goals can be accomplished by at least directing the key actors in the youth's life, such as case managers and family representatives, to relevant resources that can increase their access to educational programs and other aids that can meaningfully minimize the impact of established life stressors or risks that contribute to the acting out of certain criminal and delinquent tendencies.

Public Prosecutors and Public Defendant

Public defenders and public prosecutors have the right to participate in treatment team meetings, and indeed they can play important roles in the rehabilitation of the offender. However, it is important to note that treatment teams meet about youth who have been adjudicated and committed to a correctional facility or placed on probation; thus, there is very little for a public defender or prosecutor to do other than to demand the enforcement of a particular court order in cases where the offender is a significant threat to the public. It is therefore not surprising that these people hardly ever attend multidisciplinary meetings except when the meeting is designed to decide the fate of a high-profile offender's request for parole or absolute discharge from a correctional institution.

When public defenders or prosecutors attend treatment team meetings, their roles at such gatherings can logically promote meaningful rehabilitation of offenders. At the same time, however, public prosecutors' presence at a treatment team meeting may discourage the free participation of particularly the offenders because the prosecutors' presence may cause a youth to not freely speak about their offending behaviors, fearing that doing so will adversely affect the outcome of their dealings with the court or the juvenile justice system as a whole. The same self-restraints may inhibit the ability of mental health teams, correctional staff, and family representatives to freely speak.

Welfare Service Providers

Correctional case managers, especially probation and parole officers, work closely with welfare and service providers. It is therefore highly logical for welfare service representatives to attend monthly correctional treatment team meetings in secured facilities or in the community, especially for youth with risk and needs scores indicating they are at greater risk of engaging in serious delinquent and criminal behaviors. However, with the exception of child protective services, these people rarely attend treatment meetings except in cases where their respective agencies are planning to provide or are already providing services to the offender. Service and welfare providers include family resource specialists, mental health service providers, medical service providers, educational support services, employment services, and residential care services, particularly for sex offenders, substance abusers, and violent offenders. The phrase "welfare service providers" also covers other social service agencies who work with at-risk youth in the juvenile justice system.

Community or intuitional case managers working with youth already on probation or parole or who are likely to be placed on probation or parole typically maintain ongoing contact with specific welfare and services providers. The presence of welfare service providers at a treatment team meeting is therefore important because at such gatherings, welfare service providers can easily inform the team about what their expectations are, which service or program may be beneficial to a particular youth, and the likely challenges a youth should expect to face and the successes a youth can expect to achieve. Service providers also use the occasion to explain their respective programs and to give all participants at the meeting some understanding of how the service they provide works and how likely such services are to help the youth achieve treatment goals and objectives.

Victims and Victims' Rights Advocate

The cry for victims' rights gained ground in the 1970s, and by 1985 the movement had produced many useful laws as well as changes in the United States, especially in the criminal justice system where the pioneers of the victims' rights movement argued that victims of crimes such as sexual assault and domestic violence were not fully recognized or given audience by the criminal justice system (Hanser & Gomila, 2015; Young & Stein, 2004). Consequently, states passed laws that created an independent participatory role for victims in criminal justice proceedings. In fact, every state has some sort of victims' rights legislation that gives victims the right to attend meetings specifically designed to discuss appropriate responses to particular criminal or delinquent behaviors. Victims' rights laws give victims the right to information about the offender's behaviors, the right to attend criminal justice proceedings, and the right to be heard at important criminal justice proceedings.

Victims attend treatment team meetings to voice dissatisfaction with a pending decision by juvenile justice institutions such as the courts or correctional facilities, to protest the granting of parole or absolute discharge, or to help the offender achieve the collective goals of not reoffending. To foster these efforts, correctional institutions have victims' rights units that are responsible to inform each victim of record about offenders' release dates, escape, or death, and any upcoming hearings or meetings that make decisions about releases and parole or probation status, as well as any major change in the youths' physical locations. In addition, each agency has a victims' rights advocate that directly or indirectly monitors institutional respect for victims' rights.

Youth Advocates

There are many types of youth advocates, but the main ones are court appointed *guardians ad litem*, institutional youth advocates, and tribal representatives. A *guardian ad litem* is appointed by the court and given specific duties to work with the court, welfare and service providers, and the youth and their families with the goal to give the offender the best opportunity to fully benefit from the services offered. The institutional youth advocate makes sure that basic hygiene, food, and shelter are provided and that educational and medical and mental health needs are fully respected. Thus, to ensure that each secured care offender's right to be treated with respect and love without reference to race, gender, language, national origin, religion, disability, sexual orientation, gender identity, or personal beliefs, the institutional advocate reviews most disciplinary actions against a particular youth. Where necessary, a youth advocate may also assist youth with legal matters such as appeal and with preparation for treatment team meetings or administrative review board hearings. The advocate is responsible for making sure that correctional staff are not violating the basic constitutional rights of the child, and thus the advocate works with offenders and correctional staff to ensure that the youth's mental and medical health, religious, disability, and educational rights are not violated.

The Indian Child Welfare Act (P.L. 95–608) of 1978 provides specific protections for Native American children, especially those who are receiving child protective services within the juvenile justice system. That is, if "a child is affiliated with a tribal organization, the tribe has the right to intervene in proceedings" (Jones, 2006, p. 19). Consequently, although tribal representatives may not always attend treatment team meetings, they are responsible for educating team members about the services that are available to tribal youth and for ensuring that Native American youth are being treated in accordance with their culture, traditions, and values.

ADMINISTRATIVE REVIEW BOARD

The main functions of the correctional administrator are to review, approve, or deny matters agreed upon at a treatment team meeting and recommended to the administrative review board. Typically, treatment teams make recommendations for release or denial of release from secured care custody and for absolute discharge to the correctional administrative head for approval or denial. For example, a youth seeking parole would generally have the request first reviewed by a treatment team who would conduct a preliminary analysis of the petitioning youth's thinking and behavior. If the team finds that the youth is ready for parole release or absolute release, recommendation for approval is sent to the administrative review board, which is led by the head of the correctional institution or the specialized branch of the correctional agency.

Administrative review boards are convened to examine treatment team recommendations for continuous detention, parole release, and absolute discharge release. Hence, at the administrative review board meeting, the correctional or community case manager speaks on behalf of the treatment team. The youth is then directly quizzed by the administrator in front of everyone in attendance. During the same meeting, the administrator reviews reports and listens to comments from all treatment members present, including and especially the youth, the case manager, family representative, educator, and the mental and medical representatives.

The presiding administrator's legal responsibility at the administrative review board meeting also includes the review of the offender's risk and needs assessment reports and the treatment team's reports, and the examination of corresponding interventions, services, and resources available to the youth and reports by the respective probation or parole officer. At the conclusion of the meeting, the presiding administrator approves or denies the recommendation regarding whether the youth should be released, where the youth will reside upon release, and the services and resources that are in place or should be in place to mitigate the youth's chance of recidivism.

CONCLUSION

The goals of every multidisciplinary or treatment team are clearly to reduce each youth's risk and needs levels, as well as to match each youth's risk and needs to the best clinical and legal responses available to minimize the potential for future delinquent, criminal, and incorrigible behaviors, particularly those that brought the youth into contact with the juvenile justice system. The achievement of these goals can, however, be complicated by factors such as weak participation of treatment team members, the lack of adequate resources at the disposal of the treatment team, and the failure to fully address the youth's risk and needs from the moment of admission into the juvenile justice system.

Indeed, it is often difficult to secure the active participation of the most critical members of the team, such as family representatives and social services providers. Secondly, the lack of adequate resources at the disposal of the treatment team can undermine their ability to adequately attend to each youth's risk and needs and thus to positively impact the youth's thinking and behaviors. Thirdly, for treatment team interventions to produce the desired results, preparation for transition from secured care into the community must begin immediately after a youth enters the juvenile justice system. That is, from the moment a youth is detained, the respective treatment team must start looking for appropriate clinical ways to release the youth back into the community by identifying the youth's risk and needs by helping the youth acquire the skills and resources needed for mitigating such risk and needs.

Finally, the ability of the treatment team to prevent future delinquent and criminal acts heavily depends on the extent to which members of the team remain committed to evidence-based interventions and, of course, the quality of the risk and needs assessment tools that inform treatment team decision-making. Such practices certainly produce a better outcome, especially when the case manager is well familiar with risk and needs that inform delinquency, criminality, and corresponding evidence-based interventions.

DISCUSSION QUESTIONS

1. Which of the correctional treatment team members is most important and why?
2. Except in a few cases, juvenile courts, in reality, do not closely monitor youth's treatment progress, as that responsibility is usually delegated to the institutional administrators. Should the court play a more active role in the post adjudication correctional treatment process?

3. How does an emphasis on therapeutic interventions impact the overall tendency of juveniles to engage in delinquent and criminal behaviors?
4. Which treatment team has the most realistic impact on delinquency and criminality, the pre-adjudication, post adjudication, or community correction treatment team?
5. What are some ways to improve the goals and functions of any of the treatment teams discussed in this chapter?

REFERENCES

Burke, J. D., Mulvey, E. P., Schubert, C. A., & Garbin, S. R. (2014). The challenge and opportunity of parental involvement in juvenile justice services. *Children and Youth Services Review, 39*, 39–47. doi:10.1016/j.childyouth.2014.01.007

Davies, H. J., & Davidson, H. A. (2001). *Parental involvement practices of juvenile courts: Report to the Office of Juvenile Justice and Delinquency Prevention, U.S. Department of Justice.* Washington, DC: American Bar Association, Center on Children and the Law. Retrieved from https://www.americanbar.org/content/dam/aba/migrated/child/PublicDocuments/full_report.authcheckdam.pdf

Garfinkel, L. (2010). Improving family involvement for juvenile offenders with emotional/behavioral disorders and related disabilities. *Behavioral Disorders, 36*(1), 52–60. doi:10.1177/019874291003600106

Hanser, R. D., & Gomila, M. D. (2015). *Multiculturalism and the criminal justice system.* San Francisco, CA: Pearson.

Jones, W. G. (2006). *Working with the courts in child protection.* Retrieved from the Child Welfare Information Gateway website: https://www.childwelfare.gov/pubPDFs/courts.pdf

Smith, P., & Schweitze, M. (2014). The therapeutic prison. In F. T. Cullen, C. L. Jonson, & M. K. Stohr (Eds.), *The American prison imagining a different future.* Thousand Oaks, CA: Sage.

Steiner, B., & Meade, B. (2014). The safe prison. In F. T. Cullen, C. L. Jonson, & M. K. Stohr (Eds.), *The American prison imagining a different future.* Thousand Oaks, CA: Sage.

Weissman, M., Cregor, M., Gainsborough, J., Kief, N., Leone, P. E., & Sullivan, E. (2008). *The right to education in the juvenile and criminal justice systems in the United States.* Retrieved from the American Civil Liberties Union website: https://www.aclu.org/files/images/asset_upload_file164_38663.pdf

Young, M., & Stein, J. (2004). *The history of the crime victims' movement in the United States.* Retrieved from the National Criminal Justice Reference Service website: https://www.ncjrs.gov/ovc_archives/ncvrw/2005/pdf/historyofcrime.pdf

CHAPTER NINETEEN

Evidence-Based Treatment Interventions

THE PRIMARY DUTIES of probation, correction, and parole officers demand the ability to recognize at-risk behaviors and tendencies, assess related risk and protective factors, classify and predict the likelihood of future behaviors, and rehabilitate and evaluate the effects of interventions on offenders' risk and needs. The task of assessing risk and needs is important because it is the process that identifies the precise behavior that should be targeted by treatment activities.

Indeed, one of the key purposes of the risk and needs assessment process is to identify the most effective interventions for each juvenile offender who ends up in the care of the juvenile justice system. Fortunately, there is a long list of behavior modification programs that address nearly every major antisocial thinking and behavior and every core risk or protective factor. The availability of multiple programs for every behavioral domain means that criminal justice professionals can easily find behavior-specific therapeutic interventions for each troubled youth in the juvenile justice system.

This chapter covers evidence-based therapeutic programs that are used to correct delinquent and criminal thinking and behavior and to increase protective factors that are critically relevant to each youth's success in school, in correctional settings, and in the community. Select evidence-based behavioral modification programs for sex offenders, substance abusers, violent offenders, offenders with mental health issues, and general offenders are presented as examples of the programs used by criminal justice professionals to revise antisocial behaviors. Evidence-based programs are practices that have been rigorously researched and found to be effective for behavioral modification with the potential to significantly alter certain antisocial thinking and behaviors and to positively impact specific behaviors, thoughts, risk, and protective factors.

LOGIC OF CORRECTIONAL TREATMENT PROGRAMS

One of the core legal and theoretical aims of the juvenile justice system is to reduce the frequency and effects of young offenders' antisocial behaviors, especially delinquent and criminal acts. Agencies accomplish these goals by providing offenders with behavior-specific interventions using behavioral modification programs. A number of scientific and theoretical assumptions dictate the content, structure, and delivery of each treatment program that aims to modify offenders' thinking and behaviors.

It is well-established that the likelihood of criminal and delinquent activities exists when conditions or risk factors that inform such behaviors are present. The opposite is also true: when criminal or delinquent activities are present, the conditions or risk factors that make such behaviors possible are also present. Second, there is no such thing as zero risk for engaging in criminal, deviant, or delinquent acts because everyone is at least at minimum risk of committing most offenses on the books, including behaviors that are deemed deviant, such as substance abuse, sex, or violent offenses.

Third, most offenders have a need for treatment in more than one behavioral domain (sex, violent, substance abuse, and mental health-related behaviors). As a result, most behavioral modification programs address two or more domains. For example, sex offender treatment programs address violent behaviors such as rape and other forms of sexual violence. Fourth, behaviors are products of thinking; therefore, antisocial behaviors are direct products of antisocial thoughts, and prosocial behaviors are influenced by prosocial thinking. Lastly, delinquent and criminal behaviors flourish in environments that are inhabited by antisocial, delinquent, and/or criminal environments.

Behavior modification programs generally focus broadly in terms of behaviors because treatment programs are informed by specific sociological and/or criminological theories that address behavior in general rather than specific acts. For example, social learning theory argues that antisocial behaviors can be learned through social interactions. Differential association theory holds that the techniques required for most criminal, delinquent, and deviant behaviors can be learned through interactions with others, primarily people within intimate personal groups. That is, both theories argue that offending behaviors, including substance abuse, violent, sex, and general offending behaviors, can be learned through social behavior and that the skills required for each antisocial behavior can be honed through social interactions with close friends and family members (Akers, Sellers, & Jennings, 2017; Williams & McShane, 2018). These logical assumptions inform the proposed behavioral modification goals and actions and the samples of evidence-based programs provided under each domain.

A PROPOSED BEHAVIORAL MODIFICATION GOALS AND ACTIONS APPROACH

Table 19.1 contains a proposed behavior modification goals and actions (BMGA) method that can be used to address a wide range of behavioral problems including sexual, violent, substance abuse, mental health-related, and general offending behaviors. The program is based on the premise that antisocial behaviors can be unlearned and prosocial behaviors learned through concerted effort that recognizes primary behaviors, identifies the sources and patterns of antisocial and prosocial behaviors, develops prosocial behavioral goals and objectives, uncovers steps to correct or modify behaviors, and offers methods to evaluate interventions.

TABLE 19.1 *Example of a Behavior Goal and Action Sheet*

STEPS	ELEMENTS
Behavior	I pass notes to my friends during class
Factors	Passing notes to my friends during class is a dynamic risk factor that can be stopped
Source	I am unwilling to wait for break to communicate with my friends.
Goals	I will stop passing notes in class to my friends.
Objectives	I will communicate with my friends before or after class.
Actions	I will tell my friends that I will not pass notes during class
Evaluation	I will keep track of talking to friends before class and during break.

As shown in Table 19.1, BMGA has seven elements: the primary antisocial behavior; whether the behavior is a static or dynamic risk factor; the source of the antisocial or prosocial behavior; the goal, objectives, and actions that will be taken to further those goals or objectives; and the methods that will be used to evaluate such actions. The extent to which an offender successfully completes these steps obviously depends on the level of guidance rendered by that offender's correction, probation, or parole officer or the criminal justice professionals charged with modifying the offender's behaviors.

The behavior refers to allegations that are typically filed against an offender or behavior observed by authorities including the police, school authorities, parents, or correction, probation, and parole officers. The factors answer questions about whether the behavior is revisable. Indeed, in order to adequately address a primary behavior, it is necessary to identify the effect and types of the behavior. Furthermore, the types of therapeutic responses generally needed to correct an antisocial behavior depend on whether the behavior is a static or dynamic risk factor. For example, certain acts of aggression are dynamic risk factors; therefore, the appropriate therapeutic response would be to stop such behavior. Unlike dynamic factors, such as the tendency to engage in delinquent activities or unwillingness to find gainful employment, static risk factors such as violent criminal history do not change; therefore, BMGA focuses on minimizing the impact of such factors on offenders' future behaviors.

Most primary behaviors are symptoms of other underlying behaviors or specific risk factors; therefore, identification of the source is a critical step in the modification of such behaviors. Of course, the identification of sources requires a great deal of knowledge about how various risk and protective factors inform certain behaviors. In the case of substance abuse, violent, or sexual offending behaviors, offenders must be helped to discover the underlying factor or behavior that informed the primary behavior or the substance abuse, violent, general, sexual, and mental health-related offending behavior. For example, attraction to children is a source of child molestation. Similarly, drug use is a likely source of shoplifting behavior or theft if an offender shoplifts and uses the proceeds to fund drug abuse habits. In some cases, drug use can be a source of prostitution if the offender is prostituting to buy drugs. Prostitution can also be a source for drug use if a prostitute uses drugs as a way to manage pain and suffering associated with being a prostitute.

Some behaviors have more than one source, but BMGA focuses on the source that has the most impact on the offender's antisocial behaviors. For example, failing a class can be caused by not paying adequate attention in class, being absent from class, not understanding class materials, or not having required resources for the class. Similarly, the reason a youth becomes a gang member could include peer pressure, living in gang-infested environments, or lack of a sense of protection in the community. In these cases, the task of a correction, probation, or parole officer, and indeed any criminal justice practitioners assessing an offender, is to pinpoint the precise source that has the most impact on the offender's behaviors.

The desired results for behavior modification programs are to ultimately enhance protective factors, stop dynamic risk factors, and to minimize the effects of static risk factors. The behavioral goal is therefore the opposite of the primary behavior if the primary behavior is a risk factor. The goal is the same as the primary behavior if the primary behavior is a protective factor. Hence, if the primary behavior is daily consumption of marijuana, then the goal will be to terminate the daily use of marijuana. If the behavior is showing respect for authority, then the goal is to continue to show respect for authority.

The objective addresses the source. That is, the objective is the same as the source if the source is a protective factor, or conversely, the objective is the opposite of the source if the source is a risk factor. The assumption is that the primary behavior can be resolved by addressing the sources of the primary behavior. For instance, if the source of truancy is fear of being assaulted at school by peers, then focusing on eliminating the potential for assault at school will address the truancy problem.

The most effective way to impact an antisocial behavior is by undertaking actions that directly impact the target behavior. Therefore, the aim of the activity is to minimize or eliminate the source if the source is a risk factor or to enhance the source if the source is a protective factor. For instance, if the primary antisocial behavior is "failing a history class" and the source of failing a history class is "not paying attention in class," then the goal is to pass the history class, the objective is "to pay attention in history class," and the action would be a behavior that furthers the goal or objective. The prosocial behavior in this case would therefore be the actual act of paying attention in history class. The behavior may also include actions such as taking good notes during history class, asking the history teacher at least two questions for clarification, and working with one or more partners who do well in the history class.

Behavioral modification activities must have a clear way of knowing the extent to which a promised action is carried out as planned and the effect on the primary behaviors or on the source if the source is different from the primary behavior. This continuous evaluation of behavioral modification goals is critical because the process measures the extent to which the offender is making efforts to correct his or her antisocial behaviors or whether the BMGA interventions are working. Hence, the evaluation assesses whether the steps being taken are working or not working.

There are also few dos and don'ts with regard to how BMGA should be completed and administered: behavioral modification goals should not be used as a tool for compelling an offender to change or to engage in a particular behavior. Behavioral modification goals must therefore avoid phrases like "you must" do this or that. Rather, the offender should be clinically guided by their correction, probation, and parole officers or their criminal justice practitioners to recognize the primary behavior and, most importantly, to discover its source.

Offenders must also be encouraged to develop their own goals, objectives, actions, and methods of evaluation. As a matter of general rule, each step of the behavioral modification goal must also be time-bound and realistic. The problem, source, goal, objective, action, and evaluation must contain action verbs that bind the offender and not a third person. For example, the source of failing a class should not be listed as "the teacher speaks too fast," but instead should be identified as the "offender not asking for clarifications." Finally, the process of identifying sources must rule out or consider the contribution of distorted thinking to the primary antisocial behavior. Furthermore, although goals must be specific, they can be broad and need not be crafted in measurable terms. However, the objective and actions must be stated in behaviorally measurable terms.

While some criminal justice intervention programs focus on patterns of behaviors, many criminal justice intervention programs focus on thought patterns. Specifically, some criminal justice interventions programs focus on antisocial thoughts such as distorted thinking, sometimes referred to as thinking errors, criminal thinking, or neutralization. Programs that address thought patterns assume that antisocial thoughts are consequences of distorted cognition, which increases the chances of criminal or delinquent behaviors (Cechaviciute &

Kenny, 2007). Therefore, programs that focus on helping at-risk youth use logical thinking instead of thinking errors or distorted thinking can reduce adolescences' chances of engaging in future acts of delinquency and criminality.

"CRAZY" THINKING LEADS TO "CRAZY" BEHAVIORS

Every behavior has a trigger event that may occur without the aid or special effort of the offender. Knowing the events that trigger a particular behavior is therefore vital because such knowledge makes it easier to control the progression or continuation of unwanted behaviors. To identify the trigger event is also to understand the thinking process of a typical delinquent and criminal mind, the stages of thought that make antisocial and prosocial behaviors possible, the ways offenders move from noncriminal activity to criminal activity, and why some offenders gravitate toward antisocial behaviors. In this respect, this box shows the steps delinquent and criminal minds take to complete a delinquent or criminal behavior and the steps taken to avoid, escape, or cope with situations that create opportunities for delinquent and criminal behavior.

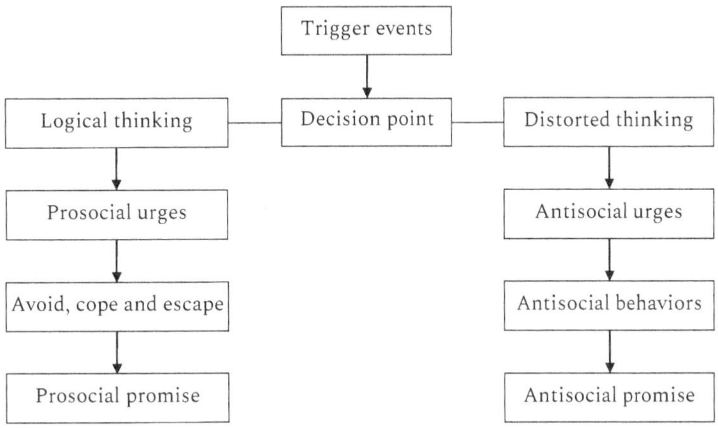

FIGURE 19.1 Patterns of prosocial and antisocial thinking and behaviors.

Trigger events are stimuli that come to the attention of offenders through one or more of the five senses: touch, smell, taste, sight, and hearing. For example, an offender may be triggered to think about marijuana use if he or she smells or sees marijuana or simply hears something about marijuana. The most crucial stage after a trigger event is the decision point because at this level in the behavior pattern, the offender either engages in logical thinking that will lead to prosocial activities or engages in distorted thinking that leads to antisocial urges and behaviors.

A prosocial activity in this case includes escaping, coping, and avoiding high-risk situations. To escape is to physically leave a high-risk environment or situation in order to avoid the possibility of engaging in unwanted behaviors. For example, if a youth with normal behavior attends a party with no expectation of drug use at the party but upon arrival at the party suddenly finds himself or herself in the midst of other youth using drugs, he or she can escape the temptation of using drugs by physically leaving the party. Alternatively, the youth could remain at the party but refuse to participate in the drug use by simply coping with the temptation to use drugs. The youth could also avoid such situations by refusing to attend any future party that the same group of friends may organize.

As Yochelson (1976) notes, the "criminal thinking process precludes responsible thinking and actions" (p. 187). Instead, criminals or delinquent youth will do everything within their means, including the use of distorted thinking, to legitimize their actions. Distorted thinking, in relation to a potential delinquent or criminal behavior, leads to antisocial behavior because offenders use distorted thinking to reinforce their negative thinking or emotions or to illogically convince themselves that an inappropriate behavior is justified even though ample evidence exists to suggest that such behavior is illogical, prohibited, or inappropriate.

Distorted thinking generates antisocial urges to engage in antisocial behavior partly because distorted thinking allows offenders to justify their antisocial behavior and to make excuses for it. Furthermore, the use of distorted thinking such as blaming other people or justifying and minimizing behaviors makes antisocial activities appear harmless or reasonable at the time of the act, during the delinquent or criminal act, and even after the antisocial behavior. Sex offenders, for instance, may convince themselves that their victims want to be sexually victimized. Substance abuse offenders may minimize their behaviors by convincing themselves that they are using a less harmful substance compared to other abusers or that their use of drugs is more measured than others. Violent offenders may blame their victims, arguing that their victims provoked them into a violent rage.

One of the routine tasks offenders perform after the completion of a delinquent or criminal act is to reflect on their delinquent or criminal behavior. In some cases, that process ends with an antisocial or prosocial promise to repeat or not to repeat an antisocial behavior. Antisocial reflection takes place after the completion of a delinquent or criminal act and involves self-assurance that the behavior in question will be repeated with improved skills when the opportunity to engage in such behavior arises. Prosocial reflection also occurs after the completion of a particular criminal or delinquent act and involves self-assurance that steps will be taken in the future to escape from, cope with, or avoid a high-risk situation in order to not engage in a particular delinquent or criminal behavior. For example, a speeder who drove 65 miles per hour in a 45-miles-per-hour zone and promises himself or herself to speed at 70-and-above miles during the next drive is making an antisocial promise. The same driver makes a prosocial promise if he or she admits that speeding at 65 in a 45 zone is illegal and dangerous and thus promises not to exceed the speed limit during the next drive.

EVIDENCE-BASED TREATMENT PROGRAMS

The behavior modification programs listed in Tables 19.2 through 19.6 are samples of a long list of evidence-based programs catalogued by the National Institute of Justice and the Office of Justice Programs (CrimeSolutions.gov, 2018). The process of labelling a program as evidence-based involves a careful evaluation by experts in the relevant field of the extent to which a program achieves its stated goals and the extent to which a program is likely to produce the target results when that program is adopted or duplicated by another agency.

Evidence-based and indeed juvenile justice treatment programs in general share common characteristics with regard to the behavioral issues they target, how they address antisocial thoughts and behaviors, and the strategies and procedures they use to properly implement such programs. Treatment intervention programs for sex offending behaviors, anger and aggression, substance use disorders, mental health-related problems, and general offending behaviors use group-based cognitive-behavioral therapy (CBT). Studies have shown that group psychotherapy and cognitive-behavioral therapy are effective behavioral modification tools, and sometimes even more effective than individual psychotherapy (Driessen & Hollon, 2010; Hofmann, Asnaani, Vonk, Sawyer, & Fang, 2012; Jennings & Deming, 2013, p. 7; Söchting, 2014), which is why group therapy is being increasingly used for even common mental health problems (Söchting, 2014).

Irrespective of the behaviors (violent, sexual, substance abuse, general, or mental health-related behaviors), a typical group therapy approach holds a meeting of several offenders with common behavior backgrounds. The groups are supervised by a criminal justice practitioners with knowledge about a particular behavior and experience in conducting such group therapy. The groups are generally designed for offenders to help one another learn about their own behaviors and to develop ways to deal with future opportunities to engage in antisocial behaviors. In these groups, offenders can confront flaws in statements made by other offenders in relation to their offending behaviors, and members can point out distorted thinking; explore ways to prevent the repetition of antisocial behaviors; help each other fully understand the impact of their behaviors on victims, society as a whole, and themselves; encourage each other to accept responsibility for their behaviors; and improve or build interpersonal relationships and skills.

Sex Offenders

Treatment programs for offenders with sexual behavior problems are generally delivered in peer-group settings. Sex offender treatment programs, in particular group therapy, are run by criminal justice practitioners with specialized knowledge in working with youth with sexual behavior problems. Typically, the aim of sex offender treatment groups is to help sex offenders take responsibility for the harm they cause their victims, develop skills for managing future deviant sexual impulses, learn techniques for managing healthy sexual urges or desires, recognize distorted thinking that facilitates their offending behaviors, understand the patterns of their deviant sexual behaviors and urges, and learn core social and legal rules that govern sexual behaviors (Allen & Berliner, 2015; Jennings & Deming, 2013).

Treatment programs also help offenders identify their own specific risk factors, develop a personalized plan for preventing future sexual offending behaviors, and reduce or eliminate thinking errors in relation to sex offending behaviors. Consequently, sex offender treatment programs emphasize truthful and complete self-disclosure of all documented and undocumented deviant sexual urges and acts and demand full acceptance of responsibility. Evidence shows that these group approaches reduce the risk of future sexual offending behaviors. Fortunately, plenty of evidence-based sex offender treatment programs, including those listed in Table 19.2, fit these profiles.

TABLE 19.2 *Evidence-Based Sex Offender Programs*

PROGRAM NAME	PROGRAM AIM	PROGRAM IMPACTS
Children with Problematic Sexual Behavior-Cognitive Behavioral Therapy (CPSB-CBT)	CPSB-CBT is an outpatient treatment program that aims at reducing inappropriate sexual behaviors among school-age children.	Studies find that CPSB-CBT reduces the rate of sexual offending behavior among youth.
Juvenile Sex Offender Treatment (JSOT)	JSOT targets juvenile sex offenders who have been adjudicated for sexual offenses and who are at risk of committing sex offenses, including rape, child molestation, incest, and exhibitionism.	Studies show that this program positively benefits youth with multiple delinquent or criminal behaviors, including sexual offending behaviors.
Multisystemic Therapy for Youth with Problem Sexual Behaviors (MTY-PSB)	MTY-PSB targets adolescents who have committed sexual offenses and who demonstrate other behavioral problems.	A study shows that participants reported significant reductions in behavior problems and were less likely to be arrested or to commit property offenses.

Most offenders find comfort in talking about their behaviors because such acts lighten the heavy burden of walking around with the secret of sexual offending on their minds. Most offenders also benefit from the support they receive from their peers in their treatment groups and from the agency conducting the groups, all with the hope of helping themselves build a nonsexual offending life. These groups and treatment programs help juvenile sex offenders freely talk about past behaviors, current urges, how their behaviors impact their victims, and how to fully accept responsibility for past and present sexual offending behaviors.

Substance Abusers

Substance abuse group therapy and individual psychotherapy aim at changing offenders' alcohol and substance abuse habits. Hence, substance abuse treatment programs, including the sample of programs listed in Table 19.3, and self-help group-based programs such as Alcoholics Anonymous, Mutual Aid, LifeRing Secular Recovery, and Smart Recovery emphasize verbally acknowledging the harmfulness of substance use and abuse behaviors and the gravity of individual substance abuse behaviors. Offenders who participate in these groups try also to identify factors that lead each them to engage in substance use and abuse and the events that trigger individual acts of substance use or abuse. Group members also focus on identifying people, such as relatives and peers, who enable offenders' substance abuse habits.

Substance abuse programs help offenders craft ways to avoid circumstances that increase their use of substances, recognize how to deal with cravings and other triggers that lead to substance abuse, and develop better ways of solving problems without resorting to substance abuse. Programs also address how to develop alternative activities and how to find or identify friends and relatives that can help minimize the chances of substance use.

TABLE 19.3 *Evidence-Based Substance Use and Abuse Programs*

PROGRAM NAME	PROGRAM AIM	PROGRAM IMPACTS
Adults in the Making (AIM)	AIM uses a family-centered preventive intervention approach designed to enhance the ability of family to positively impact youths' behaviors.	A study found that AIM reduces the risk of substance abuse and participation in other at-risk behaviors.
Family Matters (FM)	FM aims to reduce tobacco and alcohol use among youth age 12 to 14 years old.	A study found that FM is effective at reducing the habits and chances of smoking and drinking among youth age 12 to 14 years old.
Multidimensional Family Therapy (MFT)	MFT is a family-based treatment and substance abuse prevention program designed to address adolescents' drug use and behavior problems.	Studies show that this program significantly decreases adolescent substance abuse and related behavior problems.
Multisystemic Therapy-Substance Abuse (MT-SA)	MT-SA targets adolescents with substance abuse and dependency problems.	Studies show that adolescents who participated in MT-SA were less likely to use marijuana and to engage in criminal or delinquent behavior.
Positive Family Support (PFS)	PFS is a family-centered intervention program that targets children at risk of engaging in problematic behaviors or substance use.	Studies show that PFS participants report significant reduction in tobacco, alcohol, and marijuana use and in antisocial behaviors, thus fewer arrests.

Evidence-based treatment programs also help offenders identify their strengths as well as their problems and deficits. Programs help offenders recognize the severity of their substance abuse and related problems including the behaviors that brought them into the criminal justice system. Groups encourage participants to freely speak about their alcohol and other drug habits, articulate what they like about the substance they abuse, examine their level of drug use and related harms, explore how their habit affects friends and family members, and make informed decisions about ending substance abuse behaviors.

Violent Offenders

Violent acts are serious behaviors with grave consequences that can be particularly costly and painful for victims, society as a whole, and indeed for offenders. Consequently, many treatment programs, including those listed in Table 19.4, address violent tendencies and behaviors with the aim of reducing the rate of recidivism among violent offenders. Programs achieve this goal by teaching offenders how to verbalize their anger and how to express themselves through healthy physical and emotional outlets. Programs prepare offenders to take steps to reduce the severity and frequency of anger outbursts or behaviors and teach offenders how to deal with frustration, disappointment, and provocation.

In a typical therapeutic group setting, program participants are indeed encouraged to freely talk about their feelings, learn how to take responsibility for their violent behaviors, and articulate the harm they cause victims, society, and themselves. Members also learn how to identify factors that provoke them into angry outbursts, lead them to engage in acts of aggression, and cause them to use violence as a tool for mediating conflicts or navigating life's difficulties in general.

TABLE 19.4 *Evidence-Based Violent Offender Programs*

PROGRAM NAME	PROGRAM AIM	PROGRAM IMPACTS
Aggression Replacement Training (ART)	ART promotes prosocial behavior among aggressive and violent adolescents by helping them learn social skills and develop emotional control.	Studies find that ART improves offenders' social skills and reduces felony recidivism and problematic behavior in general.
Group Violence Reduction Strategy	GVRS aims to reduce gang violence and homicide.	A study shows that GVRS reduces homicide rates, firearm-related violence, and gang violence.
Operation Ceasefire (OC)	OC uses a problem-solving police strategy designed to reduce gun and gang violence and illegal possession of guns.	Studies show that OC decreases the rate of youth homicides, citywide gun assaults, and calls to police for service.
Project BUILD (BUILD)	BUILD is a violence prevention program aimed at helping youth in detention centers stay away from gang activity, violent offenses, controlled substances, and general criminal and delinquency behaviors.	A study shows that those who participated in BUILD reported lower rates of recidivism.
Second Step: A Violence Prevention Curriculum for Elementary School (Second Step)	Second Step is designed to reduce impulsive and aggressive behaviors among youth and to increase social competency.	Studies show that Second Step improves social competence among youth

Programs designed to address violent behaviors and tendencies offer offenders the opportunity to improve their prosocial skills, reduce the rate of impulsive and aggressive behaviors, and to enhance their overall social competence. Therapy groups for violent behaviors also help offenders identify and confront thinking errors or distorted thinking, identify and verbalize the consequences of their violent behaviors, disclose past violent behaviors, and examine underlying issues such as a history of being victimized. Most importantly, treatment programs help offenders develop and implement realistic plans for living a nonviolent life.

Mental Health-Related Offending Behaviors

Assessment and classification of mental health-related behaviors by criminal justice practitioners, including correction, probation, and parole officers, generally focus on the symptoms of mental illness and on factors that generate such symptoms. Certainly, oftentimes the behaviors that bring many youth into the juvenile justice system are known symptoms of mental illness that require evidence-based interventions that account for factors that contribute to adverse mental health conditions as well as address the manifested symptoms. Therefore, mental health-related treatment programs such as those listed in Table 19.5 approach mental health needs in many ways, depending on each offender's exhibited mental health symptoms and, of course, the underlying factors that inform the mental health-related behaviors.

TABLE 19.5 *Evidence-Based Mental Health-Related Behavior Programs*

PROGRAM NAME	PROGRAM AIM	PROGRAM IMPACTS
Cognitive Behavioral Intervention for Trauma in Schools (CBITS)	CBITS offers cognitive and behavioral therapy designed to reduce symptoms of post-traumatic stress disorder (PTSD) and depression.	Studies have found that CBITS significantly lowers self-reported PTSD and depressive symptoms as well as psychosocial dysfunction.
Cognitive-Processing Therapy for Female Victims of Sexual Assault (CPTFVSA)	CPTFVSA is a cognitive therapy program that helps female victims of sexual assault cope with or address post-traumatic stress disorder (PTSD).	Studies found that CPTFVSA decreases symptoms of depression.

Some offenders manifest their mental illness through various behaviors including sexual, violent, substance abuse, and other general antisocial behaviors. In addition, some offenders engage in self-injurious behaviors such as suicidal ideation or behavior and other self-inflicted harms. To address all of these factors, mental health treatment programs focus on events that cause offenders to think about or engage in self-harm, violent, sexual, substance abuse, and general offending behaviors. Mental health therapy sessions also serve as venues for offenders to freely verbalize their symptoms of mental illness, the contributing factors such as a history of being victimized by others sexually, physically, or emotionally, and the ways the abuse they suffered have impacted them. Programs also help participants improve their ability to address factors that increase their chances of engaging in mental health-related antisocial behaviors.

General Offending Behaviors

An overwhelming number of delinquent and criminal behaviors are general offending behaviors. Consequently, the majority of juvenile offenders commit general delinquent and criminal offenses, although the underlying causes of some general offending behaviors can easily be traced to substance abuse behaviors and mental health needs. That is, substance abuse habits and mental health needs are behind many of the offenses for which juvenile offenders are brought into the criminal justice system. It is therefore not surprising that a significant number of evidence-based programs, including those listed in Table 19.6, address a variety of behaviors.

TABLE 19.6 *Evidence-Based General Offending Behavior Programs*

PROGRAM NAME	PROGRAM AIM	PROGRAM IMPACTS
Adolescent Diversion Project (ADP)	ADP diverts juvenile offenders from formal juvenile justice processing and provides them with community-based services.	A study indicates that ADP reduces the number of youth who are formally processed by courts.
Big Brothers Big Sisters Community-Based Mentoring (BBBSC-BM)	BBBSC-BM offers one-to-one mentoring services to at-risk youth between the age of 6 and 18 living in the community.	Study shows that BBBSC-BM significantly reduces the number of youth who start using drugs and alcohol and who engage in antisocial behavior.
Functional Family Therapy (FFT)	FFT is a family-based prevention program that serves at-risk youth age 11 to 18.	Studies show that youth who participate in the program FFT show low recidivism rates
Juveniles Breaking the Cycle (JBTC)	JBTC uses comprehensive risk and needs assessment tools to identify and provide individualized services for youth at a high risk of drug use and abuse.	A study shows that offenders who participated in JBTC were less likely to recidivate and thus less likely to be arrested.
Multidimensional Treatment Foster Care–Adolescents (MTFC-A)	MTFC-A is a behavioral treatment program that targets youth with chronic antisocial behavior, emotional disturbance, and delinquency, and who may be considered for residential placement.	Studies have shown that MTFC-A reduces the rates of official criminal referral.
Multisystemic Therapy (MST)	MST is a family- and community-based treatment program that serves adolescent offenders with serious antisocial problems and delinquent behaviors.	Studies have found that MST participants were less likely to be arrested and thus spend less time in secured facilities than those who did not.

Collectively, treatment programs in this domain aim at lowering recidivism rates and reducing the rates of delinquent and criminal referrals. That is, general programs target multiple antisocial behaviors and tendencies with a focus on reducing the risk of general criminality and delinquency as well as the severity and frequency of antisocial behaviors. Thus, evidence-based programs in this category help offenders develop strategies for minimizing the possibility of delinquent behaviors and for developing and implementing behavior modification plans. Programs help offenders identify and utilize community-based and individualized services. Some programs also address emotional disturbances and serious antisocial problem behaviors including drug and alcohol use or abuse.

CONCLUSION

No program is a magic bullet for any particular behavior. Furthermore, every behavior is unique. Every offender is special, socially and cognitively. Every behavior takes place within a context and under circumstances unique to the time, place, and events surrounding each behavior. Naturally, offenders also respond to specific treatment interventions in their own ways. Treatment programs and their unique approaches may also benefit offenders in different ways depending on the approaches, interventions, and the level of each offender's motivation to benefit from such services and resources. It is, however, clear that irrespective of the program, the core goals that drive treatment programs, approaches, and indeed sessions are to prevent juvenile offenders from engaging in delinquent and criminal behaviors including violent, sexual, substance abuse, general offending, and mental health-related behaviors and to redirect the antisocial behaviors of youth at risk of committing serious delinquent and criminal behaviors.

DISCUSSIONS QUESTIONS

1. How many public resources should be directed at providing cognitive-behavioral therapy to minimize the rate of delinquency and criminality?
2. Do juvenile sex offenders, substance abusers, violent offenders, or general offenders pose more of a threat to society and cause victims more harm than do adult offenders?
3. What are some disadvantages associated with group therapy, and which behaviors (violent, substance abuse, sex, or general offending) are better served by such an approach?
4. There are many ways the juvenile justice system tries to correct juvenile antisocial behaviors. Which of the treatment interventions or methods of response, besides the individual or group therapies discussed in this chapter, are more effective and which are less effective?
5. In the name of prevention, argue for or against nondelinquent youth participation in evidence-based treatment programs that focus on cognition.

REFERENCES

Akers, R. L., Sellers, C. S., & Jennings, W. G. (2017). *Criminological theories: Introduction, evaluation, and application* (7th ed.). New York, NY: Oxford University Press.

Allen, B., & Berliner, L. (2015). Evidence-informed, individual treatment of a child with sexual behavior problems: A case study. *Archives of Sexual Behavior, 44*(8), 2323–2331. doi:10.1007/s10508-014-0460-6

Cechaviciute, I., & Kenny, D. T. (2007). The relationship between neutralizations and perceived delinquent labeling on criminal history in young offenders serving community orders. *Criminal Justice and Behavior, 34*(6), 816–829. doi:10.1177/0093854806298210

CrimeSolutions.gov. (2018). *All programs & practices.* Retrieved from https://www.crimesolutions.gov/Programs.aspx

Driessen, E., & Hollon, S. D. (2010). Cognitive behavioral therapy for mood disorders: Efficacy, moderators and mediators. *Psychiatric Clinics of North America, 33*(3), 537–555. doi:10.1016/j.psc.2010.04.005

Hofmann, S. G., Asnaani, A., Vonk, I. J. J., Sawyer, A. T., & Fang, A. (2012). The efficacy of cognitive behavioral therapy: A review of meta-analyses. *Cognitive Therapy and Research, 36*(5), 427–440. doi: 10.1007/s10608-012-9476-1

Jennings, J. L., & Deming, a. A. (2013). Effectively utilizing the "behavioral" in cognitive-behavioral group therapy of sex offenders. *International Journal of Behavioral Consultation and Therapy, 8*(2), 7–13. http://dx.doi.org/10.1037/h0100968

Söchting, I. (2014). *Cognitive behavioral group therapy: Challenges and opportunities.* Hoboken, NJ: Wiley-Blackwell.

Williams, F. P., & McShane, M. D. (2018). *Criminological theory* (7th ed.). New York, NY: Pearson.

Yochelson, S. (1976). *The criminal personality.* New York, NY: J. Aronson.

Glossary

Adjudicated Delinquent A child whose delinquent or criminal behavior has been examined by a court and found to be a violation of one or more criminal laws or statutes.

Antisocial Behavior Antisocial thoughts typically lead to antisocial behaviors or behaviors that are unlawful, unacceptable, and frowned upon by the public. Thus, stealing, smoking cigarettes in places where smoking cigarettes is prohibited, skipping school, and hitting other people against established rules are all examples of antisocial behaviors. Indeed, these behaviors also show disregard and a lack of respect for the law and socially acceptable norms.

Antisocial Thought A pattern or set of thought processes that are favorable to violations of rules, norms, or laws or that are likely to enhance the chances of engaging in antisocial behaviors. For instance, believing or thinking that school or good grades are not important, obeying laws is a waste of time, drug use is not all that bad, or selling drugs is a quicker and more fruitful way to make a living are antisocial thoughts because such thoughts or beliefs increase the chances of criminal or delinquent behaviors.

Assessment Systematic examination and analysis of an offender's psychological well-being, thought processes, past behaviors, and socioeconomic standing. Assessment is motivated by the desire to understand an offender's patterns of thinking and behavior, predict an offender's future behavior, identify the most fitting therapeutic interventions for an offender, and to appraise an offender's suitability for a specific treatment intervention.

Case Plan A carefully developed blueprint for the rehabilitation of an offender. A case plan is usually developed based on risk assessment and classification results. Such plans outline actions that must be undertaken by an offender and the services that must be provided by criminal justice practitioners with the goal of correcting an offender's antisocial thoughts and behaviors. Case plans are sometimes referred to as treatment plans.

Classification The purpose of classification is to categorize an offender's behavior (sex, violent, controlled substance, general, and mental health-related offender) and to predict the likelihood of his or her reoffending in a particular behavioral category. Classification answers the question of whether an offender is a sex, violent, general, substance abuse, or mental health-related offender and whether an offender is less, somewhat, or most likely to reoffend in any of the five areas of delinquent and/or criminal behaviors.

Clinical Classification The categorization of a youth based on his or her deviant or prohibited act, irrespective of whether such behavior is recorded by law enforcement. For example, a youth with a history of violent confrontation or altercation is clinically a violent offender irrespective of whether he or she is adjudicated or convicted for such acts.

Clinical Staff Typically, clinical staff are correctional staff charged or concerned with the rehabilitation of juvenile offenders. These staff are tasked with helping juvenile offenders correct their behaviors. Institutional psychologists, therapists, and probation, parole, and correctional staff that assess and prescribe interventions are clinical staff.

Cognitive Ability The mental capacity of a person in terms of the ability to foresee the consequences of prosocial and antisocial behavior. An example of healthy cognitive ability is the capacity to articulate the consequences of specific criminal or delinquent behaviors.

Cognitive-Behavioral Therapy A treatment approach driven by the belief that antisocial thinking often leads to antisocial behavior. Hence, cognitive-behavioral therapy (CBT) programs seek to correct offenders' thinking and behavior through activities designed to help offenders reevaluate the mental processes that inform their behaviors. An example of cognitive-behavioral therapy is Thinking for a Change.

Commitment A decision by a juvenile court judge ordering the detention of a youth in a secured facility is known as a commitment order. A committed youth is therefore a youth who has been ordered to spend days, months, or years in a juvenile detention facility so as to receive treatment for a specific delinquent behavior or to protect such youth from specific adverse conditions that are likely to increase the youth's chances of engaging in consequential antisocial behaviors.

Co-occurring The word *co-occurring* is often used in the context of an offender having two or more categories of behavioral needs. An example of co-occurring needs is someone being a substance abuser and at the same time having a serious mental health disorder that informs the substance abuse behavior.

Coping Skills Specific cognitive, physical, verbal, and social skills required to resolve conflict in a manner that results in a desirable outcome. In most cases, the term refers specifically to offenders' ability to appropriately deal with emotionally and physically stressful situations and to resolve conflict in ways that lead to good outcomes.

Criminal Justice Practitioner A trained professional who works for any criminal justice agency and who is charged with or concerned about the rehabilitation of offenders who involuntarily make contact with any criminal justice system.

Criminogenic Factors Behaviors and thought processes that increase an offender's participation in criminal and delinquent activities. Criminogenic needs therefore refer to resources and interventions that will reduce the offender's risk of future criminal or delinquent behaviors.

Delinquency The violation of a criminal law or the commission of a status offense by a person under the age of 18. The juvenile court judge determines whether an offender is delinquent or criminal in accordance with the offender's deeds.

Deviant Sexual Arousal Sexual stimulation in response to a person or thing that is prohibited by law or social norm from being viewed as a source of sexual gratification. Getting sexually excited by close family members, children, animals, and objects are examples of deviant sexual arousal. Behind most deviant sexual arousals are deviant sexual fantasies.

Diversion A formal removal of a juvenile offender from formal processing by the criminal justice system into a nonformal criminal justice program that is charged with correcting specific behaviors manifested by that youth.

Dynamic Risk Factor Most factors that predict behaviors are dynamic factors that change as a result of treatment or a decision by an offender to alter or put an end to a behavior or factor. For instance, controlled substance use is a dynamic risk factor because the risk will cease to exist when an offender quits. Similarly, not having a college education is a dynamic risk factor because an offender can easily change that status by simply enrolling in college and pursuing a college education. Unemployment is also a dynamic risk factor because the status of joblessness changes once a person acquires a job.

Evidence-Based Many programs and practices are marketed as being able to correct antisocial thoughts and behaviors. Among such practices and programs, those that have been studied, tested, and found to have the potential to significantly reduce an offender's chances of engaging in specific antisocial behaviors are known as evidence-based programs or practices. The Office of Juvenile Justice and Delinquency Prevention maintains an up-to-date *Model Programs Guide* listing evidence-based programs.

Family Reunification A treatment process that involves the reestablishment of the relationship that existed between an offender and his or her victim prior to the initial act of victimization. Family reunification is often necessary in cases involving sexual victimization of close family members with whom an offender must interact upon discharge from a treatment facility or custody.

Grooming A carefully developed plan that is designed to trick a potential victim into going along with acts of victimization. Most grooming, especially by juvenile sex offenders, involves manipulation of the victim including the coaxing of the victim either to go along with their victimization or to keep their victimization secret. An offender may use tactics such as gaining a victim's trust by giving compliments, attention, or gifts and by progressively victimizing the offender.

Incest Any sexual activity that involves an offender and a family member.

Intake Officer When youth are detained by police officers, they are initially taken into the custody of a juvenile court. Upon arrival, they are interviewed by an intake officer who determines whether the youth should be sent home until it is time to appear before a juvenile court judge or should be diverted to a nonformal criminal justice agency to address the youth's behaviors. Alternatively, an intake officer can hold a youth in a secured facility until he or she is seen by a juvenile court judge.

Intervention Any criminal justice response to a delinquent or criminal behavior that is intended to end a particular behavior. Thus, commitment, placement in group homes or with family members, and an order to pass the General Educational Development Test (GED) or participate in a particular programming activity are examples of criminal justice interventions.

Involuntarily Contact Any contact with the criminal justice system as an offender or suspect or in relation to any incorrigible, delinquent, or criminal behavior

Legal Classification The designation of behaviors or the labelling of offenders in accordance with existing law or classifications created by legislators. Legal classification uses objective scales; therefore, offenders and behaviors are classified without regard to individual circumstances and contexts in which a particular behavior occurs. For example, legally a youth who sell drugs at school is a law-abiding person until he or she is caught and adjudicated or prosecuted. Youth with a history of violent confrontation or altercation are not legally violent persons until they are caught and adjudicated or convicted.

Mental Health Disorder Any mental or cognitive condition that enhances an offender's ability to engage in antisocial activities or any serious psychological condition that is characterized by recordable or measurable symptoms of distress, mental impairment, or decreased functioning or that significantly increases the risk of engaging in antisocial behaviors.

Needs Resources and interventions that an offender must have in order to reduce the risk of criminal or delinquent behavior as well as to increase the number or strength of protective factors. Common needs include a high school diploma, job, tutoring, transportation, prosocial peers, a safe home, and behavior-specific counselling or treatment.

Needs Factor A set of specific services, skills, treatment, interventions, assistance, resources, and knowledge particularly needed to avoid future participation in delinquent and criminal behavior. Some offenders have needs for developed beliefs and thoughts that are favorable to law- and rule-abiding behaviors. Needs assessment is therefore a process that identifies treatment goals, a treatment plan, and the appropriate level of supervision and resources an offender must be afforded in order to avoid a relapse.

Pedophilia A sexual attraction to children, mostly by older persons. Pedophiles are sexually attracted to or get sexually aroused by the thought of engaging in any sexual activity with children.

Predictive Value The term *predictive value* is used to describe factors that studies show can impact individual ways of thinking and behavior. Factors that have predictive value encompass risk, responsivity level, and protective and needs factors. Examples of factors with predictive value include family, educational, and employment history as well as the types of friends and acquaintances an offender keeps and history of any past violent, deviant sexual, substance abuse, general offending, and mental health-related behaviors. Studies show that these factors can be used to predict offenders' future thinking and behaviors.

Prosocial Behaviors Behaviors consistent with the rules, norms, and values of a society. They are behaviors that are expected by law and that do not conflict with societal expectations. Generally, prosocial behaviors promote noncriminal or nondelinquent behaviors and are more likely to produce a noncriminal or nondelinquent outcomes.

Prosocial Thinking Positive or good thinking that supports compliance with rules, norms, and publicly held values. Examples of prosocial thoughts are held beliefs that education is important, respect for law is necessary, hard work is beneficial, and crime and delinquency often lead to undesirable outcomes.

Protective Factor A variable in the form of event, behavior, thought process, history, view, or belief that reduces the chance of criminal or delinquent behaviors. Certain characteristics such as a good academic track record, no history of controlled substance use, supportive family background, and association with nondelinquent and noncriminal peers are known protective factors.

Psychosocial A comprehensive report generated by clinical staff detailing an offender's history of offending and ways of thinking. Psychosocial reports typically cover matters such as an offender's psychological and physical well-being, residential status, employment history, family situation, and social history. Psychosocial reports are written by trained clinical and correctional staff such as psychologists, psychology associates, and probation and parole officers.

Recidivism This term is used to describe delinquent or criminal behaviors by offenders who have been treated or addressed for the same or similar behavior in the past.

Responsivity The cognitive and material readiness of an offender to fully benefit from a rehabilitative intervention. The principle of responsivity insists that cognitive behavioral treatment programs must be tailored to each offender's learning style, motivation level, cognitive and physical abilities, and strengths.

Risk Factor A variable shown by studies to increase the likelihood of a specific future offending behavior or to predict the likelihood of antisocial behavior. Most risk factors are cognitive, behavioral, attitudinal, and historical factors that can increase the likelihood of future delinquent and criminal behaviors. Examples of risk factors are having friends who are delinquent, not completing high school, and experiencing sexual, physical or emotional victimization as a child.

Service The average youth who enters the juvenile justice system has a lot of needs, including the need for help with medical attention, education, and future employment. Any of those resources or assistance qualifies as a service. Common services include medical and mental health services, educational services, and other services such as assistance regarding readiness for employment and/or finding a school.

Sexual Abuse The subjection of child, especially someone younger than the offender, to any sexual activity. Examples of sexual abuse include child molestation or the use of a child in any sexual activity or in any manner so that the abuser derives sexual gratification or financial benefit.

Sexual Misconduct This term generally refers to any sexual behavior that is viewed as deviant, inappropriate, or prohibited.

Static Risk Factor Although most risk factors can be manipulated or completely eliminated, some risk factors do not change irrespective of efforts by offenders. Such factors are known as static risk factors. Examples of static risk factors include a history of being arrested, spending time in a controlled environment, growing up in a single-parent home, and a history of being physically, sexually, or emotionally victimized by others. Similarly, static protective factors such as the achievement of a high school diploma and growing up in a supportive and healthy family environment do not change.

Status Offender A juvenile offender who commits status offenses or offenses that only apply to people under the age of 18. Thus, a youth who violates curfew, engages in truancy, runs away from home, or drinks alcohol is a status offender.

Status Offense A less serious law or rule violation that applies only to persons under the age of 18. Examples of status offenses include nondelinquent and noncriminal offenses such as curfew violation, incorrigibility, running away, truancy, and underage drinking.

Substance Abuse A pattern of controlled-substance use characterized by the repeated use of controlled substances to achieve intoxication despite physical evidence of adverse consequences associated with the controlled-substance use behaviors. Examples of negative consequences of controlled-substance use include serious and minor behaviors such as missing classes or work and failing to satisfy social and legal obligations.

Substance Dependence A pattern of controlled substance use characterized by the continuous and increased use of controlled substances to achieve a level of intoxication that allows the user to avoid the discomfort associated with withdrawal symptoms. Another documented symptom of substance dependence is when an offender feels continuously pressured to use higher and higher doses of a controlled substance to achieve similar levels of intoxication.

Thinking Error Distorted or illogical thinking or a specific thought process that normalizes, rationalizes, facilitates, or reinforces delinquent and criminal behavior. Common thinking errors used by offenders are blaming other persons for their own actions, justification of antisocial behaviors, minimization of antisocial behaviors, and claiming to be a victim of their own wrongdoing.

Treatment This term is used to describe any delivery of correctional service, opportunity, intervention, or assistance or the provision of opportunities and similar services to offenders with the sole purpose of helping them avoid future antisocial thinking and behaviors. Examples of treatment are requiring an offender to attend counselling sessions or to acquire a high school diploma.

Violent Crime Unlawful acts that are violent in nature. Violent crimes are often directed at persons or property and include offenses such as murder, forcible rape, armed robbery, kidnapping, and aggravated assault.

Waiver A process by which a juvenile offender is transferred to the adult criminal justice system for prosecution of certain crimes. Most states have laws that allow juvenile offenders of certain ages to be waived over to the adult criminal justice system for crimes such as murder, aggravated rape, armed robbery, and mass shootings.

Youth Advocate A criminal justice practitioner who fights for better or improved criminal justice responses that are favorable to the best interests of a juvenile under the custody or jurisdiction of a state agency, including detention facilities.

Index

D

E

N

O

P

R

S

CPSIA information can be obtained
at www.ICGtesting.com
Printed in the USA
FSHW021747121219
65023FS